Raine and Johnnie

Raine and Johnnie

The Spencers and the Scandal of Althorp

ANGELA LEVIN

Weidenfeld & Nicolson
LONDON

To Robert

First published in Great Britain in 1993 by
Weidenfeld & Nicolson
The Orion Publishing Group Ltd
Orion House,
5 Upper Saint Martin's Lane,
London, WC2H 9EA

A catalogue reference is available from the British
Library

ISBN 0 297 81325 0

Filmset by Selwood Systems, Midsomer Norton
Printed in Great Britain by Butler & Tanner Ltd, Frome
and London

Contents

Illustrations

The Illustrations appear between pages 122 and 123 and 154 and 155.

The Author and Publishers are grateful to the following for supplying photographs: Raine, aged five, by Dorothy Wilding (National Portrait Gallery); Barbara, Raine, Ian and Glen (Associated Newspapers); Johnnie on his first day at school and Johnnie in his corps uniform at Eton (Lady Anne Wake-Walker); Johnnie in Australia (Michael Transenster); Johnnie's wedding day (Associated Newspapers), Raine as a deb (Tom Hustler); Raine's wedding day (Associated Newspapers); Raine and her sons (Associated Newspapers); Raine and Barbara (Tom Hustler); Sarah's christening (Press Association); Raine and Johnnie outside Althorp (Tim Graham); Diana's wedding (Syndication International); signing books (Associated Newspapers); Diana and Johnnie (Syndication International); Raine and Johnnie inside Althorp (Derry Moore); The Long Room at Althorp (Derry Moore); The Marlborough wine coolers (British Museum); painting by Sacchi (Metropolitan Museum of Art, Enid A Haupt Gift, Gwynne Andrews Fund, and Purchase, 1871, by exchange. (1981.317)); painting by Hamilton (Tate Gallery); painting by Rosa (National Gallery); Diana after Johnnie's death (Tim Graham); Raine after Johnnie's death (Associated Newspapers).

If, inadvertently, copyright has been infringed in any of the other photographs used the author and publishers will be happy to make due acknowledgement in subsequent editions.

Introduction

'The hangings, carpets, glasses, sofas, chairs, tables, everything is not only beautiful but contains a vast variety. The carving and gilding is unrivalled; the taste in which every article through the whole house is executed is just and elegant.'

This is not a comment on the Althorp of Raine and Johnnie Spencer's time, but was written by Arthur Young in 1772 in his book *A Six Weeks Tour through the Southern Counties of England and Wales*. Few could say the same today. Many feel Raine and Johnnie have wreaked havoc and destruction on a family inheritance. A vast number of Spencer heirlooms have been sold, many in secretive circumstances. Between two and three hundred paintings have gone, along with many fine pieces of antique silver and furniture, china and porcelain, valuable Spencer archives, manuscripts, drawings, and some property, adding up many millions of pounds. Part of the proceeds was used to redecorate Althorp in a manner that has caused widespread controversy: controversy that initially aroused my interest in writing this book. How, I wondered, could there be such a wide divergence of opinion, ranging from those who are full of praise for the manner in which Althorp, a Grade I stately home with a four-hundred-year old history, has been restored to those who feel it had been desecrated and looks like a 'summer pudding'? Have family heirlooms been sold for a fraction of their worth? And what has happened to the proceeds?

Finding out has been an absorbing and difficult treasure hunt, not least because most art dealers, claiming confidentiality to clients, have a vested interest in keeping quiet. Art experts and museum curators would often only talk in riddles, as many also work for government bodies, such as the Reviewing Committee which grants export licences for works of art and other valuable objects and which is covered by the Official Secrets Act. Eventually I managed to gather and piece together enough clues, and to find sufficient experts who felt so strongly about what has happened at Althorp, to form what, I believe, is the most comprehensive list of *objets d'art* sold during Raine and Johnnie's marriage.

I

Analysing the two main characters in this most extraordinary of love stories proved equally fascinating. People loved Johnnie but were in two minds, although never indifferent, about Raine. The message about Johnnie is clear: here was a warm, rather shy, simple man, easily pleased but used to having his own way. Although I did discover a bullying side to his character that I hadn't expected, first impressions were largely correct.

One look at Raine, however, and you could get quite the wrong idea. She has carved out an appearance that is deliberate but misleading. Her hair is so sculptured that it could win first prize in a topiary competition, her face is carefully painted, her smile professional, her manner regal, and her choice of clothes and jewels are reminiscent of a fictional bygone age. Here, you would think, is a woman who had done nothing in her life but cultivate her image. You could not be more wrong. Below the surface is a sharp mind and plenty of ability. A well-respected worker for local government for many years, few doubt that if she had been better educated she could have been a successful professional woman. Indeed, many have compared her abilities to those of Margaret Thatcher.

Instead she concentrated much of her formidable energy on acquiring wealth and status. Society's loss was Johnnie's gain; he adored her and there is no doubt that she loved him although some also felt there were other factors at play. Most outsiders acknowledged, however, that she was by far the brighter and more dynamic of the two. She is a woman who excites strong emotions in both women and men, ranging from fear to adoration so much so that when I began my researches a couple of months before Johnnie Spencer died in April 1992 someone who knows Raine well said to me, 'Be careful. Raine can spell D for Danger.'

Although I made several attempts to secure her cooperation, she refused to see me, but her correspondence was never less than immaculately polite and often handwritten. She also tried to stop others from talking, although her choice was arbitrary. Of those who discussed the matter with her, several who were connected with her work at the British Tourist Authority were not discouraged from speaking, while those with a personal connection were. Only a few, I'm happy to say, followed her wishes, although some, including close members of the family preferred to speak anonymously. Her influence on those who knew Johnnie was less easy to understand. Apart from fathering the girl who married the Prince of Wales, he had not done very much in his life, yet she did not wish his commanding officer in the Royal Scots Greys to speak to me even though he thought very highly of Johnnie.

Despite this I have tried to be scrupulously fair in telling the story of their lives through the accounts of contemporaries and have interviewed well over a hundred and fifty friends and colleagues.

I have tried to select the influences on Raine's childhood that helped form the woman she became, particularly those of her mother, the romantic novelist Dame Barbara Cartland, to discover whether her life has been a series of calculated manoeuvres to reach a set number of goals, or whether she has responded to what Fate had in store for her. Few doubt that Raine saved Johnnie's life after his near fatal brain haemorrhage in 1978 and nursed him back to health. After the stroke, however, their lives were filled with controversy particularly over what happened to the Spencer heirlooms. I have tried to find out why Johnnie felt obliged to turn much of his inheritance into cash. I have also attempted to discover where the truth lay in the stories about the allegedly appalling relationship between the Earl's children, one of whom became a princess, and their stepmother.

Despite the opposition of Johnnie's family to his remarriage, and the bitterness this caused, Raine and Johnnie's love for one another prevailed. A love that for them both was sweeter second time around. This is their story.

I

Death of an Earl

At 5.30 p.m. on Sunday 29 March, 1992, a newsflash interrupted television programmes and ITN newscaster Carol Barnes announced the death of the 8th Earl Spencer: 'darling Daddy' to the Princess of Wales, and Johnnie to his friends. The 68-year-old Earl had been in the Humana Hospital Wellington, St John's Wood, north London, recovering from 'mild' pneumonia. But earlier that afternoon he had suffered a massive and fatal heart attack. It was a sad and unexpected end to a week that had seen such an improvement in his condition that he had been planning to return to his stately home of Althorp, pronounced Altrup, in Northamptonshire, the centrepiece of the 15,000-acre family estate, in another couple of days.

In retrospect, however, his timing could hardly have been better. Amid strict security, including a guard posted outside his room in case the Princess of Wales should make an unexpected visit, all Johnnie's children and grandchildren, including one-year-old Kitty, daughter of his son and heir Charles Althorp, had visited him during what was to be the last week of his life. They had been loving and concerned and the family rows over the desecration of the family inheritance, that at times threatened to tear children from parent, were temporarily set aside.

The grand five-storey Mayfair townhouse which Johnnie had bought for his second wife, Raine, had been refurbished and provided her with a suitable home to retreat to after his death. And most of all, he was spared the media's exposure of his daughter Diana's failed marriage to the Prince of Wales. He had called her his 'fairy-tale princess' and would have been terribly upset by the publicity following Andrew Morton's book and tapes of alleged conversations between her and James Gilbey.

The Earl had been admitted to the £300-a-day suite on the second floor of the hospital on 21 March. On the same day Raine Spencer had taken a room for herself on the fourth floor which she changed three times. It enabled her to be near Johnnie, keep him cheerful and ensure that he was receiving the best attention. A lady of high standards, on one

5

occasion she spent a good fifteen minutes extolling the virtues of freshly – 'it must be freshly' – squeezed orange juice to the Filipino nurse in the ward kitchen.

Although the Earl had been suffering from a heart condition for some time, it was thought to be under control, and there had seemed no reason to prevent Princess Diana from leaving for her planned week's holiday in the Austrian skiing resort of Lech. She had been to see her father in hospital on Wednesday 25 March, the day before she left, spending twenty-five minutes at his bedside with Prince William, reassuring herself that it was safe to leave him. (The ward sister said that during her visit she had never seen so many patients taking exercise outside their rooms.) The Prince of Wales was to join the Princess and their two sons, William and Harry, in Austria, in a brave attempt at family togetherness in their increasingly cold marriage. They also hoped the break would provide a welcome respite following the publicity surrounding the marital break-up of Andrew and Sarah, the Duke and Duchess of York. The young princes had invited some friends to join them – eight-year-old Harry Soames and seven-year-old George Grumbar, and their cousin, eleven-year-old Laura Fellowes, daughter of Princess Diana's sister Jane. Viscount Linley, the Prince of Wales's cousin, was also to be there.

The holiday in Lech began as a great success. The young princes thoroughly enjoyed skiing and tobogganing in the snow. Diana contacted the hospital every day. She heard that her father was doing well and happily monitoring England's progress in cricket's World Cup. She was told, as late as Friday night, that he was sitting up laughing and joking.

The news of his death came just three days into the holiday, on a day that began with all the family skiing together for the first time. The Princess was in an excellent mood, even laughingly offering reporters piggyback rides down the mountain. She, the Prince of Wales and their sons had lunch together in a mountain chalet undeterred by flurries of snow whipped up by a biting wind. The Princess then retired to her room at the Hotel Arlberg and soon afterwards appeared on the balcony with wet hair and dressed in a white towelling bathrobe. She was watching her sons enjoying a snowball fight with their father and friends when the telephone rang. She answered it and went back to the window, looking distraught and anxious. She told the photographers who were snapping the happy scene to go away and asked her husband to come in. Soon afterwards a Palace spokesman informed the gathered members of the press that Diana had just received the news of her father's death and that she was with the Prince.

Johnnie had suffered his heart attack at 2.00 p.m. He died almost immediately and, the hospital said, peacefully. He also died alone.

Although the Earl hated hospitals, his condition had so improved and he seemed so bright and lively that it had seemed perfectly safe to leave him with the attentive staff for a few hours. Raine had gone to Althorp to supervise three Mothering Sunday events – part of her fund-raising activities for Althorp. About six hundred guests in all were due for lunch, tea or dinner and she did not want to let her paying guests down. It was there that the hospital telephoned her advising her to return to her husband as quickly as she could.

Johnnie's son Charles was with his newly pregnant wife, the former model Victoria Lockwood and their baby daughter at their home, The Falconry, on the Althorp estate when the news reached him. Instead of travelling the sixty-five miles to London together, Raine was rushed to the hospital in her Rolls-Royce and Charles drove himself in his Range Rover. The Earl died before either arrived. Johnnie's other two daughters, Lady Jane Fellowes, wife of the Queen's Private Secretary, Lady Sarah McCorquodale, married to a landowner, remained with their families.

The press soon gathered at the hospital entrance. When Charles, now the 9th Earl Spencer, and Raine later emerged to face the barrage of press photographers and reporters, Raine was holding on to her stepson's arm. Charles, whose dislike of his stepmother would not be out of place in a children's story, was so overwhelmed by events that, at first, he could hardly speak. Then, mastering his emotions, he said, 'Until this afternoon my father was in very good condition and he was improving all the time.' His death had come as 'an enormous shock' and it was a matter of 'deep regret' that his father had died alone. It was a small consolation, however, that 'there was no pain whatsoever'.

By contrast, Raine appeared immaculately made-up as usual and with not a hair out of place. She wore a scarlet coat and showed no shred of emotion. The more observant, however, noticed her intense grip on Charles's arm, the one indication that something was wrong as he led her to a black Rolls-Royce that whisked her away. Raine's 91-year-old mother, Dame Barbara Cartland, was asked for an instant obituary. 'He was a most wonderful man. A sweet, kind amusing son-in-law,' she said. 'I have never known two people so happy. I suppose it was like one of my books.'

Dame Barbara revealed that although Raine was terribly distressed she was keeping her composure. 'One of her strengths is that she is like me. She does not believe in death. She believes that she will meet him again.'

Meanwhile in Lech, the Princess of Wales remained behind closed shutters with her husband, although how much comfort he was able to give her at this point in their marriage is questionable. Diana wanted to return home immediately, but no plane was available and they had to wait until the following morning. They decided, however, to spare the young princes, their grandfather's pride and joy, the trauma of the funeral and left them behind to enjoy the rest of their holiday.

When Diana emerged from the Hotel Arlberg at 9.00 a.m. the following morning dressed in black, she looked as if she had been crying all night and cut a lonely and forlorn figure. Keeping her head well down, eyes blinking rapidly, she slid into the back seat of the waiting car. Once inside she flung back her head and closed her eyes. When Charles emerged from the hotel a few seconds later, wearing a grey suit and black tie, and got into the back seat with his wife, she did not even glance at him. As the chauffeur-driven car sped off to Zurich airport, where a special aircraft of the Queen's Flight was laid on to take them to RAF Northolt in north-west London, tears rolled down her cheeks.

Soon after the Prince and Princess left, at 10.00 a.m. the children went out for a skiing lesson with instructor Markus Kleissl and then romped in the snow with a friendly dog before being called into the hotel for lunch by their nanny, Jessie Webb.

The Spencer family announced that the funeral service would be held at midday on Wednesday 1 April at the 800-year-old sandstone church, St Mary the Virgin, in the village of Great Brington, Northamptonshire, close to Althorp. Johnnie's children had asked for a quiet family service, to be followed by a public service of thanksgiving, but Raine knew that her husband wanted his funeral to be more like a memorial service and was keen that anyone connected with the Spencer estate could come. 'My late husband loved us dearly and hated gloomy people,' she said.

Despite their differences, the children agreed. The day after the Earl's death, a gloomy, blustery day that was more like winter than spring, Raine emerged from the door of her £1.6 million house in Farm Street, dressed in mourning and announced to the waiting press, 'We are all missing him very much already. Charles has been splendid doing lots of arrangements.' She added, 'From now on this is my home.'

It is not customary for a dowager to stay on in the family stately home, but Raine's speedy declaration that she had already moved out of Althorp, some said, was a desire to go before she was pushed. Later in the day she came out of the house again, shielded from the pouring rain by a vast umbrella. She was wearing a black coat with grey fur cuffs and matching fur-brimmed hat, that had been sent by car from Althorp. Since the Earl's death, the stately home had remained close to visitors. She was smiling broadly. 'Thank you very much for your interest,' she said to the waiting band of reporters and photographers. 'He would be very touched and flattered.' The contrast between her and her stepdaughter Diana could not have been more marked.

Whereas Diana had made no attempt to hide her obvious distress, Raine's emotional mask was firmly in place. Pro-Raine-ites saw this as an example of her control, discipline and deliberate politeness. Anti-Raine-ites saw it as another example of her determination never to let herself go and reveal her true feelings. 'We are now going to church to say a prayer,' she added. With that she walked the twenty yards to the Catholic Church of the Immaculate Conception to join lunchtime worshippers in the middle of Mass. There she sat for ten minutes in prayer and lit a candle, an action that later led to speculation that she was to convert to Catholicism. Returning home shortly before 6.00 p.m. she told the press, 'I have been with my family. My husband's family have been constantly in touch. They have been marvellous.'

Lord Spencer had made generous provision for her. As well as the Mayfair house, there were luxury homes in Bognor.

On the following day – Tuesday 31 March – the new Earl and Countess Spencer visited the country church where they had been married two and a half years' previously, to confirm arrangements for the funeral service. The Vicar, the Revd Norman Knibbs, said they had seemed calm and intent on sorting out the seating arrangements for the family. Half muffles were put on the church bells. Organist John Townley, a 43-year-old farmer, went through the hymns he would play during the service. Royal Protection Squad officers used sniffer dogs to search the church before sealing it off; officers remained on duty overnight.

Despite the forecast of cold winds and squally showers, Wednesday 1 April, was one of those idyllic spring days with postcard-blue sky and marshmallow clouds. Great Brington is a pretty village with yellow- or red-brick houses. The daffodils were in full bloom along the hedgerows and, in neighbouring fields, the newly born lambs snuggled up to their mothers, or frolicked in the bright spring grass.

Barriers had been erected the previous day on either side of the yellowstone church, its colour emphasised by the brilliant sky. By 9.00 a.m., three hours before the funeral service was due to begin, the photographers, with their stepladders and lightweight metal equipment, had already gathered behind one barrier. They all had telephoto lenses to make sure of catching their shot of the future Queen of England – or so they believed – at her father's funeral. Two fields had been allocated to take visitors' and press cars and one was already completely full. The police, who were directing the steady stream of cars, were helpful and friendly. 'It's a low-key operation,' one said. 'We've been asked to make the event as near as we can to a family funeral.' The village pub had opened early and was serving coffee, banana and chocolate cake and apple pie to the hordes of press who might have missed their breakfast.

At about 10.30 a.m. the villagers and some guests began to congregate in the driveway to the church, talking in small clusters. It was a gathering reminiscent of *Upstairs, Downstairs*, of cashmere versus Crimplene. However, the women immaculately dressed in designer black and with large hats and the men in bespoke dark-coloured suits were outnumbered by women in comfortable tracksuits and trainers and men in short fawn macs or suits that had seen better days. This was obviously the funeral of a lord of the manor, where feelings were more important than fashion. There were also numerous royal watchers who saw this as a not-to-be missed event, one or two of whom had brought flowers which they hoped to be able to give to the Princess of Wales. 'I came here for Charles Althorp's wedding,' said one elderly lady. 'And I wouldn't miss this for the world. I'm pleased it's not raining today, like it did then.'

Rippling through all the groups were anecdotes and happy memories of Johnnie, and several spoke openly of their affection for him. Whereas Raine Spencer was often criticised, Johnnie was much loved. 'He was a very, very nice man, he always asked how you were whenever you saw him,' said an ageing villager. 'Whatever they say about Raine – she saved the house completely,' said Sue, a heavily-made-up young lady who had taken the day off work to pay her respects and was dressed entirely in black.

Laura, from Luton, was a particular fan of the Countess. They had met when she went with a friend to Althorp in 1986 and chatted to Raine who was serving behind the counter in the shop. They got on so well that, when Laura left, Raine took her address, kissed her on both cheeks and gave her a 'very expensive' bar of chocolate. Two days later a handwritten letter from Raine arrived at her home, inviting her to a free drinks party at Althorp. This was followed by an invitation to a Christmas party which, even at the price of £65 a ticket, Laura felt was 'well worth it'. 'Her Ladyship always recognised me instantly,' she said. She had brought the Christmas invitation along with her in case it would help her to get into the funeral service. It did.

There were also rumours circulating around the groups that Charles, the new Earl, had already sacked most of Raine's staff and halted his father's proposed sale of cottages on the Althorp Estate.

Nobody seemed to mind the long wait and those waiting outside the church eagerly strained their heads, like spectators at a tennis match, whenever a wreath or a bunch of flowers was delivered.

At 10.30 a.m. a family friend, the Rt Revd Dr Mervyn Stockwood, former Bishop of Southwark, notorious in his day for being a maverick, arrived. Also present was the Revd Norman Knibbs. At 1.30 a.m. the heavy wrought-iron gates at the end of the driveway to the church were opened and the huddles of mourners immediately separated to re-form into an orderly queue. But it wasn't quite so simple. Far more people had gathered to pay their respects than the little church could hold. Almost inevitably those wearing designer clothes walked through with ease, while villagers and several current and former members of the Althorp staff were asked to wait. They began voicing their disapproval, but their anxiety did not last long. Within half an hour they were called back to the gate and allowed in. Sir Robert Fellowes, Johnnie's son-in-law and a member of the Queen's staff, helped show people to their seats.

There were two notable omissions from the congregation: Johnnie's first wife, Mrs Frances Shand Kydd, stayed at her home on the Isle of Seil, near Oban in Scotland, and his mother-in-law, Dame Barbara Cartland was in Spain to appear on a TV chat show. She said before she went that she was sorry not to be attending, but could not disappoint her Spanish fans. 'I sell very well in Spain. I cannot chuck them at the last minute. Either you are in show business or you are not. And as I'm the star it would throw out the whole programme.' Later interviewed by *Hello!* magazine in Spain, wearing her trademark pink dress with matching hat, she added, 'They tried to persuade me to go to the funeral. But although Earl Spencer was my favourite son-in-law, and a very charming person, I had to come.' She denied that she had upset her daughter. 'Raine is very brave. She understood my obligations to the television.'

By 11.50 a.m. the church was packed with over one hundred relatives, friends and Althorp employees. Mourners were even allowed to stand at the back. All sat or stood in silence facing the church's richly coloured William Morris east window of praying angels and listening to the selection of hymns being quietly played on the organ.

Earlier that morning, the oak-wood coffin had been escorted to the church by a guard of honour made up of gamekeepers and estate workers. On top were two wreaths, one of yellow daffodils, the other of white lilies and freesias.

Meanwhile Earl Spencer's cortege of seven black limousines crawled at walking pace up the estate road from Althorp, preceded and followed by Range Rovers full of plain-clothes police. In the first car sat Raine, who had been driven in her Rolls from her Mayfair home that morning. At the other side of the car sat her stepson Charles, now the ninth Earl, and between them sat Victoria, who had taken Raine's place as chatelaine of Althorp. In the second car were Sarah and Jane and in the third Diana, who sat behind tinted windows. She had earlier driven herself from London in her brand-new Mercedes. Beside her sat the Prince of Wales, who had dashed up from London by helicopter, after a private meeting, and was about to dash back again to take tea with the Crown Prince of Bahrain. Some onlookers believed that Diana had persuaded the Prince of Wales to cancel that day's schedule of engagements, but when he left soon after lunch it was one more indication of his increasing lack of support for his wife.

The cortege drove through the Lord of the Manor's entrance at the back of the churchyard so that the mourners could compose themselves before the service unobserved by the crowd of tenants, villagers and newsmen crowding the gates. At 12.05 p.m. Sir Robert Fellowes, who had kept his eye on the main door, jerked his head and mouthed, 'They're ready.' Everyone stood to attention. Raine came in first. Dressed in black with matching veiled hat and white gloves, she held her head high and walked slowly down the aisle, past her husband's coffin, and took her seat to the left. Later Viscount Lewisham, her son from her first marriage, joined her. Raine was followed by the Princess of Wales, with downcast eyes, and her husband. She was wearing a black Chanel suit and a large-brimmed black hat that partially hid her face from the press and public. She took her seat across the aisle from her stepmother and kept her head bowed throughout the service.

Raine occasionally turned to smile to people she recognised in the congregation. Sitting as she did on the opposite side of the church from her stepchildren suggested that the rift that had divided the family for sixteen years would not end with Johnnie's death, even if today they were all gathered in the same place.

Just as the service was about to start, the sun shone through the small high windows to form a pool of light at the far end of the coffin. By special request of the family, the funeral service was not broadcast on loudspeakers for the benefit of the crowds outside. The opening hymn was 'The Lord's My Shepherd', chosen by the late Earl himself, the first of three cheerful hymns sung by the congregation during the forty-minute service.

The new Earl, Charles, had intended to read the lesson from 1 Corinthians 15:20–58, beginning 'but now is Christ risen from the dead . . .' the passages read at the funeral of the seventh Earl – but he was so overcome with emotion that he was unable to take his place in the pulpit and his brother-in-law Sir Robert Fellowes read it instead.

Then a lone trumpeter in the bright red uniform and black busby of the Royal Scots Greys, with whom Lord Spencer had served during the Second-World War, played a lament. Family friend Lord St John of Fawsley, the former Conservative MP Norman St John-Stevas, who had known Raine a great many years, rose to give the address. With a low bow to the nave and a short bow to the coffin, he walked to the pulpit. Clearly and slowly his voice echoed round the silent and packed church.

He spoke of Johnnie's life and his warm and loving personality. 'He was in many ways not a twentieth-century figure, not even a nineteenth-century one but an illegal immigrant from the eighteenth century, when the aristocrats lived freely and at ease with their neighbours,' he said. 'He was the perfect gentleman, but one never afraid to speak openly about his emotions. The words of love were on his lips.' He declared, 'Johnnie loved his family, his son Charles, to whom he remained devoted always, his daughters – the three Graces – and his grandchildren; their love is witnessed by their presence here today.'

He spoke briefly of the row over the sale of heirlooms which had threatened to split the Spencer family. 'Of course there is bickering in every family ... Birds twitter and peck in their nests be they large or small. And if the nest is gilded, it is sometimes bathed in the glare of media light. But love is not so easily disarmed. Its fruits are peace, forgiveness and reconciliation.'

He spoke also, as the Earl would have wanted him to, in defence of Raine. It was she who had saved his life when he suffered his serious stroke fourteen years previously. 'She did not waste time in idle tears and wringing of hands, but acted with resolution, courage and intelligence.' That Johnnie lived to see the proudest moment of his life – the marriage of his daughter to the heir to the throne – was, he said, thanks to Raine. 'All of us, his friends, his family and the nation, owe her a deep debt of gratitude for that.' He spoke of the moment when the Earl – a little unsteady on his feet – led Lady Diana Spencer up the aisle of St Paul's Cathedral. 'From that moment, the British people with their superb instinct took him to their hearts and he has remained there since.'

Lord St John remembered once asking the Princess: 'How do you manage to get on so well with so many different kinds and types of people?' She had replied: 'I learned it from my father.' The Earl's countenance, he said, was 'suffused with joy and gratitude' when he heard the story. He had a special affinity with Diana and a pride in the way she discharged her duties.

He told how Johnnie's greatest love was his grandchildren, then numbering nine but with two more on the way which he had heard about just before his death; of the 'wonderful' children's Christmas parties which he enjoyed as much as the children: 'the boy in him was never extinguished.' Raine strained forward, smiled and nodded. Diana kept her head low. Lord St John spoke of Johnnie's love of food, positive outlook and most of all, his love of life itself. When he had finished his address he repeated his bows and returned slowly to his pew.

The service finished at 12.50 p.m. and eight grey-suited pallbearers placed the oak-wood coffin on to their shoulders and, led by the Bishop and the Vicar, shuffled, arms entwined, out of the church. They were followed by Raine and Diana who instinctively clasped gloved hands. It was a gesture that caused much speculation. Was it a public statement of friendship, the healing of a rift, or just a moment's bond as they shared the feelings of love and grief for the same man? For a few seconds Raine's composure faltered. She pursed her lips tightly and blinked furiously.

13

Diana, visibly distraught, bit her bottom lip as she too fought to regain her composure before facing the cameras trained on the church door. The two women walked together behind the coffin to the strains of Princess Diana's favourite hymn, 'I Vow To Thee My Country'. They were followed by the Prince of Wales, other members of the family and the rest of the congregation.

Outside the family stood for a few emotional moments with bowed heads as the coffin was lifted into the hearse to start the Earl's last journey, towards the crematorium at Milton Malsor. His ashes were to be placed in the family vault beneath the floor of the Spencer chapel, which contains the remains of members of the family dating back to 1522. Only the Earl's immediate family – his widow Raine, her youngest son, Henry, Diana, her two sisters Sarah and Jane, and Johnnie's older sister, Lady Anne Wake-Walker – attended the cremation, but the population of Great Brington turned out to line the streets and pay their last respects to the lord they had all loved. The Prince of Wales went back to the house with Charles and Victoria and stayed on for lunch with Diana and all the family. Raine joined them, but spent most of the time alone in her former bedroom.

Despite Johnnie's request that there should be no flowers, but donations instead to the National Association of Boys' Clubs, a charity he had worked for for many years, thirty-five floral tributes lay on the fresh spring grass outside the church. Even here etiquette was observed. The first in line was a wreath of freesias and chrysanthemums from the Queen and Prince Philip with a card which read: 'In memory Elizabeth and Philip.' Attached to the same wreath was a handwritten message from the Prince of Wales: 'In most affectionate memory.'

Next came Diane's floral tribute of lilies and sweetpeas with the touching message: 'I miss you dreadfully darling Daddy, but will love you forever ... Diana.' Two policemen stood guarding these wreaths and the handwritten notes. The fact that the messages from Diana and the Prince of Wales were on different wreaths was seized upon as evidence of the split between them, although later Palace bungling was blamed for this: Diana and Charles were said to have written personal messages on cards to be attached to their joint wreath, but by an unfortunate mistake Charles's card was pinned to the flowers sent by the Queen and Prince Philip. Next to Diana's flowers was a wreath of grape hyacinths and tulips from the Queen Mother and further down the line, Dame Barbara Cartland's traditional pink carnations with a note that read: 'In loving memory of a wonderful man who we all loved.'

Having had to snap the royal mourners at great speed – 'I didn't have much time but at least I was clear on Diana,' said royal photographer Tim Graham – the band of photographers could take their time over the floral tributes. Journalists stood around dictating the story on their portable telephones, then, to friendly police shouts of 'Don't leave any litter now', some moved on to the pub which was doing a roaring trade. The satellite dishes on the vans were taken down, the fields emptied of cars and the little village gradually recovered.

On Saturday 11 April the Princess of Wales returned to Althorp to inter the ashes of her father. With head bowed and accompanied by her brother Charles and her sisters Sarah and Jane, she carried the black box containing the eighth Earl's ashes to place them in the family vault at the church. A flagstone was raised to provide access to the burial vault and then cemented back in place. Raine did not join them and Diana was hardly noticed during the brief visit. On the surface the village had returned to normal, but everyone knew that life in the great house would never be the same again.

2

Early Days

Edward John Althorp, known as John or more commonly Johnnie, was born on 24 January, 1924 at 24 Sussex Square in London, a house which his father Jack, the seventh Earl, had rented for the winter. Jack Spencer, a gruff, introverted, difficult man with little idea about how to communicate at a personal level, exerted considerable influence on his son, although not always of a positive sort. Although father and son got along reasonably well when Johnnie was small, and then much later when he was involved with Raine and his father was old, their relationship was always formal and there were often long periods when they were not on speaking terms. By all accounts Johnnie was a great disappointment to the demanding Earl; the two were very different in temperament and had little in common. Johnnie didn't inherit his father's intellect, share his passion for antiques or show much concern about his inheritance. He preferred outdoor activities and was altogether a more easy-going character.

Interior designer David Hicks believes, 'They weren't each other's cup of tea. His father was more of a London person and Johnnie was a country man.'

The Spencer godparents have often been royal; Jack was a godson of King Edward VII, Johnnie of Queen Mary and the Prince of Wales, later King Edward VIII. The Prince, however, didn't attend Johnnie's christening, but sent a silver mug. Johnnie used to see him as a boy in the school holidays and got on with him 'jolly well'. A generation later, Johnnie's daughters Sarah and Jane had royal godparents, and the Queen is godmother to Charles, the new Earl Spencer. Ironically only Diana, the Princess of Wales, who disappointed the family by being a girl, did not have royal godparents.

Jack's sister Margaret, twenty years younger, lived with the family at Althorp. She was only fifteen when their father Charles, the sixth Earl died, and despite his brusque manner Jack had no hesitation when he succeeded to the title and moved into Althorp about letting Margaret continue to live there. Now Lady Margaret Douglas-Home, she says: 'Although my brother was very sweet to me, he had a very peculiar temperament, didn't like people and certainly didn't see the point of ordinary people. He was a loving father when his children were young, but not when Johnnie grew up.'

Looking at Jack's upbringing, however, one could hardly have expected anything different. He was born Albert Edward John Spencer in May 1892 but was always known as Jack. His father, Charles Spencer (1857–1922), was an eccentric who became a Liberal MP in 1880 when he was only twenty-two. He followed in the steps of several Spencer ancestors, including Henry (1620–43) who supported Charles I in his campaign against the Roundheads and was made Earl of Sunderland; the devious and amoral Robert, Lord Spencer, 2nd Earl of Sunderland (1641–1702) who regularly changed his political allegiances and successfully cultivated three kings, Charles II, James II and William III; and John Poyntz, (1835–1910), Johnnie's great-uncle, the fifth Earl, known as the 'Red Earl', who served Gladstone as Viceroy of Ireland, Minister for Education and First Lord of the Admiralty and was Gladstone's choice to succeed him as prime minister. (Queen Victoria sent for Lord Rosebery instead.) When the Red Earl died his title passed to his half-brother Charles, Jack's father. Charles made his mark not from contributing to debates, but by his appearance. He liked to wear high, stiff collars and elaborate cravats and the royal offices he held were ones concerned with court etiquette and dress. He was made Groom-in-Waiting in 1886, Vice-Chamberlain in 1905 and, later that year, Lord Chamberlain of the Household. He was a formal, meticulous man, whose priorities lay in appearance rather than feelings.

In contrast Jack's mother, Margaret Baring, daughter of Lord Revelstoke, was a plain, shy woman who was widely read in both English and French and was a talented violinist who had studied at the Royal College of Music. Although it seems an unlikely union, the pair married in 1887, had three sons and three daughters and apparently lived together quite happily. Margaret made no attempt to compete with her husband's stylish dressing, was unsnobbish and disliked parties.

Jack, who inherited his mother's shyness and reticence, was educated at Harrow and Trinity College, Cambridge and, later as a captain in the Life Guards, was wounded during the First World War. He was only fourteen when his mother died and almost simultaneously his father withdrew from the family, having almost nothing more to do with his children until his death in 1922. Any parental care was left to Jack's eldest sister Delia, who was only sixteen and in need of mothering herself. Nor did Charles ever speak of his late wife to anyone, but retreated behind his polished façade of meticulous dress and manners. He often accompanied

Edward VII abroad in his position as Lord Chamberlain of the Household and shared the King's mania for punctuality. After the King's death, he continued as Lord Chamberlain to George V but in 1911 resigned due to ill-health and retired to Althorp. When he died he left an estate valued at £1,197,826 gross.

The double blow of effectively losing both parents at once must have had a traumatic effect on an introverted boy like Jack, and no doubt influenced his behaviour throughout his life. Although he could be kind and considerate to those who responded to his interests, he had no time for those who did not and put all his energy and suppressed emotions into the pictures and treasures of Althorp which he inherited when he was thirty. He became so passionate about his collections that he was nicknamed the Curator Earl. Margaret says of him: 'There was nothing my brother didn't know about the house and everything in it, from the smallest locket to the largest chair. The house was his life.'

He was equally knowledgeable on the history of the Spencer family whose fortune was founded on sheep and good marriages, the most spectacular of which was that of Charles (1675–1722), 3rd Earl of Sunderland, to Lady Anne Churchill, in 1700. The second of his three wives, she was the daughter of the Duke and Duchess of Marlborough, who were enormously rich. Sarah, Duchess of Marlborough, passed on her estates and wealth to her favourite grandson, Hon. John Spencer (1708–46), who also inherited Althorp, with the proviso that neither he nor his eldest son, yet another John, should enter politics. Instead, his son John (1734–83), who became the first Earl Spencer, developed a passion for books, art and architecture, became a close friend of Sir Joshua Reynolds and built Spencer House, the magnificent mansion overlooking Green Park, as the family's London home. It was recognised as one of the most ambitious private palaces ever built in London and is the city's only great eighteenth-century house to survive intact.

In 1927, however, Johnnie's father decided that Spencer House had become too expensive to run. He leased it to the Ladies' Army & Navy club and moved the contents to Althorp. In 1942, during the Second World War, he returned for the last time to remove all the fixed furnishings – including fireplaces, skirting boards and chimneypieces – in case they were destroyed in bombing raids. It was lucky he did. Two years later, in 1944, the house was damaged in a raid.

Johnnie's mother, Lady Cynthia Hamilton, daughter of the third Duke of Abercorn, possessed many of the human qualities her husband lacked; she was sensitive, generous-spirited and compassionate as well as beautiful. Edward, the Prince of Wales had fallen in love with her during the First World War, but the mere fact she was not of royal blood prevented the marriage. If they had married, the history of the Royal Family would have been very different. Instead, after several other love-affairs, the Prince married the American divorcée Wallis Simpson, abdicated and became the Duke of Windsor. Soon after their romance ended, Cynthia was introduced to Jack Spencer by Elizabeth Bowes-Lyon, later Queen Elizabeth the Queen Mother, who was a close friend of another of Jack's sisters, Lady Lavinia Spencer. They married in 1919, and had a daughter Anne born some three years before Johnnie. By all accounts it was not a happy union. Jack was either unable or unwilling, or perhaps a combination of both, to fulfil the emotional demands of marriage. He treated Cynthia with coldness, bullied her and, according to a family friend who knew them well, 'was often very rough with his wife'. Countess Spencer, however, bore her often unhappy life with great fortitude and would hide her own personal sadness by immersing herself in good works, in much the same way as her granddaughter, the Princess of Wales, was to do later.

Johnnie adored his gentle mother and her sister-in-law, Margaret, found her 'the sweetest, most generous woman I have ever met. She was an angel and wouldn't have rows with anybody.' When Elizabeth became Queen, she invited Cynthia to become a Woman of the Bedchamber in 1936 and later a lady-in-waiting. The King and Queen were friends with the Spencers for years; George VI admired Jack who in turn managed to curb his sharp tongue in his presence. Mostly, however, Jack was a man who followed his own path regardless of the feelings of others or the niceties of convention. In 1947 he had the centuries-old family vault in Great Brington parish church opened, having decided that the general disintegration was beginning to cause an unpleasant smell and that his ancestors should be brought up for cremation. The bodies of the earls, lords and ladies of the Spencer family that had lain in the vault for hundreds of years were loaded on to a lorry and taken to Milton Crematorium. With the ashes now in urns and returned to the Spencer tomb the Rector of Great Brington held a special committal service. The lead from the coffins was re-cycled for lining the church roof.

Some felt the Earl's action was brutal and insensitive, but Jack defended his decision. 'There is nothing morbid about what I have done,' he said. 'The family vault is full. It had not been used for about a hundred years since my grandfather was placed there. My parents lie in the churchyard. The vault was very untidy and I decided it was time the place was cleared up a bit ... I am sure my ancestors would approve ... The urns will take up far less room than the lead coffins.'

Jack Spencer was a right-wing Tory and involved himself in local affairs; he served as Lord Lieutenant of Northamptonshire from 1952 for fifteen years and was chairman of the Northampton General Hospital Management Committee when it changed from voluntary to National Health status. He was also president of the local Trustee Savings Bank, the

Territorial Association, the Old Contemptibles, (an association of ex soldiers of the original British Expeditionary Force sent to France in 1914) the Northampton Town and County Association for the Blind, the St John Ambulance Council, the Antiquarian Society and the Association of Boy Scouts, a trustee of the Pytchley hunt and a fellow of the Royal Society of Arts.

Jack Spencer did not confine his artistic interests to Althorp alone; he became chairman of the advisory board of the Victoria & Albert Museum, and a trustee of the Wallace Collection and took advantage of free consultations from the curators of both organisations.

It was Jack who opened Althorp to the public although he had mixed feelings about strangers walking through his home. He would often insist on checking the underside of their shoes to make sure they were not bringing any dirt on to his precious carpets and follow them around with duster in hand. If, however, a visitor was obviously interested, or an expert in antiques, he happily acted as guide and would talk for hours about his possessions. He enjoyed the company of scholars and writers whom he encouraged to use the family archives at Althorp. He happily lent valuable pictures to exhibitions and had his own portrait painted by Augustus John.

He relaxed by doing, of all things, embroidery – 'the finest relaxation I know – it is as good as a nightcap before one retires after a worrying day,' he said. It was also an economy measure and some of the chairs at Althorp are covered with his work. He reluctantly had to give it up when he was seventy because his eyesight had deteriorated. His crusty manner and short temper increased as he became older, but although local residents feared him they respected his knowledge and love of Althorp.

In complete contrast to her husband, Countess Spencer cared very much about people. 'Everyone absolutely loved her,' recalled one local resident. She would spend considerable time bringing comfort to any of the estate tenants or villagers who were sick or in difficulties. She herself died of cancer in 1972 at the age of seventy-five and although her husband treated her well in the last months of her life, her gentle qualities were not generally valued by him.

Johnnie was aware of his parents' difficult marriage and the gulf between his irascible father and kind and gentle mother were to have a fundamental affect on his own relationships. He grew up in the twenties, a period when aristocrats did not show their true feelings and, in accordance with tradition, he and his sister Anne were placed in the care of the strict but much-loved Nanny Stackwood, who stayed with the family for twelve years. The children spent most of their time with her in the day and night nursery on the first floor of Althorp House and little Anne readily accepted the restrictions on her behaviour. 'In those days there was tremendous discipline and that was it.' Johnnie, however, 'was a wicked little boy and full of spirit'.

However, unlike many aristocratic families who only saw their children scrubbed and suitably dressed for a formal half-hour after tea, Anne remembers going off for family outings. She insists, 'We were a very happy family and did a lot with our parents, going to the zoo and things like that. Our mother had a beautiful nature and adored both her children.' As for her notoriously difficult father, she says, 'He had a strong personality but I was devoted to him and got on with him very well. I saw his weak points. He didn't suffer fools gladly, but he was highly intelligent and knowledgeable and adored the house, absolutely adored it. A lot of people were frightened of him, but I never saw him lose his temper.' She believed Johnnie and his father never got on well because 'they were probably too alike'. Others feel that Johnnie's dislike stemmed from fear of his father's bullying of both himself and his mother.

Althorp was Jack's priority not only for his time and energy but also for his finances. The children were brought up not to waste anything, whether it was food or electric light, and he often kept his wife desperately short of funds. Although Anne and Johnnie had enough to wear – hems were regularly let down and clothes carefully darned – Countess Spencer had barely an adequate wardrobe to equip her for her position in society. Although Jack was not interested in maintaining an elaborate social life, there were occasional visitors. When Johnnie was three, Winston Churchill came to stay and was put in the magnificent Oak Bedroom. 'He was a cousin,' says Johnnie, 'but my mother was not very keen on him because he was writing *Marlborough: His Life and Times* in bed and got ink everywhere.' Although he was so young he remembers his mother saying, 'We don't want that young man again.' Jack agreed. When he caught Churchill smoking a cigar, 'I ripped it right out of his mouth and stamped it out on the floor,' he said.

The Earl did have one extravagance, however: a dark green Rolls-Royce with a red and white line painted round the middle and the family crest painted on each door, which he used when he wanted to be chauffeur-driven to London. Anne found it quite out of character. 'I never knew why my father had it because he wasn't ostentatious.' A traditional aristocrat, he ruled his staff with a rod of iron. They feared and respected him and dared not disobey his orders. After one visit to Buckingham Palace Jack climbed into his Rolls-Royce dressed in his official attire as Sheriff of Northampton – feathered hat, great boots and red coat – for the return journey to Althorp. His chauffeur was under strict instructions never to turn his head when the Earl was in the car, but to start the car and move off when he heard the door slam. Some distance from the Palace, the Earl tapped on the window. The car stopped and

Jack went into the bushes to relieve himself. It was a windy day and a strong gust slammed the door closed. The car moved off, leaving the Earl stranded and he had to hitch a lift in full regalia from a passing motorist.

To compensate for the austerity of the childrens' daily lives, they were surrounded by beautiful countryside and some of the most priceless heirlooms of an English heritage. Portraits of their ancestors stared down at them from walls lined with silk. When Anne reached the age of nine and Johnnie was about seven, they were allowed to go down and eat lunch with their parents. Anne remembers, 'It was quite an excitement.' They ate with silver cutlery and when Johnnie was small, he was bathed in a vast 1701 solid silver wine container which was part of the famous Marlborough collection.

Brother and sister lived a country life surrounded by dogs and bantam hens. In the summer they would sometimes cycle together in the grounds of the great house, or play tennis, badminton or bumble puppy – a game of hitting a ball attached to a piece of elastic. When the winters were cold enough, they skated on the Althorp lake.

Occasionally, for a treat, the groom would take both children for rides in a pony cart round the local lanes. When friends came, a favourite game was having races round the top passages of Althorp but there is no record of one shy young visitor, Princess Elizabeth, taking part. She would come to see Johnnie and Anne when her parents, the Duke and Duchess of York, later George VI and Queen Elizabeth, took a house in Thornby, Northamptonshire, for the hunting season.

Every Sunday morning at 11.00 a.m., the children went to the parish church in Great Brington, when their father always read the lesson. 'There was no question of not going,' says Anne. Johnnie said his prayers every day, a habit that continued into adulthood.

Christmas was a particularly happy time at Althorp, which Johnnie continued to celebrate on a grand scale. Relations came to stay and there would be a huge Christmas tree with real candles, usually in the front hall. The servants would appear in order of seniority to be given their presents and the family would eat a traditional Christmas lunch. Although Johnnie's children later said they found Althorp 'spooky', Anne disagrees and always loved the house.

Summers were often spent in the family house in North Creake near Holkham Bay on the Norfolk coast. 'It was near the sea, we had picnics on the beach every day and there were lots of other children to play with,' Anne recalls.

A governess by the name of Miss Manning was employed to teach both children. Anne was a good and willing pupil. Johnnie, however, was not and when he saw Miss Manning walking towards the schoolroom, would often run away. Miss Manning would try to catch him by chasing him along the Althorp corridors. She rarely succeeded. When Johnnie felt trapped, he would jump out of the window and run off into the vast grounds.

Such freedom, however, was not to last long. Although Anne continued to be educated at home throughout her childhood, when Johnnie was eight he was packed off to board at St Peter's Court School in Broadstairs, catering for about sixty boys. Like most traditional prep schools in the thirties, it had strict rules. Boys had to attend chapel every morning and twice on Sundays and eat all of their 'not very good' food. The dormitories, shared between three and ten boys, were unheated and without curtains which meant they were freezing cold in winter and had to go to sleep in broad daylight in the summer.

Great emphasis was placed on sport at St Peter's Court and, with so many schools in the Broadstairs area, rivalry was considerable. Boys who gave illness as an excuse for not playing games were frowned upon and to reduce the risk of infectious diseases, necessitating periods in quarantine, parents were only allowed to visit their offspring once a term. Even then, restaurants, cinemas or other public places were considered a health hazard and ruled out of bounds.

Despite these restrictions, St Peter's Court maintained a happy atmosphere and in general the masters were 'marvellous'. The boys were divided into four sets – Alpha, Beta, Gamma and Delta – and competed in these sets for games, work and even good behaviour. Johnnie was in Gamma with Christopher Pease, now Lord Wardington, who remembers Gamma as being the best set when he and Johnnie were there. 'Johnnie was always very competitive, very forceful, full of ideas but sometimes a bit of a bully,' he says. He does not ever remember him being homesick. 'I think he was quite happy to be away.' Lord Montagu of Beaulieu, however, who followed Johnnie to Eton, remembers him as being 'extremely kind to younger boys like me'.

In the summer of 1937 when Johnnie was thirteen, he was sent to Eton and no longer had to sleep in a dormitory. Like all Eton schoolboys, he was allocated his own room with coal fire. His contemporaries included the young Gerald Legge, later to be Raine's first husband.

Johnnie was never an outstanding pupil and apart from his achievements in the school Corps, the Eton experience was probably a disappointment for him. 'He wasn't very bright but nor was he a fool and in those days none of us worked terribly hard. But he was terribly competitive and didn't like being beaten,' said Lord Wardington who went on to Eton from St Peter's Court with Johnnie.

He was an enthusiastic games player, especially keen on cricket, and quite good at football, but without being in the top flight. Wardington, who was captain of games, remembers that in December 1941 Johnnie 'was very annoyed that I didn't give him his football colours. There was an atmosphere between us that you could cut with a knife for weeks.' Johnnie also enjoyed rifle-shooting and was 'a good but not exceptional shot'. He did have a tiny sporting triumph at Eton, however. It was he who rekindled interest in a game called passage football – a football game played along the passages in the school house after lessons had finished – that had temporarily slipped from schoolboy memory.

Johnnie's favourite subject was history and he got on particularly well with the stand-in history tutor, Geoffrey Agnew, of the Bond Street family of art dealers. Agnew encouraged seventeen-year-old Johnnie to deliver what several fellow pupils remember to this day as a 'marvellous' lecture with slides showing the treasures, and particularly the paintings in the Althorp Collection. It was the beginning of Johnnie's lifelong passion for photography although sadly, not for the family treasures. Despite his keenness, Johnnie failed to win the history prize which upset him deeply.

The popularity of a boy at most public schools, and particularly at Eton, often depended on academic and sporting prowess. As Johnnie did not distinguish himself in either direction, he was never particularly popular. This was not helped by the emergence of a bullying streak that affected his behaviour towards some, but not all, of his fellow pupils. 'I was sometimes the target,' Lord Wardington admits. The streak took the form of verbal rather than physical abuse, which he used against fellow pupils and younger boys when he felt he could get away with it. Sir Roger Cary, who arrived two years after Johnnie, remembers: 'When I first arrived in 1939 Johnnie was rather spiky and spiteful, particularly towards new boys who he liked to tease. I think his father used to bully him a lot at home and he came across as being very bitter, but he gradually matured and behaved slightly better. All in all I don't think Johnnie found himself at Eton.'

Others, however, never saw that side of Johnnie, including Lord Montagu of Beaulieu. 'He was always a very gentle sweet person. I never heard him raise his voice against anybody,' he says.

When the war started in 1939 life at the school changed. All the boys were given a gas mask in a tin canister which they were trained to use and were shepherded into 'cold and miserable' air-raid shelters during air raids.

Eton was the target of some incendiary bombing. The upper school was hit once, but no great damage was done. Several of the staff were called up. Even Johnnie's housemaster, Reggie Colquhoun, although over forty at the time, left to join the Home Guard, leaving behind his pretty twenty-year-old wife, Ruth, to continue managing the catering. Now Ruth Birchall, she worked 'wonders' with vegetables, including nettles, and even, she recalls managed to make tasty omelettes out of dried egg:

24

You had to be a bit crafty. Some of the food was very dreary, but luckily boys are always hungry. They had potatoes in their jackets a few times a week. I managed to get kippers sent by train from Grimsby. I used local milk which wasn't pasteurised, so I suppose I took a risk. I found some mushrooms growing locally which I collected. They were blue and looked poisonous but, in fact, were perfectly safe. And I tried to grow salad. Sometimes parents helped out. One kind parent sent us a whole stag from Scotland which I remember arrived on the kitchen table late one very hot Saturday afternoon. I had a terrible job trying to find a butcher to cut it up.

She was particularly fond of Johnnie. 'He was a very nice, good-looking and helpful boy who left Eton as a handsome young man. He was one of the gentlest people in the world,' she said.

Like many young patriotic boys of his age, Johnnie wanted to help the war effort and in the summer of 1940 organised a group of five friends, including Henry Bruce (later Lieutenant-Commander) and Christopher Wardington, to work in the woods on the Althorp estate for a month, chopping trees for use as pit-props in the mines. The estate woodman marked all the trees and helped the boys fell and chop them up. 'It was terrific fun,' Bruce remembers 'although I think most of us were pretty useless. But Johnnie's mother was like a mother to us. The old man, however, struck us as being pretty mad and would fly off the handle very easily.' Wardington agrees. 'I think you could say his father was bonkers in a nice way, but he had the most enchanting mother that ever lived.'

The friends had not been at Althorp long when Johnnie and his father had a fierce argument, which resulted in the Earl confiscating his son's ivory hairbrushes. Johnnie was so angry that he was determined to take his revenge that same evening. He concocted a plan, aided and abetted by his friends. That night, after the Earl had retired to bed, they crept along the corridor and into his father's bedroom where he slept alone. Johnnie poured large quantities of the effervescent indigestion remedy, Eno's Fruit Salts, into the chamber pot kept by the bedside. Muffling their nervous giggles, the boys then ran back to their bedrooms and, after a lot of excited whispering, finally fell asleep. They were woken a few hours later by a raging, furious Earl. He had got up in the night to relieve himself in his chamber pot and had a terrific fright when the liquid foamed up and cascaded over the pot on to the floor. Fearing he had some dreadful ailment, he called his doctor who rushed over, examined the Earl and the contents of the pot and discovered the prank. Bruce recalls: 'There was the most almighty row. We were all called from our beds and told we had to leave first thing in the morning.'

The boys packed immediately and although they were down for a very early breakfast, couldn't bring themselves to eat as they waited anxiously for Johnnie to appear. He, however, was calmness itself, told them not to take any notice of his father's orders and to carry on as if nothing had happened. To the friends' surprise the episode was never mentioned again and they remained at Althorp for the full month. Bruce remembers 'Johnnie was thrilled with the prank. It absolutely delighted him. Not everybody would let their mates do that to their father.'

At that time much of Althorp was shut down and in part used by the Natural History Museum in South Kensington to store some of its collection of animals, including all the stuffed gorillas. It was also used as a stopping-off point for soldiers on their way to France, and the boys would often wander down to talk to them. Bruce remembers, 'The park was a mass of tents, one of which was a big NAAFI tent and it was one of Johnnie's main pleasures to go and help serve the tea and he often persuaded us to join him. He particularly enjoyed egging on the troops to say something dreadful about the Earl without letting on who he was, saying things like "What are the people in the big house like?" He liked a bit of fun.'

The old Earl, however, was not so keen on the troops in his grounds. He claimed that they blocked his view when they walked past and demanded that they ran past instead. Johnnie's friends witnessed him many times sitting waiting by the window in case any of the soldiers dared to disobey his order. If he caught anyone walking there would be the 'most colossal row'.

All senior boys at Eton were entitled to a fag, a younger boy who was at their beck and call, to run errands and do small chores. Johnnie's fag was John Bovill who has 'no complaints' about how Johnnie treated him. 'He wasn't as fierce as some one heard about and didn't beat me much. I had to light the fire in his room, make his toast for tea and run his errands. There was a tuck shop where you could get some fried bread which we called rafts with an egg or sausage on it, but in wartime there weren't that much available.' Making the fire was more demanding. Because boys were only allowed a meagre ration of coal and sticks in their room 'woe betide you if you didn't get it going first time because there weren't any spare sticks'. Toast was cooked in front of the fire and when on one occasion Bovill burnt it, Johnnie gave him 'six of the best'.

Although Johnnie was liked in his school house, he was not elected to 'Pop', the élitest Eton society, responsible for much of the discipline and the running of the school. He was so disappointed that he said to Wardington, 'I will get into every club in London so I can blackball every member of Pop who tries to get in.'

The aspect of Eton that Johnnie liked best was the Corps. He became company sergeant major and took to it as to the manner born. Here, at last, was something he could excel at and his manner relaxed accordingly. 'He really shone, and I think it was what made Eton worthwhile to him,' says Sir Roger. 'He became very fatherly towards the boys in his platoon and so different from the John I had first known.'

One of the reasons why Johnnie took the Corps so seriously was that soldiers stationed in Windsor would regularly come to Eton and talk to the boys about the Army and the war. After Johnnie left Eton at the age of eighteen, in July 1942, he was called up, and later joined the Royal Scots Greys in Europe for the last part of the war when he had several opportunities to put his fighting spirit to the test.

3

War and Peace

Johnnie Althorp, after an initial period of training, arrived at Sandhurst on 10 July 1943 with his schoolfriend John Dawes, later to be his best man when he married Frances Roche. He received his commission the following January and in the spring of 1944 joined the Royal Scots Greys, first as a subaltern but soon becoming a lieutenant and then captain. He was one of several reinforcements joining the Greys who had lost many officers during the war. Most of his fellow soldiers were experienced fighters and Johnnie was sensible enough not to pull rank. Sergeant Jim Randall who served in the Greys throughout the war says: 'Johnnie came straight from Sandhurst into our Recce (reconnaissance) troop. He was rather shy and retiring and very youthful-looking and quickly became very popular.'

The Scots Greys had been in the Middle East for about three years but were at the time brought back from fighting in Italy for the Normandy battles. Despite the losses, regimental pride was very high; their motto was 'Second to None' and the troop instruction was 'Push on the Recce, but don't get involved'. Johnnie was soon as fiercely proud of his regiment as the next man, was mentioned in dispatches and after the war regularly attended regimental reunions.

The Recce troop used light Stuart tanks affectionately called 'Honey' tanks and during the latter stages of the war moved from Normandy through France, Belgium, Holland and Germany. The tanks were not heavy enough to take on the German tanks and when there was a major battle the troop sat on the flank and passed information through. When the regiment was static they would go out and watch enemy activity.

The shock of war was traumatic for any young man and particularly for someone whose life had been as sheltered and comfortable as Johnnie's. He wrote about his experiences in his diary describing how he had not experienced the comforts of civilian life for over ten weeks. 'We had been existing in a world of noise, ruin and the choking dust of a boiling summer. Evil sights and the stench of burnt flesh had become more and more commonplace...' In August, when fighting west of Caen, Johnnie found himself face to face with the horrors of war. The roads around Falaise were blocked by wrecked German equipment and he said 'everywhere in ditches, in carts, in streams and on the roads lay scattered hundreds of German bodies rapidly decaying under the August sun.'

Sergeant Randall remembers one particularly hair-raising time when the troops were trying to cross the narrow River Orne on the approach to Caen. 'The Recce troops were in their tanks working with the 15th Scottish division at the time and their infantry had made a corridor through the enemy positions. On the far side of the Orne there was some very high ground we called Hill 112 which was very hotly contested. Johnnie and I were shelled for a long time. It wasn't the Hollywood movie stuff by any means. We were surrounded by dead bodies and nearly frightened to death ourselves. It was very unpleasant.'

Johnnie became a tank commander working with another two men in his tank with four tanks under his control. Opinion is divided as to how effective a commander he was. Jim Randall and Pat O'Rourke, who fought closely with him, felt he commanded his tank well. 'When a young officer comes straight from Sandhurst into a fighting regiment he has to tread carefully, nor is he used to fighting in tanks,' said O'Rourke. 'Johnnie wisely took it steadily for a couple of weeks and the NCOs in the regiment looked after him. But once he settled down, you couldn't have wished for a better troop leader. He knuckled down, got the hang of commanding the tank and was very good at it. He was a very nice chap, never pulled rank and never bullied anyone.'

One of Johnnie's senior commanding officers was not so impressed. 'He had all the signs of never having been given his head. He was very nice but very stupid, very slow and lacking in go. He was never the brightest of people. It was all squashed out of him by a domineering father. He had beautiful manners and was always very correct, but was one of the stupidest officers I had at that time ever met. I recall a private soldier remarking to me that you could set his trousers on fire and it would be ten minutes before he realised his bum was burning – though the word used needless to say was not bum.'

Conditions for the Recce troop, as with other members of the regiment, were pretty rough. Whenever there was shelling, they slept in cramped conditions in the tank. If all was quiet they slept side by side in the open air and sometimes under a tarpaulin. Sergeant Randall remembers Johnnie trying to fill any spare space in the tank with enemy equipment and weapons. 'We wondered if he was dreaming of establishing a private war museum at Althorp.' His driver, a little Lancastrian known as Snacker Goulden, was not amused. He and I agreed that any spare space was needed, not for enemy weaponry, but for carrying the contents of looted wine-cellars. In civvy street Snacker had been a butcher and during a quiet spell we caught and killed a pig and soon every tank in the troop had a joint of pork hanging from the gun breech, but Johnnie's tank had the biggest.'

The fresh meat was a welcome change from the tinned and dried rations that were normal fare. Men shared a water-pack and rations came in boxes which contained tins of beans, bacon, jam and, if you were lucky, treacle or plum pudding. The contents were heated by knocking a hole in the top and boiling the cans in water. Because of the cramped conditions inside the tank, Johnnie, like other tank commanders, welded an empty ammunition box on to the outside of the tank as a space-saving container for rations. Occasionally, however, the ammunition box would be hit by a piece of shrapnel and the tins congeal together. 'It was a big tragedy,' says Randall.

The Recce troop often operated far from the regiment, gathering information – an experience Randall describes as 'bowel loosening'. He remembers one occasion in Germany when a camouflaged tank came swiftly round a bend heading straight for him. 'I felt great consternation until I realised it was Johnnie. We were both lost, an easy thing to happen after a cross-country ride, but neither of us would admit it.'

The plan was for the Army to cross the Seine and advance as rapidly as possible to Belgium. It was not as easy as it seemed. Nearly all the bridges over the Seine had been destroyed by the Allied Air Forces and those that were left were blown up by the retreating Germans. They did not, however, meet with fierce opposition.

According to a history of the Greys, *Second to None*, it was at this time that the Reconnaissance troop commanded by Captain Sprot came into its own. 'Its speed and accuracy quickly won the confidence of all squadrons and its dash and cunning made many valuable openings for the regiment.' Once the troops reached the town of Le Quesnoy, one Recce section under Captain Sprot and another under Johnnie were sent ahead to recconoitre crossings over a stream which flows into the River Somme at Longpré. Johnnie reported the presence of abandoned enemy infantry and guns, but when the troops crossed the only opposition they found was 'desultory small arms fire'. On seeing the tanks approaching the Germans fled, once again leaving behind a number of guns and mortars, and Johnnie took several prisoners.

They also met innumerable very relieved French people who gathered round them offering hospitality. Few surpassed the kind residents of the little town of La Neuve Lyre on the banks of the River Risle, however, who brought out bottles of Calvados and champagne, eggs, flowers and fruit. Johnnie records how they were all 'kissed, embraced, shaken and shoved'. The troop stayed for several hours until 'the combined effect of wine, women and song was beginning to tell'.

The tanks continued to move forward with no sign of the enemy for about a hundred miles but the fighting was not yet over. In the process of seizing bridges over the River Somme they lost several men and tanks.

By the following spring Johnnie had reached Germany. Here they encountered some of their heaviest resistance when they tried to capture the town of Bremen. Johnnie and his men were subjected to sniper fire and shelling from 88-mm anti-aircraft guns. According to the regimental history, two of Johnnie's tanks were knocked out by Panzerfausts, anti-armour weapons.

Johnnie, now Captain Viscount Althorp, had had a good war. It had brought out many positive aspects of his character and given him a new confidence. After the rarefied atmosphere of Eton and Sandhurst, he had learned how to mix with people from a different class and how to live in uncomfortable and often dangerous conditions. His first major problem when he came home in 1947 was to think of something to do. He decided he didn't want to stay in England, a shrewd move that enabled him to escape from the country's post-war austerity and the constraints of life at Althorp. He therefore applied to go to Australia for a three-year stint from 1947–50 as one of two ADCs required by Lieutenant-General Sir Willoughby Norrie, Governor of South Australia. His application was successful and he met his fellow ADC, Michael Trasenster, a former captain in the 4th/7th Royal Dragoon Guards for the first time at a special party given by Sir Willoughby in London. 'There were about twelve of us,' remembers Major Trasenster. 'Sir Willoughby took us to see *Oklahoma!* and then to dinner at the Dorchester.'

Soon afterwards the Norrie family – Sir Willoughby had two children from his first marriage and three from his second – Johnnie and Michael sailed off on the P & O liner *Stratheden* for the four-week journey to Australia. 'Although we had a lot of fun on board it wasn't like a cruise,' Michael says. 'In those days lots of people travelled by boat for their work and it was full of normal people going about their business. Johnnie and I hadn't really known life at all. We had gone straight from school into the Army and we were both rather shy. The mores of the time were different from now and the Norries were so sweet to us young people.'

Johnnie's three years in Australia were fundamental to his development. He blossomed and matured in the unstuffy atmosphere of Sir Willoughby's household and developed interests: a passion for photography, a fascination with wine and a love of people that were to stay with him all his life. He also discovered girls.

The Norrie party arrived to a warm welcome. 'Poms were very popular at the end of the war,' said John Darling, an Australian and fellow aide. They soon settled down to life at Government House, a vast colonial building, in Adelaide. Johnnie and Michael were installed in a wing over the offices, where they each had their own small bedroom and shared a bathroom.

As Governor-General, Sir Willoughby represented the Sovereign, then King George VI, and fulfilled part of the monarch's duties like unveiling plaques, opening schools, planting trees and, as it was Australia, occasionally making forays into the outback. Johnnie as Sir Willoughby's right-hand man had to make all the necessary arrangements for his visits throughout the state, ensure that everyone and everything was at the right place at the right time and then accompany the Governor-General on his travels. These broad-ranging duties brought him into contact with everybody who was anybody in South Australia as well as those who lived in remote country areas. Sir Willoughby expected proficiency and enthusiasm. A 'daily file' of the following day's activities and itinerary was given to both Johnnie and Michael with their morning tea and they were expected to check and confirm last-minute arrangements.

It was hardly an arduous job but by all accounts Johnnie did it efficiently and well. Apparently the only time he showed any reluctance to fulfil his duties was when he had to accompany Sir Willoughby on his regular weekly trip to the races. 'Sir Willoughby was mad on racing,' says Michael Trasenster. 'Johnnie, however, didn't like it much. Unfortunately I didn't either and the only thing we used to argue over was who was going to the race meetings.' If the work was up-to-date Sir Willoughby encouraged his ADCs to go out and enjoy themselves and Johnnie developed a taste for both nightclubs and, despite the strict licensing laws, beer.

There was a tremendous amount of social activity at Government House, including official receptions, three large garden parties a year run on Buckingham Palace lines and numerous formal and less formal dinner parties. Johnnie and Michael maintained a card index of potential guests based on the visitors' book at Government House. 'In terms of catering it was rather like running a hotel,' says Michael. The food, particularly on formal occasions, was 'wonderful'. After the deprivations of war and rationing, it was, Michael felt, like 'going from a state of siege to a land of plenty'. Johnnie was in charge of the cellars, which is where his interest in wine began. Much later he would market Château Althorp wines, champagne and port.

Another aspect of his work was to help put visitors to Government House at their ease. Johnnie, who was himself shy and rather awkward, initially found this endless socialising a strain. 'He used to try to hide it by being over-matey and more Australian than the Australians,' remembers Michael, 'and used such phrases as "Good on yer cobber" all the time.'

But by encouraging others to talk, looking after visitors who were equally diffident and making sure no one was left out of a conversation, he soon cured himself of his own shyness. A symbol of his newly acquired confidence was that he grew his first moustache at this time.

Every major British occasion was celebrated at Government House and when Princess Elizabeth married Philip Mountbatten on 20 November 1947, a gala dinner party was held.

Many British VIPs visited Adelaide during Johnnie's stay including Helen Keller, the blind, deaf and mute writer; Sir Laurence Olivier and his wife, Vivien Leigh, leading a company from the London Old Vic; Jean Simmons, then a shy eighteen-year-old actress; Marie Rambert of the Ballet Rambert who used to do cartwheels on the lawn; and Anthony Eden, then Deputy Leader of the Opposition. It was not surprising that in such distinguished company Johnnie quickly developed an enviable social manner and found he could be witty and amusing which, with his natural good looks, made him very popular, particularly with young women. 'He liked pretty girls – no doubt about it,' says an Australian friend, 'and the girls liked him for being tall, handsome, charming and a viscount. He seemed the perfect example of an aristocrat.' He was expert at remembering names and personal details, an ability which stayed with him throughout his life even after his life-threatening brain haemorrhage. It endeared him to the Australians and later to fellow aristocrats as well as staff and tenants on the Spencer family estates.

Perhaps encouraged by the successful lecture and slide show of the Althorp treasures which he gave in his last year at Eton, Johnnie developed his interest in photography which was to become a lifetime's hobby; indeed, he first came to the nation's notice when, after his daughter Lady Diana announced her engagement to Prince Charles, he was to be found outside Buckingham Palace clicking away with his camera to capture the moment for the family album. He began presenting slide shows to women's institutes in Australia, the most popular of which was of the marriage of Princess Elizabeth. When accompanying Sir Willoughby on tour, he also took photographs on behalf of idle newspaper photographers, who, rather than endure a rough ride in the outback, preferred to stay at home and thank Johnnie by giving him lots of film.

While in Australia Johnnie was visited by his mother who came out to Adelaide on her own in 1949. As well as seeing her son she came to convalesce after being involved in two nasty accidents: a car crash followed soon afterwards by a train crash. Some felt she also wanted a break from her difficult husband. She was a guest at Government House for several months and, despite the fact that she had injured her back and was in obvious pain, never complained. As always, her natural elegance and charm endeared her to everyone who met her. She was delighted to see her son happy and doing well and left for England feeling relaxed and content.

When Johnnie's three-year assignment came to an end in 1950, Sir Willoughby gave him a large green scrapbook and a briefcase as mementos of his stay. He was returning to become Equerry to the ailing King George VI, a friend of Johnnie's father.

The position of royal equerry was offered to those who had performed public service duties well or who came from well-connected families. Johnnie had both qualifications and the position would enable him to put into practice, albeit in a more formal atmosphere, all that he had learned in his time with Sir Willoughby. One of his duties would be to accompany the King on a proposed tour of Australia and New Zealand, which had been planned despite fears for the King's health and during the course of which his experience in Australia would be particularly useful. Two doctors were to travel with the party and the trip was to have been a family event as Johnnie's mother had been invited to go as lady-in-waiting to the Queen. Few then thought that the 56-year-old King would die in 1952 and Johnnie little expected to revisit Australia not with the King, but with the young Queen Elizabeth on the first foreign tour of her region.

A new, confident Johnnie returned home to find that England had still not recovered from the after-effects of the war, although in Johnnie's élite aristocratic circle the deprivations were felt less than most. Despite the fact that food and clothes were still rationed, the season was in full swing and he was pitched into a heady whirl of balls and dinner parties. The most popular party venues at the time were the house at 23 Knightsbridge and the old Berkeley Hotel in Piccadilly. Balls started at 10.00 p.m. – with dinner beforehand – and finished in the early hours, with everyone being served eggs and bacon. The girls dressed in whatever finery their ration books allowed or in dresses retrieved from the family trunk and skillfully altered.

As the good-looking heir to a famous earldom and one of the great stately homes of England, Johnnie, now twenty-six, was the catch of his generation. 'When Johnnie came back from Australia, the girls fell in love with him in droves,' remembers his aunt, Lady Margaret Douglas-Home. 'He was such an attractive type. I think he was a man who found it fairly easy to fall in love, particularly when someone was in love with him.' Nor was his appeal lost on many a young girl's father. One of the first to make a move was the Earl of Leicester who invited Johnnie to his own stately home of Holkham in north Norfolk to introduce him to his slim, golden-haired, blue-eyed seventeen-year-old daughter, Lady Anne Coke (pronounced Cook).

Anne, now Lady Glenconner, remembers Johnnie as a very attractive young man. 'Although he already had lots of girlfriends, I fell very much in love with him. We saw each other a lot over the season and I went to stay at Althorp. It was a wonderful time. There were weekend parties and two or three dances a night. We used to go from one to the other. It was incredible.' Her own coming-out ball at Holkham was attended by King George VI and Queen Elizabeth and their daughter Princess Margaret. (In May 1992, Lady Glenconner represented Princess Margaret at Johnnie Spencer's memorial service.) 'My father had saved some very good champagne and my coming out party was one of the first great balls after the war,' she says.

Johnnie, like the other young men, wore black tie rather than uniform. Anne found him 'sweet, amusing, charming and a very good dancer'. Johnnie proposed to her when they were both guests at the Royal Ascot house party at Windsor Castle soon after the ball. Anne accepted immediately, with the idea that they would marry before the King's proposed tour of Australia in 1952 so she could accompany Johnnie as his wife. 'We got engaged. I told my parents. He told his. Sadly, however, it didn't work out.'

Opposition came from Althorp, where Johnnie's father was absolutely against the match, and made allegations about the Coke's family's health. He bullied his son to break off the engagement which put Johnnie into a terrible dilemma. He still did not quite have the inner resources to stand up to his father, yet he did not want to be seen to give in meekly to his father's wishes. Fate stepped in. At one of the coming-out parties when Johnnie was at his most vulnerable and indecisive, another blonde, blue-eyed beauty walked into his life. The Hon. Frances Roche was, like Anne Coke when she and Johnnie first met, only seventeen, but already possessed of a steely charm and iron determination. Just as she fell headlong in love with Johnnie, so he was completely entranced by her. Her family, the Fermoys (her father was the fourth Baron), also had strong Norfolk connections and her mother, Lady Fermoy, was a close friend of the Queen. Johnnie broke off his unofficial engagement, leaving Anne heartbroken. 'It was a terrific scandal,' recalls an onlooker. Frances was delighted and, ignoring her parents' anxiety over the difference in their ages, insisted that he was the man for her. At the time Johnnie saw no reason to disagree.

4

Married Life

Johnnie Althorp announced his engagement to the Honourable Frances Roche, younger daughter of Lord and Lady Fermoy, on 16 October 1953. This time there was no opposition from his father: the family could be traced back to the Stuart kings of England. The match was generally thought to be a good one although many recognised that, despite the age difference – Johnnie was, at twenty-nine, twelve years older than Frances – she was a much stronger and more determined character than he was.

Frances's father had inherited a fortune from his American grandfather. He was educated at Harvard and sat as Tory MP for King's Lynn from 1924 until 1935 and again for two years during the Second World War. In 1931, when he was thirty-six, he became Mayor of King's Lynn and married Ruth Gill, a professional pianist, that same year. She was only twenty, setting a precedent for daughter Frances and her granddaughter Diana to marry considerably older men.

Soon after their wedding near Ruth's home in Bieldside, Aberdeenshire, George V offered the couple Park House on the Sandringham estate as their home. Here Ruth raised their three children, Edmund the son and heir, Mary and Frances in a happy and lively atmosphere. A generation later, the house became home, although not always such a happy one, to Frances's own four children, Sarah, Jane, Diana and Charles.

Frances Roche was born on 20 January 1936, the same day that King George V died in the main house nearby, and it is said that Queen Mary, despite her own sadness, remembered to enquire after the health of Ruth Fermoy and her new baby. Lady Fermoy was a great friend of Elizabeth, the Duchess of York whose husband would, following the abdication in December of that year, become King George VI. Ruth later accepted the position of an Extra Woman of the Bedchamber when her friend was widowed and became Queen Elizabeth the Queen Mother. Many believe that it was these two old friends who hatched the plot to marry two of their grandchildren, Prince Charles and the Hon. Diana Spencer.

Johnnie and Frances had not been engaged for long, however, before

Johnnie's royal duties forced them to part. He had been working as Equerry to King George VI but, on 6 February 1952, the ailing king, who had been suffering from lung cancer, had a heart attack and died in his sleep at Sandringham. (Johnnie's future father-in-law, Lord Fermoy, was out hare-shooting with the King the day before he died.)

Johnnie was asked to continue to work for the royal household and to accompany the new Queen to Australia and New Zealand, as she wanted to take her father's place on the proposed tour. As his schoolfriend Sir Roger Cary recalls, 'Johnnie was a brilliant Equerry at the key time.' Not only did he know Australia, but it was reassuring for the young Queen to be able to rely on someone she had known since childhood. Her friendship with Johnnie, however, was to have its ups and downs. If its high point came when Diana married the Prince of Wales in 1981, the relationship deteriorated when, in the last years of Johnnie's life, he exploited his royal connection to make potentially lucrative commercial deals in Japan.

Just before the Australian tour, Johnnie went into King Edward VII's Hospital for Officers for a minor operation on his back (his father was at the same time in Guy's Hospital having his gall bladder removed). He recovered quickly and, in April 1954, as acting Master of the Queen's Household, Johnnie sailed on the royal tour liner *Gothic*, taking with him a life-size portrait of his new fiancé. The painting was a last-minute idea and Frances sat for a whole day as Hampstead artist Nicholas Egon completed the work in twenty-four hours. It was framed the following day and rushed to the docks before the ship sailed.

Frances filled in the time of Johnnie's absence by taking 'finishing courses' in Florence and Paris and buying a trousseau for her wedding, planned for June 1954. She purchased 'delicate lingeries, hand-made and trimmed with fine lace', glamorous cocktail dresses and the sort of smart, casual clothes a pretty young aristocratic wife should be seen in.

Much to everyone's relief the tour was a huge success. As the Queen was the first reigning monarch to tour both Australia and New Zealand there was a very pro-British atmosphere wherever she went. 'Everyone was absolutely thrilled to see Her Majesty, particularly as she had not been Queen for long,' says Russell Nash an ADC at Government House. She stayed in Sydney for two weeks where the welcome in 1954 was very different from her two-day stay in 1992 when she was subjected to considerable anti-royal feeling. 'She was radiant and mixed amongst huge crowds,' Nash remembers. 'The streets were packed with people ten deep trying to get a glimpse of her.'

Because the Queen knew of Johnnie's enthusiasm for photography, she entrusted him with her own cine camera and Johnnie took several films during the tour, even jumping off the royal dais to get the shot he wanted. When the Queen was off-duty she would film for herself.

Johnnie found plenty of time to amuse himself outside his royal duties and once again responded to the Australian extrovert attitude to life. He made his name as a fisherman; in Tauranga, New Zealand, he landed a 200-lb mako shark after a twenty-minute tussle and, off the coast of Sydney Harbour, a 222-lb marlin. He went to several dances at the Royal Sydney golf club and, when the Queen retired for the night after an evening engagement or a film show at Government House, he would quickly change and be off to a nightclub. Russell Nash says: 'It was a pretty social time and he was very much liked by everybody, especially the girls. He was a real ladies' man.' It was a foolish girl who took Johnnie's charming chatter seriously, however, for his heart now belonged to Frances. He wrote to her every day and telephoned her whenever he could get a decent telephone connection.

The young Queen had known Frances since childhood although some friends said that she had never particularly liked her. She fully understood, however, Johnnie's wish to be reunited with his future bride as soon as possible and gave him special permission to leave the royal tour at Malta. Although he was sorry to say goodbye to his friends in Australia Johnnie happily returned home to Frances and to prepare for what was billed as the wedding of the year.

For several weeks before hand, hundreds of presents piled up at the Fermoys' London home in Wilton Street, Belgravia, and during the week leading up to the big day, Lady Fermoy held 'open house' so that friends could see the carefully guarded gifts.

The wedding, which was held at Westminster Abbey on 1 June 1954, was a spectacular occasion. Frances looked radiant in a full-skirted camellia faille gown embroidered with cascades of silver sequins, rhinestones, crystals and hand-cut diamonds. Her tulle veil, which formed a short train, was held in place by her mother's diamond tiara. She carried a crescent of stephanotis, lilies-of-the-valley and white roses, and was followed by a procession of ten. There were three small pageboys: David Wake-Walker (nephew of the bridegroom), Viscount Raynham and James Dawnay who wore white satin suits buttoned down the front and stiff muslin collars with pale blue moiré sashes based on a Reynold's painting at the Spencer family home. (Johnnie's son Charles followed the same theme when he married Victoria Lockwood in September 1989.) There were three child bridesmaids: Elizabeth Wake-Walker (niece of the bridegroom), Lady Margot Cholmondeley and Bridget Astor, and four grown-up bridesmaids: the Hon. Mary Roche (sister of the bride), Sylvia Fogg-Elliot, Fiona Douglas-Home and Rowena Combe who wore long dresses of white-spotted Swiss muslin with a fichu neckline, full skirts and pale blue moiré sashes. Their headdresses and bouquets were made up of the same flowers as those carried by the bride.

Members of the Royal Family present included the Queen and the Duke of Edinburgh, the Queen Mother, the Duke and Duchess of Kent, Princess Alexander, the Duchess of Gloucester and Princess Royal; the Bishop of Norwich officiated, assisted by the Dean of Westminster, the Revd H. D. Anderson and the Rev Grenville Morgan, and the Bishop's address to the newly-weds included a prophecy: 'You are making an addition to the home life of your country on which above all others our national life depends.' Captain John Dawes of the Royal Scots Greys was best man and warrant officers and NCOs of the regiment formed a guard of honour as the bride and bridegroom left the Abbey.

The ceremony, attended by 1,700 guests, was followed by a large and extravagant party for nine hundred at St James's Palace loaned for the occasion by the Queen. Following the wedding, Frances and Johnnie left for a month-long honeymoon in Europe, the highlights of which Johnnie later said were sitting in cafés in Vienna and driving through the splendid mountain scenery of the Dolomites.

Once Johnnie was married, he decided to give up his court duties, having worked for George VI and then Queen Elizabeth for four years. He later told interior designer David Laws that he could not have continued working for the Royal Family as the heavy demands made of courtiers meant that it was almost impossible to have a life of one's own. He could not lead a life of aristocratic leisure, however, because the meagre allowance his father gave him was not enough to keep a wife and – as Frances, later emulated by her daughter Diana, became pregnant immediately – certainly not a child as well.

First of all he approached his old schoolfriend Lord Wardington for a job. 'Johnnie came to me and asked if I thought he could join Hoare & Co., the stockbrokers I was working for, but I said no, partly because there wasn't a vacancy and partly because mathematics was never his strong suit.'

Instead in September 1954 Johnnie went to the Royal Agricultural College at Cirencester for a year's course on farming and estate management which he knew would be useful to him when he inherited Althorp from his father. He wanted to buy a house near the college but could not find one that was suitable so rented a rather modest house for a year some eleven miles away in the little Gloucestershire village of Rodmarton.

In March 1955, just nine months after their wedding, their first child, a girl, was born at the Barratt Maternity Home in Northampton. She was named Sarah and christened three months later in St Faith's Chapel in Westminster Abbey with the Queen Mother as one of her godparents.

Life for the young married couple was working out perfectly, except for one thing. Soon after Sarah's birth Johnnie and Frances moved from Rodmarton to Orchard Manor, a house on the Althorp estate at Little

Creaton. The close proximity to his father only served to highlight the tense and uneasy relationship between the two men. They had little in common and now that Johnnie was a married man he was not prepared to tolerate the kind of treatment he had had from his father as a child. Nor could he rely on his young, inexperienced wife to help smooth things over. Frances did not have the sort of temperament or inclination to act as a conciliator between father and son, nor did she treat the Earl with the delicacy and tact that his gruff manner demanded. The relationship deteriorated to such an extent that the two men were soon no longer on speaking terms.

Fate, however, took a hand. Frances's father died in 1956 and his widow offered to turn over the lease of Park House on the Sandringham estate to her daughter and Johnnie. Frances was delighted at the idea, bringing up her own family in the house where she had been so happy as a child. Johnnie was equally pleased with the offer as it would enable him to get away from his father. They moved in as soon as was practically possible. Lord Spencer refused to let Johnnie take any furniture from Althorp, so Frances filled the house with Fermoy family heirlooms; he did, however, increase Johnnie's allowance once Sarah was born, but not by much.

The young family settled down easily in Park House. Johnnie loved his role of traditional English landowner and country aristocrat and quickly became well respected and liked by other landowners in the 'squires and spires' county of Norfolk.

The Sandringham estate, near the Norfolk coast, had been bought by King Edward VII, then Prince of Wales, in 1861 and has been a holiday home for the Royal Family ever since. Park House, with ten bedrooms and ample servants' quarters, had been built to accommodate the overflow of the vast numbers of friends the King liked to have around him at Sandringham, particularly when he organised shooting parties. It stood at the end of a short curving drive by Sandringham church, sheltered from the road by mature trees and rhododendron bushes that provided a vibrant red screen in late spring. Built in the local stone, the north-facing front of the house is weathered and grey but the private side is altogether softer, a peaty brown undamaged by the weather. The front door was painted in 'Sandringham blue', marking it as a royal property. The large garden looked out over acres of parkland and backed on to the Sandringham cricket ground. Many years later, well after the Spencers had moved on, the Queen donated Park House to the Leonard Cheshire Foundation who turned it into a £1.5 million hotel for the disabled, which she officially opened in July 1987. Diana, who grew up in the house, took the Prince of Wales to see her childhood bedroom and nursery just before they were turned into guest bedrooms. Still untouched was the window-frame where she and her sisters used to write their friends' telephone numbers. This was later removed and sent in its entirety to the Princess at Kensington Palace. Preserved in the house for guests to see is an architrave on which Diana's height was marked.

Not long after Johnnie and Frances moved in, Frances became pregnant again and Jane, their second daughter, was born six weeks prematurely in 1957 in the Queen Elizabeth Maternity Hospital in King's Lynn. One of her godparents was the Duke of Kent.

Johnnie had by this time completed his agricultural course and bought 240 acres at Ingoldisthorpe, almost adjoining the royal estate, for £16,000. The following year Frances gave him a further 236 acres at Snettisham which she bought for £20,000. More land was later acquired at Heacham, bringing the total to about 650 acres. The land was farmed for beef cattle, but as Johnnie was never one to push himself too hard and largely left the running of farm in the hands of foreman, it was not a particularly lucrative venture.

Although Johnnie was no longer working for the Queen, they continued to have a special relationship. She was so delighted with the colour films that he had taken of her tour in Australia and New Zealand that she gave him permission to show them publicly with his own commentary. Johnnie first showed his three forty-minute films at the fifteenth-century Guildhall Theatre in King's Lynn in July 1954 as part of the arts festival, initially set up by his mother-in-law in 1950 and now an important annual event. There were three showings and the tickets, priced at 3s 6d (17p) and 7s 6d (37p), sold out within half an hour of going on sale, with a long list of people waiting for returns. As well as covering all the more formal aspects of the tour, the films contained some delightfully informal shots, including some of the young Queen wearing jeans and driving a horse-and-cart. Because of their popularity the Queen allowed Johnnie to continue showing them, which he did almost a hundred times, raising some £2,500 for charity.

The Queen and Johnnie did not see each other often but when she was in residence at Sandringham over the New Year she would often ride through the park and chat to Johnnie's children. Tea parties would be arranged for her younger children and Johnnie's daughters and she would sometimes visit Johnnie and Frances at Park House. The Queen Mother would also occasionally drop in unexpectedly. She used to enjoy walking round the cricket ground and would sometimes stop for a cup of tea with Johnnie, especially if her great friend and lady-in-waiting Ruth Lady Fermoy was staying at Park House.

It was an annual tradition that the Spencer family, along with many other residents from the Sandringham estate, would be invited to attend the presentation of books to the Queen's Sunday-school children. Everyone would gather at the school in the picturesque village of Dersingham on the estate early in the afternoon. First they would all sing a hymn which would be followed by the presentation, with a lavish tea and an opportunity for everyone to take photographs afterwards.

Frances and Johnnie's social life was active, but limited to a narrow group of well-bred friends, and mainly centred in and around the estate. Since his school-days Johnnie had loved shooting and took his hobby very seriously. He was a regular and enthusiastic member of the Sandringham shooting parties and had actually been with George VI when he had shot his thousandth woodcock. He was also a keen, although not a very good cricketer.

One of the highlights of his social and sporting year was to organise a match against the workers on the estate. A close neighbour (now Sir) Julian Loyd, who was the land agent at Sandringham, recalls: 'Everyone looked forward to the annual cricket match. It was good fun and fairly casual. We were always beaten by the estate side and then we all had tea together afterwards. Johnnie wasn't a great cricketer, although he was better at bowling. We were all knocking on a bit and none of us were very fit.' He does, however, remember Johnnie as being very popular, although not very energetic. 'He was quite a big chap, a little ponderous and not ambitious.'

Frances, who had little in the way of domestic concerns to occupy her – the Spencers had six full-time staff including a cook, a butler and a private governess – contented herself with the gentle charitable work of the well-heeled upper classes. She did 'a lot of good work' for the local branch of the NSPCC and the Parochial Church Council, 'the focus for everybody'. 'She seemed to enter into Norfolk life like anybody else,' says Sir Julian. 'It was a friendly estate, a fantastic place with a great feeling of family support. Although the Royal Family are not there all that often, at the time they had a devoted staff many of whom had clocked up fifty years of service.'

Following in his father's footsteps and in preparation for when he inherited Althorp, Johnnie involved himself in the Northamptonshire community by becoming a councillor for the Brington division in 1952, a position he only relinquished in 1981 although he was no longer active after his stroke in 1978. But unlike his father, who was very active, he approached his work for the Council in much the same laid-back way as he tackled all other aspects of his life. Apart from serving as High Sheriff of Northamptonshire in 1959, he never held a position of any authority. He was never a chairman or even deputy chairman of any committee although, in mitigation, he did have a three-hour drive from Sandringham in order to attend meetings. According to John Lowther who was leader of the Council from 1970–81: 'Unlike his father Johnnie only did what he had to do which was attend four meetings a year and that was about it.'

He also held the post of Deputy Lieutenant for Northamptonshire from 1961 until his death in 1992, but he was one of forty deputies serving the Lord Lieutenant and his duties were mainly ceremonial. Sir William Morton knew Johnnie for thirty-five years and served on various committees with him. He was impressed that despite his long journey from Sandringham to Northampton he was always punctual, arriving at Council meetings 'often earlier than the members who lived five miles away'. Johnnie often attended the same meetings as his father but, as Morton remembers, 'They were at loggerheads and wouldn't speak to each other.'

Johnnie and Frances rarely visited Althorp, and the Earl never came to Park House. Johnnie's mother would occasionally come to visit her grandchildren, particularly when the Queen Mother was also at Sandringham. One occasion she always tried to attend was the annual cricket match which Johnnie organised against the estate workers. Sir Julian cannot remember Johnnie once mentioning his father, but his schoolfriend Lord Wardington recalls:

> When I saw [Johnnie] I got a sense of his great frustration that his father was still alive. He was waiting to take over. I don't think he had any respect for his father. He felt frustrated that he was in Norfolk in a small house on the Sandringham estate and felt that his children should be growing up in Althorp. He got more imbued with a love of Althorp, once he had a family, which I don't think he had before. At school it didn't seem such a vast amount of wealth, but by then he was the heir to what had become an enormous estate.

When Johnnie's mind strayed to Althorp and his inheritance it was a mere thought away to consider his own link in the Spencer chain and, after the birth of two girls, his need for a son and heir. Frances became pregnant again two years after Jane was born. She looked forward to having a new baby in the house and proudly told neighbours, 'It will be the first baby born to the wife of a High Sheriff of Northampton during his term of office. Usually High Sheriffs are much older men than my husband.' Her enthusiasm soon turned to anguish. On 12 January 1960 a male child was born, delivered in her bedroom at Park House, but was so badly deformed that he only survived for ten hours. They called him John and his grave with the message 'In loving memory of John Spencer' is alongside that of his grandfather, Maurice Fermoy, in the west corner of the churchyard at Sandringham.

It must have been a harrowing and traumatic time for Frances. Up until that moment she had had everything she wanted and her life had been a series of happy and positive experiences. This was her first taste of failure and it was on a grand scale. Not only had she failed to produce a healthy child, but she had failed in her duty to produce a male heir. (In those days it was not well known that it was the man who established the sex of a baby.) She knew only too well that without an heir the impressive stately home of Althorp and its enormous estates, and, in the next generation, all the titles, would pass to another branch of the family. The depression that inevitably followed the tragic event must have been deep and overwhelming.

Johnnie made no secret of his disappointment and it brought out an aspect of his character that few had seen. Although he was the sweetest, gentlest man to many and loved by all ranks, behind closed doors he revealed the more unpleasant side to his nature. A few of his schoolfriends had been subjected to his verbal bullying, which now began to surface again. Johnnie liked to get his own way and often pursued it with great obstinacy. Now that he was thwarted in his wish to have a son, he felt frustrated and angry and lashed out at the person closest to him, his wife. A friend who knew him for twenty years commented: 'He was very kind and generous when he chose to be, but he could be extremely selfish and stubborn. When he wished to exert his position he would.'

Frances was dispatched to Harley Street for various gynaecological tests – an experience which she found deeply humiliating – to see if there was any medical reason why she had produced only girls. Johnnie had no instinctive understanding of how to help his young wife who had undergone a severe emotional and physical trauma and his own background did not help. He had often seen his father bully his mother and watched her accept it with quiet and dignified resignation. In those days, wives were not brought up to work and the stigma of divorce was for most too awful to contemplate, so they had little choice but to make the best of an unhappy marriage.

Frances, however, was of a different generation and far less placid than Johnnie's mother. Nor was she any longer the impressionable teenager who had been swept off her feet by a handsome captain with a vast inheritance like a heroine in a fairy story. Now, although still only twenty-three, she felt a mature woman. She loved her role as a mother but was becoming aware of the limitations of her relationship with Johnnie. The romance had gone out of their marriage and the tragic loss of a baby boy, and Johnnie's insensitivity to her plight, opened her eyes to the reality of her situation. Like many a young woman who settles down too soon with an older man, she still wanted a full and exciting life, while Johnnie was content with a comfortable and undemanding routine.

Frances began to find their social life dull and Johnnie middle-aged and boring, although she was too well-brought-up to reveal her dissatisfaction in public. Johnnie, on the other hand, had no idea that he was fertilising her seeds of discontent with his bullying ways, like his father before him.

His son Charles is quoted by Andrew Morton in his controversial book *Diana: Her True Story*: 'It was a dreadful time for my parents and probably the root of their divorce because I don't think they ever got over it.'

Frances, however, understood her role and dutifully became pregnant again later that year. Johnnie was determined that the baby would be a boy, his long-awaited son and heir. Frances was so anxious about the impending birth that she persuaded Joy Hearn, the midwife who had delivered her two earlier babies and baby John, to fly back from Canada where she had emigrated. This time the birth went smoothly and in the evening of Saturday 1 July, 1961, a little girl was born at Park House weighing 7 lb 12 oz. Although her arrival was initially a great disappointment to her parents, and especially Johnnie, he soon succumbed to her baby charms, later calling her a 'superb physical specimen'. This time they had not given any thought to names for girls, but they eventually settled on Diana Frances. Sarah was then six and Jane four.

Diana was christened on 30 August at the Sandringham church of St Mary Magdalene by the Rector, the Right Revd Percy Herbert. The nursery on the first floor of Park House, which overlooked grazing cows and a patchwork of fields, was newly decorated with cream wallpaper. Although Diana very quickly became a much-loved addition to the household, the problem of an heir to ensure the survival of the family's 200-year-old title had still not been solved and Johnnie grew increasingly anxious for a son.

When Diana was nearly three years old, Johnnie's wishes were finally granted. Amid much rejoicing, a healthy son and heir, Charles, finally arrived on 20 May 1964. He was born at the London Clinic and even Johnnie's undemonstrative father ordered the flags to be flown at Althorp. In marked contrast to Diana, Charles had an elaborate christening in Westminster Abbey and the Queen agreed to be one of his godparents.

Frances and Johnnie ran their home along the traditional and formal lines of the English upper classes, a world away from the powerful influence of the Swinging Sixties in London. Sarah, Jane, Diana and Charles were taught to be self-disciplined, well-mannered and to think of others as well as themselves. All the family would go to church most Sundays. Sarah and Jane were at first educated at home by Miss Gertrude Allen, a governess who had earlier taught Frances and her brother and sister. She arrived at Park House punctually every weekday morning from her cottage a couple of miles away in Dersingham and taught the two girls, who called her Ally, in a ground-floor room, between the drawing room and the kitchen. Diana later had her lessons here too and became very fond of Ally, who sadly died just a month before Diana's wedding.

Lessons over, there were plenty of opportunities for the girls to let off steam; they shared a pony called Romany, which they rode in the park, and had lots of pets including dogs and hamsters; sometimes they would visit their father's farm where the new-born calves were a particular attraction. In summer they would go off to the seaside at Brancaster, about twenty minutes' drive away, where the family had a beach hut.

Johnnie always enjoyed special occasions with his children; part of him never grew up and he had as much fun as they did on his children's birthdays. There was always a party with lots of friends including Charles and Alexandra, the children of their neighbour, the Queen's land agent Julian Loyd, Penelope Ashton, daughter of the local Vicar Patrick, and William and Annabel Fox whose mother, Carol, was Diana's godmother. Johnnie particularly loved fireworks and always gave a Guy Fawkes party, when he would insist on letting off vast numbers of these himself. He was less interested in the day-to-day care of the children which was left to the nanny and Frances.

By the time Charles was born Frances and Johnnie had been married ten years and, to all outward appearances, the family had recovered from its earlier tragedy and was complete. But now that Frances had produced a Spencer heir, Johnnie's attitude towards her grew increasingly cold and dismissive. Lord Wardington remembers: 'Frances caught the other side to gentle Johnnie. He had a bit of a cruel streak as he got older.' She in turn lost her respect for her husband. She felt increasingly unappreciated by him, unloved and terribly bored.

A member of the Spencer family says, 'Johnnie was boring beyond belief. Nice to his friends, soppy and sentimental with his children but achingly dull.' While several peoples have commented on Johnnie's sweet and gentle nature, no one has ever said he was a live wire. One friend of many years comments: 'Johnnie was a reasonably intelligent man, who never had his brain taken out of its box. It was never used or stretched.'

No-one knows what happened privately between Frances and Johnnie; but in public they continued to put on such a brave face that no one was aware of their disintegrating marriage. Sir Julian Loyd says: 'There was no indication to an outsider that they were anything but very happy.' Frances often used to take Diana out for walks in the large pram with her two elder sisters riding their bicycles or running alongside. Neighbours remember that she always seemed glad to stop for a friendly chat. The conversations, however, were spoken through a stiff upper lip, her disciplined upbringing preventing her from showing her true feelings. It was a difficult position that soon became untenable. As was the tradition of the day, she had no career to immerse herself in and a full complement of staff to ensure the smooth running of the house and to care for the children. Time hung heavily.

In 1966, when Charles was a lively and active two-year-old, Frances began to go increasingly to London, leaving Johnnie behind in Norfolk.

She built up an active social life and regularly went to smart dinner parties. Johnnie was with her, however, at a dinner party one warm summer evening when Peter Shand Kydd, a fellow guest, breezed into her life.

A graduate of Edinburgh University, Shand Kydd had inherited the family wallpaper business but resigned from the board in 1963 when he emigrated to Australia. There he ran a sheep farm for three years before deciding to return to Britain. He was a natural extrovert, a touch bohemian and, unburdened by the strictures of the upper echelons of the aristocracy, openly charming. He had been married to artist Janet Monro Kerr for sixteen years and was the father of three children.

For 31-year-old Frances, who must have been very vulnerable, the attraction was instant. She was overwhelmed by Shand Kydd's charm, and his attentions flattered her and made her feel light-hearted in a way she had not done for years. They decided to meet again and were soon planning a ski-ing holiday together with their respective spouses. One can only guess at the complex undercurrents that passed between the four of them during that holiday. Frances must have controlled her emotions sufficiently well to fool Johnnie, never the most sensitive of men, as he always claimed he had no idea that Frances was unhappy with him.

The burden of the charade proved too much for 42-year-old Shand Kydd, however, and he moved out of the London family home soon afterwards. For a while he and Frances met secretly at an address in South Kensington. For Frances, the liaison highlighted the deficiencies of her own marriage and as she fell increasingly in love with Peter, she found it intolerable to maintain her double life of intrigue and deviousness with Johnnie.

In September 1967, shortly after Sarah and Jane, aged twelve and ten respectively, were sent to boarding school at West Heath in Kent, Frances told Johnnie that she wanted a trial separation. He was astounded but had no alternative but to agree. She then moved into a rented apartment in Cadogan Place just off Sloane Square, taking with her most of the furniture she had brought into the family home. It left Park House bleak and empty of both life and chattels. 'It is very unfortunate,' Frances said at the time. 'I don't know if there will be a reconciliation or anything like that.'

Diana, who was now six and still being taught by Ally in the schoolroom, and Charles, a toddler of three, followed their mother the next day with their nanny. Frances quickly found local schools for both children and Johnnie came to London to see and approve them: a girls' day school for Diana and a kindergarten for Charles. The marriage had lasted thirteen years. Frances's move marked the beginning of a most acrimonious period that must have exceeded her worst nightmares.

47

5

An Unhappy Family

Johnnie was so traumatised by Frances's departure that for a while he could do and feel nothing. As he slowly recovered from the shock itself, waves of self-pity, despair and incredulity overwhelmed him. He had seen his mother put up with much worse from his father, and she had stayed. He hadn't been nearly as cruel to Frances, yet she had gone. He had never dreamt that Frances was unhappy, let alone ready to leave him. 'How many of our fourteen years were happy? I thought they all were until the moment we parted. I was wrong. We hadn't fallen apart, we'd drifted apart,' he said.

According to Sir Julian Loyd, 'It was a bolt out of the blue and knocked him flat.'

The younger children, like others of separated parents, then began their double life. During the school term they lived with their mother in London, returning to Park House most weekends to stay with their father. They also saw him when he came up to London, although these were not always happy reunions. Charles said his earliest memory was playing quietly on the floor with a train-set while his mother sat sobbing on the edge of the bed, his father smiling weakly at him in a forlorn attempt to reassure him that everything was all right.

In October 1967, a month after the separation, there was an awkward and tense family reunion when Frances took Diana and Charles to Park House where they were joined by Sarah and Jane for the half-term holiday. At the end of the week Frances took Diana and Charles back with her to London and the family were not to be together again until Christmas when they joined forces at Park House for the festivities. Although both parents tried to make Christmas a happy time for all the children, the strain of playing happy families was all too apparent. It was obvious that the marriage had completely broken down. What Frances was quite unprepared for, however, was the change in Johnnie. He had managed to pull himself together and had galvanised himself into a series of actions that surprised not only his wife, but most of those who knew him.

He was ferocious in his insistence that Diana and Charles should not return with their mother to London in the New Year, but stay with him at Park House and be sent to Silfield School in nearby King's Lynn, a school run by Jean Lowe with small classes of a maximum of fifteen pupils.

It was Frances's turn to be devastated. She could not believe what was happening. She tried to persuade Johnnie to let her have the children back, but he had always had a stubborn streak and he was utterly immune to her pleas. She returned alone and bereft to London. Her only hope was to begin legal proceedings for the custody of the children and the dissolution of the marriage.

The case was set to be heard on 12 December 1968. Frances was confident that she would win. In those days custody of children was almost automatically granted to the mother, unless there were special and extreme reasons why it should not be. In May 1968, however, eight months before the case was heard, Janet Shand Kydd divorced her husband, citing Frances as 'the other woman'. Peter did not contest the divorce and Janet was given custody of the children.

In the sixties courtiers like Johnnie modelled their behaviour on that of the Royal Family, which at the time was impeccably discreet – divorce was unthinkable. (Princess Margaret created a precedent when she and the Earl of Snowdon were divorced ten years later in 1978.) Therefore, in the context of the times and of their class, Frances's decision to divorce Johnnie and fight for custody of the children was a terrific scandal, made worse by the public branding of Frances as 'the other woman' in another divorce case.

A member of the county set comments: 'Divorce was quite traumatic in county life at the time, particularly amongst the Viscount's gossipy hunting friends. Everyone knew Frances and Shand Kydd were involved in a major love-affair which wouldn't happen if someone was even reasonably happy at home. We all took sides. People have never forgotten it. Although a lot of people felt sorry for Johnnie at the time, many also liked Frances which later made it difficult for Raine when she came along.'

Far more people, however, shunned Frances for what she had done. The bitter custody case, as is routine, came up in the courts before the divorce proceedings themselves and, as usual, was heard behind closed doors in the Family Division of the High Court. To most people's astonishment Johnnie fought his corner with uncharacteristic energy and drive. He asked a selection of friends to appear as character witnesses on his behalf, and snobbery was to play an important part in the outcome of the case. When the proceedings came to court he had wall-to-wall support from some of the bluest blood in the land. His hand was also strengthened by support from Jean Lowe, Diana and Charles's headmistress, and by

Frances's mother who turned against her daughter and said that the children should stay with their father. According to a family friend, Lady Fermoy was appalled that Frances had chosen to run off with a common wallpaper merchant and would have taken a very different view if she had gone off with a Duke. Frances was horrified by her mother's actions and had nothing to do with her for a long time afterwards.

One of Johnnie's friends maintained that several of the aristocrats who appeared on his behalf did so because he was a viscount, in line to become an earl and take possession of one of England's great stately homes. 'People will say and do anything to stay in a great stately home,' he said. 'The British have the disease of social climbing, which they see as a virtue, like no other country in the world.' All in all, it was an unbeatable combination. A leading divorce judge commented at the time that in reaching a decision, the children's interests would also have been paramount and that as Johnnie was staying in the family home, it would be seen as a stabilising influence for the children to live there with him. The judgment on the case was clear. Custody of the children would be awarded to Johnnie. He took on the role of single parent long before the position became socially acceptable.

Frances, who desperately wanted to keep her children, felt destroyed, but on taking further legal advice realised that she stood a chance of reversing the decision when her divorce case came up on 15 April 1969. She alleged cruelty, and Johnnie cross-petitioned on the grounds of her adultery with Peter Shand Kydd at an address in Queen's Gate, South Kensington, in April and May 1967. When the case was heard by Mr Justice Wrangham, the allegations of cruelty were denied by Johnnie. Frances had no defence against Johnnie's petition as she had already been named in Janet Shand Kydd's undefended petition and did not proceed with her own. Frances was branded an adulteress and lost the case. Johnnie was given a decree nisi on the grounds of Frances's adultery and retained custody of the children. Mr Geoffrey Crispin QC, his counsel, told Mr Justice Wrangham: 'Lord Althorp entered upon this course with hesitation and reluctance. He would much rather have his wife back, but he recognises now that this marriage has broken down completely.' The judge ordered that Frances and Shand Kydd should jointly pay £3000 towards costs. Johnnie, however, didn't wish to prevent his children from seeing their mother and Frances was officially granted access to the children and allowed to have them with her in London at weekends.

One month after her divorce, on 2 May 1969, Frances married Peter Shand Kydd. She exiled herself from public life and the couple moved to West Itchenor on the Sussex coast. Three years later, in 1972, Frances and Peter bought a farm on the Isle of Seil in Argyllshire where she bred Shetland ponies as well as running a gift shop in nearby Oban. The Shand

Kydds also had a 1,000-acre sheep station in Australia in New South Wales, Australia, where Diana had a secret holiday in 1981 shortly after the Prince of Wales proposed to her. The Shand Kydd marriage, however, broke down in 1988.

After the acrimonious and bitter Althorp divorce, rumours abounded about France's behaviour and attitude towards her children. Some were under the mistaken belief that Frances was so in love with Peter that she had walked out on her children when she left Johnnie; others, that she was so desperate to get away from Johnnie that she was willing to pay the price of leaving her children.

The wounds caused by the divorce never completely healed but what neither party could have foreseen was that their daughter Diana would marry the heir to the throne and be the subject of innumerable biographies which would pick over that painful and difficult time of their life. In April 1982, a year after the royal wedding, Frances, then forty-six, decided to give her version of the story by inviting former ITN newscaster Gordon Honeycombe to Oban. She explained that she had not abandoned her children, but had wanted them to live with her in London. Earl Spencer professed himself shocked that she should speak publicly about their divorce. 'It is very unkind to speak in that way about our separation,' he said. 'I was totally surprised that she should bring it up in public and it can only hurt Diana. I don't know why my ex-wife felt she had to do such a thing. This kind of thing opens up old wounds and is very hurtful ... It doesn't matter about my feelings, but she should have thought about [the children.] How will they feel about this kind of thing being aired publicly? I feel sure it will upset them deeply.'

Johnnie said he would never consent to discuss such personal aspects of his life in public, although later, in 1991, he publicly criticised his children for opposing the changes he and Raine had made at Althorp. Also, in a radio broadcast in July 1988, when hosting *Your Hundred Best Tunes*, he talked about his feelings after the separation. 'There was a time after the break-up of my first marriage to Diana's mother when I was terribly unhappy and felt very down. Though I had nice girlfriends I didn't want to marry any of them. They were not lasting relationships.'

At the time he readily admitted to friends that he was 'pole-axed' by Frances's behaviour. Lord Wardington remembers: 'He was very disillusioned when his wife left. It hurt him dreadfully.' Sir Julian Loyd feels Johnnie 'was in a state of shock for some time. He said several times to me "where did I go wrong?"' And Lady Margaret Douglas-Home, who was a regular visitor of Johnnie and Frances during their marriage, says: 'I don't think Johnnie could believe what happened. It was absolutely unexpected and he was devastated. I don't think he ever mended. The children were very badly affected by it. He tried to put everything right with them but of course it was never possible.'

Just before the divorce came through, he took all four children to a party at Spencer House to celebrate his parents' golden wedding anniversary. Johnnie, now an unlikely single parent, did his best to look after their welfare. In practical terms he succeeded, although he was still imbued with old-style aristocratic methods of child-rearing. The nanny would take the younger children to see him in the morning around 9.00 a.m. and in the afternoon they were again brought down from the nursery brushed and tidy.

The children were very aware of the acrimony between their parents and felt pulled in both directions. It was difficult for Johnnie to overcome his own feelings of wretchedness and it didn't help that, by coincidence, the nanny who had looked after Diana and Charles for two years left during the fateful Christmas of 1967 when the family were together for the last time. She was followed by a succession of nannies and au pairs, which didn't help to create a stable atmosphere when the children needed it most.

Some of the nannies were very tough, even cruel. When Sarah or Jane were naughty, one of them used to give them strong doses of laxative. Another nanny would bang Diana and Charles's heads together if they did something wrong, or individually bang their heads against the wall.

Johnnie now joined the seven-mile school rota run by about four sets of parents on the estate, including Sir Julian Loyd. 'We all had children about the same age so it was very convenient and of course they all went to each other's parties.' When it was Johnnie's turn to take or collect, he was meticulously punctual. He kept a paternal eye on the children's school work and made a special point of chatting to the other parents. He gave the children every possible practical compensation for the loss of their mother. For Diana's seventh birthday, soon after the divorce, he persuaded the officials of Dudley Zoo to relax their rule forbidding the hire of zoo animals and let him have a camel called Bert for the afternoon so that the party guests could have rides.

Johnnie also installed a swimming pool, the only one on the Sandringham estate. Diana in particular loved it and the pool was a great hit with the local children. He generously organised swimming lessons, not only for his own family, but also for his neighbours' children and the butler's son Paul. Sir Julian remembers: 'He was most generous with the swimming pool. Our children kept asking if they could go and he always made them welcome.' There was a diving board, a blue slide and revolving underwater lights that flashed different colours by night. Prince Andrew, Prince Edward and Princess Margaret's children Viscount Linley and Lady Sarah Armstrong-Jones became regular visitors whenever the Royal Family were staying at Sandringham. Johnnie was said to cherish secret hopes that Diana and Prince Andrew might marry one day and particularly encouraged their friendship.

At Christmas, Johnnie's favourite time of the year, the children had piles of presents. He would order a huge Christmas tree which was put in the dining room and on Christmas morning the children would come down to find over a hundred red candles alight on the tree and all their presents piled around it. When it came to dealing with the children's emotional void and their feelings of devastation at the loss of day-to-day contact with their mother, it was not so easy for him. His own upbringing having been formal and emotionally restricted, he was naturally reserved towards them and found talking about feelings and emotions very difficult. 'He wasn't such a great saint to his children,' says a friend. 'He was a bit bad-tempered.'

It helped that after a couple of years of constantly changing staff, Mary Clarke joined the family as nanny and brought some stability and common sense into their lives. She suggested that relationships between father and the younger children might be improved if Johnnie joined them for tea in the nursery, but as she recalls, 'it was very hard going. In those early days he wasn't very relaxed with them.' The conversation was stilted and awkward and after a few rather formal remarks about their welfare, he would often make his excuses and leave. Mary further suggested that the children should join their father for lunch downstairs, rather than eating all their meals upstairs in the nursery. Johnnie agreed to this, and the change of routine certainly helped, although the atmosphere of Park House was still rather formal. Charles later described his upbringing to Andrew Morton: 'It was a privileged upbringing out of a different age, a distant way of living from your parents ... It certainly lacked a mother figure.'

The children missed their mother dreadfully. Although they were distracted during the day with school and outside activities, they wanted her to tuck them up in bed at night and read them stories as she used to do. Johnnie was often out in the evenings, and in any case had asked the nanny to read the bedtime story. As both children were afraid of the dark, their bedroom doors were kept open and the landing light left on. Four-year-old Charles found it the hardest and would often cry pitifully, 'I want my mummy, I want my mummy.' Diana, three years older, tried to be a surrogate mother to him during the day, but her courage deserted her at night, when she lay awake so frightened of the dark that even though she tried to summon all her willpower she could not bring herself to leave her warm bed to go and comfort Charles. She hated herself for it as she lay there listening to his cries. 'I just couldn't bear it,' she later recalled 'I could never pluck up enough courage to get out of bed. I remember it to this day.'

The children certainly absorbed their father's unhappiness. Charles said that his father was 'really miserable after the divorce – basically shell-shocked. He used to sit in his study the whole time. I remember occasionally, very occasionally he used to play cricket with me on the lawn. That was a great treat.' It was also hard for both Diana and Charles at school. They were the only ones in their class whose parents were divorced and like most children they hated feeling 'different'.

Lady Fermoy tried to fill the vacuum caused by her daughter's departure. She moved in to Park House to help look after the children until she felt life there was a little calmer, and afterwards regularly came to stay and spent Christmas Day with the family. In particular she tied to pass on to them her love of music and they always went to some of the concerts at the annual King's Lynn Festival which she founded.

Nonetheless all the children felt very insecure. Sarah and Diana were the worst affected, both suffering later from serious eating disorders. Sarah was a victim of anorexia, Diana of bulimia. Although there is no wide agreement among psychiatrists and psychologists about the true causes of either, many believe that these disorders arise from an unconscious wish in the sufferer to generate anxiety in parents and force them to take control. Full recovery from both conditions can take many years of psychiatric care.

At the time when the seeds of later problems were being sown, Sarah was often virtually uncontrollable. She even once rode her pony into the drawing room at Park House to surprise Lady Fermoy. Diana, who hero-worshipped Sarah when she was a child and used to dress up in her sister's clothes, followed her lead and also became rebellious and sulky. Jane, the quietest of the four, had the calmest nature and seemed on the surface to cope reasonably well. Little Charles became taciturn and introverted. A close relative says, 'They were allowed to run loose as kids, with no discipline or control which could be one reason why Diana later separated from her husband. She couldn't cope with the discipline of the court.'

Meanwhile Frances felt torn apart from her children; Diana and Charles spent most weekends with her in London but she saw much less of Sarah and Jane who were at boarding school. Like any divorced parent who does not live with her children she tried to make up for her absence in the short time they spent together by giving them her undivided attention. The children felt their emotions pulled in two directions and guilty because they loved both their parents.

Apart from trying to be both mother and father to his children, Johnnie also had to take over the duties of running the house. Needing a new butler and cook, he asked around the estate for personal recommendations and was told about an experienced couple called Bertie and Elsie Betts whom he had seen working at various shooting parties on the Sandringham estate. Bertie, who kept a diary of his time with the Althorp family, which his elder son David discovered after he died many years later, remembered Viscount Althorp from these parties and liked him and 'his very charming wife' Frances, a lot. 'He always made a point of asking how I was.' The diary records their first proper meeting: 'Lord Althorp came round personally after the break-up of his marriage and said he was looking for a butler and a good cook to look after the children. He said he was badly in need of a couple to run the house and offered the large carrot that whoever came to work for him now, he would take them with him when he inherited the family stately home of Althorp on the death of his father. He said his wife had left him and made such a touching story we really felt sorry for him.'

When the Bettses went round to Park House for a further interview, they were surprised at the informality. Johnnie himself answered the front door and showed them into the drawing room. They were even more surprised a short while later to hear shuffling noises behind the door while they were talking. Johnnie kept looking round awkwardly and on two occasions got up to open the door to see what was happening, but found no one there. On the third attempt, however, he found Sarah and Diana eavesdropping on the conversation. Bertie and Elsie took the job of butler-valet and cook-housekeeper respectively and worked at Park House from 1971 until Johnnie's father died in 1975 and Johnnie became the eighth Earl. Other staff at the time were a nanny or au pair to look after Diana and Charles, two daily cleaning women and an odd-job man.

The relationship between the Bettses and Viscount Althorp began happily enough, but was to end in bitterness for the Bettses. Bertie, Elsie and their younger son Paul moved into a flat overlooking the park with views of the cricket ground and newly installed swimming pool and, in the distance, the huge Sandringham lake. The first thing that struck Bertie when he moved in was the emptiness of the house. Johnnie had not replaced any of the furniture that Frances took with her when she left and Bertie recorded in his diary that Park House 'looked as if it had been ransacked. There were only a few things left. It didn't look like a home.'

He wasn't, however, aware of too many problems with the children. 'They seemed happy kids,' he wrote, 'although they all seemed quite spoilt.' Even as a young girl, Bertie saw special quality in Diana, whom he found very different to her two sisters. 'She was very domesticated [and] spent lots of time washing and ironing her own clothes, whereas the older two would have theirs done by the local dailies.' Elsie cooked plain simple food. 'Diana's favourite was bread and butter pudding but she also liked chocolate cake and home-made ice cream especially raspberry and blackberry. Apart from desserts, her favourite food was smoked salmon, game and chicken.' All the family enjoyed cooked breakfasts, especially Lord Althorp. 'He started with fruit juice then four rashers of bacon, two eggs, some tomatoes or mushrooms and always drank milk for breakfast rather than coffee.' Johnnie liked plain food and for Sunday lunch always ate roast beef with all the trimmings, followed by pear and creamed rice, cheese and coffee.

He lived very simply. 'When he was alone for lunch or dinner he would drink orange squash with meat and lemon squash with fish, although he had two cellars of wine,' remarks Bertie. Johnnie didn't do a lot of entertaining after Frances left him, but often went shopping himself, looking a forlorn figure as he trudged with his back bent and hunched shoulders, round the shops. In the evening Diana and Charles would have their baths and come down in their dressing gowns at about 6.30 p.m. to eat their supper in the drawing room watching television, in winter wrapping themselves up in large blankets. Although Park House had central heating, Johnnie was not keen on the rooms being too warm. The open fire kept the drawing room relatively cosy, but Bertie and Elsie often used to freeze in the staff flat. All the children had been brought up to be polite to staff, but Diana was particularly friendly to Bertie and Elsie and their son Paul who 'had a very soft spot for her'.

When she went to visit her mother in Scotland she would ask Paul to feed and clean her pets: a vast menagerie that included pet hamsters, rabbits, guinea pigs, goldfish and a ginger cat called Marmalade. In turn she always remembered to send Paul a postcard when she was away, which would include an inquiry about the pets and end 'with lots of love and kisses, Diana'.

As Charles grew up he developed a love of cricket to equal his father's and would invite friends round during the summer holidays for cricket matches in the grounds. Bertie and Elsie would provide them with tea and Bertie always noticed how Charles's friends 'would all swarm round Diana'.

During this time Johnnie tried to find relief from his loneliness by burying himself in good works. He had been born to serve, and like many aristocrats knew he should use his title and what wealth he had for the benefit of others, even though he had had no formal training. He had long been involved with the National Association of Boys' Clubs, of which he became chairman in 1962 on the retirement of Sir Guy Russell, and also with the Schoolmistresses' and Governesses' Benevolent Institution.

Now, in addition to serving as a JP for four years from 1970, he became Honorary Colonel of the Northamptonshire Territorials, chairman of the Nene Foundation, a charity to relieve poverty and promote education and religion, a trustee of King George's Jubilee Trust and later of the Queen's Silver Jubilee Appeal Trust. None of these roles were very demanding, however, and he found himself at home alone for much of the time, which he hated. He therefore accepted every invitation that came his way, particularly to shooting parties organised by the Queen and Prince Philip or other tenants on the estate.

Occasionally Johnnie invited friends to stay at Park House, including Clive de Paula who worked with him for the Schoolmistresses' and Governesses' Benevolent Institution. De Paula remembers: 'After Frances left him he lost his bounce and it was very tough for him. He was a shy man who took life as it came and when people caused difficulties he tended to walk away from them or go round them rather than push through them.'

Rupert Hambro, banker and businessman, who became treasurer of the NABC in 1973, also worked closely with Johnnie and found him a combination of shy and naïve. 'He didn't have an enquiring mind. He was cocooned in his lack of self-confidence and shyness. I think he had perfectly good judgment but was never able to demonstrate it outwardly and communicate what was going on inside his mind in a way others could benefit from.'

Johnnie's interest in the NABC lay not in raising money for the movement but rather with the boys themselves. 'The part that interested him most was visiting the clubs,' says Hambro. 'He also contributed a lot of his time to promoting the movement within itself. He would appear at boys' clubs where a representative was required and at the same time run the NABC council of quite difficult rather dyed-in-the-wool people which he did efficiently and well.'

Brigadier Davies-Scourfield, general secretary until 1982, found Johnnie totally committed to the NABC. 'He was very courteous, good at putting one at one's ease and he had a good sense of humour.' Like many people who worked with Johnnie, however, he became aware that his gentleness and charm concealed an obstinate and determined nature. Davies-Scourfield says: 'He had marked leadership qualities and was quite a strong-minded person behind all that friendliness and if he felt strongly would become very obstinate.'

Hambro comments: 'He wouldn't stand any truck from anybody. If anyone questioned his decisions he would be inclined to say "that is the way it is." ' He remembers Johnnie as 'quite an imposing figure', but as he was equally a shy one, the mix could give the wrong impression.

Sometimes he appeared arrogant which he wasn't, and sometimes his shyness would make him sound diffident which equally he wasn't. When he went to a gathering of boys many of them couldn't quite understand what he said because his shyness made him mumble and swallow his words at the end of a sentence. Johnnie was born into the old school and had the belief, which wasn't at all snobbish, that the boys wanted to meet a lord and that it was very important that someone with a title came to a boys' club so that the boys could see that they were human. I got the feeling he was quite easily influenced and that he had been starved of love and affection, ignored or bullied by his own father, which showed itself in the time and trouble which he took over the movement and particularly the boys in the clubs. He always had lots and lots of time for them and particularly for the very poor inner-city boys who perhaps lived on the eleventh floor of a fifteenth-storey block.

As chairman of NABC Johnnie often had to entertain people officially, which Davies-Scourfield would help organise. 'I would remind him that it was time we invited the new Chief Scout or some such person for lunch and always knew his opinion of the person depending on where the lunch took place. If he asked me to book a table at the Turf Club, I knew he thoroughly approved; at Brook's, he quite approved. If he thought the idea a thorough bore, but agreed it was necessary, he would ask me to book a table at the Bedford Corner Hotel.'

Hambro remembers the change in Johnnie after Frances had left him. '1969 – 1975 was a very bad period in his life. His body language was appalling. He walked with a stoop and he wasn't concentrating on what was going on. He would stare into space for long periods of time. He had been hurt by his father and was now hurt by his divorce and particularly suffered pain from a lack of understanding of why people treated him as they did. He was a very lonely man and kept himself to himself.'

No one seems to know why Johnnie took an interest in the SGBI, a charity to help old and ill women teachers, unless it was his way of making up to Miss Manning, the governess who had had such a hard time teaching him when he was a small boy at Althorp. The SGBI runs a home for retired teachers and governesses in Chislehurst, Kent, where Miss Manning contentedly lived out her last years, entertaining fellow retired schoolmistresses with stories of Johnnie's youthful escapades.

Johnnie had also become chairman of the SGBI in 1962 and it was the only outside activity he kept up after his debilitating brain haemorrhage in 1978. He remained an active member on the board of management right up to his death and left the organisation £1,000 in his will. Richard Hayward, now director and secretary, worked with Johnnie for twenty years and was most impressed with his record as chairman. 'He was a good working chairman, not just a figurehead, and rarely missed the monthly board meetings. He was a big man in every sense – in stature, belly laughs and temper. When he felt I was doing something I shouldn't have done, he rapped my knuckles in front of the whole board. He liked things done well and wanted the charity to be as efficient as a business, but with a human touch. He understood the needs of the ladies we

helped and that they would not necessarily be answered just with money.'
Johnnie's memory for people's names and interest in the minutiae of their
lives enchanted the old ladies who always looked forward to his visits.

The repercussions of the Althorps' divorce extended beyond Johnnie
himself and the four children to Johnnie's father. Despite the fact that
father and son did not get on, a male heir is still a male heir and in 1967,
not long after the separation, the 75-year-old Earl took several steps to
ease the amount of duty that would have to be paid after his death. He
gave to Johnnie personally, and not as part of any trust, the majority of
the Althorp estate, about 7,700 acres worth at the time about £10 million.
He also set up a discretionary trust – of which Johnnie's son Charles later
became the sole beneficiary – that included some 2,750 acres of farmland
at North Creake which had been acquired by the Spencer family through
the will of Sarah, Duchess of Marlborough, and 2,300 acres at Wormleighton in Warwickshire. There was also some property in London
adjacent to Spencer House, the London home of the Spencer family since
the eighteenth century. Spencer House itself had been part of the marriage
settlement when Johnnie married Frances, for the benefit of their children.
These trusts meant the old Earl left himself with relatively little disposable
income. The following year, in 1968, Johnnie himself set up a discretionary trust into which he put five tenanted farms from the Althorp
estate. Their total value at the time was about £200,000 and the bene-
ficiaries were his children and their issue. Johnnie also sold his six hundred
and fifty acres near Sandringham in order to concentrate on farming the
family estate in Northampton.

A couple of years later, Johnnie asked Viscount Coke, heir to the Earl
of Leicester and the stately home of Holkham Hall with 26,000 acres of
farmland in north Norfolk, to be a trustee of Charles's part of the estate.
The two men had first met in 1968, the year after Frances had left Johnnie.

> He was rather low, [recalls Coke]. It took him some little while to get over
> it, if indeed he ever did. I am sure he would have preferred to have remained
> married to his first wife. It was pretty devastating. I was never a very close
> friend. The reason I was asked to be a trustee was he and I found we got
> on well together when we went with a party of about twenty other Norfolk
> landowners on a week's study tour of Denmark looking around estates
> there. It was an interesting trip but Johnnie was very unhappy. During our
> time away we naturally discussed our estates and found ourselves in a
> similar position. Johnnie's father was running the Spencer family estates.
> My father's first cousin, who I succeeded, was running Holkham. Both
> men were friends with well-known estates with the same sort of problems.

Coke had no control over Althorp House itself, which when Johnnie
began selling off vast numbers of family treasures, was a source of great

frustration to him. 'We were trustees of the lands that went to Charles which Johnnie only retained an academic interest in,' says Coke. 'We were working, while Charles was a minor, to try to do what he would wish for the estates and we used to take decisions, which were related to Johnnie by the professional advisors. He very seldom attended trustee meetings which was very unusual . . .'

Although Johnnie was happy to give the trustees who also included John Floyd, a former chairman of Christies and Viscount Hood, a free hand in later years, and particularly towards the end of his life, he regularly complained that far too much had been handed over to Charles and that he did not have enough to live on. Viscount Coke thinks the whole thing is relative. 'If you live at the rate that he was living for fifteen years, once he married Raine, then of course he didn't have enough. It is well known that he had a fairly extravagant life style which frankly not many of us do.'

By coincidence the older male relatives of both men died within a year of each other, Johnnie's father in 1975, Coke's cousin, the Earl of Leicester in 1976. 'Our position continued to be comparable when we both had to take on the estates,' says Coke. It was a relationship that worked very well for some years, but finally broke down in the early 1990s when Johnnie tried to sell cottages on the Althorp estate.

Although the family finances were being tidily organised, the lives of Diana and Charles continued to be disrupted. Not only did they have to cope with the emotional upheaval of their parents' divorce, but there were other changes to be faced up to.

A year and a half after the divorce, in September 1970, nine-year-old Diana was sent to Riddlesworth Hall, a boarding school set in thirty-two acres of Norfolk countryside near Diss, some two hours' drive from Park House, where she was to stay for three years. Catering for girls aged between seven and thirteen, its headmistress was Miss Elizabeth Ridsdale, known as Riddy to the girls.

Diana, who felt rejected by her mother, was anxious about staying away from home. Her fears were partly relieved when she was told she could take her pet guinea pig called Peanuts with her, which she kept in one of the hutches at the school's Pets' Corner.

Both Frances and Johnnie took a keen interest in Diana's work, and wanted to see as much of her as possible. At that time, however, they found each other's presence so intolerable that they always came separately to see her, bringing with them her favourite treats of Twiglets, cream eggs and ginger biscuits. It was a source of sadness and embarrassment to her that, unlike most of her fellow pupils, she never had the pleasure of both parents visiting her at the same time. She found the reality of her situation so hard to bear that, to save face with her schoolmates, she always dedicated her paintings and drawings to 'Mummy and Daddy'.

The teachers at the school were full of praise for Johnnie's efforts on Diana's behalf and his interest in her welfare. 'Such a nice man. Always very caring and anxious to do the best thing for her. He was so interested in how she was getting on and whether she was happy,' says one. Charles, meanwhile, was sent to board at Maidwell Hall in Northampton at the age of eight which was not an altogether happy experience for him. 'I must say I was fairly miserable at the beginning of each term, because it's just too young to be sent away,' he says.

In the autumn of 1972, when Diana had just about got used to boarding school, Johnnie's much-love mother died as a result of a brain tumour. Johnnie and his children were heartbroken, especially Diana who adored her grandmother and from whom she inherited her instinctive compassion.

Despite the fact that Countess Spencer had a major operation to try to remove a tumour and was a very sick woman for the last two years of her life, her main worry was Johnnie and, characteristically, she put his predicament and sadness before her own. Johnnie's sister, Lady Anne Wake-Walker, was full of praise for the way her father, despite his often irascible behaviour towards his wife, looked after her during her fatal illness. 'My father was wonderful to he and thought of everything to make her life more comfortable,' she says.

When Countess Spencer died, the Queen visited Park House to offer Johnnie her condolences and to make arrangements for a memorial service at the Chapel Royal, St James's Palace, which was held at the end of January. Bertie, Johnnie's butler, recalls: 'Although he rarely showed his feelings, Lord Althorp was delighted about the Queen's visit. He was devoted to his mother.'

Not long after Lady Spencer's funeral, Diana's mother and stepfather moved to Scotland. It could not have happened at a worse time for the children. Their mother was now a long way away and the feeling of rejection, at such a difficult time in their lives, was overwhelming, particularly for Diana and Charles. The older two girls, who were by now teenagers, reacted in very different ways. Sarah was still wild and extroverted and began drinking heavily, anything she could get hold of, but particularly vodka as it didn't make her breath smell. Jane became even more quiet and reserved.

All four children also had to learn to cope with two very different life styles. Although they were at boarding school and off Johnnie's hands during term-time, in the holidays they spent half their time with their mother in Scotland and the other half at Park House. In Scotland they were mainly outdoors, despite the often wild weather. Life was very casual and no one changed for dinner. At Park House they were surrounded by servants and every material possession they could wish for.

Unfortunately Johnnie, who had made such an effort to get close to the children when their mother left, was no longer often around even in the holidays. A neighbour who knew him well comments: 'Even though he had custody he wasn't with them very much and when he was, the children ran him. He used to go away for the weekend and leave the house to Sarah and her friends. She would throw wild parties and there wasn't the control there should have been.' When he was at home he often had little time for them.

Despite Johnnie's efforts to fill his time, he wasn't enjoying life as a bachelor second time around and felt insular and shy. He had been deeply wounded by Frances, fought shy of any emotional commitment and was not looking for a second wife to take her place. 'I never thought I would marry again,' he said. 'I just wanted to bring up my children and it was very hard alone ... I had my chances with the girls. I took out one or two but in London, never at home, but somehow they didn't seem, well, suitable.' It was a sentiment that would change dramatically when he met Raine Dartmouth in the early seventies.

6

The Cartland Ladies

If Raine McCorquodale Legge Lewisham Dartmouth Spencer did not exist not even her mother could have invented her. In marrying the man, who fathered the girl who married the Prince of Wales she has a unique position in the history books. She is a woman who incites strong reactions and the many contradictions in her personality have made her the source of endless controversy.

She is a lady of strong character and forceful drive, with a sharp brain, a healthy libido, determined energy and boundless enthusiasm, and has a coterie of ardent fans who love and admire her. But she can be imperious and patronising and has offended many. She has done good work, particularly during her time in local politics on the LCC and GLC. Her popularity, however, has been tarnished by two specific character traits – tactlessness and insensitivity. 'Raine has the ability to antagonise and to put her foot on people's corns with regularity,' says Rupert Hambro. Many have succumbed to her charm. 'She has always been able to charm birds off trees and some people become enchanted by her,' says a former friend who has known her for thirty years, 'but in the end most see through her. Nor does she know how to behave to ordinary people or how they think.' A close member of Raine's family finds her cold. 'It's sad that someone who is stunningly attractive, elegant, highly intelligent and has all the material trappings, has such little warmth of spirit.'

Raine has always given herself tremendous airs, likes the very grand life and is renowned for insisting on the details of etiquette. 'Even when you went for an informal lunch when she was married to Gerald Dartmouth, the footman would be there wearing white gloves,' remembers Sir Roy Strong, former director of the Victoria & Albert Museum who has known her for many years. She has an equally impressive record for putting people down. An aristocrat living in Northamptonshire says, 'Having her to dinner was a nerve-racking experience, you had to get it right or she would smile and tell you how nice it was to come to such a casual evening.' A friend who has known Raine since her single days believes she is a natural actress. 'She's always played the part of being a princess and expects everyone to dance to her tune, which mostly they do.' Sir Roy is aware of her faults: 'she often crosses people's paths' although, he says, 'never my own'. He has always been 'very fond' of her and thinks she was 'a loss to public life' when she married Johnnie. He is one of several who describe Raine as 'another Margaret Thatcher' – one of those powerful women who come to the fore in Britain every now and then. Michael Cole, public relations director at Harrods, agrees. 'There is not much difference between Raine Spencer and Margaret Thatcher. They have the same drive and the same focus, fantastic energy, huge confidence in themselves and a fair degree of conviction that they are right.'

Raine largely gave up public life to be with Johnnie and run Althorp House. She is widely credited with saving his life when he suffered a severe stroke, but her years as chatelaine of the great house have been filled with controversy, both over its refurbishment and the selling of family treasures.

In trying to understand Raine, it helps to know a little about her grandmother Polly and her mother, the romantic novelist Dame Barbara Cartland. 'She has her mother's worst attributes but not all of her good ones,' said a friend. 'In any case, can you imagine surviving a mother like that?' All three women come from the same mould, the differences in them are largely cosmetic. They are formidable, clever women with iron wills, which they decoratively package in feminine charm and frothy manners.

Barbara Cartland developed a career when it was highly unusual for a woman to do so and lists over five hundred book titles in her entry in *Who's Who*. According to the *Guinness Book of Records*, she has become the world's best-selling general-fiction author with sales of more than half a billion copies worldwide.

Yet she brought Raine up to believe that a woman's leading role was to find a suitable husband and glow in his shadow. Barbara firmly declares, 'Men matter most! ... The trouble with most women today is that they will not realise that women can only succeed when they are the inspiration or the shadow *behind* men: that men become great through them. That is the secret of women's power.' Barbara, who herself absorbed this theory of vicarious living from her mother Polly, wholeheartedly passed it on to Raine. But as with many of the Cartland theories, they haven't always worked in practice. All three women have a tidal wave of willpower coursing through their veins. It would have to be a mighty man indeed who could generate sufficiently powerful rays for any of these ambitious women to bask contentedly in his shadow.

As things turned out, all three generations have married men weaker than themselves, either in personality or in performance. Raine has learned, however, from the mistakes of her mother and grandmother, and by her two marriages, the first to the Hon. Gerald Legge – later Viscount Lewisham and Lord Dartmouth – and the second to the 8th Earl Spencer has, at least, added a title and status to her middle-class roots. All three generations have used their feminine wiles to develop superlative skills in back-seat moulding to turn their men into someone they could be proud of. Polly put this into practice with her husband Bertram, Barbara did likewise with her much-loved brother Ronald, and Raine followed suit with Johnnie over the refurbishment of Althorp.

Grandmother, mother and daughter have all deliberately surrounded themselves in a gossamer haze of romance. Curiously enough, whenever their dreams are broken by force of circumstances and they have to deal with any unpleasant reality, whether loss of money, death or illness of a loved one, they always rise to the occasion with enviable efficiency.

Another priority on the Cartland get-ahead list is keeping up a front. Never mind what goes on behind the lace curtains, the important thing is to keep smiling in public. Polly did so when she faced financial ruin, as did Barbara after the collapse of her first marriage when she was also short of money. Raine has kept smiling throughout the controversy and family feud over the sale of the Spencer heirlooms. To the amazement of the general public, she even kept her smile turned on full beam after the death of her beloved Johnnie.

When Barbara's and Raine's first marriages failed, their ex-husbands were still referred to as 'charming' and 'lovely'. Barbara said her first husband, Alexander McCorquodale, had 'the minor fault' that he drank. His infidelity was not mentioned. Raine's first husband, Gerald Legge, seems to have had no faults at all. 'I have had two wonderful husbands,' she said. 'My first husband and I are still the greatest of friends and I adore his second wife.' The marriages of both women had failed but neither felt that it fitted their image to admit it.

In an age when people feel they can, and should, speak as they really think, Raine remains a symbol of a bygone era. 'Raine courts the style of a person for whom time has stood still. Perhaps the fault lies at the door of her mother giving her the wrong set of values,' says Sir Roy Strong.

She was brought up in a mode that has just about been swept away, but is a prisoner in her period and now her whole scene, like the vast crinolines she wears, is something out of the Ark. What has been a disappointment is that she seems oblivious to the fact that things have changed. When you think of today's women, she's a throwback. She has a very good mind, but it has somehow been encompassed by the aspirations of being a Countess with a large house and changing your clothes ten times a day. In an age that has seen college and university open to women and women taking up professions, it doesn't seem to relate any more. She has a very candy exterior but underneath it, a very acute mind. The problem for her is that the surface she has adopted has made people not take her seriously, or spurn her. It's a very great shame because she has enormous energy and drive. In many ways she is her own worst enemy.

Many men have admired her style, including Tim Clifford, Director of the National Galleries of Scotland, a friend of long standing: 'When you are in the company of Raine Spencer you are engulfed by her charm – a very feminine charm. You are also surprised and impressed by her intellect.' According to another male friend, 'Raine has style. When she comes into a room she can take you over by her smile. She flirts with you even if you are years younger than herself and makes you feel she is a woman, which is very nice because most women today don't. She gushes, but in a very eloquent way.'

Although the veneer is very effective, the steely willpower underneath – which gave rise to Raine being described as a 'barbed-wire powderpuff' – should never be underestimated.

Raine's upbringing was an odd cocktail of priorities. From an early age she was drip-fed romance which real life could never equal. She has dutifully lived in the world of her mother's books and is always trying to fit her own world into those soft, pink, happy-ever-after covers. At the same time, her mother encouraged her to be a single-minded social climber even before she was out of her designer nappies and every aspect of her life was engineered to provide the right background for her social success. In addition, she had come to terms with the fact that her mother has never made it a secret that she prefers men to women and her two sons to her daughter. It is therefore no surprise that the relationship between the two women has had its turbulent moments behind the lace curtains.

First in the formidable threesome is Raine's grandmother, Polly Cartland, a vibrant energetic lady who lived to be ninety-seven, supported in her latter years by vitamins from her devoted daughter. Polly was the daughter of Colonel George Scobell and Edith Palairet. The colonel was a dictatorial husband who insisted that prayers were said in the home every morning at eight o'clock. His attitude to religion, however, like much of his life, was geared to suit himself and put no curb on his behaviour towards the many women he admired. Edith knew about this and, in keeping with the times, tolerated it quietly. The family were comfortably off and lived in a small village near Worcester.

Born in 1877 and christened Mary Hamilton, but always known as Polly, she was the couple's fourth daughter. Polly's father had not wanted yet another daughter and hardly bothered to hide his disappointment. Polly was small, lively and determined. She grew into an attractive young woman who met her future husband, Bertram Cartland, at a dance when she was twenty-two. Bertram was a handsome young man who relied on his rich father, James, to support him. He enjoyed hunting in the winter, playing polo in the summer and pursuing the expensive profession of soldiering in between. Polly was infatuated by his charm and he, by all accounts, fell in love with her at first sight. They married in 1900 despite the disapproval of the colonel, who thought his daughter deserved better than marrying into a family of financiers from Birmingham.

The newly-married Bertram gambled recklessly, running up huge debts which he believed were his father's responsibility to settle. Within a year, their daughter Mary Barbara Hamilton was born, in 1901. It was a difficult birth and there was some concern for the baby who did not immediately start to breathe. Polly was delighted with her daughter, Bertram was not. He had wanted a boy and if Polly had thought that fatherhood would make him behave more sensibly, she was wrong. He continued gambling as before. Poor Polly's romantic dreams of married life had not lasted long, nor was she able to immerse herself in the joys of motherhood as the fortunes of her father-in-law were soon to take a dramatic dive. James, supported by massive bank loans, had embarked on an ambitious business project to build the Fishguard railway which was to be the shortest route to Southern Ireland. No sooner had the railway been completed than the country plunged into an economic crisis and the banks called in their loans. James Cartland was asked to repay over a quarter of a million pounds in cash and was so appalled at the prospect of being poor that he shot himself.

The result was havoc for the newly-weds and their baby daughter, Barbara. Their house, which was part of the estate, was sold to help pay off the family debt and they could no longer afford to keep their servants. Bertram felt ashamed and humiliated. Polly, however, was made of sterner stuff. Where other women might have despaired, she showed the indomitable spirit that Barbara and Raine would inherit in full. First she turned to her father, but when he refused to help, she decided to rely on no one but herself. Polly's priorities were simple. She had to try to supplement their meagre allowance of £300 a year and keep up a public front so that they would not be deserted by the right type of friends.

As they no longer had a carriage Polly cycled everywhere, even, in winter, to and from the local hunt where she persuaded the Master of the Croome Hounds to let her ride one of his horses. One of Polly's financial priorities was to have a servant, which would enable her to give the occasional luncheon and dinner party. On such occasions the very few remaining pieces of Cartland silver were polished and put on prominent display. While Polly smiled and charmed everyone she met, at home she was frantic with worry. Bertram continued gambling, their finances were crumbling away at an alarming rate and debts continued to mount.

It certainly did not help when she became pregnant again. Having another child in such financially constrained circumstances could have been the last straw but, as this is a Cartland tale, in fact it proved an inspiration. Polly gave birth to a son, Ronald, born in 1907. This time Bertram's reaction could not have been more different. Fathering a son galvanised him into action. He stopped gambling and decided to face his responsibilities. Six years later, in 1913, a second son, Tony, was born and a stillborn daughter soon afterwards.

Barbara, meanwhile, for the first six years of her life was largely brought up on her own and, like many children without brothers and sisters to play with, lived in a world of her imagination. Having started her education at home, she later found it difficult to adapt to school, particularly the Junior House of Malvern College for Girls in Worcestershire where she was sent at the age of eleven. She had mixed so little with girls of her own age that she was perhaps disillusioned to discover that those traits which she felt were unique to her were, in fact, common among her classmates. This could well account for her general dislike of women in later life.

Polly was delighted with the change in her husband. He was now ripe for moulding and she gently began pulling his strings towards the goal she had set him – a political career. Bertram, now a compliant partner, began by becoming honorary secretary of the local Primrose League in Pershore, Worcestershire, and successfully helped to run the 1910 General Election campaign for the local candidate at Evesham, Bolton Eyres-Monsell. Soon afterwards Bertram became his political secretary at a salary of £150 a year. Polly rehearsed her husband's speeches with him just as Barbara was to do with her favourite brother Ronald, and Raine would also do with Johnnie. They went to innumerable shooting parties and balls and Polly was in her element. She loved society etiquette and made sure that her children had good manners and changed for dinner and that her sons opened doors for their sister and elders.

With her ambitions for Bertram working out so well, Polly now set herself a new goal – to get him elected to Parliament, thereby making her an MP's wife. When the First World War intervened Polly, perhaps intoxicated with her success so far, thought it would be even more wonderful if her husband became a hero before he became a Member of Parliament. Her plans, however, went dreadfully wrong. Despite his age – Bertram was thirty-eight – he volunteered for the army, crossed the Channel to serve with the Worcester Regiment, was mentioned in despatches and promoted to Major. He fought bravely, including being in the front-line trenches for a year, but was killed with the rest of his battalion in the last big German push in May 1918.

When sixteen-year-old Barbara, who was away at boarding school, heard the news of her father's death she wrote to her mother offering her love and comfort and recognising the need to keep up appearances on a budget: 'You and Daddy were an absolute ideal Mother and Father and you, my angel, were a perfect Wife and a perfect Mother ... All my love my wonderful brave Mummy. Babs. PS I have had my coat and skirt dyed black. Would you like me to have my coat-frock done?'

Polly had become a role model for Barbara who loved the romantic image of the strong woman behind the slightly wayward man. Polly had indeed manipulated her husband into becoming a hero, but the cost had been his life. She would not now become an MP's wife, and she faced widowhood with little financial support. With no husband to live through and dominate she turned to her children. Ronald would take over his father's role of politician. Tony would become a soldier. And Barbara would marry someone with money. Polly realised that this could not be left to chance and she began preparing the ground, in a similar way to Barbara's later preparations for Raine.

Barbara was an enthusiastic student and persuaded her mother to move to London. To help make ends meet, Polly opened a shop which would have been unthinkable before the war but had, by the twenties, become socially acceptable. She set about selling knitted dresses and Barbara set about meeting everyone who was anyone in London. Since she had no money the only way she could entrance a rich or titled young man would be by looking extra-beautiful and being extra-charming while, of course, remaining a virgin (an innocent state that was later the key to her fortune). Luckily she was both and was soon so much in demand that she developed a way of rating men. Four-star meant a dinner and dancing, three-star meant a lunch, two-star tea, preferably at the Ritz, and one-star entitled him to drive her to have a meal with someone else.

Barbara has made much of the fact that she received forty-nine proposals before she accepted (much to her later regret) the fiftieth. This is not, however, the delicate female equivalent of a man boasting about his sexual conquests. Barbara herself has written in an autobiography, *The Isthmus Years*, 'It was quite a common thing for a man to propose on the second time of meeting.' She also gave them irresistible encouragement by declaring: 'I invented a rule that I would not allow any young man to kiss me unless he had formally made me a proposal of marriage.' Since she turned down proposals with absolute regularity, these young men had nothing to lose, and the intoxicating prospect of several kisses to gain. It was heady but innocent enough stuff.

In fact, after five proposals Barbara became secretly engaged to a young Irishman in the Life Guards. For the first time it focused her thoughts on marriage and children and she asked her mother what one had to do to have a baby. 'I was so shocked and horrified by what she told me that I broke off my engagement immediately,' she says. 'For weeks I walked about, staring at people in the street and thinking, "Good heavens! They've done that!"'

The world of reality was too crude and vulgar for Barbara and instead she retreated into the much more agreeable world of day-dreaming about what her ideal lover should be like and how she, as a woman, should fall in love. Men, she decided, should be 'strong, silent, passionate heroes'. Women should be 'pure and innocent', and pray to God to answer all their prayers. Unfortunately the cold wind of reality could not be kept entirely out of her romantic dream.

Polly's little shop barely covered their financial needs. Barbara's brothers were still at school on assisted places and Polly suggested that Barbara should take a course in shorthand and typing in order to find a job. Barbara did not regard this as a sufficiently romantic occupation, however. She had met Richard Viner, editor of the gossip column of the *Daily Express*, and began telephoning him with stories for his column which paid her a little pocket money. By the time she was twenty-two she was writing features and had become a spokesman for the Bright Young Things of the Twenties. Lord Beaverbrook, owner of the *Daily Express*, was very taken with her and offered her his journalist's casting couch. If she became his mistress (he was already married) he would make her a star journalist. Barbara, however, was a professional virgin first and a would be journalist second. She was determined to save herself for her future husband and turned the opportunity down, a stand that so amazed Beaverbrook that he still gave her advice about writing for the popular press – that she should use short sentences and simple English. He also introduced her to Lord Birkenhead and Winston Churchill.

For a while, articles and proposals almost matched each other in frequency until towards the end of 1926 Barbara seemed to wake up to the fact that she was twenty-five years old and still unmarried. Life suddenly become 'empty and frivolous' and she impulsively accepted her fiftieth proposal. It had come from the man who was to be Raine's father, 29-year-old Alexander McCorquodale who was very rich but had no title.

The McCorquodale family came from Scotland, although the family house was a Queen Anne mansion, Coombe Hall in Shropshire. They ran the largest printing business in the world producing all the postal orders, cheque books and pensions for the Government and all the posters for the railways.

Soon after meeting Alexandra, Barbara became ill with a septic throat. Alexander sent flowers and promised that if she married him he would buy her a house in Mayfair and give her a Rolls-Royce as a wedding present. Barbara agreed but with hindsight believed that illness had weakened her resistance. 'Sachie, [her nickname for him] was a terribly, sweet, kind person,' she says. 'I was ill with this wretched septic throat and filled with poisons. You know when you are ill things are always out of focus. I was in love with Sachie, and I really believed it would be a happy marriage. I realised that many of the exciting young men I had met during the last five years were really quite unsuitable as husbands. It never entered my head that I was about to enter into a marriage that would break up within five years. I had always dreamed of marrying a powerful man. Sachie was not that but I was quite determined I would be a wonderful, wonderful wife to him.'

Barbara's mother Polly felt dubious about the match and asked, 'Is he really worthy of you, darling?' Barbara felt he was, and they were married on St George's Day, 1927, at St Margaret's Westminster (the same church where Raine was to marry Gerald Legge twenty-one years later). Barbara wrote that it was 'the church where all fashionable weddings took place. The function was identical to hundreds of others which took place that year. There was the same blue carpet, a few guineas more expensive than the red, the same full choir – very expensive – the same decorations arranged by Goodyear, the same nine extra police to control the traffic. The only detail in which my marriage was original lay in the fact that I wore the first long tulle wedding-dress which had been seen since the war.' It was made by Norman Hartnell to Barbara's design – a typical Barbara-Cartland-heroine dress with layers of tulle frills. She wore the train her mother had worn at her wedding with white fur and diamanté embroidery added to it. There were twelve bridesmaids dressed in pink.

Immediately afterwards they went off on honeymoon in the new Rolls-Royce. It was to be a romantic trip that would take in the South of France, Florence, the Italian lakes and Venice. They took a chauffeur and a lady's maid who sat in the back while Alexander, who decided he wanted to drive, and his bride sat in the front. (Not long into the journey both staff gave notice.)

Having invested so many dreams in what true love and marriage would be like, it is no surprise that the reality came nowhere near Barbara's expectations. She had prized her virginity for so long that the moment of surrender proved a bitter disappointment. Rather than being drawn heavenward in a longed-for ecstasy, Barbara found that her heart sank and her feet stayed firmly on the ground. Her sense of disappointment that her relationship with Alexander was not proving to be the blissful union for which she had hoped, was acute.

Although Barbara was no longer physically a virgin, she remained a spiritual one and began to retreat into a fictitious world of romance. She later wrote an article on honeymoons for the *Evening News* which was a thinly veiled description of her own. 'She had dreamed of a strong silent cave-man – a man of deeds but of few words – a man who underneath a deep reserve was passionate, commanding, conquering. Finally she thought that she had found him in her husband. She mistook intertia for reserve, lack of interest for silent strength and inexperience for hidden passion. She was miserably disappointed.'

She was also still suffering from a septic throat and they came home early. Many successful marriages have been built on disastrous honeymoons, but Barbara's hopes were further dampened when it became obvious that her new husband was not interested in the sort of social life she was all set to embark upon. She decided to pursue her own plans. She and Alexander set up home in a grand house off Park Lane in Mayfair, the ideal spot for Barbara to launch herself on the social scene.

Very quickly she became what *The Tatler* called 'one of London's leading social figures this season'. But like her mother before her, all was not well behind the lace curtains. Like Barbara's father, Alexander had no sense of money and by the end of the first year of their marriage, they had debts amounting to £17,000. 'We spent without thinking, quite recklessly, and although Sachie's father gave him £1,000 as a wedding present, he did not increase his allowance of four thousand a year,' says Barbara. Also just like her mother, she added to their financial instability by becoming pregnant.

The idea of influencing a child while still in the womb was a new idea in the twenties but Barbara strongly believed in its powers. 'I think a mother influences her child from the very moment of conception. I think too that how it is conceived is of paramount importance ... When I was carrying my daughter, I was determined she should be beautiful and I not only looked at Beauty but thought it. I would never read a book or watch a film which I thought could induce in me wrong or bad thoughts and might affect my unborn child.'

Alexander's reaction to her pregnancy gave her further grounds for disappointment. 'Perhaps I was being over-romantic about my baby, but I was so thrilled at having a child and went off to buy a pram as if I was going to a sacred shrine. When I came back I said to Sachie "What do you think I've done today, darling? I've bought a pram." He replied, "If you had done it through the office you could have saved ten per cent." I was cut to the quick. "How could he think about our precious baby like that?" I asked myself.'

Raine was born on 9 September 1929. It was a difficult birth. 'I was unable to take anaesthetic to help with the pain and the doctors dared not delay, so I know what having a baby is all about,' Barbara wrote in her autobiography. Raine was born with the umbilical cord around her neck and, as when her mother was born, there were many anxious moments before she began to breathe. She was covered with eczema and had to be washed only in oil for the first six months of her life and wear tiny white gloves to stop her from scratching her body. Her eczema was inherited from the McCorquodale side of the family and later Raine's half-brothers, Ian and Glen, were to suffer from it also. It is something Raine is still susceptible to if she eats too much chocolate and one of the reasons why she dislikes being out in the sun.

Baby Raine weighed into the world at 7lbs $10\frac{3}{4}$ oz. To Barbara she was just like the ideal baby she had imagined throughout her pregnancy and she chose the Gaelic name of Raine because she thought it sounded romantic. Raine McCorquodale was christened at St Margaret's Westminster by Dr Wilson, Bishop of Chelmsford, followed by what *The Lady* magazine called 'a very gay party indeed at the McCorquodales' house in Culross Street where, as usual, there were leaping flames on the hearth and flowers everywhere. Dozens of young men come to the christening parties now and try to say the right thing about the baby.'

Raine was dressed in a long, lacy christening robe with little diamond thistles running up the front among the lace frills. Her four godparents were Lady Berwick, a friend of the McCorquodales, Lady Stonehaven, a friend of Barbara's and a psychic, Sir Francis Davis, Bertram Cartland's commanding officer in the war who had given Barbara away at her wedding and the Duke of Sutherland who, Barbara claimed, had unsuccessfully proposed to her several times. A member of the family denies this, however. 'Can you imagine Barbara turning down a title in the financial circumstances she was in?'

Having done her bit for Raine in the womb, Barbara balked at some of the more unpleasant realities of a baby's existence. Not only did she find the routine wearing, but it detracted from life's fairy tale where men were handsome, gallant and romantic, girls were fresh-faced virgins and babies were rosy-faced, smiling cherubs.

Although she later campaigned for mothers to stay at home and be paid for looking after their children, Barbara employed a nanny and hurled herself back into a social and professional whirl. She began writing a novel, her second, entertained friends almost every afternoon, organised innumerable social events, especially balls for charity, and only a few weeks after Raine's birth gave a series of six radio talks on 'Making the Best of Oneself'. She did, however, in the first few months of Raine's life start the grooming process to prepare her daughter for the life she was determined she would have. Raine became a society baby, was much photographed being pushed around the park in a Rolls-Royce of a pram and probably became the youngest child to have entertained a gossip columnist. The *Daily News* wrote in March 1930: 'Yesterday I was entertained by Mayfair's youngest hostess. She is the fascinating six-month-old daughter of Mrs Archie McCorquodale who goes by the uncommon name of Raine. While her mother entertains in her beautiful Queen Anne drawing room downstairs, little Raine receives relays of guests in the nursery.'

At one level Barbara's life couldn't have been better. She had fulfilled her ambitions of having a house in Mayfair and a Rolls and being recognised as the hostess with the mostest, but none of those things make a happy marriage, or are substitutes for an unhappy one. She kept up outward appearances, but her illusions had been shattered. It was a dark time in her life, made even darker when Raine at six months, only recently recovered from the worst of her eczema, was taken desperately ill. Barbara was away in Egypt when baby Raine went black in the face and collapsed. 'Her life was saved,' she says 'by her nanny, our beloved doctor Sir Louis Knuthsen and a bottle of brandy.'

Raine was given an X-ray and it was discovered that she was suffering from an enlarged thymus gland. The gland, which increases until the child is about two slowly returns to normal by the time she is four. Until then the child can die from a sudden shock or fright. Faced with such a problem some parents might have isolated their child, and avoided any active socialising until the crucial time has passed. Barbara, however, took a strong line.

'If she survives, she will be nervous and introspective all her life,' she said. "I shall bring her up as if she was an ordinary healthy child and trust in God." Raine survived – with the help of £15,000-worth of radium which was strapped to her chest while she slept.'

It wasn't long before Raine's social life was back into top gear. She went to her first children's party when she was one year old. It was a fancy-dress party given by Dorothé Plunket at Londonderry House and Raine went dressed as a fairy. A fellow guest was Princess Elizabeth, who allegedly rushed up to her and cried, 'Oh, what a lovely fat baby. What's her name?' And on being told said, 'What a funny name!' and dashed off again.

A year later Raine presented a bouquet to the Duchess of York at a hospital fete and soon her social diary was almost as full as her mother's. And she was featured in almost as many papers. An article in *Modern Weekly* declared, 'At bye-bye time Raine sleeps under a pink silk quilt trimmed by a blue bow in which a pink rose is tied. Even her nighties are rose-coloured and made of softest washing satin.' She was, declared the *Glasgow Evening News*, 'one of the smartest babies in the park . . . Even at this tender age, she has undoubtedly inherited her smart mother's flair for clothes and coos proudly while attention is called to her pretty frocks.'

Although Barbara made sure that she and Raine kept up the right outward social appearances, after less than two years her marriage was nothing more than an empty shell. Alexander barely featured in her busy schedule. She was writing in the morning, seeing friends in the afternoon and going to dinner-dances in the evening. Neither of them saw much of Raine who spent most of her time with a nanny. Raine told Mavis Nicholson, when interviewed on the BBC2 programme *Relatively Speaking* that her earliest memory of her mother was 'always rushing out. Always coming into the room looking absolutely beautiful, always being busy.' She says it has influenced her all her life. 'I never felt parents were people who sat by the fireside doing nothing.'

Meanwhile Alexander was drinking heavily, his way perhaps of coming to terms with his unhappy marriage. He also turned for comfort to a Mrs Helene Curtis and they began an affair. Divorce carried such a stigma in the early thirties, that he and Barbara might have continued with a façade that all was well for years. Barbara, however, discovered some love letters from Helene to her husband which galvanised her into action. In one letter she read, 'Do not let us be in a hurry to run away, darling, because if we play our cards cleverly I think you will be able to get hold of your daughter and I shall be able to get my children.'

Alexander was away on a cruise at the time and, rather than waiting for his return, Barbara rushed off to confront his parents, without even telling Polly. 'If Sachie no longer loves me and wishes to leave me I am perfectly prepared to divorce him, but I must make it absolutely clear that in no circumstances would I give him custody of Raine!' she told them. Her anxiety took its toll on her health. She suffered several bouts of painful colitis 'due to unhappiness and worry', although this, too she was able to turn to positive use as it was to be the start of her interest in alternative medicine.

Alexander was not going to make life easy for her. He decided to fight for custody of Raine and employed Sir Norman Birkett, one of the most fashionable and expensive barristers of the time. He also hired a private detective in the hope of coming up with evidence against Barbara that would help cut down his costs. Barbara was dismayed by his choice of barrister. She did not have enough private funds to hire someone of equal brilliance, but fortunately a girlfriend of her brother Ronald was the daughter of another well-known barrister and playwright, Sir Patrick Hastings, who agreed to represent Barbara for nothing. The case came up for trial in the autumn of 1932 with both sides suing for divorce. Sir Patrick advised Barbara on her appearance and suggested she turn up for court in a plain black dress rather than in her usual more flamboyant clothes, which he felt might count against her.

Barbara won custody of Raine and was granted the divorce with costs on the grounds of Alexander's adultery. A few days later Helene's husband, Major Phillips Pinckney Curtis, was granted a divorce against his wife citing Alexander. Barbara's victory was far from sweet however and she was left with little to live on. She could no longer afford the Rolls or to keep up their house in Mayfair, but was desperate not to lose face by moving away. To postpone the decision, she temporarily moved into the Dorchester Hotel, but kept costs down by accepting all invitations to eat with friends. It was her mother who saved the day. She agreed wholeheartedly with her daughter's priority of status over space and rushed around until she managed to find Barbara a maisonette in Half Moon Street, for seven pounds a week with valet's quarters which she felt could be converted into nursery accommodation for Raine.

In the divorce settlement, the McCorquodales agreed to pay for a nanny for Raine, which meant that Barbara was free to work and she happily escaped from her sorrows into her writing. Initially, after the divorce, Barbara's social life temporarily went into decline as some so-called friends did not wish to be associated with a divorcee. Her daughter's social life, however, organised by Nanny, fared rather better. In 1933 *Vogue* magazine published an article on society children with the following description of four-year-old Raine:

> Raine McCorquodale sits in the nursery window on her rocking-horse: you have a fine view of Curzon Street from Raine's windows and the little daughter of Barbara Cartland is a perfect hostess for the after-tea visitor. Mrs McCorquodale believes in making her small blonde daughter a good mixer straightaway, so that the shyness and weariness of parties may not worry her later. So Raine has achieved a pretty dignity of manners which should stand her in good stead later ... Her mantelpiece is covered with invitation cards and her engagement dairy must be almost as full as her mother's. One leaves her sitting down before bedtime to write her letters, her lovely fairness gilded by the candles to make the scene, appropriately arranged against a friendly, familiar background of toys, firelight – and Nanny.'

Raine's 'pretty dignity of manners' became so ingrained in her that although it has delighted some, countless others have been infuriated by what they see as a symbol of her pretentiousness.

Barbara, like her mother before her, now had to find someone else through whom she could enjoy the Cartland brand of vicarious living. Unlike Polly she could not look to children for help and support as she had, as yet, no sons. Instead she turned to her brother Ronald, which was the beginning of a relationship that was more important to her than any other in her life. 'Ronald was like my other self,' she said. 'We thought alike, wanted identical things, and could almost have been one person ... Every man I met seemed inferior to Ronald now. I stimulated his mind and he mine. In fact we were essential to each other and we were both perfectly happy when we were together. He had a vitality which made the tempo rise and when we were together it was magnetic.'

They took holidays together in Austria, Germany and France, although never with Raine who went off to stay with her grandmother. Apart from providing friendship, Ronald also gave Barbara the opportunity to influence his career. Polly had only got as far as hoping that her husband would become an MP and, since his death, had nurtured the wish that her son would fulfil this ambition for her instead. Barbara was determined to make this wish come true. She encouraged Ronald, then twenty-six, to put his name forward as the Conservative candidate for King's Norton in the General Election of 1935. She supported her brother financially and he rehearsed all his speeches in front of her. To Barbara's delight he won the seat with a majority of 5,875. Barbara had at last achieved one of her dreams: someone she loved was successful and she was able to glow in his shadow.

7

A Difficult Childhood

After the breakdown of her marriage, Barbara continued to suffer from recurring bouts of debilitating colitis. It did not, however, stop her from working. Writing has always provided her with an escape from life's harsher realities. So successful was she as a journalist, writer and social pundit, that she became that most unusual species in the thirties, a financially independent career woman. She wrote several columns in newspapers under different bylines: Miss Tudor in the *Daily Mail*, Miss Hamilton in *Bystander* magazine, Miss Scout in *The Tatler* and anonymously in the *Observer*.

She also threw herself wholeheartedly into helping her brother with his career. She revelled in her increasing material success, a state of affairs she had been determined to achieve when faced with divorce. 'I had decided during the bitter controversy over my divorce that I would never again be entirely dependent on anyone.'

At the age of four, little Raine was far too young to grasp the full implications of her parents' divorce, but she was not entirely protected from its consequences. According to Barbara, Raine's father went into a 'home for inebriates' almost immediately he lost the battle for custody of his daughter. He was also apparently suffering from heart trouble and stayed in the nursing home for two years.

Maintenance was not an automatic right in the thirties and Barbara has claimed that, although she was the innocent party in the divorce, 'Alexander's parents confiscated his money while he was unconscious and refused to give me any'. She was left with 'only the marriage settlement of £500 a year'. When Alexander left the nursing home, according to Barbara, he made some attempt at reconciliation. 'He said we shouldn't have had a divorce but I said it was too late. He was a very nice, sweet man and there was nothing wrong with him really except that he drank.' However, Barbara claimed he now had little interest in his daughter. 'I said he could see her whenever he wanted to,' she said, 'but he never did.' His lack of interest could not have been quite as complete as she suggests, however. Alexander, who seems to have overcome his drink problem for he married again, successfully, and lived for a further thirty years. He attended Raine's first wedding and even stood in the reception line with his ex-wife. He also left Raine money in a trust fund, which, together with a generous legacy from his mother, has formed the foundation of her personal wealth.

Whatever their true feelings for each other, father and daughter rarely met. Raine must have felt rejected and, for a child schooled from birth on the importance of being socially acceptable, it must have been hard that the other children in her carefully selected social circle had both mother and father, while she did not. The intricacies of the situation were not explained to her; all she knew was that she had stigma attached to her that was nothing to do with her own behaviour. It affected her deeply. By all accounts she had an unhappy and self-conscious childhood.

She took refuge behind a veil of politeness, even better manners than her contemporaries, and elaborate charm. She kept her own counsel, confiding in no one and never speaking about her father even to her closest friends. In many ways she was a deprived child who had to cope first with the consequences of her parents' divorce and then with the family's financial difficulties. Many people have said that it is impossible to get close to Raine and that she 'always seems to be putting on a performance'.

The eminent psychiatrist John Bowlby has written: 'There is a good deal of evidence that an individual who has been prevented for whatever reason, but usually by his family, from expressing feelings of anxiety, sadness or anger during childhood and from recognising the situations that have given rise to them, is likely to have considerable problems with certain feelings in later life.' When a child is not given a chance to grieve either the death of a parent or, in Raine's case, for an absent father – one of the severest forms of rejection for a child – that child will learn from an early age to bottle up its feelings.

John Bowlby continues: 'Without understanding and sympathy there is a danger that the child's thoughts and feelings will become locked away, as though in a secret cupboard.'

Raine turned for her role models to her mother and grandmother, both of whom had had to learn to cope without a man. She says she 'couldn't have been more influenced' by her mother: a woman who displayed not only the masculine characteristics of ambition, drive and a love of success but also those gentle feminine qualities of shyness and reticence, whose eyelids would flutter and lips tremble in the presence of a powerful male. Raine was not bothered by the seeming contradiction of these two aspects of womanhood, and has absorbed them into her own life. Although she did not pursue a salaried career she became a high flyer in local politics, with a Barbie Doll style of dressing that was an important part of her public image.

Barbara might have been happy enough to spend the rest of her life with her brother Ronald rather than risk another marriage, but for the fact that she longed for a son. Her own painful experience of marriage had taught her that a perfect union between a man and a woman was only likely in books, that the ideal lover did not necessarily make the perfect husband and that the real world was one of compromise rather than euphoria. There was the added complication that any new man in her life would have to accept the presence of Raine and Barbara's close relationship with her brother.

As luck would have it, she found a second husband on her own doorstep. Hugh McCorquodale was the only member of the McCorquodale family not to side against Barbara during her divorce from Alexander. He was a close friend of Alexander as well as a cousin. They had been to the same schools and both enjoyed shooting and fishing. Hugh, as the story goes, had fallen in love with Barbara on her wedding day. He never voiced his feelings, but often came to the house and got to know Barbara well. He had never married, partly because he was in love with Barbara and partly because his life expectancy was short. He was badly wounded in First World War when, at the age of eighteen, he was hit by a bullet from a sniper at Passchendaele, where he won an MC. The bullet exploded internally, smashing three ribs and causing his lung to collapse. He was taken to base hospital, but because there seemed little chance of saving his life, he was written off by the medical team. For some weeks he wafted in and out of consciousness but slowly his body healed and he began to recover. He was to suffer from lung troubles all his life, his severe bouts of coughing occasionally producing a deeply embedded piece of shrapnel.

Barbara felt comfortable in Hugh's presence and Raine, who always called him 'Uncle Hugh', seemed to like him. Of perhaps greater significance was the fact that even Ronald approved of him. Hugh and Barbara, who was now thirty-five, decided to marry quietly on 28 December 1936 at the London Guildhall, followed by a blessing in the Church of St Ethelburga's the Virgin in Bishopsgate and a honeymoon in Paris. As the country was in the throes of the Abdication crisis it was a unique Cartland occasion, with no publicity and only Barbara's other brother Anthony and a witness present.

Barbara's reasons for her marriage to Hugh were those of a mature woman rather than a flighty young girl. 'I had known Hugh for eight years,' she said, 'and although he had been in love with me all the time, on my side it was a case of friendship and a deep affection developing through trials, difficulties and unhappiness into a firmly rooted love ... with the exception of his mother – I did not like his family and they did not like me. But finally we knew we could never be happy without each other.'

It gave Barbara considerable confidence that on the morning of her wedding Ronald wrote her a letter in which he told her how much he still loved her – 'You know what you have meant to me these last five years – much more than I can ever hope to tell you' – that he felt she was doing the right thing, and that he would hate her to marry anyone but Hugh.

Their marriage developed into a successful and happy union. A member of the family says: 'Nobody ever said a bad word about Hugh. He was sweet, gentle, easy-going and understood Barbara implicitly. She pushed him around, but he didn't mind it.' Hugh, who worked in the family printing business, was supportive and tolerant of Barbara's relationship with her brother, her need to work and to have a vibrant social life. He was also fond of his stepdaughter Raine, although twenty-eight years later when he died, he did not mention her in his will.

For her part, Barbara had learned from her past mistakes and her expectations of this marriage were more realistic. She accepted that Hugh could not give her everything she wanted, and she loved him for the fact that he allowed her to lead her own life and made no attempt to cramp her style. She continued to live in a social whirl and even to have holidays alone with Ronald which would no doubt have tested the patience of many husbands.

Barbara was equally delighted that her marriage 'looked like putting an end to my financial worries'. Despite this, she continued to write, earning substantial sums from her novels and ensuring her financial independence. She grew to appreciate and adapt to Hugh's more modest but stable qualities and learned that reticence and reserve were not necessarily signs of weakness. 'Very often men, although they do not show it, are far more shy than their very modern, self-sufficient wives. This shyness or reserve is actually one of the most charming things about an Englishman ... and the easiest way to conquer it is to love him deeply – and to show it.'

They rented a ten-roomed flat in Grosvenor Square and bought a small thatched cottage by the River Ouse in the village of Great Barford, Bedfordshire. On 11 August 1937 Barbara gave birth to a much-wanted son, whom they called Ian. 'I have a son! It is the most exciting, wonderful thing that has happened to me,' she wrote. By her account he was a pretty baby with blond curls and 'so like an angel that I was afraid he would die'. She has always claimed that having a son has been one of the highlights of her life. None the less when Ian was only a year old, he and Raine were packed off to stay with Grandma Polly while Hugh went fishing in Scotland and Barbara and Ronald holidayed together at Brienz, near Interlaken in Switzerland.

Two years later, ten minutes to midnight on 31 December 1939 her second son, Glen, was born. 'I had prayed for another boy,' said Barbara, 'and when he arrived I had, as with my other children, a very difficult confinement, but I was ecstatic in knowing I had a second son.'

Raine was ten, and had her own social life, her own quarters and a governess to educate her at home. The *Daily Telegraph* had recently reported that

> the schoolroom for her daughter Raine [had] dusty pink walls and fur-
> niture – except for a royal blue desk and chair – and dusty pink chintz
> curtains patterned with Easter lilies. She had her own piano and radio-
> gramophone and her own pale-green bathroom. An old-fashioned wall-
> paper of roses, poppies and sweet peas was chosen for her bedroom, but
> Mrs McCorquodale had to search all over London for a chintz for curtains
> and covers to match. Many hostesses like to have chintzes in the same
> pattern as wallpapers.

Although Raine had every kind of material comfort, this could not have been an easy time for her. She had been used to being an only child; now she not only had to get used to a stepfather and two siblings, but to her mother's overt declarations of how much she preferred her sons to her daughter. 'I never made any nonsense of the fact that I prefer sons,' Barbara says. 'It's never the same having a girl. Everybody has troubles with their daughters. Either they are jealous of you loving the boys or of something about the boys.' It was an attitude Barbara had inherited from her mother. 'Mummy always said she preferred her sons to me, her daughter. Of course she did. In a way I minded, but one took it as a matter of course that men are better than women. And Raine liked her boys better than her girl. I have two wonderful sons who are absolutely marvellous to me. I wish I had a dozen. Girls are also very jealous. They rather resent that you are a star and they are not. Of course they are all right when they become a star. The father should like the girl better.' In Raine's case, the father was not around.

Although Barbara employed a nanny, she insisted that the children went to bed promptly at 6.00 p.m. They were brought up to be 'grateful for small mercies' and to have 'wonderful manners'. 'They weren't allowed to play with their toys until they said "please" and always had to write "thank you" notes. Raine can sit down and write a hundred letters by hand with no trouble at all, but my grandchildren brought up by her were never taught that when they were young, because they were so much with governesses – she was busy running Lambeth and a few places like that – and they have the greatest difficulty in writing letters.'

Nevertheless, Barbara did not underestimate the value of a good nanny. 'The most important thing in a marriage is to keep your husband happy.

Therefore you have to have people to help with your children so you can spend more time with your husband and make a fuss of him.' For the same reason she claims that she stopped writing at 5.00 p.m. when her husband came home and did not work at weekends. 'I never talked about my work. When a man comes home he wants to talk about himself.'

In 1939, Raine's life was to be further traumatised by the advent of war. Both Barbara's brothers, Anthony, with whom she had never had a particularly close relationship, and Ronald went off to fight. Both men were declared missing in May 1940, but it was not until the beginning of 1941 that Ronald's death was confirmed with news of Tony's death following in 1942. Although Barbara had a premonition of Ronald's death, his loss was a blow she found hard to endure.

As the war intensified Barbara was so worried for the safety of the children that the family let their Grosvenor Square flat and moved to their small cottage at Great Barford. Work has always been Barbara's antidote to worry and she threw herself into the war effort with full vigour. She helped distribute books and magazines for the Women's Voluntary Service and organised the redecoration of the restrooms in the barracks, often in flaming pink. She later set up a second-hand wedding dress business, enabling wartime brides to save valuable clothing coupons by borrowing not buying, became active in the St John Ambulance Brigade and continued writing novels.

Her brimfull schedule came to an sudden halt in 1940, a few days after her brothers had been declared missing, following rumours that the Government was planning to evacuate women and children from the south of England overseas. Barbara's friend Irene Dunn, the second wife of industrialist Sir James Dunn, decided to take her children to Canada, well out of the war zone, and asked Barbara if she would like to join her. 'One thing stuck in my mind – that I had been told that babies were often killed by the blast of bombs and Glen was only five months old,' she said.

She was reluctant to leave Hugh but he was fully stretched at the family printing firm as well as training a detachment of Home Guards and had to stay. The following day she telephoned Irene Dunn and impulsively 'accepted her kind invitation'. Barbara, Nanny and the three children left London on the morning of 26 June to find, when they reached Liverpool Docks, that thousands of others had had the same idea. 'We were herded like cattle into a Customs shed for two solid hours. There was no possibility of buying food, no milk obtainable for the children, nowhere to sit except on the dirty, dusty forms erected for luggage.'

Eventually they were called on board the passenger ship, *Duchess of Atholl*, which belonged to the Canadian Pacific Line. Grabbing all their belongings – 'Raine was weighed down with coats and bags' – they went aboard. This was no luxury cruising liner. They all had to share a small and stuffy four-berth cabin with a cot for six-month-old Glen.

The ship was led in a zigzag pattern out of Liverpool harbour by a destroyer which saved it from attack by a submarine. There were 1,350 people crammed on board, the majority of them children. Raine has always been a very bad sailor but when she wasn't being seasick, she played with the other children, which kept her happily occupied. 'She had a lovely time,' her mother wrote, 'she was no trouble and as no one could pay much attention to her, she enjoyed a new and exciting freedom.'

Once safely docked in Montreal, they all moved into a hotel in Métis, a beautiful village in Quebec overlooking the St Lawrence River. Barbara was terribly homesick for England, Hugh, and afternoon tea. Missing tea turned out to be the least of her problems: an adaptable hotel proprietor happily agreed to provide it for Barbara and Nanny, and to give the children their high tea at the same time. 'The hotel proprietor ... quite understood Nanny's and my reluctance to break established (English) habits, and Raine and Ian had tea at 4.30 p.m. and went to bed early, at their usual hour, with a glass of milk and a cracker.'

Because Barbara had packed in a hurry she had not brought nearly enough clothes or money with her and found she missed many of her possessions. She certainly did not have sufficient funds to pay room service to keep her clothes up to standard and Raine was given the task of ironing her mother's dresses. Raine was as unhappy as her mother and hated the school she was sent to. 'The other girls kicked her with their boots,' Barbara said. 'I can't think why. Perhaps it was the way she talked.'

Matters were made worse when Barbara heard that the Government had changed its mind and would not be evacuating women and children from the country after all. Barbara felt she had been a coward and a traitor in leaving England. 'I was furious with myself for coming away, mainly because I was ashamed. Our place was in Great Britain – that little green island standing alone, defying the whole might of the victorious German armies.' She decided to return home. However, travelling back to England proved easier said than done because she had contracted to stay in Canada for a minimum of six months.

But like all Cartland women, once Barbara had set her heart on a course of action she became impossible to deflect. 'Once I had definitely made up my mind I knew nothing would stop me,' she wrote in an autobiography. She sent telegram after telegram to Hugh, a variety of friends and every influential person she could think of who might be able to help. When Hugh replied that crossing the North Atlantic at the time was very dangerous because of the threat from U-boats and German battleships she pressed on with her plans regardless.

In the end she got her way. She received the necessary travel permits in September and despite further telegrams from Hugh telling her to wait until it was safer, booked to sail on the *Duchess of Richmond* on 14 November. It proved to be a foolhardy and dangerous journey. On the sailing date Montreal was struck was by the first of the winter blizzards and Barbara, Nanny, and the three children boarded the ship 'wearing everything we possessed'.

She and Ian shared one cabin, Nanny and Glen another and Raine had a cabin to herself. The blizzard was so bad that the *Duchess of Richmond* was held up in port for twenty-four hours. Once away, she literally made 'a run for it', although even Barbara was well aware that 'our speed would be an advantage against a submarine, but we would be helpless against an armed raider which does 32 knots'.

The shipping losses for the previous week had been the worst of the war. The *Duchess of Richmond* was a valuable target as it carried much-needed supplies for Britain, including an aircraft, army lorries and munitions. By way of defence, it had only submarine- and anti-aircraft guns on board and all passengers were subjected to seemingly endless boat drills. To be ready for any emergency, Barbara took two lifebelts everywhere she went, as did Nanny, while Raine was continually in trouble for forgetting hers. In the event, it was only storms that chased the *Duchess of Richmond* across the Atlantic, although it was hardly surprising that the children's health began to suffer. Raine and Glen were very seasick and three-year-old Ian began to develop pneumonia.

Raine recovered sufficiently to stand on deck as the ship docked in Liverpool and at one point dashed back to tell her mother that she had spied 'Uncle Hugh' on the quay. Soon after returning home, probably as a result of all the strain and worry, Barbara developed a large abscess which required an operation and Raine became ill with earache which turned out to be a deep-seated mastoid and also had to be operated on. 'Raine is so brave in the case of physical pain,' her mother said, 'that when she had her operation for a mastoid the doctors and specialists could talk of nothing but her courage and patience. But Raine, having a sweet gentle nature, can be easily hurt mentally.'

8

Educating Raine

After Barbara and the children returned from Canada, Raine was sent to the fashionable Owlstone Croft School run by Theodore Fyfe and his wife. By chance the school had been evacuated to a large, imposing house a few miles from the McCorquodale cottage in Bedfordshire. This had originally been requisitioned by the RAF who had already installed a concrete drive, but plans changed at the last moment and the Fyfes were allowed to take it over. The family who owned the house were reported to be delighted as they felt the girls would do less damage than the RAF and, apart from girls' names written in lipstick on the ceiling, there was comparatively little wear and tear.

Mrs Fyfe, the headmistress, was a large, kind lady who loved her fifty or so pupils aged between twelve and seventeen but the rambling, draughty house had not been built as a school and the girls had to put up with rather cramped conditions and some particularly severe winters. Food, however, was plentiful, with a regular supply of locally-grown vegetables. When there was an air raid the children went down to the cellar, but were otherwise largely unaffected by the war. 'We didn't realise how bad it all was,' says one farmer pupil.

Raine was never mentally stretched at Owlstone Croft which did not claim to be academically inclined. She was, however, challenged by the effort of keeping up appearances on little money. In the early forties, most teenage English girls were unsophisticated but Raine, in complete contrast, paid great attention to both her wardrobe and her appearance. The iron discipline that was to be such a strong feature of her personal and public life was already well in place. As one contemporary comments, 'She never lets herself go for a second.' Following the example of her grandmother and mother when times were hard, it was almost second nature to Raine to put on a stoical front, which she has rarely let slip throughout her life.

Young girls have always been the harshest critics of each others' wardrobe and Raine's dedication to her appearance made her the envy of some pupils and disliked by others. Because clothing coupons were limited, she often wore second-hand clothes given to her by her mother's friends. These were not, however, of the jumble-sale variety. 'I loved them,' she said. 'I had things then I couldn't possibly have got new.' Compared to the complications of her wardrobe, her studies were easy. As a child she had had the run of her mother's library of over two thousand books. By the time she was twelve she had read her way through many of the classics including Dickens, Hardy and Buchan. At school she enjoyed learning poetry by heart. She was often top of the class, but on one occasion when she excitedly told her mother of her success, Barbara made her priorities clear. 'Never mind about that,' she said. 'You have a gravy stain on your skirt.'

Raine was a weekly boarder and shared a dormitory with four other girls, one of whom was her best friend Catherine de Trafford, now Catherine Walwyn, widow of the horse trainer Fulke Walwyn. 'Raine was very clever and wrote very good stories in amazing hand-writing,' she says. 'But more than anything one remembered her clothes and her hair which were always immaculate. We didn't wear school uniform but it was difficult to get clothes during the war. Raine, however, had lots of coats and skirts which took up all our cupboard space as well as her own, whereas most of us just had one suit to wear on Sunday. She had lots of shoes and even masses of stockings which were impossible to get hold of.'

Raine's concern over her wardrobe did, however, irritate some of her fellow pupils and several teased her over her insistence on curling her hair by wrapping sections of it in rags every night. Even Raine recognises her tendency to obsession over detail. 'Like Mummy I am very *détailliste*. Mummy used to say, "You'll never get a husband, you'll drive them all mad." I'm terribly difficult to live with.'

Catherine remembers Raine as 'a very alive person, and very funny' but others admit that they 'just couldn't stand her. She was such a snob even then.' Anne, Viscountess Norwich, ex-wife of the writer John Julius Norwich, was impressed with her self-discipline. 'Like most of the sixth form I much admired many of Raine's qualities. She was industrious and well-organised, up early, hair curled, pencils sharpened. Not priggish, gregarious and friendly.' One of her contemporaries felt that the four years she spent in the school were 'probably the happiest years of her life'.

Certainly her friend Catherine found her always cheerful and happy. On Sundays the two of them would often go for lunch to Raine's family cottage near by and play make-believe games in the garden. Sometimes Raine would go riding, but according to her mother 'she wasn't very keen on it'. Barbara, meanwhile, was as busy as ever – in addition to her war work and novels, she began a biography of her brother Ronald – but turned down the offer of three safe Conservative seats because of her husband and young children. Raine still felt self-conscious about the fact that her parents were divorced and never discussed it even with her best friend Catherine.

Occasionally, during the holidays, Raine would be invited to stay with friends from school, some of whom came from quite wealthy families with large houses. It made her dislike the cottage at Great Barford for being too small and not grand enough. Like all teenagers, although the word wasn't yet part of common language, Raine rebelled in a minor way. She smoked cigarettes made up of rolled-up blotting paper, but always blew the smoke out of the window or up the chimney so that the smell wouldn't give her away. 'I thought of cigarette-smoking as a status symbol,' she says. She made the fatal mistake, however, of telling her mother. 'When I told Mummy she gave me the real thing and made me finish the cigarette to the last bitter half-inch until I was finally very sick.' Afterwards Raine thoroughly endorsed her mother's rather drastic action. Speaking at a conference organised by the Chest and Heart Association in October 1962, she said: 'The moral of the story is, that I loathe cigarettes and am a confirmed non-smoker.'

Barbara ensured that Raine became a lifelong teetotaller in much the same fashion. 'One day I came home from school and said to Mummy: "Can I have a drink?" She said, "Certainly, have a cocktail." I thought it was pretty disgusting.' As a result, not since the age of eighteen has she sipped anything stronger than tomato juice.

Barbara believed in discipline as well as good manners and when Raine was naughty she was made to bend over while her mother gave her 'six of the best' using a hairbrush. 'Mummy always believed in a good beating on the behind for all kinds of naughtiness. I remember that after such beatings I was never naughty again for the same things.'

Raine couldn't wait to grow up. 'She was dying to leave school, launch herself into the deb thing and get into that world,' says a friend. But when she left school at sixteen, just as the war ended, she was almost immediately struck down by an attack of mumps. To avoid her younger brothers catching the disease, she was sent to Grandmother Polly who took her away to Cheltenham. Raine adored her grandmother, admired many of her attitudes to life and credits her with being fundamental to her upbringing. She had spent holidays with Polly since she was very young, while her mother went off with Ronald. 'She always had exciting plans arranged for our time together,' she says. 'There would be a party with organised games and competitions at which even the most inept would win armfuls of prizes so that nobody would be disappointed.'

When Raine had recovered from the mumps, Polly provided a series of treats. Raine was 'in that no-man's-land of girlhood' but her grandmother knew how to make her feel 'grown-up and important'. What could be a better start for the grooming process that was about to begin than for her grandmother to buy her own dressing-table set? It was blue enamel on silver, encased in blue morocco leather, and consisted of 'not only brushes and clothes-brushes galore, but cut-glass pots and bottles topped with the same blue enamel, nail files, a shoehorn and even a buttonhook for long white gloves.' It was, said Raine, 'the most beautiful dressing-table set in the world,' and decades later could still be found on a dressing table at Althorp.

Raine was now entering a period of her life that Barbara embraced with gusto. She had always tried to be the sort of mother to Raine that Polly had been to her. Although Barbara has made no secret of her preference for men – 'I have always found women difficult. I don't understand them' – here was her very own virgin, beautiful and clever, who she could mould into a real-life version of the romantic heroines that appeared in all her later books: one who, if everything went according to plan, would fall in love, marry and live happily ever after. Raine had been brought up to marry above her station and Barbara was determined to ensure she did just that. She gave the project the intense brand of Cartland attention.

Although Raine's unsophisticated schoolfriends were impressed with her sense of style, Raine did not yet measure up to her mother's high standards. 'Do tidy your hair and clean your face, darling,' Barbara would ng. 'No man wants a clever woman!' Barbara admits, 'At times I really used to bully her and become absolutely furious with her – as I suppose mothers often do with daughters. Hugh used to tell me "You're being beastly to poor Raine," but of course the bullying worked and soon she was starting to make the most of herself, which was really all that mattered.'

Barbara admits that the raw material couldn't have been better. 'She had perfect features and a lovely figure, so I decided I was going to produce her as a beauty.' The goal was Raine's coming-out, which was scheduled for the spring of 1947. Before the war, launching a debutante was rather like launching a ship; the bigger the splash, the better the dividend, usually in the form of marriage to someone rich and/or titled. To do it properly a girl had to have a private ball and a number of suitably ornate dresses which would set her father back several thousand pounds. After the war the mood began to change and the feeling slowly grew that debutantes and expensive 'seasons' had run their course and should be abolished. Barbara herself wrote an article in the *Leader* magazine in 1949 in which she said, 'Let us be frank. Debutantes – unless they are your particular property – are bores.' She blamed the press for hyping up the occasion. '... publicising a debutante as a beauty, or indeed as a personality, is only a Fleet Street racket started originally to fill in space.' Yet two years previously she had put all her time and energy, and a good deal of money, into launching her daughter in society and one can imagine her reaction if the press had failed to notice Raine.

The ideal springboard for Raine's imminent coming-out was the Club of the Three Wise Monkeys, better known as the Monkey Club, in Pont Street, Knightsbridge, which had the reputation for being 'London's most exclusive finishing school'. The school was founded in 1923 by Griselda Joynson-Hicks and Marian Ellison to train young society girls of good family, aged between seventeen and twenty-five, in domestic science, elocution, secretarial work and languages. The school was evacuated to Steyning, Sussex, during the war years and eventually closed down in 1969. Its motto was, appropriately, 'Speak no evil, see no evil, hear no evil'.

Attracting 'social butterflies with serious sides to their nature' and giving them something to do between parties, the Monkey Club was thought to be the ideal place where a certain class of young lady could mark time between leaving school and getting married. The modest workload was, however, too much for many young debutantes who were doing a full season with two or three parties every night and could hardly be expected to be up at nine o'clock in the morning to learn how to make potato cakes. Even the Monkey Club was not immune to the deprivations that followed the war. Recipes were carefully chosen to avoid lavish ingredients: dried egg plus two tablespoonsful of water was substituted for those that required the real thing.

Although the finishing school developed a reputation for frivolity, those few girls who wanted to learn were given the opportunity to develop language skills and a love of literature, as well as to master basic cooking. They were encouraged to rely on 'inner discipline' and taught 'to help and sympathise with their servants and not to bully them'. Despite the post-war austerity, the Monkey Club blossomed and Raine thoroughly enjoyed her time there, especially learning French and German. 'I adore languages,' she said. 'And we did cooking too and yes, of course we always swept the stairs.' Far more stimulating for Raine than symbolic acts of housework was the requirement that the girls put on evening dresses for dinner or else ate high tea in another room. It gave her an opportunity to extend and develop her carefully cultivated sartorial image.

During the school holidays Barbara continued the 'finishing' process at home. She knew how important it was that girls spoke nicely, didn't mumble, were adept at making charming conversation and at ease at social events. She wasn't going to leave Raine's success in these areas to chance. Just as Ronald Cartland, during his short-lived parliamentary career, had rehearsed his speeches in front of his sister, which he said gave him enormous confidence, Barbara decided to try the same approach with Raine. 'I used to get her to make a speech to me, rather as Ronald used to do,' she said, 'and while she was speaking I'd go into the room next door and shout "I can't hear you. Speak more clearly." ' She was delighted when Raine later won the gold medal for elocution at the London Academy of Music and Dramatic Art.

After her stint at the Three Wise Monkeys Raine was sent to a fashionable finishing school at Mürren in Switzerland. On the whole it was not a happy experience for her. Although she learned to speak good French, the food was poor due to post-war shortages and Raine told her mother that she was fed almost entirely on potatoes which gave her boils. Barbara went out to visit her and see the situation for herself and, while there, bought dozens of yards of red, green and white tulle, blue ribbon and white silk for Raine's coming-out parties. Such materials were at the time impossible to get hold of in Britain.

Barbara was determined that Raine should encapsulate all the feminine, demure and pure qualities of a debutante and, in true Cartland fashion, did everything within her power to make sure she succeeded.

For Raine's debut at the Queen Charlotte Ball, Barbara commissioned Worth to copy a dress originally worn by the Empress Eugénie to be made up from yards of the white Swiss tulle. Raine's hair was parted at the centre and curled at the sides. The society magazine *Tatler* photographed her in the dress, sitting with her back straight and her hands held neatly in her lap, as if not even sugar would melt in her heart-shaped mouth. She looked just like the romantic heroine of one of her mother's novels.

But one dress does not a season make. 'We had to think up all sorts of different ways of making Raine look striking,' Barbara remembers. To this end she used her ceaseless inventiveness and imagination. Some dresses were extravagantly garnished with frills and fripperies and two were made to Barbara's own designs: one in green tulle which had bunches of pink roses at each shoulder and another in poinsettia red tulle with white pompoms 'like snowflakes' all over it. Raine was presented to George VI in a 1934-vintage Molyneux dress of Nile-blue lace which Barbara spotted in a discreet shop in South Molton Street that sold second-hand designer clothes. 'We bought it from Mary Leigh for three and a half guineas (about £3.57). She looked quite lovely. Several of her evening dresses were also from there.'

Perhaps surprisingly, Raine has never complained about wearing second-hand clothes and later felt no qualms about putting her own dresses up for auction. A friend of Barbara's found a small Victorian crinoline in her attic and several of Raine's dresses were based on this, including a blue taffeta dress which she bought from a schoolfriend for £3 and wore over the crinoline with the neck elaborately decorated. 'Artificial flowers were free of coupons,' said Barbara. 'We bought a big wreath of daisies, poppies and cornflowers which we had sewn round the neck of the dress.' They also added a wide velvet hem. 'It looked lovely. The American Ambassador said it was one of the prettiest dresses he had seen in London.'

Raine was content to be moulded by her mother and rose to the challenge of the season as to the manner born. Barbara commented, 'The wonderful thing about Raine was that she didn't mind standing out from the others.' Even Barbara, with her high standards, could now write that 'one of the most outstanding things about Raine was that she was so neat and tidy'.

Raine had three dances given in her honour: the first by her mother and stepfather, the second by an old friend and the local MP in Bedfordshire, Alan Lennox-Boyd, and the third by Raine's godfather, the Duke of Sutherland, at Sutton Place in Surrey (later to become the home of the oil millionaire Paul Getty). This last event was reported in Jennifer's Diary, then in *The Tatler* magazine, as being a 'small' dance, although much was made of the 'huge vases of flowers in every room'. The description of the occasion went thus: 'In between dancing to Bill Savill's band which played superbly in the long gallery, guests could stroll around the beautiful gardens where the herbaceous borders were a blaze of colour or to the swimming pool in its walled garden, where delphiniums and lilies were at their best against the red-brick walls, while the scent of stocks and cherry pie filled the warm night air ... Raine McCorquodale looked enchanting in a white picture frock.'

Among the guests were Gerald Legge (heir presumptive to the Earl of Dartmouth) who was staying in the house, Lady Rothermere, Ian Fleming, the creator of 'James Bond', the Marquess and Marchioness Camden, Lady Rosemary Spencer-Churchill and the Marquess of Blandford.

As a prelude to the dance Barbara gave Raine a dinner to which she invited twenty eligible young bachelors, but no women. The young men were astonished that there were no other girls, but Barbara made her intentions quite clear. She wanted to take a close look at all the men present in order to decide who Raine should marry. Gerald Legge was high on the list. At the dance that followed, Barbara and Polly were, initially, the only women present. 'It was unusual to say the least,' says Lord Mowbray, Segrave and Stourton, 'and there were a lot of young men seething at the bar.'

Barbara, however, was unrepentant. 'I did it for a purpose. It not only meant that Raine would have a partner for every dance but also that her girlfriends would too. I can't bear girls standing around at a dance. Remember this was just after the war and we had two million surplus women in England. As each girl brought her own partner, I had made sure that there would be twenty spare men and no girl could possibly be left out.'

Barbara's hard work paid off on all fronts. Raine's tulle dance dresses were a sensation. By coincidence Christian Dior had launched his New Look that year and in contrast to the restraints imposed by the war, tiny waists and billowing skirts were now the 'in' thing.

Raine often went to a cocktail party, dinner party and dance in one night. She has always had enormous stamina and often stayed on the dance floor until three or four o'clock in the morning. 'Raine danced so beautifully and so many men were in love with her,' her mother says. She did, however, keep a watchful eye on her daughter's conduct. 'I would never let Raine drive home at night with a young man. She was kept just like my heroines, pure and cherished.' The *Leader* magazine wrote about her: 'Eighteen–years–old with a face the shape of a heart, Miss Raine McCorquodale turns dancing eyes upon the world. Eternally smiling – at Ascot, in Bond Street, at dances and at parties, she reminds us of another age, when there were courts in Europe, when a girl "came out" in a recognised manner and one of them was hailed as the Toast of the Town.'

She was less popular with some of her contemporaries, who thought her fairy-princess outfits more suitable for the top of a Christmas tree, while others sarcastically remarked that Raine became famous for looking good on a shoestring. 'She had very few dresses and they had to be changed about to look as if she had ten. She had to work terribly hard to keep going and compete in the debutante season,' interior designer David Hicks remembers. 'She irritated me frightfully with her huge crinoline dresses. She was also a frightful show-off.' One of Raine's young escorts believes that she has not changed much over the years. 'As a deb she was a younger version of what she is now. She wasn't like anybody else. Absolutely extraordinary.' Another says, 'She was a great attender of dinner parties and dances and always wore crinolines which became her trademark. She was very attractive, danced extremely well, had good manners and was never nasty to anybody. It was recognised that she was being pushed by her mother, although she wasn't the only one. She could be bossy and pushy and a lot of people considered her to be a joke character.' The Earl of Dudley remembers Raine wearing such a vast crinoline at one ball that he decided 'it must have been sustained by hoops; so much so that upon inviting her to dance I enquired – perhaps impolitely – whether I was expected to dance outside or inside the dress!'

The last laugh was certainly on Raine when she was voted 1947 Debutante of the Year. 'I made Raine the Debutante of the Year,' Barbara says. 'Wherever she went everyone looked at her because she was not only very pretty but had the loveliest dresses. She was photographed hundreds of times wearing them.'

But most important of all, Raine had come up with the required dividend to repay her mother's efforts – by falling in love. Raine had originally met Gerald Legge when she was sixteen on top of a mountain during a skiing holiday and, in true Barbara Cartland romantic heroine fashion, claimed she fell in love with him at first sight. 'We were skiing and there was Gerald standing on the ski slopes. I said to myself "God has chosen this man for you." It was love at first sight.' Sir Roy Strong heard Raine talk about their meeting on the *Thought for Today* radio programme. 'It stuck in my mind because it was terribly difficult to square it with what happened later and their breakup,' he says.

Twenty-two-year-old Gerald was the eldest son of Commander Humphrey Legge, Chief Constable of Berkshire. He had been in the Coldstream Guards and was now with a firm of chartered accountants in the City. The Legge family had a long history of serving England in various capacities. The earldom was created in 1711, but the baronetcy of Dartmouth goes back to 1682. Raine was to change her name three times before she changed her husband: from Mrs Gerald Legge she became Viscountess Lewisham and later, the Countess of Dartmouth.

Despite telling television interviewer Mavis Nicholson that 'I asked Mummy what to do on every conceivable occasion until I was already married and having children', Raine omitted to do so when Gerald proposed to her in January 1948. Barbara and Hugh were in New York on a business trip where Barbara was officially representing British authors to American publishers. Rather than wait until they returned Raine accepted Gerald's proposal with all the impulsiveness of a young girl in love and sent her mother a telegram to tell her of her engagement.

Officially Barbara was 'not particularly pleased'. 'Although I liked Gerald very much, I thought Raine was too young,' she said. 'She was only eighteen, she had not seen much of life, and as she was very pretty it seemed rather absurd to rush into marriage until she had had a good look round to make quite certain Gerald was the right man.'

Others believe that, in spite of these fine words, Barbara had put considerable pressure on Raine to marry early. 'I think her mother felt, like a lot of mothers then, that she didn't want to support her much after the season,' said a family friend. 'Now girls are encouraged to have a career but then most mothers felt relieved if their children married young.'

Conservative MP Lady Olga Maitland felt that the family were very socially ambitious. 'It was unspoken that Raine should try to marry a title and I don't think she objected. Titles were much grander than they are today. It would have been a prestige marriage.'

Raine was not put off by her mother's misgivings. As clothes were still in short supply – requiring coupons – Barbara's American friends rallied round with clothes for her trousseau and even a pretty negligée for the bride on her wedding night.

The wedding date was set for 21 July 1948 at St Margaret's Westminster, where Barbara had married Alexander twenty years previously. Raine was nineteen years old and just as she had so recently been debutante of the year so she now became bride of the year.

The *Tatler* covered the marriage in detail. 'St Margaret's Westminster has not been so crowded for many years as it was for the marriage of Mr Gerald Legge and Miss Raine McCorquodale, who had a retinue of two pages and sixteen bridesmaids.' Raine wore her white tulle crinoline coming-out dress remade into a wedding gown measuring over two metres round the hem. The neck was outlined in orange blossom and bell-shaped sleeves of tiny tulle frills were added. She wore a Brussels lace veil – a family heirloom lent by the Scobells – held in place by a fine diamond tiara lent by Lady Patricia Lennox-Boyd.

The bridesmaids included Lady Pamela Mountbatten, Raine's school-friend Catherine de Trafford, Lady Caroline Thynne, Lady Evelyn Leslie and the Hon. Joan Spring Rice. The hoops of their crinolined dresses – white tulle trimmed with sequins – were so wide that a special bus was hired to take them to and from the church. The two pages were Raine's brothers Ian, and Glen, his face swollen with mumps, who wore kilts of the McCorquodale tartan. Thirty-two ushers guided the nine hundred guests to their seats. The church was decorated with huge vases of flame-coloured gladioli, the same colour as the sweet-pea bouquets that the bridesmaids carried.

Raine's father came to her wedding and greeted the guests at the reception at Londonderry House standing in line next to his ex-wife who was dressed in an ensemble of royal blue, with a hat that looked as if it had two mop-heads perched on top. Also receiving guests were the bridegroom's parents, Mr and Mrs Humphrey Legge, the latter in pink with a pink-and-grey-striped hat.

The McCorquodales took the unusual step of having the presents on view at the reception, a procedure Raine continued at the christening of her children. These included a canteen of silver, a dinner service and two entrée dishes from the Earl and Countess of Dartmouth, who also gave the bride 'three lovely Staffordshire knots which have been in the family for three generations'. From her mother came an aquamarine and diamond clip and bracelet, and from the bridegroom a diamond watch. Raine's present to her husband was a gold cigarette-case (she had yet to take up her strong anti-smoking stance). Gerald's parents gave the young couple household linen. Not all the presents were so grand and included a ham joint and a horseshoe made in the royal stables.

Grandmother Polly was of course present, as were Raine's great-uncle and aunt, General Sir John and Lady Scobell. Amongst the guests were Earl and Countess Mountbatten, with their elder daughter Lady Brabourne, Lady Mary Alexander with her daughter the Hon. Chairman Wilson and Lord Montagu of Beaulieu. None, however, outshone the bride who looked like a living replica of the cover of a Barbara Cartland novel.

9

Marriage and a Title

The couple left for their honeymoon in France, Raine wearing a flame-coloured dress and coat with hat to match. Before leaving the reception at Londonderry House, Raine threw her bouquet in traditional fashion over the balcony to the waiting bridesmaids below.

Raine's choice of husband surprised many. 'Looking at the two of them it would be hard to imagine that there would have been any real rapport,' says one of the ushers. 'You saw this highly attractive girl and there was this rather feeble, chinless wonder standing beside her.' However Lord Wardington, a friend of both Johnnie Spencer and Gerald Legge at Eton, feels Gerald was underestimated. 'He was so very quiet you wouldn't have noticed how bright he was. From Raine's point of view Gerald had a bank balance and was going to have a title.'

In the view of another usher: 'Gerald was a very nice, quiet, unassuming person and most of us saw him as the route to her marrying a title. It was always the battleship and the frigate. She was always out in front and he was always trailing behind.' The match gave rise to the joke that although Raine had married a Legge, she was the one wearing the trousers.

According to another friend: 'Although Gerald was very nice, he was a very dull man, unprepossessing to look at and with nothing interesting to say. On the other hand Raine is very strong indeed and has been the dominant figure in both her marriages.' Even one of Gerald's cousins couldn't understand the match. 'They were chalk and cheese,' she says.

David Laws, the interior designer, a great friend of Raine's since her first marriage until they fell out in the mid-eighties, saw several similarities between Gerald and Johnnie. 'Gerald was very much a schoolboy as indeed was Johnnie. Raine talked down to them both, treating them like little boys and saying things like "Run along now and do your work." Gerald was a very uninteresting person and underneath it all Johnnie was merely a more glamorous version of him.'

On 23 September, 1949, fifteen months after her marriage, Raine gave birth to her first child, a son William. He was christened on 29 November at the Grosvenor Chapel, South Audley Street. The event was covered by *The Tatler*: 'I have never seen more friends and relations attend any christening than filled the pews of Grosvenor Chapel when the infant son of Mr and Mrs Gerald Legge was baptised William by the Revd R. G. Whiteman. The baby, who was dressed in beautiful lace christening robes which are heirlooms in the Earl of Dartmouth's family, had six godparents.' His godmothers were his great-aunt Mrs Herbert Sotheby, Mrs Bertram Currie, and Lady Inchiquin. His godfathers were the Duke of Sutherland who was also Raine's godfather, the Marquess of Northampton and the Earl of Plymouth. Raine wore a black velvet dress with a spray of small orchids pinned on her shoulder.

After the christening everyone went back for tea at the Legge home in Mayfair, followed by a cocktail party. The christening cake was decorated with miniature pieces of sports equipment made out of sugar including a fishing rod and a fish, a gun and a pheasant, a cricket bat and stumps, a football, a tennis racket, a pair of stirrups and a racing whip. Baby William's christening presents were on display and included an oil painting of an ancestor from the Dartmouth collection together with a piece of red coral mounted on a gold handle which was featured in the picture. The coral was a family heirloom which all the heirs to the earldom of Dartmouth have cut their teeth on since 1700. There were also platinum and diamond cufflinks from the Marquess of Northampton.

Two years later, in 1951, Raine's second son, Rupert, was born and christened in St Paul's Church, Knightsbridge, on 27 April. By the age of twenty-two Raine had not only achieved her mother's ambition by marrying above herself, but had produced two sons as well. Having done so much so soon, perhaps it was hardly surprising that – like her mother before her – she should begin to doubt that marriage was the answer to a young virgin's prayers. Barbara had mistaken the quietness of her first husband for a deep well of passion, only to be bitterly disappointed. Certainly Gerald Legge was never going to be as lively as his ambitious young wife. Having started his career as an accountant, he became a merchant banker and was at least able to provide her with enough funds to create the glamorous life style she wanted.

If Raine wondered what the rest of life held for her, she quickly realised it would not be within the confines of marriage. The Legges moved into a nine-bedroomed, five-bathroomed house in Chester Street, Belgravia, run by a butler, William Stone, who wore traditional uniform – pin-stripe trousers and black jacket – and with a staff of five. Raine set about decorating it lavishly and asked the interior designer David Hicks to help. 'I was a young man, unknown and struggling and thrilled to be doing any work at all,' he says. 'Raine was very gushing, but a jolly nice leg-up and always paid the bill on the dot. She is the sort of person you either like or dislike. I admire her for her intelligence and her style. I don't think she's a person with a tremendous number of friends, but there are a lot of people who admire her very much.' Hicks was particularly pleased with an eighteenth-century wallpaper which he had specially printed for the large entrance hall and staircase. 'It had a marvellous big, classical damask design in burnt orange, apricot, beige and white.'

The house provided the ideal backcloth for social climbing and Raine, like her mother before her, was soon tagged 'the elegant Mayfair hostess', 'society beauty' and 'one of England's best-dressed women'. She appeared at all the right social events and made a brief foray into the society world of fund-raising for charity, selling tickets for various charity dances and balls. For Raine, with her vast energy and ambition, this was too tame an occupation and she began to feel frustrated as much by merely socialising, as with marriage itself. She wrote a short story called 'The Spun Gold Princess' but – not wanting to compete with her mother – did not follow it up.

Where she did emulate her mother, however, was in espousing a variety of 'causes'. Was this the beginning of a conscious pursuit of power as well as a means of helping others? 'I went for a job in the library at Wormwood Scrubs, but they looked at me and said I was too young and pretty. It wouldn't be fair on the boys.' She did voluntary work in Wandsworth which she described as 'caring for latchkey children'. The experience shocked her. 'Their mothers were at work, there was mass deprivation and those haunted-looking children had to rely on strangers to unlock their front doors, because they were too small to reach the keyholes. I was turned into an Angry Young Woman by all that I saw. Yet I felt so impotent.'

Raine discussed this problem with her mother, who advised her to get on the local Council. 'That will give you a power base.' She took the advice, joined the London Conservative Union and in November 1953, aged twenty-four, made her first speech to a group of twelve Tory ladies in a small green room in St Saviour's Church Hall, Herne Hill. Wearing a bright mauve suit and a bejewelled hat she talked in spirited tones about peace, security and housing for about twenty minutes. Then she sat down to a ham sandwich, a piece of shortcake and a cup of tea. Later in her career she would often take her own tea bag to such events. She confessed to the chairwoman, Mrs R. Hyde: 'This was my very first speech. I have been in a panic all day.' Mrs Hyde told her she need not have worried and that she had done extremely well.

Raine Legge certainly enjoyed the challenge of public speaking, the feeling of adrenalin and power, and decided to launch herself on the political scene. By the following May she had won a seat on Westminster City Council in the local elections for the Knightsbridge St George's ward and became the youngest councillor: a fact that inhibited her not a jot; she was confident and energetic and quickly made her presence felt. When she realised she would have to wear the then traditional councillor's robes for her first annual meeting, she decided that the normal fore-and-aft hat didn't suit her and had a new tricorn hat designed instead, which she wore at a rakish angle. In her first year as councillor her speaking engagements multiplied until she was speaking once a week for the London Conservative Union. At the same time she continued her charity work as a voluntary schools' care committee worker in Wandsworth. Her social life also proceeded apace: in June the same year she acted in a play called *The Frog* by Edgar Wallace which was co-directed by Princess Margaret and raised funds for the Invalid Children's Aid Association.

In September 1954 she took part in a Tory brains trust at Ickenham town hall. She prepared herself thoroughly for the occasion, as she still does whenever required to perform in public, and spent days in reference libraries mugging up on current problems. She took as much care with her clothes as she did with her research, a precedent she has also maintained throughout her life. Just as her crinoline dresses became her trademark during her year as a deb, so she decided never to appear looking anything less than glamorous at public meetings. She turned up for the Ickenham Tories in a royal blue princess-line dress with matching hat decorated with a large, shocking pink rose.

Her husband Gerald was not there to hear her speak on this or virtually any other public occasion, a situation she initially defended by saying she preferred to speak to an audience of strangers. Schooled in the art of recitation by her mother, she found she could 'photograph' every page of a speech in her mind and then reproduce the words as if reading them aloud. So word-perfect was she that her secretary had to avoid numbering the pages. Once when a page number was inadvertently left pencilled in at the bottom of her script, she simply included it in her address.

Raine has kept a copy of all her speeches. After she married Johnnie and moved to Althorp she said she had two thousand of them filed away 'on every subject under the sun. You name it; I've spoken about it.'

In retrospect, all this activity turned out to be a useful prelude to her hitting the headlines two months later with an episode that became known as 'the storm in a filthy teacup'. Like MP Edwina Currie's comments about eggs in 1988, the event stuck with her throughout her political career. It happened in November 1954 when Raine, in designer suit with posies of primroses on her jacket and hat, tripped into the lounge of London airport on her way to Paris. Passing by an airport café the newly-elected Westminster councillor noticed that the tables were covered with dirty coffee cups and cigarette ash. She pronounced herself 'angry, shocked and embarrassed' by the filth that lay around her.

After politely asking various individuals to clean the tables, but having been given the usual run-around of 'it's not my job', she finally lost her temper. Holding out a half-empty cup of coffee and a brimful ashtray she walked angrily to the airline desk and demanded, 'Is no one going to clear up this disgraceful mess?' She continued with a loud five-minute volley of criticism. In true British fashion, the other passengers sank down silently into their armchairs as her voice echoed round the lounge.

Her outburst made the headlines in the following day's newspapers. By then ensconced at the Ritz in Paris, Raine felt obliged to issue a further statement. 'Untidiness and dirt are bad, not only for the public health, but because they inevitably produce a messy and inefficient attitude of mind,' she declared. 'What really infuriates me is the attitude of "It's not my job to clear it away." ' The incident created a major stir. Questions were asked in Parliament of the then Minister of Transport John Boyd-Carpenter and reporters made follow-up visits to Heathrow for comments from airline executives down to the cleaning ladies.

Raine's days as a headline-maker had begun. When she returned from her visit to Paris ten days later, a throng of reporters was awaiting her at the airport. She told them she had received 'shoals' of letters from people, many asking her to lead a campaign to raise the standards of every restaurant and café in the country. She also deliberately squashed any idea that beneath her fluttering eyelashes lurked a harridan. 'Honestly, I don't go around kicking up a fuss,' she said. 'But I feel strongly that women should speak up about things they know about. We have a part to play in seeing that things are done properly.' She then surveyed the newly scrubbed and tidied airport café and declared with a broad smile, 'What a remarkable improvement. I'm really impressed.' She even tried the coffee, which she pronounced 'lovely' but regretted she did not have time to finish. The event epitomised Raine's behaviour in public life: a devastating combination of forceful outbursts rapidly followed by lashings of feminine charm.

Raine was not one to be satisfied with her fifteen minutes of fame and accepted with alacrity the innumerable invitations that flowed in to judge, appear at and open events. She was the flavour of the year and the press took her to their heart, devoting nearly as many column inches to what she wore as to what she said. She loved the publicity, and in turn helped journalists by developing a knack, either by her choice of clothes or words, of turning the most innocuous occasion into a good story. Her love-affair with the press was later to turn very sour but in those heady days of the fifties she revelled in her new-found fame. Everything was 'marvellous', 'exciting' and 'thrilling' and nearly everyone addressed as 'darling'.

Her public smile flashed liked neon lighting. Even her appearance in a brains' trust session with her mother was deemed worthy of report. 'On tripped Mrs Legge, 26, ravishing in a sapphire blue silk dress and a mink wrap she slid off to reveal creamy shoulders.' Her mother's clothes also came in for comment: 'On came Barbara Cartland, 51, a plume of electric green feathers on her head and loaded with diamonds.'

Raine then did an early version of a *Hello!* magazine-style interview with an American glossy where she was photographed during a 'typical day'. After breakfast she was seen in a black-and-white-checked tweed suit opening mail brought in by the butler Stone. She lunched with a friend in a Hardy Amies fitted red coat with beaver collar. After lunch, as councillor of the City of Westminster, she put on her ceremonial robes of blue velvet with white lace jabot and went off to a committee meeting. Coming home for tea she changed into a coral-red wool dress with pleated skirt. For cocktail-time she changed into a black velvet suit with white ermine bow and ermine hat. Afterwards she presided over a dinner for eight, wearing a black Dior evening dress with long diamond earrings and matching necklace. Although the number of clothes changes might seem a trifle unnecessary for anyone who isn't royalty, it again set a pattern for Raine's future behaviour, particularly while she was chatelaine at Althorp. A countess says disparagingly, 'She must be one of the very few who still changes into a tea gown. Who on earth does that today?' Raine's mother even revealed her daughter's measurements in her book *Look Lovely. Be Lovely*. Raine, readers were informed, was 5 ft 8 in. tall with a 34–24–36 in. figure and weighed 9 st 7 lbs.

In March 1955 Raine made her television debut as a story-teller in a programme called *Snapshot*. She opened the 1955 Fashion in Footwear exhibition in London wearing stardust-pink and blue kid shoes trimmed with sequins and pearls. She also judged the under-fours singing section of a London talent competition. It was a harmless enough occasion which Raine managed to turn into a newsworthy event by voicing her disapproval of the suggestive song 'Walking My Baby Back Home' chosen by one of the young performers. 'It does seem so ridiculous to see these tiny children get up and sing these emotional love songs,' she said. 'I have asked the Council official to announce tactfully that at future competitions we should prefer to give the prize to the child singing a more suitable song that has taken some time to learn. There are hundreds, such as "I Saw Three Ships Come Sailing In." '

She worked hard and unceasingly, speaking at a wide range of places – even in a women's prison where she decided to talk about 'What most interests women – men'. She could always be relied on to draw a crowd. Having proved that she could talk on any subject, anywhere, she now needed to increase her credibility factor and what better way than by finding a needy case? She did just that in July 1956 with the plight of 'Helpless old people who ought to be cared for. That is the duty of the young who owe everything to them.' Her versatility at thinking up fund-raising ideas knew no bounds, a foretaste of her imaginative com-mercialisation of Althorp.

During the following three years she visited hundreds of old people's homes around the country. She organised charity balls, set up the Mrs Gerald Legge Fund for Old People, gave countless talks in public and on the radio and even managed to persuade four hundred scouts to hold 'a good-turn' week for the old in Westminster. She even made a record on the HMV label, trilling a ditty entitled 'I'm in Love' written by her mother, backed up by the Rita Williams Singers and accompanied by Geoff Love and his orchestra. Any proceeds from sales were earmarked for her fund. The record was nominated as the worst disc of 1957 by *New Musical Express*.

Within a year a gleaming red bus – the first fruits of the Mrs Gerald Legge Fund for Old People – was purchased to ferry the old folk of Hendon and neighbouring north London boroughs to and from their clubs and the seaside. Raine insisted that the bus was fitted out with a toilet and stretcher so that even the most infirm could use it. In a well-publicised launch of the bus, she poured a cup of cold tea over its bonnet, her little finger cocked in the appropriate manner. She named the bus 'Polly' after her eighty-year-old grandmother, who was the first to enter the vehicle. Several other 'Polly' buses followed.

Even this project did not take up all her time and she accepted an advertising agency's offer of a £1,500-a-year consultancy on women's interests. By May 1957 her friends in the press began to notice that Raine's husband, Gerald, nicknamed by some as 'Left Legge', never appeared with his wife in public and questions were being asked about this. Raine decided she had to take the matter in hand and at future events, although Gerald still did not appear in person, she made a point of giving him a small walk-on sentence in her speeches.

One of these occasions was the British Association of Women Execu-tives dinner at the Café Royal, where Raine turned up in a crinoline embroidered with white and aquamarine sequins. She spoke about the need for businesswomen to live in two different worlds, choosing words that she had heard at her mother's bosom. 'Men haven't changed at all. They are all cavemen at heart. They don't want to be bored by a woman talking about her job. My husband's idea of misery would be to be told details of the Westminster sewers.' At the launch of a fibreglass bicycle at the Savoy Hotel she said: 'My husband absolutely forbids me to accept money or to advertise products. I think it is absolutely wrong of famous people to say "I cleaned my teeth with so-and-so this morning." I do clean my teeth of course – but I think it's absolutely wrong.'

Someone who has known Raine since her debutante days thinks she created a forceful image of her husband as a ploy. 'Gerald couldn't have been nicer, but she completely overpowered him. Raine has to be centre stage. She would say my husband doesn't want this and that, but don't believe it for a minute. It was a convenient way of laying down her own conditions.'

Raine did, however, have a compassionate heart. When Westminster City Council tried to ban council tenants from keeping cats or dogs, she put forward a motion which she fought for furiously: that the Council would act with discretion and allow pets to be kept by old or blind people. An amendment was passed exempting the blind from the ban.

Meanwhile her television career was increasing apace. In 1957, only three years after she became a Councillor, she appeared with her mother and grandmother on an ITV programme called *Success Story*. All three indomitable ladies smiled radiantly enough to outshine any studio lighting.

The following year Raine acquired the title she and her mother had craved for. Gerald's uncle, the 7th Earl of Dartmouth, died in March 1958, aged seventy-seven. The seventh Earl's only son had been killed in action in 1942 and he was therefore succeeded by his brother, Commander Humphrey Legge, Gerald's father. Gerald, in turn, took up the courtesy title of Viscount Lewisham and, at twenty-eight, Raine became Lady Lewisham. Her popularity was rising so fast that it was no surprise when she was the subject of Eamon Andrews' television show *This Is Your Life*. Naturally Polly and Barbara Cartland were key figures and positively fell over each other in their eagerness to pay each other tributes, as well as the sparkling Raine.

It was perfectly-timed publicity for the London County Council elections due the following month, April 1958, where Raine was standing as Conservative candidate for West Lewisham. Despite a confessed dislike of the outdoors and exercise, during the three-week canvassing period Raine went out and about meeting people from 9.30 a.m. until 6.00 p.m. every day. It was a tough fight but the lady was not for beating.

After a nerve-racking re-count that lasted four and a half hours the result was finally announced at 3.00 a.m. Lady Lewisham had been elected by a margin of a mere seven votes over her Labour opponent. (at a subsequent election she increased this to a majority of 2,700.) She was dressed for the occasion in a flowing black taffeta suit with violet hat, gloves and shoes, and this time Gerald was firmly at her side. Her mother, stepfather and brothers were a mere arm's length away. When the result was announced Raine's joy knew no bounds. 'Darling . . . it is absolutely heavenly,' she cried, fervently hugging a rather overwhelmed Gerald. 'It makes all the dreary foot-slogging seem worth it.' She then added for all to hear: 'I am going to work terribly hard for all the dear people who have voted me in.'

Her euphoria was not to be dampened by an angry Socialist who did not take his party's loss in the true British stiff-upper-lip tradition. 'You're nothing but a television box of tricks,' he shouted. But Lady Lewisham could afford to be bountiful. She gave him her most fulsome beam, called him a 'silly man' and swept on her victorious way. She knew the value of consolidating her victory with the press and, in an *Evening Standard* interview that appeared the following day, admitted she had only had three hours' sleep the night before. Her enthusiasm and sharp mind were, however, undiminished. 'I can't tell you how thrilled I am,' she enthused. 'I know people have been saying: "Why should that flighty empty-headed over-dressed Mrs Gerald Legge be chosen to represent the people?" But I think now I have the perfect answer to all their criticism. I believe one must always be honest with oneself and the electorate. It is insulting to dress down to people as well as dishonest, so I always deliberately dressed up and wore all my jewellery and furs – after all, everyone knows I have them.'

To the question of whether she would now stand for Parliament she used Gerald as her excuse. 'I would love to and have been offered several seats, but my husband is dead against it ... as MPs always seem to be working between six and midnight, he would never see me.' She said that time with her husband was a priority and would determine her workload for West Lewisham. 'I had to tell West Lewisham – I never hide anything and my motto is "never complain, ever explain" – that I would not be able to do any work after 6 p.m. normally because my husband needs me. As you see, just like over the question of jewellery' (for the interview she was wearing diamonds and pearls at her throat, ears, wrists and fingers) 'they have accepted it and even liked my honesty.'

Gerald was also the reason she gave for cutting down on some of her public engagements. She told Conservative Central Office that she would no longer accept invitations in the evenings or at weekends because of her husband's disapproval, although she still managed to open an average of three fetes a week.

It's all right if I am home in time for dinner, but he doesn't like me being out later than that [she explained]. My husband hasn't forbidden me to accept public engagements in the evening, but every wife knows the warning signs – and if she's sensible she takes notice of them. I used to accept invitations months in advance to open bazaars and then we would be asked to go and stay with friends the same weekend. Either my husband had to stay at home, which was terribly unfair on him, or I had to motor miles to get to the function which was exhausting. I'd have to cut myself in three to accept all the functions to which I am invited.

However, a friend believes that Gerald could not have stopped her working any hours she chose even if he had wished to. 'She wanted to stop at six p.m. because her social life was tremendously important to her. She loved her smart dinner parties. She could get away with it when others couldn't because of the grandeur she has about her.'

Raine gave her maiden speech as candidate for West Lewisham at a meeting of the LCC in December 1958. She wore a black wool bouclé dress and had memorised her 900-word speech, choosing old people as her theme. She criticised a Welfare Committee report which wanted to improve the furniture in large council homes for old people, saying that this was only playing with the problem and that, instead, she would like to see many more small council homes where old people could take their own furniture if they wished. She hurled herself into her work with renewed vigour. She was by now an accomplished television performer and much in demand, even agreeing to appear on the pop music programme *Juke Box Jury*.

The following spring, perhaps as an acknowledgment of their increasing marital problems, Raine and Gerald decided on a deliberate act of togetherness to celebrate their eleventh wedding anniversary and Raine's birthday with a touring holiday in Europe, leaving the children, William and Rupert, with Grandma Dartmouth. Barbara Cartland romantically billed the trip as a 'second honeymoon', adding, 'They don't get much time together because they are both so busy.'

When they returned Raine continued working as hard as ever, speaking out against any perceived wrong in society. Although helping the aged remained a priority, she had by now developed an 'A to Z' of causes to support. Some were worthy, others were frivolous. There were so many that her worthwhile efforts were often lost amid her more trivial concerns. She could always be relied upon to be outspoken, let the fireworks fly, and provide eager reporters with a few well-chosen words that would make the headlines. When she was asked whether she thought her 'obvious enthusiasm' for a cause sometimes tilted her over into the ridiculous, she replied: 'No, but I think many negative people are frightened by enthusiasm and plain speaking.'

She created a predictable stir when, in a speech, she described shop assistants as 'incompetent toffeenoses' who 'hoped their customers dropped dead outside the store so they wouldn't have to serve them'. Another storm was caused by her demand that doctors should teach sex education in schools, and, failing this, that it should be the job of parents, not left to teachers whom she called 'well-meaning embarrassed amateurs'. 'It is assumed,' she declared 'that teachers will somehow sandwich sex talks in between algebra and geography. But the facts of life cannot be added up to any equation.' She even took up as a cause the current

Board of Trade regulations governing the export of lace-trimmed pet-ticoats. Exporting goods nowadays was, she said, 'like a game of snakes and ladders. The snakes are the Board of Trade and the Inland Revenue.'

Her personal swingometer of espoused causes moved so dramatically and so frequently from the serious to the superficial that she stayed almost permanently in the public eye. On the one hand she became concerned about the number of criminal assaults on children and wanted special classes to be run in LCC schools to teach girls, self-defence, on the other, she battled to abolish the gymslip, which she wanted replaced by uniforms designed by Norman Hartnell. The then Minister of Education, Mr Geoffrey Lloyd, told her in reply that he thought the matter should be left to individual headmistresses. She even attacked the prostitutes in Mayfair who, she claimed, prevented honourable men from going about their business.

Following 'the storm in an empty teacup', Raine came to be regarded as an expert in the area of catering. In this role she condemned Britain's cooks who made 'dreary, disgusting and unhealthy food' and created a furore when she opened a food research laboratory in Birmingham. Having first shaken hands with many of the staff, she announced: 'Girls in a laboratory kitchen have shaken me by the hand and now they are handling food. They should surely not handle food after receiving guests, VIPs or not.' To the stunned audience she continued, 'It is about time we realised that those who prepare and serve food can kill just as surely as dangerous drivers. If they swerve one germ away from the straight path of cleanliness, they should be properly punished by imprisonment.' The managing director, highly embarrassed by this double whammy, immediately ordered that a hand-basin should be installed in the laboratory.

Raine's confidence, forthright approach and rugged determination made her a formidable opponent and grown men were, and still are, known to quake at the knee and give in to her demands rather than challenge one of her tirades. Like her mother, Raine prefers the company of men, and from her early days as a Councillor began to surround herself with a coterie of mainly male admirers who would carry her bags and generally make themselves useful. 'She was aware of her power over men and really enjoyed it,' says a friend. Some years later, in 1968, she even admitted her skills in this direction. When testing throwaway plastic cups for British Rail at a reception at Paddington Station, she told the story of how she had once found herself sitting in the buffet car of a train with a bill for £1 5s od (£1.25p) in front of her and only 10s (50p) in her purse. 'It was the most ghastly moment of my life. There was only one thing to do – pick up a man who could pay the bill. So I looked round and saw this simply charming, sweet man, and to be quite frank, I just picked him up ... and of course he paid.'

Students, however, proved both immune to her charms and unintimidated by her presence. When she gave a talk to the Conservative Association at the London School of Economics in 1959 she was drowned by boos, catcalls and personal remarks about the shape of her legs. She was furious and the following day declared from her bed, where she lay 'exhausted', that she would never speak to such 'frightfully rude and juvenile' people again. 'When I got up to speak I realised they were all Socialists . . . and were taking the mickey all the way.' It was, however, an occasion when her tactlessness got the better of her. The rumpus appears to have reached its climax when Raine, speaking of her recent experiences of canvassing, told the students: 'Often I found that where Socialist voters lived there were dirty milk bottles on the doorstep.' Such insensitivity has, over the years, managed to offend not just students in a lecture hall but friends, colleagues and her staff.

Even if her comments failed to make the newspapers, her appearance invariably did. When she opened the sixth International Watch and Jewellery Trades Fair at Olympia's National Hall in September 1960 connoisseurs noted that she was wearing 'a William the Fourth lily-of-the-valley diamond spray with pearls, early Georgian diamond and ruby earrings, four rows of cultured pearls with a diamond clasp and an enormous diamond Louis XV ring.' She would, it seemed, do anything to get her name and photograph into the papers and in a press interview she graciously acknowledged her debt to journalists – an acknowledgment she withdrew long before the controversy surrounding the Spencer treasures reached its peak. One of Raine's colleagues said: 'When she was at Westminster City Council she had a gift for engaging the press. I would say she was made by the press, who, although they have since tried to break her, in the end, haven't been able to.'

When Raine was asked point-blank whether she sought publicity she replied,

> Not in any way. But when the press very kindly ring me up for my comments on various topical doings, then I'm often only too delighted to give them, because one can interpret what constituents are perhaps saying and feeling, but they have no platform to air their view.

She also acknowledged the importance of the press in her campaigns.

> Many years ago I discovered that no one takes any notice of people who shout at street corners. So I became a city councillor and a county councillor – that through these positions I might continually try my utmost to right injustice wherever I found it. I have received over the years many thousands of 'Thank You' letters from ordinary people whom I have helped in different ways – but none of this could have been achieved without the

press who have underlined my activities and my nuisance value towards authority.

Criticism that she was a ridiculous caricature seemed to slide off Raine like designer bath oil and she loved the fact that cartoons of her appeared regularly in the newspapers, as David Hicks recalls. 'Every time a new one appeared she would phone me up and gush "Darling, do come round and take the lovely cartoon." They all had to be mounted in ghastly viridian green.'

So rarely was she now seen in public with her husband that when he stood by her side while she opened the country gardens in Lamberhurst, Kent of the Marchioness of Dufferin and Ava – who had been a guest at her wedding – it was thought worthy of press comment. A *Daily Mail* reporter wrote: 'Viscount Lewisham was on hand to hear her speak. Indeed, many people are surprised when they learn that there is such a person.'

In July 1961 the family moved from Chester Street, Belgravia, to an even grander house in Hill Street, Mayfair. 'We wanted more room for the children [William was eleven and Rupert ten] now they're growing up,' she said. 'They'll be able to have a bedroom each and a sweet sitting room.' Raine decided she would have her new house decorated in a galaxy of gay colours – flame, turquoise blue, sunshine yellow and emerald green – and again enlisted the help of David Hicks. She has always liked walls covered in upholstery, usually damask but sometimes velvet. At Hill Street the drawing room was decorated in coral pink and turquoise with coral velvet sofas, with turquoise velvet on the gold-framed chairs. The master bedroom and adjacent boudoir were decorated in dark burgundy and shades of pink, peach and soft strawberry. 'It's all frightfully marvellous,' she enthused. 'Pink camellia in my bedroom with turquoise carpets and turquoise and white in the bathroom – frightfully David Hicksy – if you see what I mean.'

Over the years she and Gerald accumulated some beautiful pieces of antique furniture. The interior designer David Laws, who worked on the refurbishment of Althorp for Raine, says: 'She and Gerald had bought furniture that was as good as anything at Althorp, there were just fewer pieces. There were five commodes in Hill Street which could easily have been museum pieces. Raine took some of them with her when she went to Althorp.'

It was at Hill Street that Laws, then a young man working at the design company Colefax & Fowler, first encountered Raine. 'Someone else was making the curtains, and she asked me just to do pelmets, but in the end I did vast amounts.' The two became great friends. 'I would sit on the bed and she would even make up in front of me, putting Meltonian boot polish on her eyelashes with a little brush.'

Raine loved antiques-hunting and found it a useful hobby to fill the time between meetings around the country. Occasionally she and her mother would go off on expeditions together. In the early days she concerned herself with looking for etchings and engravings connected with the Legge family. Later, when she lived at Althorp, she had a ready outlet for her passion: she would pick up pieces of china, for reselling in the gift shop along with cheap jewellery and general souvenirs.

In October 1962 on the death of her father-in-law, who had held the title of Earl of Dartmouth for only four years, Gerald and Raine became the Earl and Countess of Dartmouth. Raine thus changed her home for the third time in less than fifteen years. By now her fame was such that often in the press she was merely referred to as 'Lady D.' (prefiguring the connection with her future stepdaughter-in-law, Lady Diana Spencer). She even had books of matches printed with a coronet and a golden letter 'D' for Dartmouth which were placed in the centre of each ashtray at her home. (Raine remained a non-smoker.)

Her new title did not change her life style and over the next few years her pronouncements continued in much the same vein. She was known as the Champion of Causes and Raiser of Rumpuses and had a way of routing out inefficiencies with the speed and intensity of a laser beam. Many people found it impossible to take her seriously, however, partly because of her appearance and partly because her insatiable appetite for publicity continually caused her to sidetrack into minor issues.

Having worked her way through the alphabet of causes, she now began to pronounce on basic aspects of living. She gave her Ten Commandments for family life when she addressed a Mothering Sunday service at Denton parish church, Newhaven in Sussex, at the invitation of the Rector, the Revd Victor Downs. Speaking from the chancel steps with the permission of the then Bishop of Chichester, Dr Wilson, she offered five commandments for mothers and five for children. Mothers should give their children:

'1   *Love.* Tell them as often as possible that you love them.
2   *Confidence.* Say you are proud of them and always make time to listen to their problems and their secrets.
3   *Curiosity.* Help them to discover about things, about life and God.
4   *Ambition.* Help them to make the best of their brains, their looks, their talent.
5   *A sense of humour.* Teach them to accept fair criticism and punishment and give them courage to laugh when things go wrong.'

The children, she suggested, should give their mothers:

'1 *Love.* She needs to be told you love her.
2 *Gratitude.* Without her a home would be only an ordinary building.
3 *Help.* See that you work together and find your fun together.
4 *Good manners.* Never look down your nose at her, for she is always trying to give you more than she ever had in her youth.
5 *Your secret hopes and fears.* She will never let you down.'

This set of clichés obviously pleased her and when she was asked to address more than 3,600 delegates at the Royal Society of Health Conference at Eastbourne in April 1963 she offered a set of rules for 'perfect parenthood':

'1 Tell your children about good and evil.
2 Explain sex and religion.
3 Help them with their problems.
4 Encourage them in work and play.
5 Give them your experience.
6 Teach them to live with success and failure.
7 Love both their virtues and their faults.
8 Pray for them to find faith and happiness.'

She insisted that discipline was vital:

If children are naughty, they must be punished . . . An awful lot of nonsense is talked about corporal punishment. People who even mention a cane are called sadists and it is fashionable to cloak old-fashioned naughtiness in clever talk about 'disturbed behaviour patterns'. If children understand from babyhood that 'Yes' means 'Yes' and 'No' means 'No', then parents may never actually have to hit them. But sometimes reasoning is not enough. A short, sharp beating is then an excellent thing, but the misdemeanour should not be mentioned again. Recriminations lasting for days can do no good, only immense harm.

She admitted that when it had been necessary she had beaten William and Rupert on the bottom, just as her mother had beaten her, but she chose to use a man's slipper rather than a hairbrush. She felt it was 'a great mistake that police cannot give children a good wallop sometimes instead of sending them to the juvenile court'.

Her three-golden rules for a happy marriage were:

'1 Tell your husband he's wonderful as often as possible.
2 Kiss him goodbye in the morning and when he returns each night.

3   Never bore him with your troubles until he has told you his.'

One cannot help wondering how Raine found the time to put these rules into practice herself, even though she is so highly organised that she manages to cram more into an hour than most people achieve in a day. She and Gerald somehow found time for another baby, however. A daughter, Charlotte, was born at their Mayfair home on 16 July 1963, delivered by a royal midwife, Sister Helen Rowe. She was christened at the Grosvenor Chapel, South Audley Street, and cried throughout the service, which was attended by four generations of the Cartland family: Raine's mother and grandmother as well as William and Rupert.

It took her a while to recover from the birth. At about the same time, as a result of the mid-sixties reorganisation of London, London County Council was replaced by the Greater London Council. This had much bigger boundaries, including the whole of Middlesex and parts of Kent and, as a result, many members of the old LCC changed their constituencies. Raine herself was without a political home for three years, until she stood for Richmond-upon-Thames in the local elections of April 1967 and topped the Tory poll.

She was not, however, at a loose end. She was invited to speak on a wide range of subjects and occasions, as well as appearing regularly on the *Any Questions?* radio programme and early television talk shows. During this period she complained long and loud about unscrupulous florists who put up the price of flowers on Mothering Sunday; called for an unofficial enquiry by Westminster City Council into Westminster's restaurants, declaring that the kitchens of some could only be described as 'sewers'; and campaigned vigorously for the registration of restaurants and for the number of health inspectors to be increased so that adequate standards of hygiene were maintained.

When opening a kitchen exhibition in the mid-sixties, she drew on personal experience to alert her audience to the danger of ill-designed kitchen equipment, disclosing that a 'badly balanced' saucepan of boiling water had slipped out of the hands of her mother's cook and burned seven-year-old William so severely on his shoulder that he had recently spent six weeks in hospital having skin grafts and would be scarred for life.

A new period in Raine's life began in 1964 when she became the first president of the National Association for Health (with her mother acting as deputy). The appointment gave her a fresh set of causes to fight for and marked the time in her life – that was to last until she married Johnnie – when she embraced a wide range of environmental issues. In the mid-sixties conservation was not yet a fashionable word, and Raine was an early campaigner against insecticides, bringing the problem to the public's attention in her own inimitable, headline-seeking way: 'Day after day millions give their children fruit and vegetables saturated with arsenic sprays, poultry reared on antibiotics and hormones, fish dyed with chemicals and cattle fattened by tranquillisers,' she said. 'Murder by Mouth or Death by the Pot sound like titles of Agatha Christie novels but . . . they are actual crimes we are committing on ourselves . . . Poisonous chemicals in our body can cause disease and death.'

She asked housewives to boycott any foodstuffs that had been treated with chemicals – a worthy demand but one which in the sixties was difficult to put into practice. She pursued her 'good food' campaign in a later speech to the Central London Federation of Townswomen's Guilds when she called for a national institute of nutrition. She also campaigned for the compulsory registration of pesticides and an official list of those which could safely be sold to farmers; for all vegetables that had been sprayed to be so marked; for all artificial dyes to be made illegal, with a small permitted list of tested colourings derived from natural sources; for a ban on the bleaching of bread; and for nutrition to be made a compulsory subject in schools.

In 1964, Raine also lost her father, Alexander died after thirty years of marriage to his second wife Margaret. In his will he rather touchingly left his daughter his gold wrist-watch and his grandsons William and Rupert his fishing rods. In addition Rupert was left his Purdy shotgun.

After a brief pause for an operation for the removal of her gall bladder, Raine was back at work. Although she was now a mother of three and had a burgeoning career in local government, she had not yet broken free of her mother's moulding. Having been particularly forceful in her fight for healthy eating, she now turned her attention to promoting soft feminine virtues, often repeating, almost word for word, sentiments her mother and grandmother had expressed years before. When asked to address five thousand delegates and their wives at the annual conference of the National Association of Round Tables at Bognor, she used the occasion to attack working women, in which category, curiously, she did not seem to include herself. This was a further example of Raine and her mother's practice of making pronouncements on how others should behave without seeming to apply the same criteria to themselves. 'Women are doing a man's job without his physical stamina,' she said. 'Always rushing off in the morning, rushing home at night clutching the food they must cook for supper. Rushing to clean the house. Rushing to cope with the children. There is no time for tenderness. No time for love. No time to comfort, inspire and guide . . . Every woman should say, "I will never be too tired to listen to my husband's worries and to try to help . . ." Never forget that the real power of women lies in their power to influence men, and through them, the world around them.' She failed to mention if, and in what way, she was influencing Gerald. The advent of hippydom was, she believed, partly to blame. 'Instead of delicious scented ribbon and roses, it's meant to be fashionable to wear long, dirty hair and chipped nails.'

On another occasion she told five hundred potential secretaries at Caxton Hall that 'shorthand and typing aren't all that important. The ideal secretary should have Personality with a capital P and should aim at being a combination of friend, public relations officer and nanny. A businessman needs a perfect secretary more than he needs a perfect wife.' Gerald's verdict on this pronouncement, as on all the others, is unrecorded.

Raine also, on occasion, presented herself as an amateur psychologist. At a conference of the Industrial Society in London, she pronounced that compulsive shoppers were really compensating for unsatisfactory sex lives; a statement that was guaranteed to hit the headlines. She told retail executives: 'There are many deprived, frustrated women of all income groups who find no happiness in their marriage, no fulfilment in their home life. So they go shopping to buy friendship and flattery from the assistant. A smile soothes them. Politeness charms them. Spending money gives them power.' Her remarks kept shopping in the news for several days and it was perhaps not surprising that the following year, in November 1967, she was asked to switch on the Christmas lights in Regent Street.

During a 'health and beauty' phase Raine gave an interview about her make-up routine, which perhaps explains why few people have ever seen her without make-up. 'I believe in keeping one's skin completely clean and well-protected,' she said. 'You know how dirty some people are. You've got to remember that skin is a living thing. It has to breathe, so it mustn't get caked. I do my make-up twice a day, every day. It takes me twenty minutes each time ... I take as much trouble whether I'm out or just having dinner on a tray alone. Englishwomen have a habit of letting themselves go after thirty. They seem to think once they're married they can give up trying. I would make up just the same if I were alone on a desert island: I think my powder would be my most precious possession. I hate a shiny nose.'

Raine took great pride in her skin. Anna Vinton, founder of the Reject Shop, remembers seeing her on holiday in Biarritz. 'She would only sit by the pool under a parasol. She didn't like her skin to see the sun. It's always incredibly white.' She did her nails herself twice a week, having been taught by her mother's manicurist. Her hair, 'which I am terribly fussy about', was done twice a week by 'Princess Margaret's hairdressers, René'.

In 1967, after a three-year absence from local government – she had served for eleven years on Westminster County Council and for eight as LCC member for Lewisham West, and proved herself to be able, astute, fearless and hard-working – Raine was offered a new political home at Richmond. She fought the seat with her usual vigour and tried to speak to as many of the 180,000 electorate as she could, although even she admitted that it was 'totally exhausting'. Interviewed by Max Hastings then writing for the *Evening Standard*, and now editor of the *Daily Telegraph*, she denied that power was a motivating factor in her decision to return to local politics. 'Everything seemed to be going so badly that I felt that I should come and do my duty,' she said. 'I haven't got an axe to grind. I've got a wonderful husband, beautiful children, a glamorous life, an amusing life and an interesting one. Power for power's sake is so boring. It's just that if you want to get anything done, you have to have some status to be able to do it.'

Once elected to the newly formed Greater London Council, Raine put herself forward for the Planning Committee and the Licensing Committee. Before she had even attended her first meeting, however, she plunged into controversy about a film based on James Joyce's novel *Ulysses*. Because of some sexually explicit scenes in the film, the British Board of Film Censors had made twenty-seven cuts before allowing its release with an 'X' (over eighteen) certificate. The film was banned in Australia and South Africa and got a stormy reception when it was shown as one of Britain's four entries in the Cannes Film Festival.

It so happened that, six days before Raine was elected to the GLC Licensing Committee, it had given permission for the uncensored version of *Ulysses* to be shown at the Academy Cinema in London's Oxford Street. Even though she had missed the crucial vote, Raine's outrage as defender of the nation's morals knew no bounds. Photographed in mink jacket and pink flowered chiffon dress, she expressed horror at the Council's decision. When asked if she had seen the film she replied, 'I don't see any necessity to see the film. I've read the book and that's enough for me. It's the most disgusting book I've ever read ... It's disgusting and degrading. If the characters are not doing unmentionable sex things, they're picking noses, spitting or going to the lavatory. If people want to wallow in filth let them. I like things that present life and sex in a glamorous and beautiful way.'

She lost no time in writing to the chairman of the committee, Mr Harold Sebag-Montefiore: 'As a mother I implore you to withdraw permission for this film if legally possible.' Mr Sebag-Montefiore was unmoved. 'The decision stands,' he replied. 'The film was seen by five of the fifteen members of the committee and the decision was unanimous. Lady Dartmouth is jumping to conclusions without having seen the film. I think this is an unsatisfactory method of taking up a position. I hope she will take herself to the cinema and see the film.'

Not to be outdone, Raine wrote to West End Central police station: 'I read that words censored from the film may be printed in a brochure and given to audiences. I hope our wonderful police, always the upholder of standards respected by decent people, will have legal authority to confiscate obscene literature.' The rumpus raged for almost a week. Fellow committee members were incensed that she was condemning the film without having seen it. One said, 'She encroached on an area that had nothing to do with her and didn't bother to acquaint herself with the facts. It was pure publicity-seeking.' Harking back to the incident at London Airport, film critics told her to stick to dirty cups. Raine in turn claimed to be inundated with letters, over ninety-five per cent of which agreed with her. She also saw the occasion as an opportunity to air her views on the current moral temperature of the country. 'These sort of films are having an effect on people,' she told one reporter. 'They're causing all this drug-taking which pop singers are so proud of. And why do you think illegitimacy is going up? It's all these people who are trying to degrade, debunk and disgust ... If nothing is done ... people will be making love naked in Piccadilly Circus. Passers-by won't even have to pay to watch. They'll just walk past without noticing.'

Joyce's publishers, the Bodley Head, were delighted with the publicity that Raine's outburst had brought them. 'In one day we've had orders for one thousand copies in Britain alone, plus five hundred to be sent to Australia and another five hundred to Canada,' a spokesman said. 'We've never had a day like it!'

Lord Willis, then president of the Writer's Guild of Great Britain, demanded that Raine resign from the Licensing Committee because 'she criticised the film without consulting the committee and ... without seeing it.' She fought hard for a week before graciously acknowledging she had lost the battle over *Ulysses*.

Jeffrey Archer, then a GLC councillor of twenty-six and not yet a novelist served on the Licensing Committee with Raine and remembers the terrible fuss about *Ulysses*. 'Raine was very sincere about what she felt and although we disagreed, I admired her persistence, energy and determination. If she believed in something, she really fought for it. Most times she got her way.' He does not, however, believe that she lives in the real world. 'Her ideas were based on an upbringing which none of us understood. She arrived and left meetings in a Rolls-Royce and, as her names changed, she became grander and grander. She wasn't someone I sought out for lunch, but I was in my first ever political appointment and I don't suppose she would have sought me out either.' He feels she was overpowering rather than frightening. 'She wasn't frightened of socialists –

she would get up and eat them for breakfast – but because she was so cosseted by her mother and so wealthy she wouldn't have understood what it was really like in the East End of London. But she did a lot of public service. She could have sat there with her money. She is a doer. I admire her energy, enthusiasm and desire to get things done. She also has style.'

Another well-known figure who served on committees with Raine felt that despite her hard work she lacked tolerance. 'She often made enemies on her own side which is unusual for a politician. If you disagreed with her she bore a grudge and rarely forgave you. She didn't adopt the normal politician's view of "you win some and lose some". You were an enemy for life if you opposed something she held dear.' In common with many who worked with her, he remembers Raine's appearance at meetings. 'She was always very well turned out, with never a hair out of place.'

Soon after losing the battle over *Ulysses* Raine and her husband bought a flat in Grosvenor Square (where her mother had once lived) and a sixteenth-century ten-bedroomed country house that had once been owned by Peter Sellers, Chipperfield Manor near Kings Langley in Hertfordshire. One couple who attended her regular weekend house parties remembered that during one of these Raine brought much of her jewellery down to the drawing room for her guests to admire. 'She then,' recalls the husband, 'asked my wife to show her *her* jewellery. She did, whereupon Raine told her it wasn't really worth having. She is remarkably good company, very amusing, beautiful and intelligent, but she does put her foot in it and antagonise people. She also always seems to be playing a part, which makes it very difficult to know what is going on inside her head.'

Although Raine kept her name in the newspapers with her fight against *Ulysses*, it was becoming chairman of another GLCs committee, the Historic Buildings Board, that was to have a far more permanent and dramatic effect on her life. It would lead her in the direction of meeting Johnnie, Viscount Althorp and colour her attitude to the Spencer family home of Althorp House and its unique treasures.

10

Success at Work and Play

In April 1968 Raine pronounced herself 'absolutely thrilled' to be made chairman of the Historic Buildings Board. 'My husband and I travel miles looking at buildings of beauty and historic interest,' she said. 'It is our hobby.' She was given the job partly for political reasons. The Conservative party was intending to abolish what was then the Historic Buildings Sub-committee and absorb its work into the Planning Committee of the GLC. But the proposed move was greeted with such outrage at County Hall that the Government did a complete U-turn and decided instead to give London's historic buildings as high a profile as possible. Few people at the time had a higher profile than Raine Dartmouth.

Raine and her committee were responsible for a list of five hundred historic buildings preserved by law in London and a supplementary list of another twelve thousand buildings. The committee also had the task of ensuring the preservation of parts of old London that were threatened with alteration or demolition.

In her role as chairman of the Historic Buildings Board, Raine was a round peg in a round hole and on many occasions proved herself to be a forward and incisive thinker. Many who admired the way she fought for the preservation of historic buildings later found it difficult to reconcile this with what happened later when she became chatelaine of Althorp. Whereas architect Sir Hugh Casson, who served for some years under Raine's chairmanship, was much impressed by her professionalism and punctuality, others have less warm memories. 'She was very dismissive of people unless you bowed down to her,' says one. 'She wanted your energy one hundred per cent of the time and if you didn't give it, she knew how to rub you up the wrong way.' Another colleague says: 'Raine has an iron hand in an iron glove which is so beautifully wrought people don't realise that even the glove is made of iron until it hits them.'

Raine was very clear about her role. 'We live in an age of ugliness,' she said. 'A great deal in our life is discordant and ugly and destructive. We must preserve the beauty we already have. Beautiful buildings, I am convinced, have a calming effect on the mind and the soul.'

One of Raine's first tasks was to help the young Roy Strong who had been appointed director of the National Portrait Gallery in 1967, the year before Raine became chairman of the Historic Buildings Board. 'I was in my early thirties at the time,' Sir Roy remembers. 'Mine was a sensational appointment and I was determined to put the gallery on the map. The following year, however, the National Gallery said they were going to expand and demolish us and I thought "I've got to get the National Portrait Gallery listed first as an historical building so that they cannot touch it."'

To this end he made an appointment to see Raine at the GLC. 'I remember going to have tea with her and saw this apparition with enormous bouffant hair immaculately coiffured in the late sixties way. One half of me said "How can one take this person seriously?" then a bell rang and she had to go out for a moment and the young man who was her assistant said, "She's absolutely wonderful, you know. If you brief her properly, she will take everything in and once she has the bit between her teeth, she'll never let go." And so it was. We got the building listed.'

Sir Roy also remembers sitting on a panel with Raine at a meeting on heritage at the Lyceum Theatre in London at which she had to make a speech. Raine's speeches often appeared spontaneous, but were always well rehearsed. According to Sir Roy she told the story of how she was driving through London and saw a bulldozer approaching a building. 'She stopped the car and said "My man, stop this immediately." The man stopped dead in his tracks. It was very typical of her. I have known her for thirty-five years. Like most powerful women, she is fascinated by men and whenever we encountered each other she would go "Oh Roy" and fling her arms around me.'

Raine's next major battle was over plans for an extension to the Tate Gallery which would have necessitated demolishing the portico and steps. This she opposed on the grounds that it would obscure most of the existing building. It was to be a controversy that raged on for six months, causing outrage among the art world and the general public alike. Despite being pregnant with her fourth child at the age of thirty-nine, she fought the battle energetically. The determined stand she took over the Tate Gallery put her on a collision course with some of the trustees and other proponents of the scheme, but she maintained her point of view despite accusations that the Historic Buildings Board did not know what it was talking about.

Referring to her battle for the Tate Gallery when she addressed the annual meeting of the Georgian Group at Burlington House in July 1970, Raine said: 'When my colleagues and I ... saw Ministry of Works proposals ... we could not believe our eyes. We were asked to whitewash the Ministry's decision. Instead we expressed horror and despair. We had no powers to refuse permission, but we demanded a public exhibition and the Tate was saved by public protest and press campaigns.'

She attacked planning authorities who, she said, seemed to have one law for the Ministries of the Crown and another for the general public. She was one of the first to sense 'a widening interest in preservation – in an age of tower blocks'. She spoke out against the 'hotchpotch' of new buildings in old towns which, she claimed, destroyed 'so much beauty and symmetry created by earlier architects'. She particularly disliked the newly built Knightsbridge Barracks which she called 'a monument to Government vandalism'.

In a letter to *The Times* in April 1969, she made a plea for an aesthetic approach to environmental planning and respect for the past. 'I believe that the next few years will be a crucial test for both planning committees and the public. There will be no second chance. Do we really care about our towns and villages? Do we care enough to mould a successful compromise between roads, shops, homes and offices needed for the 1970s and the charm and character of bygone eras? The fact of this compromise must be recognised and achieved in a way which satisfies both our wish for comfort and our search for aesthetic beauty.'

With a view to enlisting recruits for her fight to protect and preserve what she described as being precious to London, she wrote a book entitled *Do You Care About Historic Buildings?* Published in 1970, it was an official record of the work of the Historic Buildings Board under her chairmanship and described in detail some of the battles which the board won and lost against developers and government departments. 'Better the shabby building which is also part of the landscape than a brash modern construction which seems to shriek "notice me I am new",' she said. Ironically she singled out Spencer House, originally the London home of the Spencer family, as a fine example of a historic building converted to modern use (by Dennis Lennon for the Economist Intelligence Unit).

The tone of the book shook many members of the committee. 'When I'd finished I showed it to my board and they were absolutely horrified,' she admitted. 'They said "In twenty-five years no member has ever written anything like this, it's absolutely against council policy and there are far too many adjectives."' Not to be defeated, Raine 'got up at six o'clock one morning and rewrote the whole book in the third person'. She later described the effort of it all as 'being like giving birth'. When resubmitted the text to her board, 'This time they corrected a lot of my grammar,' she said, 'but they liked it and we've just gone on from there.' The book also contained nearly ninety photographs. She cajoled cartoonist Osbert Lancaster, an advisory member of the Historic Buildings

Board, to contribute drawings and Sir John Betjeman a new poem.

The promotion of the book was an example of Raine at her most effective. The Salvation Army agreed to distribute over a thousand leaflets publicising it. The National Portrait Gallery put it on display and Selfridges filled an entire window with copies. It was even available on the QE2. Raine has always been convinced that the personal approach pays off (she was often to be found working in the gift shop at Althorp) and sent off over four thousand letters to likely buyers. She even took orders for the book at the October wedding of her brother Ian. It was an unusual way of promoting a GLC publication, but one couldn't doubt its effectiveness. It became the GLC's only bestseller. Its first printing sold out and it even made a profit.

Raine was naturally delighted. 'I want the book to make people think "What's happening in my area?" I just want them to care because if the public really cares we shall keep everything.' Gerald, however, was less pleased with her efforts. 'The only person who is nearly climbing up the wall about it all is my husband,' she admitted. 'He's always perfectly angelic but I think if he hears the book mentioned once more he'll shoot me.'

Raine has always been a mixture of the industrious and the imperious, and never more so than during her time on the Historic Buildings Board. She was often collected by a council car to be taken to meetings. This would usually be the standard Rover and not particularly to her liking as she was used to being driven in a Rolls-Royce. Ashley Barker, surveyor of historic buildings for the GLC and the board's senior adviser, who sometimes travelled with her, remembers:

> If the car was not absolutely immaculate inside and out, there would be hell to pay. Not only would she tear into the driver, but also put in ferocious complaints to the garage about the shabby maintenance. Eventually there was only one driver who would agree to take her. Nor could she tolerate sitting in traffic jams. She would shout at the driver, 'You know I don't sit in traffic jams. Do something about it.' He would say, 'What do you expect me to do, m'lady?' and she would reply. 'Drive on the pavement, anything, but I am not going to sit here.'

Raine has always been a popular speaker at conferences and put in a tremendous amount of effort not only in getting her speeches right, but in orchestrating her entrances. 'She always had to make an entrance,' says Ashley Barker. 'If there were other speakers before her, she would refuse to sit on stage waiting for her turn to talk and would try to organise a coffee break between their speech and hers so she could make an entrance.'

Her attention to detail also extends to checking the colour scheme of the venue. For example, BTA colleague Alan Jefferson remembers Raine asking about the colour of the carpet on the podium where she was speaking at a conference for German travel agents in Harrogate. 'It was dusty pink, and Raine arrived colour coordinated in a burgundy and black outfit, with ruby and diamond jewellery.'

On 28 December 1968 Raine gave birth to her fourth child, Henry. Her son William, Viscount Lewisham, was then nineteen and at Oxford, Rupert, eighteen, at Eton, and Charlotte, whom she nicknamed Cha-Cha, only five. It was all part of a master plan. 'My husband and I always rather wanted to have two families and that's how it's worked out. We regard Henry and Charlotte as a sort of insurance policy for our old age, because at least they can push us around when we're in our bathchairs.' She also put herself on Hormone Replacement Therapy, which she has been taking ever since.

Henry was christened on 27 February 1969 in the Grosvenor Chapel, South Audley Street, by the Revd Mervyn Stockwood. His father made a rare pronouncement to the press, saying he thought it would be nice if Henry grew up to be like his namesake who was Chancellor of the Exchequer in the eighteenth century. Raine said much more. She explained how, during her pregnancy, before such things were fashionable, she had only eaten for 'half not this nonsense of eating for two which simply blows you up'; and that she took vitamin pills and was back to her normal nine stone seven pounds two weeks after Henry was born.

'Having a baby at almost forty is partly a matter of readjustment,' she continued. 'I have to switch my mind from the boys and their girlfriend problems, to the baby, his needs and feeds. But it keeps me alert and on my toes.' All in all, she said, 'it was the most wonderful thing for a woman to have a second family, like me. Before Charlotte was born ... I had forgotten the sheer joy of anything to do with babies. It took Charlotte to give me back my youth and jolt me back to life.'

Perhaps her comments inspired a Birmingham toy manufacturer to produce a 2 ft 3 in. doll based on Raine, which he intended to sell for £4.25p. She found the idea 'Amusing ... I have never thought of myself as a cuddly doll in the past, but I must say I am absolutely delighted and very flattered ... As soon as they're on sale, I shall buy one for Charlotte.'

Raine, meanwhile, was very ambitious for her eldest son William although, according to her confidant David Laws, 'neither she nor Gerald got on very well with him'. She encouraged him to stand for president of the Oxford Union debating society which was something of a personal challenge as at the time he suffered from a severe stutter. Anna Somers Cocks, editor of *The Art Newspaper*, was at Oxford with William. 'Poor William was a rather pathetic figure at the time and buckled under the weight of maternal expectation, although his brother, Rupert, managed to come out from under. During the late 1960s being a member of the

(*Left*) The young Barbara Cartland,
aged eight, with her mother Polly and
baby brother Ronald, photographed
in 1909

(*Below*) Barbara's marriage to Raine's
father, Alexander McCorquodale, on
April 23, 1927 at St Margaret's,
Westminster. She claimed to wear the
first white tulle wedding dress seen
since before the first world war. It was
made by Norman Hartnell to
Barbara's own design

Raine, aged five, just after her parents' divorce, by the
society photographer Dorothy Wilding

(*Left*) Raine and half brothers Ian (left) and Glen (right) with their mother in a St John's Ambulance Brigade uniform, taken during the second world war

(*Below left*) Johnnie dressed in his school uniform for his first day at St Peter's Court prep school, Broadstairs

(*Below*) Johnnie, second from right, with his parents, the 7th Earl Spencer, and his wife Cynthia

(*Right*) Johnnie in his uniform of the Eton corps

(*Below*) Johnnie sporting a new moustache in Australia in the late 1940s when he was ADC to the Governor of South Australia, Sir Willoughby Norrie (second from right). His fellow ADC Michael Trasenster is second from left

Viscount Althorp on his wedding day, June 1, 1954, to the eighteen-year-old Hon Frances Roche, at Westminster Abbey. The guard of honour formed by his regiment, the Royal Scots Greys

Raine McCorquodale, deb of 1947, in a dress copied from one designed for the Empress Eugénie,
taken by Dorothy Wilding

(*Below left*) Nineteen-year-old Raine on her marriage to Gerald Legge at St Margaret's, Westminster on July 21, 1948, wearing her coming out dress subtly altered for the occasion. (*Right*) Raine, now Lady Lewisham, on her way to take her seat at the London County Council in April 1958 with her sons Rupert, seven (left) and William, eight

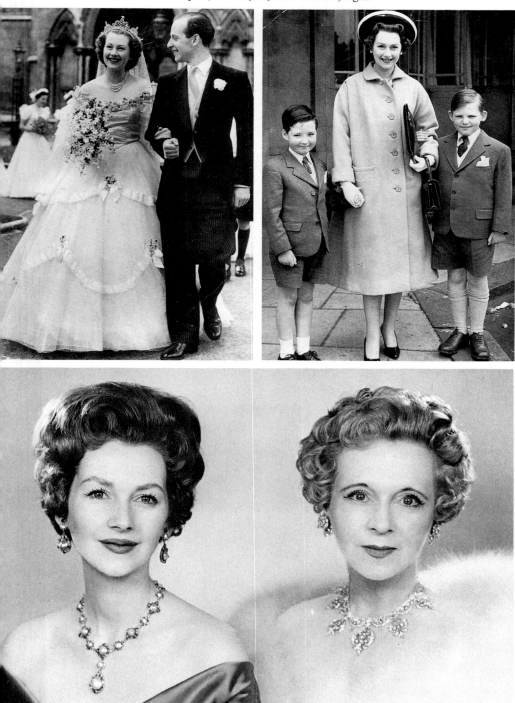

Like mother, like daughter. Taken by Dorothy Wilding

The christening of Johnnie and Frances's first child, three month old Sarah Spencer, at Westminster Abbey on June 9, 1955, with her godmother, Queen Elizabeth the Queen Mother

The golden wedding celebration at Spencer House, St James's, of the Earl and Countess Spencer (fifth and sixth from left), with Johnnie, a month before his divorce, and his four children, Sarah, Jane, Diana and Charles; and his sister Lady Anne Wake-Walker (second from left) with her family

gilded aristocracy wasn't terribly popular and those who were, didn't try to capitalise on it. Raine, however, wanted William to capitalise on it.'

In later years Raine denied that she was ambitious for her children. 'I've never tried to push my children in any particular direction, but if they want a sympathetic friendly ear, mine is always ready to listen.' According to a friend, she was furious when Charlotte became an actress: 'She thought it was a very low-grade thing for someone in her position to do and they didn't get on for some time.'

Raine's success on the Historic Buildings Board led to other appointments. In 1971 she became a member of the English Tourist Board. She was also invited by the then Secretary of State for the Environment, Peter Walker, to head an advisory committee dealing with the environment. 'I chose her because she had terrific energy, was provocative and had strong views on most topics,' he remembers. 'It didn't matter to me how she dressed or spoke. I was seeking a lively, energetic mind.'

Raine and her committee began by attacking the 'scandal' of the way planning permission was granted and she helped to write a report entitled 'Human Habitat: How do you want to live?' which was published in 1972. One of a series commissioned by Peter Walker in preparation for the United Nations environment conference in Stockholm in June 1972, it surveyed the environmental state of the nation and made fifty-four recommendations to the Government and planning authorities. These included calling for subsidies for public transport, more generous compensation for people affected by motorway building and redevelopment, a standard procedure for giving publicity to all but the most trivial planning proposals, and a national buildings conservation fund.

The Government was asked in the report to consider the whole question of tax rebates and estate duty in relation to historic buildings. It suggested that every town in Britain should have areas from which cars were banned. 'We want roots, we want security, we want to belong,' the report said. 'We want to live in a habitat which is convenient, which is human yet containing elements of beauty, which can inspire us and lift our spirit towards ambition and adventure.'

Raine visited almost every town, city centre and village green mentioned in the comprehensive report, and wrote three of the eight sections herself. Philip Larkin wrote a poem especially for it.

The cover of the report however, caused even more of a stir than the contents. Raine approached Lord Snowdon for the photograph. 'I've known him for ever since I'd go to be photographed in his dear little Pimlico basement,' she said. Initially he provided a photograph of 'some cross-looking children in Wales', which she rejected. 'Obviously they had every right to be cross. But pictures of doom and gloom and people having rotten times tend to bore one's audiences.' Instead she chose a photograph of a long-haired girl in a low-cut sepia green floaty robe emerging from a lake like a nymph. It was the first time such a picture has appeared on an official publication.

Simon Jenkins, who later became editor of *The Times*, was a member of Raine's environmental committee. 'The committee didn't realise what had hit them. She didn't brook any opposition from civil servants who wanted things toned down. They had assumed the book would have a plain white or blue cover which would contain the title of the committee and its report on the front. Raine organised the photograph and then summoned the hapless official responsible to her mansion in Mayfair. The idea of this photograph appearing on a government paper was completely beyond him. But she got her way.'

Jenkins, who at one time regularly dined with Raine, remembers her as 'very dynamic, extremely vigorous and absolutely determined to get her way'. He did feel, however, that 'like many people she was probably the victim of her public manner. Many people have a fortunate public manner and an unfortunate private one. I think Raine had an unfortunate public manner. She was a figure of some ridicule partly because of the way her mother brought her up. She was much more her mother's daughter than she was the wife of a peer and the Tory lady she seemed. She wasn't really a snob, although that was her image. She took people very much as she found them. What she didn't like was dull people.'

Jenkins remembers that she was 'very ambitious politically'. Peter Walker agrees. 'There was a time in the sixties when she wanted to be a Conservative candidate. She was a great publicity seeker in those days. She enjoyed hitting the headlines and was also always being featured in the social columns. I couldn't have cared less about all that. She was the sort of woman that if you asked her to do something, she would do it well with no stone unturned.' Raine invited Walker to dinner several times. 'She was an enthusiastic hostess, totally extroverted and rather dominated the scene. Gerald was quiet although one got the impression that he was supportive of all her crusades.'

Raine admitted that Gerald complained about the amount of time she spent working on the human habitat. He'd say 'What about this human habitat? Your own family home?' She advised her friends and colleagues not to take his complaints too much to heart. Gerald was, she said, 'the Rock of Gibraltar and divine. So steady and strong and yet such humour.' In retrospect, however, this might have been the moment when their marriage finally began to crumble. Within a couple of years Raine had fallen in love with Johnnie Spencer.

Raine at this time seemed unable to resist self-publicity and was regularly sought out by journalists who could rely on her to say something controversial or amusing on the most trivial of subjects, despite having created a serious and worthwhile platform for herself – she was even called the Florence Nightingale of London's architectural heritage. She criticised the actress Elizabeth Taylor for not curtseying properly before Princess Margaret at a royal film performance. 'You should not cling on to anyone for support, having a straight back and not bow one's head,' she said firmly. 'When you curtsey to the Queen you must get your right knee to the ground. But for other members of the Royal Family the curtsey is not quite so low.'

The *Evening Standard* featured her in its series called 'Favourite Things' – Raine's were a mixture of the nutritious and the idiosyncratic. Her favourite things included a pot of honey 'because I always have honey for tea', peppermint tea, wholemeal bread and non-battery eggs. She loved bottled Malvern water: 'It is truly my favourite drink. I don't drink London water and I'm a teetotaller.' Another favourite was a pale aquamarine embroidered evening dress she had bought three years previously for the wedding of Crown Princess Margaret of Denmark, which she later sold. She also chose a Scout's brooch from her own troop, the 59th Westminster, two china pigs which had been wedding presents, a Victorian tortoise footstool, a lucky china cat which she bought after her father died 'when I was feeling gloomy', with the words 'When things are grim, Good luck I'll bring', written on the bottom, and a fan her grandmother used when she was a girl.

Her favourite book, she claimed, was 'The Town and Country Planning Act' adding, to appease cynics, 'Honestly it is, because it has done such a lot to protect historic buildings.' Her favourite memory was of meeting her husband for the first time on top of a mountain in Switzerland.

In another article of this period she praised her mother for giving her so much. 'I learned early a lot about duty to others. Above all, Mummy taught us never to feel that the world owes us anything – it's the other way round. I may not be creative like Mummy, but I can certainly see, when a city council shows me high-rise flats for married couples, how some young mother is going to have to climb fifteen floors with her baby and her toddler (gosh that might be me with Henry) and her pram and the bag of groceries when the lift's not working.'

In May 1971 she stood down from the Historic Buildings Board to take charge of the planned £140-million redevelopment of Covent Garden, a position that was regarded as the equivalent of a junior Minister's post. She was partly given the job, according to one of her committee members, because 'It was believed that she could put her devastating charm which has melted the frozen hearts of many a planning committee to good use to charm aggressive property developers and anxious residents in the area.' Her appointment was particularly welcomed by conservationists who were anxious about the fate of the many fine old buildings in the area, including the Opera House, after the market moved to its new site south of the river at Nine Elms, Battersea. Raine found her new post 'a great challenge. My heart is very much in saving the best of our buildings, but when modern buildings are right, they are very exciting.' Her declared aim was to see the mixed character of the area continued.

At first she was positive and enthusiastic about the GLC plans that included offices, hotels, shops, a leisure centre and new housing. She was unable, however, to win the support of those individuals or bodies which represented the general public. Her Mayfair house was besieged by angry demonstrators and she gradually came to realise that the GLC proposals were unacceptable and wrong. Having failed to gain permission from the GLC to approach Peter Walker with an alternative scheme, she took the only action she felt was honourable and, just over a year after she had embarked on the redevelopment project, resigned. Many felt it was Raine's finest hour. She said at the time, 'I am not by nature a resigner – I have been in local government for seventeen years – but in the long run it is a matter of conscience.' She declared that she could not work for something she no longer believed in and which would do unnecessary and irreparable damage to an historic part of London.

In her letter of resignation to the GLC leader, Sir Desmond Plummer, she said, 'I have felt increasingly that our proposals are out of date and out of touch with public opinion which fears that the area will become a faceless concrete jungle.' Her resignation brought praise from members of the Covent Garden Community Association. In a letter to *The Times* several signatories declared: 'It has become increasingly rare for public figures to admit that they have changed their minds, let alone that they may have been seriously wrong and the courage of Lady Dartmouth in making both admissions will not be soon forgotten.'

The timing of her resignation was described as 'lethal', coinciding as it did with the arrival on Peter Walker's desk at the Department of the Environment of the report on the Covent Garden public enquiry. The public enquiry found against the scheme on the grounds that it was too big, not thought out with sufficient care, and that another two hundred buildings not on any conservation list should be listed and preserved. When Geoffrey Rippon took over as Secretary of State for the Environment in a cabinet reshuffle in 1972 he agreed with the enquiry's findings. He felt there should be a comprehensive plan for the area, but one that was less drastic and had the approval of the local population.

William Bell, who served with Raine on both the Historic Buildings Board and the Covent Garden committee, says: 'As a result of her resignation the matter was brought to the public's attention and her action precipitated the abandonment of the comprehensive policy for a much more low-key type of development. It takes a lot of courage to resign as she did.' He is a devoted fan of Raine's, although he admits, 'She's a very efficient lady and sometimes efficient ladies scare people. She was a very good chairman, punctual and conscientious and got the best out of people. Committee meetings were very amusing, almost as good as a play, but they could also be very serious.'

Her resignation was also praised in the national press. 'It is all too easy to dismiss this particular woman ... as a good-looking, immaculately dressed, effusive member of the aristocracy who somehow gets offered positions of power,' wrote the *Guardian*. ' ... Behind the saccharine image there stands an extremely able politician, a feminine but tough bargainer who is prepared to fight for the moon to get half. She is also loyal to the Party and would much prefer to work within the system, than shake Conservative London government by something so ostentatious as a resignation.' Lynda Lee-Potter in the *Daily Mail* called Raine 'a titled professional charmer, [but] you've got to admit it's only surface gloss on a shrewd relentless toughie.'

For all Raine's achievements, something was missing in her life. She was bored with Gerald and felt personally unfulfilled. David Laws remembers, 'He was no longer important in her life.' Not that she ever let it show on the rare occasions they were seen together in public. 'Publicly she always made the most tremendous fuss of Dartmouth,' says a friend who was at their wedding. 'But then she always makes the most tremendous fuss of everyone and everything. It was "darling, darling" all the time and you never really knew what she was really thinking or feeling. She later played a similar role with Johnnie Spencer.' At home, however, things were very different. A cousin of Gerald's was 'shocked' at how Raine treated him. 'She was beastly to him and so dismissive,' she says.

In 1972 Raine was asked to become chairman of the United Kingdom Executive Committee for European Architectural Heritage Year 1975, a major inter-European event before such things became commonplace. She threw herself into this three-year project 'with gusto'. Under the auspices of the Civic Trust, its objectives were to awaken European interest in a common architectural heritage, to protect and enhance buildings and areas of architectural or historic interest, to conserve the character of old towns and villages, and to ensure that ancient buildings had a living role in contemporary society. It was to be a full-time occupation that would require Raine to travel and speak widely in Europe. Because of its demands Raine announced in November 1972 that she was 'terribly sad' but she would not be running for re-election for her GLC seat in Richmond the following April.

The idea for Architectural Heritage Year arose from a proposal made by Conservative MP Duncan Sandys to the Council of Europe in 1969. Over twenty-three countries were involved, including several in Eastern

Europe. The project was launched at a glittering reception at Lancaster House, St. James's where the distinguished guests included the Duke of Edinburgh, the Duke of Westminster, a clutch of lords, and Ministers from the Scottish and Welsh Departments and the Departments of Housing and the Environment. The Duke of Edinburgh agreed to become president of the United Kingdom Council and the Civic Trust was nominated to undertake the detailed administration.

National committees for Scotland, Wales and Northern Ireland were set up with the Queen Mother and the Prince of Wales accepting the presidency of the first two respectively. In Britain individual local authorities made a commitment to strive for conservation, a campaign for environmental education for schoolchildren and adults was instigated, and a national Architectural Heritage Fund formed. Notable conservationists like Sir John Betjeman, Sir Hugh Casson, Sir Roy Strong and Mr Henry Moore were involved. Conservation was not then a popular cause, but the campaign helped to awaken the public to its importance and to re-educate attitudes towards caring about the environment. As well as important national schemes, various smaller schemes were launched by individual local councils. These included competitions for the best guidebook and suggestions for the restoration and use of neglected buildings. Grants of between £14.00 and £10,000 were made available for over a hundred conservation or restoration projects which covered schemes ranging from the renovation of an old millstone, to the restoration of cottages. The Victoria and Albert Museum ran a major exhibition on 'The Destruction of the English Country House' and the Post Office issued special commemorative stamps.

Raine announced plans to raise £1 million to save Britain's most historic buildings and attacked modern architecture as 'a new form of pornography', destroying towns and cities. She declared, somewhat ironically in view of what later happened at Althorp: 'To save our heritage is also to save our souls.' Derek Waring, a member of Raine's executive committee, believes 'She handled a very difficult task in a very competent way and was capable of working very hard.' She amazed him at the launch party at Lancaster House, attended by between three and four hundred people, by standing by the door and 'greeting everybody by name'.

He was equally impressed with her performance abroad. 'She was always marvellous at getting across the English point of view.' When she gave a speech at a reception attended by fifty people, she made a point of mentioning everyone by name and giving each of them a word or two of encouragement. She had to give a great many speeches during the three-year period which, as usual, she would learn by heart but present as if they were off-the-cuff. 'A wonderful accomplishment because each one came out so naturally,' says a colleague. She was equally effective in encouraging local councils up and down the country to make efforts to ensure the year was a success.

As ever, she used her charm as well as her determination. A member of her committee remembers: 'She would arrive with her entourage beautifully turned out, looking extremely attractive, and charm even the most left-wing councils to improve their environment or make some great gesture to European Architectural Heritage Year'. Throughout this period Raine was also pursuing more personal goals.

Raine's and Johnnie's paths had crossed at the occasional social function when they were young, but they had not seen each other since Johnnie married in 1954. They met again in the early seventies at a party in Kensington when Johnnie was at his lowest and most vulnerable after his divorce. Forty-six-year old Raine entered his life as forcefully as a tornado. Tall, striking, with creamy-white unblemished skin and sculptured hair, she was dressed to perfection and her powerful presence and strong personality knocked Johnnie sideways. His comment that 'We sort of hit it off straightaway' was a classic piece of understatement as he probably did not then realise the full force of what had hit him. The event was certainly unforgettable for Raine: 'It was a hot day and everyone was in the garden,' she recalls. 'When I went inside there was only one person there – John. "I haven't seen you for twenty years," he said. 'Things in life are so coincidental aren't they?' Their meeting was to radically change their lives.

Opinion varies as to whether or not Raine and Johnnie fell headlong in love with one another like one of Barbara Cartland's romantic novels. A friend recognises that 'from the moment she saw him she channelled all her energies into him'. Some have found it hard to believe that the shy, ponderous, not terribly bright Johnnie – 'a bear of very little brain' – had quite what it took to overwhelm her. Certainly Althorp enhanced Johnnie's value and encouraged her to pursue him with a passionate fervour. A member of the Norfolk gentry comments: 'If Raine wants something she will get it. When she took up with Johnnie everyone said poor Gerald didn't stand a chance. He didn't have a stately home.' Sir Roy Strong remembers: 'She always wanted to have a great house and one of the great disappointments was that Dartmouth didn't have one.' In mitigation, a friend claims, 'She is not a gold-digger in the traditional sense. Raine was genuinely fond of Johnnie, but it certainly helped that his father was already in his eighties and he was heir to a stately home which she had always set her heart on.'

Criticisms of Raine as a social climber prompted Dame Barbara to dismiss these as 'very unfair and very untrue. She gave up a sixteenth

Earl for an eighth Earl – hardly social climbing. Everything gives the impression she came out of the gutter. It is not true.'

Michael Middleton, who worked with Raine on European Architectural Year, feels there was an additional aspect to the relationship. 'I suspect that from the beginning there might have been an element of mothering. As well as being fond of him, she felt sorry for him and felt she could help him.' He does not underestimate her tenacity. 'I'm sure it's in her character to be ruthless, if that is how she felt things should go. There was an element of iron about her.'

A close relation believes Johnnie found a kindred spirit in Raine: 'Someone he could laugh with.' He was not, however, one of those men who, having met a woman he liked, would pursue her ardently, and initially was as laid-back about his relationship with Raine as he was about running his farms. Although he was overwhelmed by her presence when he saw her, he made no great effort to see her again. He also still felt deeply depressed and hurt by France's departure which he made little attempt to hide. Raine invited him to dinner when Gerald was present. One regular guest at Hill Street commented, 'He was awfully sweet, but not an exciting person and slightly heavy weather at a dinner party. It was rather embarrassing to see Raine all over him.'

Raine apparently spent other dinner parties talking about him. Rupert Hambro, whose link with Johnnie was through the National Association of Boys' Clubs, recalls one of these. 'There were sixteen people for dinner and to my surprise I found myself sitting next to Raine in her very hot red dining-room. Throughout the meal we had only one topic of conversation, which was Johnnie Althorp. I was rather confused until about halfway through when I realised what was afoot. I remember she treated her husband as if he was a nonexistent fool most of the time. It always mystified me how Raine and Johnnie got together. I presume she decided what she wanted and went for it.'

Gerald was not always present at these social events. Lord Wardington remembers: 'For years Raine gave dinner parties or had meetings at home without him and he would creep into the house through the back or basement door.'

Raine realised, however, that inviting Johnnie for dinner at her Mayfair home was only scratching the surface of their relationship and she set out to make herself indispensable to him. With her meticulous planning and characteristic efficiency she slowly began to hook him like a skilled fisherman trying to land a rather large marlin. Her mother had taught her as a child how to be entertaining and there is no doubt that she brought life, enthusiasm, vigour and humour into what had been a dull and miserable life. She lent a sympathetic ear when Johnnie confided in her his worries about his children and tried to make helpful suggestions.

She seized her chance to be invaluable to him in March 1973 when Johnnie's eldest daughter, Sarah, turned eighteen. Johnnie, who was always very generous to his children, bought Sarah a green MGB GT for her birthday and arranged an enormous ball for her at Castle Rising in Norfolk. The castle was floodlit for the occasion and flew the family standard which her grandfather sent from Althorp. A dinner party was held for about forty guests and nearly four hundred attended the ball itself.

Guests were asked to come in period costume and, if possible, to arrive in a coach and horses which a large proportion managed to do. Johnnie had no idea what to wear or, more importantly, where on earth to find a suitably original dress for Sarah. Raine came to the rescue. She suggested to a delighted Johnnie that he attend the ball as King Henry VIII. She also pulled several strings to borrow for Sarah the dress worn by Geneviève Bujold in the 1969 film, *Anne of the Thousand Days*. Johnnie, whose fatherly concerns did not extent to his daughter's wardrobe, thought this, too, a wonderful inspiration. Sarah, who at the time had no idea that Raine would become her stepmother, readily agreed. She was very anxious that everything should be done properly for her party and telephoned Peter Townend, now social editor of *The Tatler* and an expert on upper-class etiquette, for advice. 'She telephoned me several times for help which she said she needed because she didn't really have a mother to organise it for her.'

Two ladies were hired for two full days to fill the castle with flowers. A vast marquee was set up in the castle grounds. One half was for the ballroom and the other for the running buffet which had a theme of red and gold with silver candelabras on each table. For those who preferred to be more robust in their dancing, a disco was laid on in the castle itself. The ball, which went on until dawn the following day, was a great success although Raine's presence was the source of much gossip among the Norfolk gentry. Sarah, with her hair curled down to her shoulders, looked beautiful in the pale grey ballgown decorated with pearls.

One positive aspect of Johnnie's relationship with Raine was that she was responsible for mending the long rift between him and his father. Jack had known Raine very well in the past and, although initially astonished that she and Johnnie had come together, found her as irresistible as ever. Raine, for her part, knew how to get round the rather irascible old man. Each birthday and Christmas she would buy him a walking stick to add to his collection. Johnnie attended his father's eightieth birthday party at Althorp and the Earl in turn held a sumptuous party to celebrate Johnnie's fiftieth birthday in January 1974. Jack brought out much of his unique collection of Marlborough silver for the occasion, as usual cleaning it himself so that it would be 'properly done'. Also on display was a large proportion of the Spencer collection of candelabra and candlesticks – enough to hold fifty red candles, one for each year of Johnnie's birth.

Four butlers wearing white gloves served the four-course meal which consisted of soup, fresh salmon with cucumber salad, roast pork with four different vegetables and all the trimmings, followed by Bombe Alaska. As soon as dinner was over, the butlers went round with gold dishes full of rosewater and the ladies present delicately dipped their fingers in the scented water and dabbed it on their ears.

If Johnnie and Raine's social lives were becoming increasingly inter-twined, Fate gave a helping hand to enable them to work more closely together too.

Several specialist committees were established to help promote European Architectural Heritage Year. They included leading representatives of business and industry, films and television, education and youth. Raine thought that Johnnie Althorp, as chairman of the National Association of Boys' Clubs, would be the ideal person to serve as chairman on the Youth Panel along with representatives of the Girl Guides, Boy Scouts, Duke of Edinburgh's Award Scheme and Boys' Brigade; she probably also saw the appointment as a way of providing them with a legitimate basis to meet and travel abroad together. She put her idea first to Michael Middleton, Secretary-General of the Executive Committee and Director of the Civic Trust.

Having secured his agreement, she talked to Johnnie. He found her inimitable combination of enthusiasm and flattery hard to resist and readily agreed to the proposal. Raine's delight added an extra sparkle to her role as chairman of the Executive Committee. 'Every meeting she chaired was always upbeat,' Middleton remembers. 'She used to say "Always bring the good news, never the bad." She had a particular ability of being able to drop things instantly if there was no future in them. She would get a sudden rush of blood to the head and get terribly excited about an idea and if you could prove it wasn't a runner, she would drop it, forget it and never refer to it again.'

On her travels at home and abroad, Raine would always go first class, even when others, including MPs, were travelling second. 'She would insist on it even when we were only flying London to Paris,' says a colleague, 'and never minded paying for herself.' Occasionally her behav-iour was astonishing. On one train journey another colleague remembers how 'suddenly, in full view of everyone, she took out her make-up case, took off her entire face and put it back again. One was really rather put off by that private ritual performed in full view of everyone. It looked exactly the same to me afterwards. She was very conscious of her public role, would always turn up impeccably dressed and sometimes changed her outfit three times a day. Her face was always made up to look exactly the same too.'

To commemorate the project Raine conceived and wrote a book called *What is Our Heritage?*, published by Her Majesty's Stationery Office and translated into French and German. The book was a further example of her growing expertise at coaxing and enthusing the rather lazy Johnnie into action. She knew of his passion for photography and suggested he took the pictures for the book. It provided another opportunity for them to spend time together.

The book was regarded as a modest success; the Youth Panel under Johnnie's chairmanship, however, was not. 'He was not a ball of fire,' says a member of the committee, 'I wasn't impressed with him although he was very charming. Nothing much happened from his group as compared to some of the others.' In fact, the only mention in the forty-page final report to the United Kingdom Council on European Architectural Heritage Year is a note that '£5,000 was allocated for small grants towards environmental improvement projects undertaken by youth organisations'.

Raine's relationship with Johnnie was by now the source of much speculation. 'We were very aware that there was something between them,' says a member of the campaign. 'She was very open about everything that was going on and became more so as time passed. By 1974 it was clear she was in love. It was equally clear that she was much brighter than him.' Johnnie was not, however, the only man interested in her. The power of Raine's personality and her regal manner, even before she became mistress of Althorp, meant that throughout her years of public work she nearly always had several male admirers and an entourage of eager helpers. 'Weak characters in particular were always attracted to Raine,' says a colleague. 'During those three years there were quite a few who flocked around her. The thrust came entirely from the chaps, who tended to be rather dopey doggy-type characters. I don't think she necessarily encouraged them, but I think she felt it was nice to have a chap around all the time to open doors for her and pay for the taxi.' According to one of her friends, 'All sorts were absolutely mad about Raine but Johnnie was the one she always talked about.'

It was clear to Johnnie's friends that he was very much in love with Raine, too, and they were delighted to find him so much more cheerful. Brigadier Davies-Scourfield of the National Association of Boys' Clubs remembers when Johnnie tried to organise a discreet lunch for Raine that rather backfired on him. 'During his work for Architectural Heritage Year he said he thought it would be nice if the Youth Panel entertained Lady Dartmouth to lunch, but he didn't want any publicity about it for obvious reasons and asked me to book lunch at the Bedford Corner Hotel in central London. Lady Dartmouth arrived at the hotel in an enormous chauffeur-driven Rolls-Royce and almost immediately a crowd gathered on the pavement to watch her. When she went into the restaurant everyone else fell silent because they were all trying to listen to the conversation on Johnnie's table or merely just watching them.'

Although Raine approached her responsibilities as chairman of the Executive Committee with her usual professionalism, there were occasions when her relationship with Johnnie took precedent over all else. Colleagues recall that at a Council of Europe weekend conference at Zurich Raine suddenly announced that she would be unable to fulfil a long-standing speaking engagement in England a day or two later as she was going on to Rome with Johnnie. It took a considerable amount of effort to find an appropriate replacement at such short notice.

The three-year campaign leading up to Architectural Heritage Year was judged to have been reasonably successful, although newspapers reported at the end of 1975 that one listed historic building was still being pulled down every day. The overall verdict on Raine's efforts was so positive that many people were amazed that she was not given any public recognition for her work.

'I was surprised she didn't get an honour because she put such a lot of effort in,' says Derek Waring, who personally wrote to Downing Street suggesting that she should receive one. 'She had put three years of her life into the work and I felt her efforts deserved something. Having her own title is not the same as being officially recognised for services to conservation.' Michael Middleton agrees: 'When it was all over, I remember her saying that she didn't even have a letter of thanks from the Government.'

One reason given for Raine's efforts not being acknowledged was that by the time the slow process of governmental red tape had been set in motion, Raine's marital affairs were in such disarray that disapproving tongues were wagging in places that mattered. Then, soon after she was married for the second time, many felt that the difference between Raine's public work and private actions made it inappropriate to give her an award for conservation.

If she was upset she didn't show it. Other matters of a more domestic and romantic nature were on her mind. At the end of 1974, soon after a theft of £7,000-worth of silver from the family home, she and Gerald put their eight-bedroomed house in Hill Street on the market. She said it was too large for her family's needs and that she wanted something smaller. It was sold for a little under £200,000 to a Kuwaiti businessman. Raine put as much effort into the sale of the house as she did into every other aspect of her life, inviting the Kuwaiti to a formal dinner for which, according to David Laws, 'she got all dressed up, put her best brooch on and charmed him to ensure that the deal would go through'. She and Gerald retained their flat in Grosvenor Square.

By this time rumours were rife that her marriage to Gerald had broken down. David Laws remembers sitting, with other visitors, in Raine's boudoir when the telephone rang and a reporter from a national gossip column asked her if her marriage had collapsed. 'She very politely told her the rumours were untrue,' says Laws. 'But over the next five minutes I could see the anger mounting in her face. She then excused herself and went into the next room, called the reporter back and shouted at her down the phone. She was too well-mannered to do it in front of visitors.'

The reporter was, however, on the right track as events were soon to prove. Early in June 1975, Johnnie's father complained of feeling unwell. He was taken into a nursing home, where he died of pneumonia on 9 June at the age of eighty-three. 'He was very lonely in the home,' says his daughter, Lady Anne Wake-Walker. 'Luckily for him he was only there a few days, he wouldn't have liked being ill for a long time.'

After the merest nod to convention by not acting too fast, Raine was again involved in packing up the family home, this time Chipperfield Manor in Hertfordshire. She then filled a Land-Rover and a triple horse-box with her possessions and drove to Althorp to move in with Johnnie, now the 8th Earl Spencer. The two younger children, Charlotte, then twelve, and little Henry, who was six, remained with their father.

Many friends and acquaintances who had seen the way Raine had treated Gerald during the latter part of their twenty-seven-year marriage thought he would be only too pleased when she left him. Johnnie's schoolfriend Lord Wardington, who was also a friend of Gerald's, said, 'I thought Gerald would breathe a sigh of relief when Raine left him for Johnnie, but he was terribly hurt. He did, however, have her painted out of a lovely picture of the two of them and the children with the house in the background. She was replaced by a mysterious tree.'

11

Raine at Althorp

Johnnie's children were initially unaware of how much their father was beginning to depend on Raine, as all four were away at boarding school and spent much of the holidays with their mother in Scotland. Charles was at his prep school, Maidwell Hall, in Northampton. Diana was sent, in September 1973, to join Jane at West Heath, one of Britain's best-known girls' boarding schools, set in thirty-two acres of parkland and woods outside Sevenoaks in Kent. A close relative remembers, 'Diana was quiet and demure at school, but very strong. She got a lot of her own way by pretending to be helpless. She was a manipulative little madam.' She was following in the footsteps of both Sarah and Jane, whose scholastic achievements were very different.

Jane was a model pupil, reliable and enthusiastic and a sixth-form prefect when Diana arrived. She was also a member of the school's lacrosse and tennis teams and was to leave West Heath with eleven O-levels. Sarah was much more fiery. Although she passed six O-levels, loved riding, amateur dramatics and swam for the school team, she did not take kindly to the restrictions of a respectable girls' boarding school. She drank and became rowdy and disruptive and left abruptly.

Johnnie was so besotted with Raine that he decided to introduce her to his children. He arranged a dinner at the Duke's Head Hotel in King's Lynn where he hoped they and Raine would find lots to talk about over a leisurely meal. It was not a success. Raine felt self-conscious and unsure of how to handle such a delicate situation. She took refuge, as she often does when feeling awkward, in being effusively polite. The children became quiet to the point of being sullen and quickly made up their minds about her. 'We didn't like her one bit,' said Charles. 'As a child you instinctively feel things and with her I very much instinctively felt things.' A close member of Raine's family believes that the Spencer children never gave her a chance. 'They had had their father too long to themselves. It wouldn't have mattered who it had been, they would never have accepted her. Nor do I think Frances Shand Kydd was conducive to Raine being accepted. She didn't want another woman to take over her teenage children. Another reason why they were never likely to get on is that Raine is not a terribly warm person and at the time wasn't close to her own children. Had she been a maternal type, someone like Diana, who wasn't getting a great deal of support from her own mother, might really have benefited from the relationship.'

Although Johnnie had not yet officially proposed to Raine, she was the only woman friend to whom he had introduced them since their mother had left and the children could work out the implications for themselves. At first, the older pair, Sarah and Jane, gently tried to persuade their father to cool the relationship. When he refused, they became more outspoken and, it has been said, told him he could marry anyone but Raine. A family friend comments, 'The children didn't stand a chance. Raine can be ruthless. If she makes a beeline for a man she's difficult to resist.'

Johnnie was upset that his children did not like Raine, but equally determined that they should not be allowed to rule his life. Raine made him laugh and feel much more positive about the future. He was also emotionally committed to her. Sex was a very important and powerful part of their relationship. They had several secret assignations at the houses of friends and on one occasion when giving a lift to a friend in the Rolls, stopped their car at a service station motel on the M4 and, leaving their friend in the back, disappeared inside for a cuddle.

Johnnie, on his father's death, moved almost immediately to Althorp and gave his butler, Bertie Betts, instructions about moving his possessions from Park House as he wished to return the house to the Queen as soon as possible. At the same time he told him that he would not, after all, be requiring the services of Bertie and his wife Elsie at Althorp and they were given a month's notice. It is not known why he changed his mind and Bertie, just two years away from retirement, was shocked, both at not being needed at Althorp and having to leave Park House at such short notice. The shock turned to indignation, however, when soon after Johnnie's departure the heating was turned off and the Betts family had to resort to boiling water in a saucepan to wash. Bertie was then told by Johnnie's solicitor that he would be taken to court unless the house was vacated immediately.

Betts wrote in his diary: 'While this was going on it was very hard to pack up His Lordship's pictures, silver and two cellars full of wine ... I feel very bitter now after giving my whole life to private service. I was treated very badly by this great lord. Everyone thinks he is so charming, but there is another side to him that the public don't see.' Luckily an offer of council accommodation turned up for him and his family just in time. That Christmas a newly furnished Park House was used by Princess

Anne and Captain Mark Phillips when they joined the Royal Family for the end-of-year celebrations.

Moving to Althorp drastically altered Johnnie's life as it was now that his relationship with Raine took on an entirely different momentum. As he walked slowly along the corridors and into every room at Althorp, stopping in each for several minutes to let his childhood memories flood over him, he found it hard to believe that, at fifty-two, the family stately home was finally his. He remembered the happy family Christmases and the great Christmas tree covered in red candles that his father had insisted upon every year; how he had chased his governess Miss Manning along the corridors; and how he went to his mother for comfort when his imperious and domineering father used to make him feel worthless and small. Even though he would never have to endure his father's temper again, he could feel his presence in every room, which despite the warm June day, made him shiver with past fear and future anticipation. Some members of the family and staff believed there was good reason for Johnnie's reaction. 'I know there is a ghost,' says Jack's sister, Lady Margaret Douglas-Home. 'The butler's wife said she saw Jack on the great staircase not very long after he died. He smiled at her and apparently she said "Good morning my lord." She was rather delighted to see him and not at all frightened.'

It is a moot point whether or not Jack came back to haunt his son or if, in fact, Raine ever saw him, but she certainly felt uncomfortable enough in later years to have the house exorcised.

Jack had been a stickler for detail, Johnnie was laid-back and easygoing. Although Johnnie's relationship with the Bettses had soured, the staff at Althorp found that the atmosphere in the house changed dramatically with Johnnie's arrival and life below stairs became much more fun. 'The early days were very happy ones and jolly good fun, with no bowing and scraping,' remembers Betty Andrews who began working at Althorp as a cleaner in 1975 and later became cook and housekeeper. 'No one was in charge, only the butler. His Lordship didn't mind what you did.'

At first, life in the stately home was very quiet. Johnnie didn't even go into the staterooms let alone use them, preferring to live in the smaller, less elaborate ones. He also kept a minimum of staff: a butler and his wife, a footman, a cook and two cleaners. It did, however, burst into life during the holidays when the children came home from boarding school. 'One by one they used to run into the house, drop their things, then come rushing into the kitchen to find something to eat,' says Betty. They were not fussy eaters and often Diana or Charles would do their own cooking. 'Diana even used to cook for the staff. She loved to make bread-and-butter pudding for us and rice or milk pudding for herself.' She also did her own washing and often Charles's too. 'She would put his things in the washing machine and then iron them for him. She was lovely with him,' remembers Betty. It was partly a reaction to their mother leaving them; a combination of Diana's desperate need to be loved and her strong maternal feelings towards Charles. 'She was also quite tidy. You didn't have to do much tidying up after her,' Betty says. All three sisters got on well together too and the atmosphere was 'happy-go-lucky'. Diana would often fly down the seventeenth-century front staircase on a tea-tray or practise her dancing in the black-and-white marble entrance hall, known as Wootton Hall.

It was, however, the lull before the Raine storm. To all intents and purposes she easily shook off her old Dartmouth skin and replaced it with an even more glamorous one. Being at the magnificent stately home was like arriving at the end of her personal rainbow. Its endless rooms were bursting with treasures. There was some of the finest eighteenth-century furniture in the country, unrivalled collections of silver and porcelain, vast antique tapestries hanging on dusty walls, chandeliers as large as fountains, walls lined with portraits of noble ancestors and works of art by Van Dyck, Joshua Reynolds, Gainsborough and Rubens.

Here for the taking was a tailor-made *Upstairs, Downstairs* situation which, hopefully could become Raine's very own. She liked nothing better than a challenge and felt that her experience of redecorating her marital homes with Gerald had been a preparation for what might lie ahead. She saw how much there was to be done and how indispensable she could become to Johnnie who was facing inheritance taxes of over £2 million. Not only could she add sparkle and colour to his surroundings, but by using the commercial skills she had accumulated from her years in public life, she could put the place on a sound commercial footing.

Raine, however, is a shrewd woman and knew she had to tread carefully. This wasn't merely a business proposition. She told her mother, 'I am wildly in love and there is nothing anyone can do about it.' Dame Barbara was, as always, supportive of her daughter, even though she had always liked Gerald. 'What can you do?' she asks. 'You've got to stand by your daughter. There was nothing wrong with Gerald. He was a sweet person and very gentle. He hadn't done anything wrong at all. She just fell madly in love with Johnnie and that was her happiness.'

When Raine first began staying at Althorp, Johnnie asked the butler to put her in the India Silk Bedroom right across the landing from his own room. As her presence became more frequent, the butler no longer checked where to put her, but automatically kept the room ready for her.

Johnnie felt uneasy living in his father's private suite of drawing room, bedroom and bathroom, and Raine suggested that it should be redecorated. She called in interior designer David Laws, who had helped transform her Mayfair house and was later to play such a prominent part in redecorating the whole of Althorp, to help her advise Johnnie. It was the first trickle of her decorative influence that was later to flood through the rest of the house.

'When she was married to Gerald she was used to a lot of ready money,' Laws says. 'Johnnie however didn't have available cash in those early days, so Raine paid for the scheme herself. She asked me to keep notes of everything she bought and, even before his illness, I had to ensure that everything she paid for was written down. She realised if he died she would stop living there. Although Johnnie put lots in her name, she spent a lot of her own money.' Her influence at Althorp began immediately. She did her best to reduce the amount of death duties Johnnie had to pay and also vigorously negotiated with representatives who had come on behalf of the Treasury to value Spencer heirlooms. It wasn't for herself but to protect the Spencers' money,' says Laws.

Johnnie, easy-going as usual, was delighted to fall in with Raine's decorative ideas, as with her suggestion that she help him write a guide-book to the house. She was becoming invaluable to him, although he had not yet proposed marriage. Johnnie's children were doing their best to ensure that he never did. Twenty-one-year-old Sarah, in particular, made no attempt to hide her dislike of Raine and her disapproval of the relation-ship, even to curious reporters. At the time, before Diana married the Prince of Wales and Johnnie became one of the most famous fathers-in-law in the land, it was Raine Dartmouth's comings and goings that excited reporters' interest. When one telephoned Althorp and asked to speak to Lord Spencer about his current liaison, Sarah replied that her father was in bed with Lady Dartmouth and she wasn't going to disturb them. She told another reporter: 'Since my grandfather died last June and we moved from Sandringham to Althorp, Lady Dartmouth has been an all too frequent visitor.' And to a third, who cheekily asked why Lady Dartmouth was spending so much time at Althorp, she replied icily: 'She is helping my father open the house on a commercial basis. In my grandfather's time he did not care for the idea of the public walking around his house. Lady Dartmouth is writing a guide for it with my father.'

When the children were together in the house, they would walk along the corridors pointedly singing the children's ditty 'Raine, Raine go away' within Raine's earshot. Johnnie tried to ignore it. A close relative comments: 'Johnnie was like many men with his daughters. He adored them, but was extremely lax and let them get away with murder. They ran rings round him and resented Raine when she tried to put a stop to it.' One of the areas where the girls and Raine clashed straightaway was over dressing for dinner. Raine would always come down in evening dress, while Johnnie's girls often appeared in jeans. A relative comments:

'Raine hadn't been brought up that way and didn't understand. She resented the jeans and they resented being told to dress up.'

Johnnie had still not proposed when Raine's divorce came before the court. Having been outraged and humiliated by France's adulterous behaviour eight years previously, he was about to have a similar charge thrown at him by Gerald Dartmouth. On 29 May 1976, Gerald named Earl Spencer in his divorce petition. Raine, however, confessed to adultery in a sworn statement and the court was not asked to make a finding against him. Gerald was therefore granted a decree nisi by Judge Everett because of his wife's adultery with a man 'against whom the charge has not been proved', and given custody of their younger children, Charlotte and Henry. Raine made no attempt to fight this according to a member of the family who points out the difference in reaction between the Dartmouth and the Spencer children. 'During Raine's divorce from Gerald, I never heard her children criticise Johnnie. They never said a word about what was happening despite the fact that, unlike the Spencer children, their home had been broken up. Gerald was a nice, decent man, who could be very witty and amusing. He was not well treated and certainly got the rough end of the deal.' After the divorce, Gerald used to ask his sister-in-law Anna McCorquodale to buy Charlotte's clothes for her and then send him the bill.

Raine was relieved that her marriage was over, but slightly alarmed that Johnnie had still not proposed. She had invited David Laws to keep her company on the day her divorce went through and he recalls how she confided her vulnerability to him. 'I am not saying anything to Johnnie. I know he loves me, but I have told him he must not feel because of the divorce he was committed in any way.' She added with brutal honesty, 'He might not want to take me on.'

Her patience, however, was soon rewarded. Johnnie was so deeply in love that he put his children's feelings to one side and asked her to marry him. He received an immediate and positive response and on 14 July 1976, just two months after Raine's divorce came through, Raine and Johnnie took their marriage vows for the second time.

None of the children knew about the wedding in advance, and Charles was told by the headmaster of his prep school. The simple ten-minute ceremony at London's Caxton Hall was very different from the grandeur of both their first weddings. There were only two witnesses present – one of them Lady Dartmouth's brother Glen. The marriage was later blessed by Raine's friend Dr Mervyn Stockwood, Bishop of Southwark.

When the news of their marriage broke, the press inevitably contacted Barbara Cartland. 'It was such a quiet wedding that even I didn't go,' she admitted. 'They rang me immediately afterwards and just said "Hello. We're married."' As always, she supported her daughter. 'When it's your second marriage I don't think you should have a reception.' Raine, however, admitted that her mother found the news a bit of a shock. She was pleased she was supportive, but added firmly, 'She is not allowed to interfere.'

It was a match of opposites. 'We are both very different, but we compromise,' said Johnnie. 'My wife is a very forceful personality, but easy to get on with once you know her ... She's a town woman. I'm a country man. She's a saver, I'm a spender – I suppose good champagne, brandy and port are my biggest extravagances ...' Later he revealed his traditional view of women, explaining that he chose to marry Raine because 'she has brains and beauty and she came to me an older and wiser woman. She's much better now than when she was rushing about getting half a page in *Who's Who* long before she met me. She's got that out of her system.'

Naturally the marriage was a source of gossip everywhere and the word went round that 'Raine didn't marry Johnnie, she married Althorp.' Raine herself put an innocent, romantic gloss on the affair worthy of her mother's novels. 'When I met Johnnie his marriage had been over for years and he was a very lonely and unhappy man. I started helping him with his work and later with the house-opening. I never thought falling in love would happen, but you know how these things happen gradually until you discover you just can't live without the other person.' It was, she said, simply a case of 'two very lonely people who found each other and found happiness together'. A well-known lord remembers the gossip that surrounded the match: 'Common parlance at the time was that although Johnnie was a very nice man, he was not a good picker of women. Both Frances and Raine made an absolute beeline for him.'

Although the actual wedding had been quiet, Raine has always loved a grand occasion and in September she and Johnnie threw a massive celebratory party at Althorp; her first as hostess and chatelaine. There were about a thousand guests. The radiant newlyweds, Raine and Johnnie, sat next to each other at the long top table in the State Dining Room where the most distinguished guests were seated. 'They looked like the king and queen at a medieval feast,' says David Hicks. His wife, Lady Pamela Mountbatten, had been one of Raine's bridesmaids when she married Gerald. The other guests were placed at round tables throughout the ground floor.

After twenty-six years in public life, eighteen of which had been spent in local government, Raine temporarily lost interest in her career and turned her energies towards Johnnie and Althorp. 'The experience of falling in love with and marrying him and going to Althorp was so overwhelming that she couldn't do both,' says former *Times* editor, Simon Jenkins. 'I think she decided to devote the rest of her life to him.' She told her friend Michael Cole, public relations director of Harrods, that her relationship with Johnnie was 'a total love-affair'.

Some people believe that Raine fell equally in love with being a countess. A friend says, 'She was completely carried away and played the role as if it was something out of her mother's novels. She was rude, grand, patronising and condescending.' To Johnnie, however, she was 'part nanny, part goddess. The nanny took care of him, the goddess was for him to worship.' She looked after him to the point of over-protection and, to their fury, friends, colleagues and even his children found it difficult to get through to him. Rupert Hambro says, 'It was as if she had put an iron fence around him. She also had a way of making people who played a part in his life before she arrived feel small. She was totally insensitive to Johnnie's family, his life and his interests. Everything became "ours" and "mine". When you did see him she became his mouthpiece and if you asked him anything, she would answer. A lot of people are incredibly happy in an environment that takes any pressures away from them. I would describe Lord Spencer as being pretty close to that environment.'

Although Hambro believes 'Johnnie was very weak to allow it to happen', after his lonely years as a bachelor Johnnie luxuriated in the attention and was mesmerised by Raine's immaculate regal style. This dependency dramatically increased with his near-fatal brain haemorrhage in 1978, two years after their marriage.

Johnnie was so involved with Raine that he loosened his ties with the National Association of Boys' Clubs, although he would occasionally make a speech at an important function. Raine's influence was felt even here and had echoes of her mother's behaviour with her brother Ronald. 'Johnnie wasn't a good speaker and often got things wrong until Raine took him in hand,' remembers Brigadier Davies-Scourfield. 'We noticed a significant improvement once she was around.'

Johnnie's father had been a widower for the last three years of his life and Althorp reflected this when Raine arrived. The new Countess Spencer disliked the subdued decor of her stately surroundings and felt that the place needed a woman's touch and hauling into the twentieth century. Once the ring was on her finger, she wasted no time in stamping her influence on Althorp and before very long the wind of domestic change swept through the house. Several members of staff and estate workers at all levels left soon after the wedding, including the cook, the footman, and the land agent John Edwards, who had looked after Johnnie's part of the estate as well as his father's. He and his wife Janet also had to leave their home in the Falconry, later occupied by Charles Althorp. Edwards was replaced by Richard Stanley, who became the most powerful man in Earl Spencer's retinue and ran the estate for fifteen years until his contract was abruptly terminated in November 1990. Some staff were loyal to

Raine, others did not work for her for very long and during her reign at Althorp the staff turnover was high. A senior adviser said, 'She was appalling at managing people and could never get anything done by persuasion. She had to give orders, which is a sign of weakness and many of the staff were frightened of her. When she first became Lady Spencer she was terribly concerned about her position and the need to assert it all the time. Although she could manipulate and handle Lord Spencer very well, fundamentally she feels inferior about not having been born an aristocrat.'

Several members of staff reported that the discipline at Althorp was far stricter than at Buckingham Palace and most employees had to sign a document that they would not talk about their time at Althorp. Johnnie, however, apart from a lapse of behaviour towards the Bettses, knew the importance of treating servants in the proper manner, a lesson he felt Raine needed to learn. One day early on their marriage, they were being served lunch in the private dining by the butler and footman. Raine who does not drink alcohol, was having difficulty in getting either of them to bring her some water. She became increasingly agitated, turned to Johnnie and said, 'Darling Johnnie, will you tell them to get what I want. This is all too absurd.' The butler hearing this remark, put back his shoulders and walked out. Johnnie turned sharply to Raine and said, 'You will never be so rude in front of servants again. You will learn to behave correctly.' Raine knew to eat humble pie immediately and replied, 'Darling, I didn't mean it.'

About twenty staff were employed to run the house and the estate plus a further twenty casuals. Some of the staff who worked in the house were paid net of tax and National Insurance contributions. Unfortunately due to an oversight no-one informed the estate office about the situation and the relevant amounts were not paid to the authorities. This state of affairs was discovered by the Inland Revenue during a visit to Althorp in 1983. An amicable agreement was reached.

Some staff fared well under the new regime including Betty Andrews who was promoted to cook and took Raine's demands in her stride. Betty worked a ten-hour day for £15 a week with rarely a day off. She only cooked English food and each day would make suggestions for meals which Raine would often alter when there was to be a big dinner. She was not very particular about day to day meals, however, although preferred soft foods that did not need much chewing. Favourites for lunch were shepherd's pie, moussaka and lasagne. Johnnie liked homemade soup or a fish starter and a savoury to finish with such as 'devils on horseback,' (prunes wrapped in bacon) or scrambled eggs with anchovies. For dessert he liked lemon meringue pie. Johnnie would get up for breakfast, between 8.30 and 9.00 a.m. and eat a large cooked breakfast, sitting on his own at the head of a long polished table in the Tapestry Dining Room surrounded by antique silver figurines. 'I love my breakfast – it's my favourite meal,' he said. He liked freshly squeezed orange juice, poached egg, and bacon which was specially sent up for him by Fortnum and Mason. For several years after his brain haemorrhage he would go back to bed after breakfast to rest. At mid-morning he liked a glass of champagne: 'a real pick-me-up and a wonderful tonic. I always have one at 11.30 a.m.' He enjoyed a light lunch: 'just a plate of cold ham or chicken salad and a glass of lager.' His favourite dish was roast partridge and, like the Princess of Wales, he loved bread-and-butter pudding. Dinner was usually at 8.00 p.m. after which Raine and Johnnie usually went their separate ways. At the end of the evening Johnnie would take a bath before going to bed at around 11.30 p.m.

In contrast, most days Raine would have breakfast brought to her in her huge salmon-pink and turquoise bedroom. Propped up in her emperor-sized bed surrounded by photographs of her family in diamond-encrusted frames, she would start the day with yoghurt and fresh orange juice. If anything was wrong with her food Raine would phone the kitchen, where a white warning light would flash. A member of staff said, 'We dreaded that light because when she was angry it was always "bloody this and bloody that." The Countess can be difficult at times. She does go off people. The Earl is okay. He's good to his staff, but leaves the running of the household to his wife.'

Although Raine had always been punctual for council meetings, she regularly disregarded the unwritten aristocratic rule of being prompt for meals in consideration of the staff. 'Johnnie liked lunch at one thirty,' says David Laws who frequently joined the two of them. 'Raine would often not come down until about two fifteen. Johnnie would get very cross and stamp his foot like a schoolboy. Instead of taking tea at five, she would arrive at six thirty despite the fact that some of the staff should have been off by then. It was the same at dinner which the staff expected to serve at 8.00 p.m. so they could go off at 9.00 p.m. I've been there waiting for Raine to appear until 9.45 p.m. which meant the butler, footman and all the kitchen staff had to hang around. Johnnie was a great lord, but she had no sense of noblesse oblige.'

Johnnie's early lesson to Raine on how to deal with staff did not have a lasting effect. When she was angry she took no account of a person's sensibilities. At one of her paying dinners the chef made a caramel dessert with a fruit coulis which was not to Raine's liking. She strode into the kitchen and, in front of the under-chefs and all the assistants, complained loudly, not about the quality of the dessert, but about his choice. 'How dare you serve anything like that,' she was heard to bellow. 'You don't have that kind of food in the country.' The chef was mortified and left soon afterwards. There were repeated troubles with chefs and David Levin, owner of the Capital Hotel in Knightsbridge and a BTA colleague states: 'I have never had a good meal at Althorp.' Sometimes Raine would ask to borrow staff from other landed gentry and if she liked them was known to offer them more money to work for her. In May 1984, after five years' service, the chauffeur John Harmon, who had been watched by millions of television viewers helping Earl Spencer up the steps of St Paul's Cathedral on the day of Diana's wedding, was given notice – a hastily scrawled note on the back of a postcard.

Raine insisted that both her and Johnnie's bed-linen was changed every day. The white linen sheets, edged with lace and embellished with the Spencer monogram, were taken home by a member of staff to be washed and ironed by hand in her tiny cottage. There would be at least fourteen sheets a week, more if there were guests, and each sheet took over half an hour to iron. In the winter the condensation would run down the windows and the room would be full of steam. However, although Raine could be a hard taskmaster and rude to employees, she could also be kind and generous. She would often buy presents for the staff and when Betty had a frozen shoulder she paid for her to have private treatment.

Although Raine's general health is good, she suffers from migraines and bronchitis. Betty, who also worked as Raine's lady's maid, looked after her through one particularly nasty attack of bronchitis and was given a pressure cooker as a thank-you present.

'Countess Spencer had some jolly good points and was kind in her way.' She would not let herself be intimidated. 'If she shouted at me I used to shout back.'

One of her jobs was to look after Raine's vast and expensive wardrobe. This kept her busy as Raine maintained her practice of changing her outfits several times a day when she went to live at Althorp. She always dressed in something long for dinner, often choosing dresses with crinoline skirts that had been her trademark when she was a debutante. They did not have quite the same allure now that she was in fifties. A friend comments, 'Sometimes when she dresses up she looks amazing, but her penchant for crinoline dresses is entirely inappropriate. Some of us called her Come Dancing.' Betty's tasks included hand-washing Raine's underclothes and nightclothes, and ironing everything from day clothes to ballgowns which Raine liked to be done as soon as she had taken them off. 'She had a lot of evening dresses which were devils to iron. I used to hold my breath in case the iron was too hot,' Betty remembers.

She used to pack for Raine when she went away. 'She would give me a list of what she wanted to take and the accessories and I would take them out of the special wardrobe room. I used to pack them in layers of tissue paper and had to get it just right. She had jewellery to match her outfits, but she would get that out herself. Each piece would be wrapped separately in little chamois bags. Her evening dresses would be put in big covers and carried out.'

Raine would also leave a note at night of the clothes she wished to wear the next morning. 'I would run her bath at about nine and then call her. If she wasn't going anywhere she would do some work in the bedroom after breakfast. She used an awful lot of talc which would have to be cleared up and then I would hang her clothes in the bathroom. She would leave them there at night after her bath. I would press what she had worn that day and put it back into the wardrobe room and take underwear away for washing. She was always immaculate. I never saw her in anything that didn't match.'

Betty often looked after Lord Spencer's clothes too, putting all his day clothes and underwear ready for him on his valet stand. She also laid his pyjamas out at night. 'He was no trouble,' she says. 'When they went away Her Ladyship would say which day and evening suits to pack and you knew which shirts and ties went with them.'

Raine has always loved jewellery and collected some fine pieces during her two marriages. A member of her family says: 'Although Raine is very wealthy in her own right she loves to be given jewels. Johnnie was very generous to her and enjoyed buying her jewellery, which she always chose herself, because she appreciated it so much. He got a lot of pleasure from seeing how happy she was when he gave her a present. The thing about Raine is that whereas most people think of the thought not the value, she thought of the value as well as thought.' David Laws remembers her telling him about new purchases. 'She was particularly excited about a diamond brooch Johnnie bought her which she told me cost £40,000.' Raine keeps most of her important pieces under lock and key in London, looked after by the antique dealers S. J. Phillips, who handled much of the sale of silver from Althorp. She regularly drops in to change items of jewellery.

Raine enjoys nothing better than a major project to get her teeth into and had already given considerable thought to her proposals for Althorp while she was working for European Architectural Heritage Year. 'She used to talk to me a lot about what she was going to do at Althorp soon after she and Johnnie got together, which was well before he married her,' one colleague remembers. 'She knew exactly how she wanted to redesign it.'

She was equally determined to make Althorp pay for itself. 'We got the show on the road right away, no hanging about,' she said. She attacked the problem with all the zeal and enthusiasm that marked her success at the LCC and GLC. With her entrepreneurial talent, her ideas for money-making schemes multiplied like Mickey Mouse's brooms in the 'Sorcerer's

Apprentice' sequence of Walt Disney's *Fantasia*, and if they did not become quite so out of control, they went well beyond the boundaries of good taste.

Within a couple of months of their wedding Raine set up a souvenir shop at Althorp on, she claimed, a budget of £500. In it she sold jewellery, knick-knacks, old china, much of which came from her tours of junk shops in the Bognor area, and her mother's romantic novels. (The removal of Dame Barbara's novels was one of the first but most significant changes Charles made after his father's death.) Raine also revamped the tearoom which she called the Georgian Stables Restaurant. She declared it 'an enormous success. You can sit on nice chairs at tables with damask tablecloths.' Whereas £500 might have been the cost of initially stocking the gift shop, the overall cost of the alterations to the stable block which housed the tearoom and gift and wine shops was many times that amount.

Johnnie recognised that his wife had a sharper sense of business than he and happily let her take charge. Richard Stanley, Althorp's longtime estate manager, says, 'Lord Spencer simply was not financially aware. He did not know the value of money. Raine Spencer did know its value but had little business sense – she found difficulty in understanding the difference between turnover and profit.' Johnnie adopted the same laid-back attitude to his estate as he had to his farm in Norfolk. According to another employee, 'he was interested in the estate but perfectly happy for other people to handle it for him.'

On one level Raine conscientiously watched every item of expenditure while on another she behaved with unbridled extravagance. One of her early money-saving schemes trod on several aristocratic toes. In 1973 Lord Montagu of Beaulieu founded the Historic Houses Association for owners and guardians of historic houses and their 'friends'. Althorp was a member along with other great historic houses such as Longleat, Woburn and Blenheim. One of the small perks of belonging to the association was that members were allowed into each other's houses without having to pay. Raine, however, refused to go along with this on the tenuous grounds that it would lose valuable revenue. At the time, the entry charge at Althorp was £1.00 a head and Johnnie's fortune estimated at £12 million. Her action was considered 'extremely mean and odd' and resulted in Althorp being expelled from the Association. (Within a couple of months of Johnnie's death Charles applied to rejoin.)

One of Raine's first commercial ventures was a money-making shoot. Johnnie offered, through property dealers Savills, three days' pheasant-shooting over half his 8,500-acre estate for eight guns a day at £4,500. All the game would remain the property of the estate although guns would be given one brace a day. The shooting party were to be the guests of the Earl and Countess and dine with them. There was an extra charge of up to £50 a night, including VAT, for staying at Althorp.

Although Raine was happily involved with Johnnie and running Althorp, problems were looming with her stepchildren. It is never an easy matter becoming a stepmother to children who have had their father to themselves for some time, as Johnnie's children had for eight years. They had become used to mothering and protecting him and felt abruptly ousted when Raine arrived on the scene. Girls in particular can be very jealous if they feel their father's love and attention has shifted to another woman.

The situation in which Raine found herself was one that required tact, subtlety, patience and understanding, not characteristics for which she is particularly noted. Some women in her position might have tried to become the children's substitute mother, others might have slowly become their friend. Raine became neither, but both sides are to blame for the chasm that divided them. A senior employee at Althorp for many years says, 'With the exception of Jane, who wasn't too bad, the children could not have been more difficult or cold to Raine. There was open hostility not just to her as a person. They also disliked the way she dominated and became so possessive of their father which made them feel they had to compete with her for his attention.'

Sarah and Jane could not stand Raine's effusive manner or seeing their father fall increasingly under her spell. Jane, who has always been the most self-reliant and least controversial of the two older girls, coped better, although even she cut down on her visits to her father and, when she was at Althorp, behaved as if Raine wasn't there, totally ignoring her even when they passed on the stairs. After leaving West Heath, she went to Italy to study history of art in Florence for six months. When she returned she took a secretarial course and, in common with many other aristocratic young ladies at the time, went to work at *Vogue* magazine as an editorial assistant.

The red-headed Sarah, who was the more volatile, found it hard to control her fiery temper. She would countermand Raine's orders to the servants in front of her stepmother and was deliberately rude to her. Diana felt as strongly as her sisters about the woman who had entered their lives and also cut down on her visits to Althorp. Twelve-year-old Charles played her up when he came home from Eton.

In her own way Raine tried to bridge the distance between them, not least for the sake of Johnnie who was, she said, 'very upset at the children being so antagonistic towards me'. She suggested that he should make a point of telling them that Althorp was their home, too, and that if they wanted to organise a weekend party for their friends, they should feel free to do so. Sarah decided to take advantage of this offer and invited lots of eligible young men to Althorp one weekend. Johnnie and Raine tactfully absented themselves during Saturday but Raine returned in time for dinner. When she went into the private yellow-and-blue drawing room to say hello, the whole room fell silent. She told David Laws, who was with her at the time, that she knew Sarah had been talking about her. She dealt with the occasion by telling her how 'absolutely marvellous' she looked, at which Sarah was apparently nonplussed. Raine then went round to each of the guests in turn, smiled, shook their hand and introduced herself. As she left the room she said to Laws, 'I fought council elections in the East End. I could have them for breakfast if I wanted to.'

In the early days of his remarriage, Johnnie's aunt, Lady Margaret Douglas-Home, used to visit Johnnie frequently at Althorp and saw the problems for herself. 'I don't think Raine went about it in the right way. I don't think she is made to be a stepmother. She hasn't the right temperament. She must be the only pebble on the beach and wasn't willing to take second place to Johnnie's children. She used to claim all of him the whole time and didn't like them interfering in her life with Johnnie. The children never liked it and they were old enough to know. I was very sorry for them. They looked so miserable.'

In April 1991 Raine admitted to the journalist Jean Rook that being a stepmother 'was bloody awful' and that she was 'absolutely sick of the Wicked Stepmother lark'. She told Rook, 'You're never going to make me sound like a human being because people like to think I'm Dracula's mother, but I did have a rotten time at the start and it's only just getting better.'

Nor did Raine see much of her own children. Peter Townend, social editor of *The Tatler*, remarks, 'The family didn't seem to be close and I don't think any of her children got on with her all that well at that time. They were a bit afraid of her and she would shout at them. William has a stammer and wasn't best man at his brother Rupert's wedding. Charlotte became quite a rebel, and wanted to become an actress which was very low on her mother's scale of values. Henry the youngest, however, was the apple of her eye.'

It wasn't long after her father's marriage that Sarah started to suffer from the eating disorder anorexia nervosa, where young girls see themselves as fat and go on compulsive diets, in some cases until their lives are threatened. Sarah began to live on Coca-Cola and cigarettes and like many girls suffering from this condition, her weight plummeted, dropping from a comfortable eight stone to a desperate five stone twelve pounds. Her condition was not helped by the breakup of her relationship with the Duke of Westminster with whom she had been going out.

Eventually she was persuaded to go into a clinic near Regent's Park where she was treated by the psychiatrist Dr Maurice Lipsedge, who later also treated Diana for her bulimia. The Prince of Wales was instrumental in helping Sarah to get over both her relationship with the Duke of Westminster and her anorexia. Sarah had met him at Ascot in June 1977 and the two became good friends. He invited her to watch him play polo at Smith's Lawn, Windsor, during the summer and she invited him to a shooting party at Althorp in November. Diana, then a shy sixteen-year-old, was given the weekend off from school for the occasion and it was at this party that she officially met her future husband for the first time. On that occasion Charles had merely found Diana 'an amusing and jolly – and attractive – sixteen-year-old.' Diana, however, found him 'pretty amazing' even though she had to call him 'Sir'.

The following February Charles asked Sarah to join him on his skiing holiday at Klosters in Switzerland. It set newspapers buzzing that Charles was in love, but Sarah publicly stressed that the relationship was platonic. 'I am not in love with him . . . ' she insisted, 'and I wouldn't marry anyone I didn't love . . . If he asked me I would turn him down.' If Charles harboured secret hopes in her direction, her public statement nipped them in the bud.

Diana left West Heath school without distinguishing herself academically. Fortunately the school prides itself on its welfare work and once a week Diana would visit old people and play with handicapped children. Although at the time she was still shy and gawky like many teenagers, she had a natural ability to make people feel comfortable with her. She was a good swimmer but had to abandon her ambition to be a ballet dancer as she had grown too tall. She was also very romantic and an avid reader of Barbara Cartland's novels even before she became her step-granddaughter.

After leaving school Diana went to a Swiss finishing school, returning in April 1978, much sooner than expected, as she felt so homesick. She initially lived with her mother in Cadogan Place, but in the summer of 1979 Johnnie and Frances bought her a flat in Coleherne Court, South Kensington, and she moved in with three friends.

In the same month that she returned from Switzerland Diana was chief bridesmaid at the wedding of her sister, Jane, and Robert Fellowes. Jane was just twenty-one, Robert thirty-six. Johnnie was delighted with the match as Robert's father, Sir William Fellowes, had been the Queen's land agent at Sandringham and Johnnie had known Robert since he was a little boy. Robert had even been taught by Ally, the governess who had taught his own children. Jane, now a fashion assistant at *Vogue*, told the press on her engagement: 'We have known each other all our lives and have gradually grown closer.' The wedding was held in the Guards' Chapel, Wellington Barracks in central London and a reception, paid for by her mother, followed at St James's Palace. It was attended by several members of the Royal Family including the Queen Mother, the Duchess of Kent, the Duke and Duchess of Gloucester, and of course all the family and staff from Althorp.

The tension between Frances and Johnnie, parents of the bride, was noticeable. They could not even manage a frosty politeness. As a friend says, 'There was no love lost between them.' Although they had both remarried, Johnnie could not forgive Frances for leaving him and Frances could not forgive Johnnie for depriving her of the children. Frances and Raine managed to skirt round each other and the biggest problem was persuading Raine not to be in the family photographs. By all accounts she put up quite a fight despite explanations that it was customary for step-parents to stand to one side on such occasions.

After their wedding Jane and Robert, a member of the Queen's staff, moved into a grace and favour apartment at Kensington Palace. After nine years as Assistant Private Secretary to the Queen, Robert became the Queen's Deputy Private Secretary in 1986 and her Private Secretary in the autumn of 1990 on the retirement of Sir William Heseltine. As Jane was Johnnie's first child to marry, he also gave the couple a house in the grounds at Althorp. Sarah, Diana and Charles were as delighted as Jane. It meant they did not have to stay at Althorp and see Raine when they came to visit their father. They could invite him to come and see them. Jane and Robert gave up the house in the late eighties when they bought a house in Norfolk.

The following year, in August 1979, 24-year-old Sarah announced her engagement to 28-year-old former Guards officer Neil McCorquodale, ironically a distant cousin of Raine's, after a whirlwind romance. 'I am a whirlwind sort of lady,' she said. A secretary in Savills, the upmarket estate agents, Sarah had known Neil McCorquodale for a couple of years but had only been going out with him for five weeks. She broke the news to her father during one of his cricket matches at Althorp. The McCorquodales farmed in Lincolnshire where Sarah could enjoy riding and shooting. Although Johnnie agreed to the marriage at once, the relationship was not all plain sailing. After announcing her engagement, Sarah broke it off, then changed her mind and finally made it up the aisle on 17 May 1980. Frances paid for Sarah's reception too and there was a repeat performance of trying to steer Raine away from the official family photographs. 'She kept saying she had to be in them as Johnnie's wife. It was really hard to persuade her that it just wasn't the done thing for a step-parent to be in the formal wedding photographs,' says a family friend.

Raine loves entertaining and now had the grandest setting for her many parties. At first she mixed their friends and acquaintances. As the traditional English landowner, Johnnie chose his from fellow landowners, the county set, and the rural aristocracy, among whom he was well respected and liked. Raine had a 'Who's Who' of contacts including politicians and colleagues from her days in local government. 'Raine was wonderful at creating a good atmosphere and guests were made to feel marvellous,' says a regular visitor. 'Sometimes however people came just to send her up. They would make spiteful comments behind her back. English society can be very uncharitable.' It was a habit that Raine herself didn't descend to. 'She might be very selfish, but she was never a bitch,' says someone who knows her well.

She and Johnnie regularly gave balls for as many as a thousand, when guests tended to be 'people by numbers' rather than friends. David Laws remembers some marvellous weekend parties in the early eighties. 'There were some very grand people at the balls, from the Duke of Marlborough to Joan Collins. There were smart shooting parties too, with Sir John Mills, Lord St John of Fawsley, Prince Michael of Kent and the Queen of Denmark.' The woods surrounding the great house were full of pheasants. There was also a herd of fallow deer in the park which were regularly culled to control numbers.

Over the years, however, some friends began easing themselves out of the Spencer social circle, including Lord Wardington. On one of his last visits Johnnie sat him next to his son Charles, with the specific brief that he was to try to 'make peace between him and Raine.' Lord Wardington remembers, 'I got the subject on to Raine. Charles, who was still at Eton, told me he hated her. We had a long conversation during which I said "she isn't your mother. Don't try to treat her as such, treat her as someone who is living here. Then you will get on better with her." I didn't do any good'. Another friend of Johnnie's who stopped going to Althorp says: 'Johnnie was always sweet but my wife and I felt we could no longer go there because of what was going on. We couldn't be part of something that we felt was morally very wrong'.

Raine also dropped some of her own friends. The cynical view of this was that she discarded those she felt no longer had a role in her new life. A peer says 'I would be very surprised if there is a single person who is a real friend of hers unless they kowtow to her. I don't think she's generous in spirit.' Social commentator Peter Townend adds, 'She is the sort of person whose eyes were always looking for someone more interesting in the room.'

Raine was certainly not interested in cultivating close women friends. She defined a friend as 'someone from whom you can expect warmth, affection, appreciation and a certain amount of loyalty ... I don't care what people say behind my back – all I want is for them to be nice to my face.' She admits to very few close friends but 'several hundred' less close friends. Someone who knows her well and has watched her change over the years remarks, 'She had a great many acquaintances and her relationships with them were often very shallow.'

Interviewed by the author Angela Huth, Raine said, 'I approach close and absorbing friendships between women with great suspicion. The idea of a best friend to me is a disaster. One: She'll always steal your husband, or try. Two: The best friend is the only person who can make a dangerous enemy. Three: Best friends nearly always become jealous of some aspect of your life – perhaps you are cleverer or prettier or have more money in which case, due to jealousy, the best friend cannot help but be disloyal ... If you absolutely must have a best friend make it your husband or your mother. But even with them there should be some reservations.'

She added that she believed 'the only perfect and lasting friendship is a platonic friendship between a man and a woman'. Raine had several of these, as she had always managed to draw a coterie of sexually neutral men, or those who were not sexually interested in women, around her. She modified her views slightly once married to Johnnie. As she told *Woman* magazine: 'It's wonderfully lucky to find someone who you actually want to be with who's a great friend. I'm always complaining to Johnnie that I never have time to see my friends but he tells me "I'm your best friend" which is true. I adore his sense of humour. He makes me laugh more than anybody. In fact I can't even get very cross with him because he defuses it by making me laugh. I can't bear it when he's not in the house.'

In point of fact Johnnie was around so much of the time that Raine began to find it somewhat claustrophobic. To give herself more space, she decided that he should have a special room where he could amuse himself with his photographs. She chose the room Johnnie's father had used as a study, which had a big library desk, and decided to convert it for his use on a rare day when he went out for lunch. As soon as he had left she rushed to clear out his father's desk before he returned, pulling out and tearing up everything the old man had hoarded away, including old bus tickets, ration cards and electricity bills. In one of the drawers she also found a very valuable seventeenth-century folio edition of Shakespeare. When Johnnie returned he was delighted with his new room.

Despite the distractions of Althorp, Raine soon found she was becoming bored and this led her to establish a pattern of going to London twice a week, usually on Tuesdays and Thursdays. Although she loved Althorp itself she was not a country person and much preferred London. The flat at 48 Grosvenor Square, which had been made over to Raine as part of the divorce settlement, was later sold back to Gerald. She and Johnnie subsequently bought a flat in the same block, much it was said to Gerald's anger. This was later sold and a larger flat bought. Raine also had a tiny-

Raine and Johnnie outside Althorp, the Spencer estate in Northamptonshire, in January 1981

Johnnie bravely leading Diana up the aisle of St Paul's Cathedral on her wedding day, July 29, 1981

(*Above*) Raine and Johnnie on the whirlwind author tour to promote their joint book, *The Spencers on Spas*, published in 1983

(*Right*) Johnnie and Diana at a gala in Northampton in 1988

Raine and Johnnie matching their glamorous surroundings in
the newly-refurbished Althorp

(*Right*) The Picture Gallery, where the antique chairs have been reupholstered in orange dralon, the globes restored at a cost of about £10,000, the picture frames regilded and the seventeenth-century oak floor covered with a beige fitted carpet.

(*Below*) 'Witches at their Incantations' by Salvatore Rosa acquired by the 1st Earl Spencer in 1761 and sold by Raine and Johnnie in 1983 to the London dealers Wildenstein, whose attempts to export it were blocked. Now in the National Gallery

'Apollo crowning the musician Marcantonio Pasqualini' by Andrea Sacchi originally acquired by
the 1st Earl Spencer in 1758 for the Great Room at Spencer House. It was bought as a pair with
'Liberality and Modesty' by Guido Reni. Both had frames designed by Athenian Stuart. Both were
sold by Raine and Johnnie in 1980 to Wildenstein. The Reni is owned by a private collection in
New York. The Sacchi is now in the Metropolitan Museum of Art in New York

A pair of seventeenth-century gold wine coolers from the
Marlborough collection, believed to have been given to the Duke of
Marlborough by Queen Anne after his victory at Blenheim. The sale
was negotiated by S. J. Phillips for about one million pounds to
the British Museum

'Agrippina with the ashes of Germanicus' by the Scottish artist Gavin Hamilton commissioned by
the 1st Earl Spencer in 1765. Bought by Colnaghi's in 1983 who sold it to the Tate Gallery, London

A contrast in styles. Diana and Raine on the day after the death of their beloved Johnnie

one bedroomed apartment in Whitehall Court near St James's Park, which few knew about and which she bought when she was married to Gerald, kept for her own private purposes and has since sold. David Laws says, 'She told me it was private and not to be talked about and that she had it as a little investment.' Johnnie hated her going to London and was, David Laws says, 'pathologically jealous'.

12

A Dramatic Illness

The lives of Raine and Johnnie took a dramatic turn in 1978 when, on 19 September, the 54-year-old Earl collapsed with a massive cerebral haemorrhage. He had not felt well when he woke in the morning and on seeing his land agent Richard Stanley walk by, called out of his bedroom window asking him to postpone a meeting they were due to have that morning at the estate office. Raine, assuming her husband's upset was minor, went off to Claridge's for a lunch date with her mother.

Despite feeling wretched, Johnnie struggled to pull himself together and later that morning managed to walk the hundred yards to the office. He signed a batch of cheques and was just about to return to the main house when he was suddenly very sick and collapsed. Richard Stanley rushed to help him. As Johnnie could hardly walk Stanley supported the portly Earl on his shoulders and they struggled back to the house.

Once there, the butler rushed to his aid and the two of them strained to get Johnnie upstairs and on to the bed. 'It was a mighty problem as he was very heavy,' remembers Stanley. They rang Mr Banham, a surgeon who lived in a nearby village, and Johnnie's own doctor, Dr Dalgliesh. Mr Banham arrived first and said immediately that he thought the Earl, who was now unconscious and a pale shade of metallic grey, had had some form of stroke.

An ambulance was summoned and took Johnnie to Northampton General Hospital, a six-mile journey from Althorp, where several doctors rushed to his aid. After his blood pressure was taken and he had been given several tests, the diagnosis was confirmed: Johnnie, a moderate drinker and non-smoker, had had a major stroke.

Strokes, at least half of which are the result of high blood pressure, can be caused either by a blood clot forming and blocking the flow of blood to part of the brain or, as in Johnnie Spencer's case, when a blood vessel bursts and blood pours into the brain. The latter, a brain haemorrhage, is often the cause of immediate death. The victim's chances are improved, however, if he can be operated on to remove the pool of blood from the brain, relieve the pressure, and prevent the leaking spot from a further fatal bleeding.

The blood pouring into the brain, which has the consistency of soft margarine, causes considerable damage. The stroke can result in permanent paralysis of arms and/or legs on the opposite side of the body from the affected part of the brain and twisting of the face. Speech, hearing, control of bladder and bowels, understanding and concentration can also be affected. All the symptoms of a stroke are caused by brain damage. Brain cells that are destroyed never recover, but other cells, which were only partially damaged, can start working again within a few weeks of the stroke and can, to some extent, take over from the damaged parts of the brain.

Raine was telephoned at Claridge's. She abandoned her lunch and was driven straight to the hospital where she arrived just over an hour later. Johnnie's four children were also contacted and rushed to the hospital as soon as they could. At the time Diana was staying with her friend Caroline Harbord-Hamond, the daughter of Lord Suffield, at their Norfolk home. Charles was collected from Eton and driven to Northampton by Jane's new husband, Robert Fellowes.

Raine immediately tried to take charge of the situation and, rather than the crisis uniting the family, the tension between the children and their stepmother only increased. The news was grim. Raine was told that her husband's chances of survival were slim and she and the children maintained an all-night vigil at the hospital. Somehow Johnnie clung on to life as the medical team fought to stabilise his condition and bring down his sky-high blood pressure.

Many new wives faced with such a poor prognosis for their husband would have wept in despair, but not Raine. Instead she relied upon her iron control, steely determination and, most of all, her courage – the characteristic she believes most epitomises her life. 'If you have courage – moral and physical – you can overcome any disadvantage,' she once said.

Here was her chance to prove it. Despite the devastating nature of her husband's illness, she did not allow herself to shed a tear, either on discovering how ill he was, or as he hovered between life and death in the months that followed. 'I didn't cry once through that crisis,' she said. 'Crying is selfish. When you're in a crisis, you have to detach yourself, find a logical solution.'

Instead she made up her mind that Johnnie would not die and, as history has proved, what Raine wants Raine usually gets. She cajoled and pressurised the doctors at the hospital to do all they could, but as Northampton General did not have the specialised equipment needed, she also contacted everyone she knew with medical connections to find the best place for him to be treated. The following day Johnnie developed pneumonia, a dangerous complication. Despite this Raine said she wanted him taken to the renowned National Hospital in London's Queen Square where he would have a better chance of recovery. He was so ill, however, that the two-hour journey to London could well have killed him. She contacted Dr Nigel Southward in London who sent a private ambulance and late on Wednesday night, 20 September, Johnnie was driven down the motorway with a police escort.

On his arrival at the National Hospital he was immediately given a brain scan. This shows in three dimensions exactly where a haemorrhage has occurred, whether it is in a part of the brain that is operable and how much damage has already been caused. He was also given an angiogram, which outlines the blood vessels in dye. The scan revealed that Johnnie had suffered bleeding in the back part of the brain which controls balance and articulation and suggested to the doctors that the haemorrhage had been caused by high blood pressure.

Johnnie was by now deeply unconscious. He was put on a life support machine and his vital bodily functions, such as blood pressure and pulse rate, were constantly monitored. A catheter to remove body fluids was inserted, although this proved to be quite difficult due to his size. He was also given a routine chest X-ray and an electro-cardiogram (ECG). By that Wednesday evening even Raine had lost confidence in his recovery. 'When Lord Spencer arrived here he was extremely ill,' says a doctor. According to a close relative, he was not expected to live and the atmosphere between the children, who had remained at the hospital, and Raine was explosive. 'Only Jane said "Hello" to Raine, the other three first ignored her completely and then were terribly rude. It was awful for her. She was doing what any loving wife would do and didn't need little brats coming in and saying "we don't want you here".' Efforts were also made by Johnnie's solicitor, Hugo Southern, and his land agent, Richard Stanley, to minimise taxation in the event of Johnnie's death. (Some time later when the immediate crisis had passed, application was made to, and granted by, the Court of Protection for Johnnie's affairs to be administered by Raine, Southern and Stanley, both jointly and individually.)

The doctors decided that an immediate operation was needed to save his life, but this was going to be additionally risky because of the pneumonia. Although Raine knew that the pneumonia would reduce Johnnie's chances of survival, she realised that, untreated, his chance of life was even slimmer and so gave the surgeons the go-ahead to proceed.

'We decided to treat the pneumonia with antibiotics, but ignore it as far as the operation was concerned, otherwise he wouldn't have had any hope at all,' says a doctor. A further non-medical problem caused some anxiety: Johnnie was found to be too large to fit into the normal operating chair used by the surgeon, but this was solved by placing him on a makeshift table instead.

The four-hour operation – Johnnie's first since he had had his tonsils removed as a child – was delicate and dangerous and, as with all such operations, carried the risk of further brain damage. Afterwards Johnnie was moved to the recovery unit, as the hospital did not then have an intensive care unit. For the next two weeks he was kept ventilated, sedated and unconscious in order to rest the brain and allow it to recover. Throughout that period his life hung by the thinnest of threads.

For patients on a life support machine, good post-operative nursing care is vital to survival. Johnnie had his pulse, blood pressure and temperature taken every fifteen minutes day and night. He was fed through a tube that went from his nose down the oesophagus into his stomach. Another tube passed from the breathing machine through his mouth down into his lungs. Because of the pneumonia it was vital to keep his chest as clear as possible and secretions from his lungs were continually suctioned from the tubes. He was also given regular physiotherapy to keep his limbs supple.

His position was changed every couple of hours to help prevent bedsores, and blood clots from developing in his legs, and to keep his chest clear. Nurses also performed the daily tasks he could not do for himself, including brushing his teeth and putting drops into his eyes to stimulate the action of blinking. Daily lumbar punctures were performed to drain the blood away from the brain to reduce the risk of hydrocephalus, water on the brain.

At the end of the fortnight, during which time the dedicated staff managed to keep his chest 'relatively clear', Johnnie was gradually weaned from the ventilator. Over a period of a few days, the doctors managed to get him to breathe spontaneously and he was then taken to a room in the private wing.

If Raine's work for the Historic Buildings Committee and Covent Garden were her finest hours professionally, this was to be her finest hour in personal terms. While Johnnie lay day after day deeply unconscious, she sat by his bed and hung on to his life by sheer willpower. 'When he was so terribly ill there was not a lot she could do apart from encouraging him,' says one of the medical team. She also encouraged the nurses and doctors. 'She got on very well with the staff and was very, very supportive to the surgeons, doctors, anaesthetists, physiotherapists and everyone concerned. She wasn't overpowering at all and all of us who worked with her liked her. Although she was desperately worried about her husband, she could still be very amusing to talk to.'

Raine initially mounted a round-the-clock vigil, then, as Johnnie's condition gradually improved, she was with him every morning and early evening, tearing herself away in the afternoon to rest after which she was usually picked up by her brother Ian and his wife Anna and taken back to the hospital. At night she mostly stayed with her other brother Glen in his London flat as she could not bear to be on her own.

'Raine was determined that he wouldn't die,' says a doctor. 'She never broke down once but it was obvious she was extremely happy when we managed to get him to the ward upstairs.' Raine would sit for hours by Johnnie's bed, repeating: 'Johnnie, I love you. You are going to get well. Come on, Johnnie.' A close relation remembers her talking to him one night. 'She said "If you can hear me Johnnie, squeeze my hand." To our amazement his fingers moved just slightly round her hand.' One of Raine's major worries was that her husband would be left with brain damage. The doctors tried to be reassuring. 'The bleed was nowhere near the area of his mind that controlled rational thought processes,' says a member of the medical team. 'We felt his speech and the coordination of his arms would be fine, but that he would have neurological symptoms in his legs, would be unsteady and unable to walk without assistance.'

These symptoms – reeling gait, slurred speech and shaky legs, similar to someone who is drunk – were very marked in the first year or so of Johnnie's recovery. Although they gradually improved, there was still tremendous concern for him at Diana's wedding to the Prince of Wales nearly three years later when he bravely walked up the long aisle of St Paul's Cathedral.

True to her word, Raine never let herself go. She was always immaculately made up and her hair perfectly in place. She did not dress ostentatiously when visiting the hospital and told the admiring staff that the jewellery she was wearing was 'all fake or fun stuff'.

While the medical staff were doing everything possible to save the Earl's life, Raine, leaving nothing to chance, also appealed to the heavens. She was a great believer in the power of prayer and asked everyone she could, whatever their religion, Church of England, Catholic or Muslim, to pray for Johnnie's recovery. She even asked the Revd Victor Malan, Vicar of All Saints Church in Northampton, to come round to Althorp one evening and exorcise the ghost of Johnnie's father, as she felt his presence there was preventing Johnnie from making a good recovery. Raine also turned to her mother. 'Raine rang her every day and was very much encouraged by her,' says a member of staff. Dame Barbara recommended the services of a renowned faith healer, Elizabeth Gibson. Gibson, who lives in Scotland, said that Johnnie was so near death that his spirit was only connected to his body by a very fine thread and, according to a member of the family, 'worked very hard to put the spirit back in his body'. Raine also went to church several times herself while Johnnie lay critically ill in hospital. On one occasion she decided to light fifty-four candles, one for every year of his life. 'Then,' she said, 'I thought "why stop?" so I lit eighty-four. Then I noticed this priest watching what he obviously thought was a mad arsonist. So I explained and put ten pounds into the box.'

In August 1988, a recovered and buoyant Johnnie revealed, when he hosted *Your Hundred Best Tunes* for Raine 2, that Raine 'then asked for a sign. As it happened there was a wedding in another part of the church. As the bride came out of the registry, the organist started to play Widor's Toccata . . . one of my favourite tunes. From that moment she knew I would recover.'

At first Johnnie's progress was slow but steady. Once the tubes were removed and he could eat normally, Raine ordered special food from the Connaught Hotel, one of her husband's favourite eating-places, to encourage his appetite. She organised an intensive-care private nurse to help the regular nurses look after him. When he had progressed a little more, she encouraged the nurses to take him in a wheelchair outside to Queen Square. She felt that showing him something different from the four white walls of his hospital room would help him feel that life was worth living.

Because of his condition visitors were kept to a minimum. Among those who came regularly were the historian Sir John Plumb, Dr Mervyn Stockwood – who had blessed their marriage only two years previously – Raine's brother Ian and his wife, Raine's son Henry who was nine, her daughter Charlotte and, of course, Johnnie's three daughters. Charles, who was boarding at Eton, did not come often but was kept closely in touch with his father's progress.

According to one doctor, 'all three daughters were very shocked. Their father had been taken ill so suddenly. Sarah came most frequently and was also the liveliest. Jane usually brought her husband. She was obviously very attached to her father, but very quiet and shy. Diana, who had just left school, was also quite shy. She was the most tearful of all the girls and the one who most strongly felt he would die. I remember one day when she was obviously very upset, one of the doctors took her to one side and tried to reassure her that her father would get better.'

The three sisters' relationship with Raine, not easy at the best of times, buckled under the strain. Although they could see that she was doing her utmost to help their father recover, they resented the fact that she was masterminding his recovery with a cavalier disregard for their sensitivities and a lack of understanding of how important he was to them and they to him. Sarah, in particular, often lost her temper and she and Raine had heated and bitter exchanges, often in fierce whispers, along the corridors.

A doctor admits, 'Raine was very protective of Johnnie and didn't want his first family visiting the bedside at the same time as her.' The girls tried to work their visiting times around her but on at least one occasion she was heard to ask them to leave and not overtire their father.

Initially Johnnie seemed to be progressing reasonably well, although his pneumonia was proving extremely difficult to shift. Once he was conscious he tried hard to cooperate with his physiotherapists. 'He was always keen to get well and resume his life again,' says one of his doctors. 'Raine helped with a lot of the hard work like getting him to walk.' Gradually, anxiety was replaced by cautious optimism over his condition. But about six weeks after the operation he developed an abscess on his lung. He coughed it up one day when was in the toilet and some of the poisonous fluid went back down into his lungs and made him extremely ill. Tubes were again inserted to suction up as much as possible but he remained gravely ill. Now, not only did he have to fight to recover from the stroke, the trauma of the operation and his persistent pneumonia, but he had also contracted pseudomonas, a rare virulent bacterium which was unresponsive to normal antibiotics.

It was decided to transfer him to the intensive care unit at the Brompton Hospital in South Kensington. There Johnnie was put on a whole range of antibiotics, but the bacteria proved very resistant. He remained on the critical list for several weeks and almost died eight times. The strain on the family and their relationships was intense.

It has been said that Raine gave instructions to the hospital staff not to allow Johnnie's children to visit him and that the staff would sneak the girls into his room during Raine's absence, and they often waited outside for her to leave, but a close relation believes Raine's action could be justified. 'The girls used to shout at her at Johnnie's bedside over whose time it was to be with him. Good God, the man was dying. You didn't need teenagers throwing tantrums.'

The doctors were by now very pessimistic and indicated that Raine should prepare herself for Johnnie's death. But after the initial shock of his illness, she never once gave up or allowed her emotions to get the better of her. She again clung on to his life and mounted a round-the-clock vigil, leaving his bedside only to eat and sleep. He was unconscious most of the time and kept alive by a breathing machine. Johnnie later admitted that he almost lost the will to live several times, but, even though he was in a coma, he could feel that Raine simply would not allow him to die.

He told Jean Rook of the *Daily Express*, 'I couldn't talk to Raine but I knew she was there, holding my hand. She just sat there hour after hour, week after week, holding my hand and talking about our holidays and my photography, things she knew I liked ... She used to shout at me sometimes, bless her. "Can you hear me?" she'd yell. I nodded because I couldn't answer. But she was always there at my side and I could feel her great strength, her determination that I should live even when the doctors said she must lose me. Raine won . . . ' He said he wasn't afraid of dying. 'I'm not the sort of person who is afraid. I think, at one very bad stage, I had a choice of life or death and I knew at that moment I didn't want to die. Anyway Raine wouldn't have let me. She stops at nothing.' He later acknowledged, 'There is no doubt that I have Raine to thank for my full recovery. Without her I wouldn't be sitting here today. I would be dead.'

Raine explained her ability to cope: 'I'm a survivor and people forget that at their peril. There's pure steel up my backbone. Nobody destroys me and nobody was going to destroy Johnnie so long as I could sit by his bed – some of his family tried to stop me – and will my life force into him. The doctor kept saying there was no cure for pseudomonas. The obvious solution then was to find a cure.' She turned to her good friend Lord William Cavendish-Bentinck, subsequently Duke of Portland, the head of a drugs research company in Germany. She asked him if the company had anything in the laboratory stages that might save Johnnie's life. She was told they had a new drug but that it was not yet on the market and that she needed the approval of Johnnie's doctors before it could be tried out on him. Raine turned to the doctors. 'You say nothing can be done,' she said. 'Well I'd rather he died my way, doing something, than your way, doing nothing.' As she succinctly put it, 'I won. So did my husband.' Samples of the new drug, Aslocillin, were flown over from Germany and collected by Raine herself and, despite the fact that it was unlicensed in Britain, she persuaded the doctors to give it to her husband. Miraculously it did the trick.

It much amused Johnnie to discover he had been the 'guinea pig' for the drug. 'They had only tried it on rats before. It worked on the rats and I'm glad to say it worked on me.' One of the team of doctors who looked after Johnnie admits, 'It was very lucky that she knew about the trials of this drug.' Even so, expert opinion believed that if Johnnie had been a smoker he would not have survived.

Raine described Johnnie's recovery in characteristically romantic terms, claiming that one afternoon she was maintaining her usual bedside vigil and was playing him music from *Madame Butterfly*, when he suddenly opened his eyes 'and was back'.

She had sat at his bedside for four months talking him through coma after coma. Even her fiercest critics admit that she dragged her husband back to life, although some also believe that she was very well aware that if Johnnie had died in 1978 she would have had to leave Althorp without adequate provision for the future. A close member of the family has no doubts about her motives. 'One night when Johnnie was so ill she said to me, "Life is so unfair. I have waited twenty-eight years for the man I really love. I simply adore him and now it looks as if he is going to die." '

By Christmas, the drugs Johnnie was given to control his high blood pressure and reduce the risk of a further stroke seemed to be working well. This time there were no setbacks, although the stroke had caused some damage to his heart which was only discovered on his death in 1992.

In January 1979 he was discharged from hospital and continued his recovery in the comfortable surroundings of the Dorchester Hotel where Raine took a £90-a-night suite. 'After such strokes,' says a doctor, 'your blood pressure and your life style has to be controlled. When someone has something like this it is almost impossible to go back to their normal hectic life style. Lord Spencer was wheelchair-bound for a while and it was obvious that Raine kept all stresses away from him.'

During the months in the quiet luxury of the Dorchester, under Raine's guidance and with the care of a bevy of private nurses, Johnnie made steady progress. Raine gave a small party to celebrate his recovery and he astounded some guests by thanking them for visiting him when he was unconscious. 'I knew you were there,' he said. 'You didn't think I could hear you, but I could. I couldn't speak but I could hear.'

By April he was well enough to travel to Monte Carlo for a recuperative holiday. Raine also bought a two-bedroomed flat in Brighton because she thought the sea air would do him good. This marked the beginning of Johnnie's love of the south coast which culminated six years later in the controversial purchase of three houses in nearby Bognor Regis. In May he returned to Althorp and an emotional reception from the staff. Housekeeper Betty Andrews remembers: 'When he came home after his illness we all stood in the hall to greet him. His Lordship came up to us all and asked after our families. He knew all our names. Just his speech was a little slurred. He even kissed some of us which he'd never done before and was just as kind as he'd always been.' He gave several of the staff small enamel boxes inscribed with 'Be Happy' and dated 5 May, the date of his homecoming.

In the middle of May 1979 Raine and Johnnie celebrated his recovery with a thanksgiving service at All Saints Church in Northampton for about a hundred invited guests including friends, neighbours and all those who had been involved in his recovery. Dr Mervyn Stockwood took the service in the packed church and a lesson was read by the actor Sir John Mills. Norman St John-Stevas made a speech and was generously thanked by Raine with a present of an etching of Queen Victoria at her Jubilee in 1887 to add to his collection of her portraits.

Two special tunes were played – 'All Things Bright And Beautiful', which Raine promised the nursing staff they would sing if Johnnie recovered, and Widor's Toccata, the music that Raine had heard in the church when praying for his life. Johnnie said later, 'You can imagine what that music means to me and my wife.'

When the service was over, the congregation burst into spontaneous applause which brought tears to Johnnie's eyes as, leaning heavily on Raine's arm, he walked slowly up the aisle. The crowd of well-wishers that had gathered outside the church also clapped so furiously that Johnnie was initially quite overwhelmed. However, his natural ease with people helped to calm him. Walking slowly and deliberately he went up to several individuals in the crowd. Richard Hayward, director and secretary of the Schoolmistresses' and Governesses' Benevolent Institution, remembers the occasion well. 'He looked very drawn but he walked up to several of our members who were waiting outside the church to see him, smiled, said "Hello" and even remembered everyone's names.'

The service was followed by lunch at Althorp which was held in the State Dining Room and library. Johnnie told everyone, 'There is no doubt in my mind that my wife saved my life. She willed me to live and even now she watches over me, urges me to take care and not to overdo it.'

Once back at Althorp Johnnie's progress to health continued to be slow but steady and Raine took great care to see that he did not overtire himself physically. Rupert Hambro believes that his recovery was in part due to his strong sexual attraction to Raine. 'I think that sex was the winning combination that got him back on the road to recovery. She was able to give him physical enjoyment which got him mentally up and going.' He tired easily, however, and as he had never been one for a hectic life, did not find it difficult to take life gently. A friend says, 'Johnnie didn't continue his previous activities, or take part in country life any more but concentrated on the house.'

He did not, however, notify the various charitable organisations that he would be giving up his involvement with them. Rupert Hambro remembers the problems it caused for the National Association of Boys' Clubs. 'When Johnnie was ill we had a very difficult hiatus period for a year and a half when we didn't have a chairman. No-one replied to our letters asking what was going to happen. Johnnie was obviously ill, but we didn't know how ill and we couldn't get any form of answer. I don't think he wanted to retire, but it wasn't possible for him to carry on in the light of his illness. He became deputy president which was just a figurehead title.' Brigadier Davies-Scourfield even had difficulty speaking to Johnnie on the telephone. 'When I tried to ring him Raine would take the call and say he was far too busy to talk to me. I know she felt I was calling on his time too much.' Surprisingly, the one area of interest which Johnnie maintained, was the Schoolmistresses' and Governesses' Benevolent Institution. Clive de Paula, who was honorary treasurer when Johnnie was chairman, remembers that he started attending meetings again as soon as he was able. 'Although after his stroke he was slower, his way of working was the same. It was remarkable that his mind was still as straight-thinking as it had been before.' The Hon. Lady Goodhart, current president of the SGBI, bears this out. 'He looked very fragile, old and doddery but he wasn't. He used to go round talking to all the old ladies with great charm and remembered all their names.'

One of his favourite old ladies in the SGBI residential home was 84-year-old Grace Randall, an invalid. He never failed to seek her out after meetings or the lunch parties he attended to mark a resident's 100th birthday. 'I knew him for twelve years,' says Miss Randall. 'He would bring up a chair and sit beside me and talk. He never ceased to tell me that Raine saved his life and would always ask if I thought his speech was improving.' He made a point of telling Miss Randall when he or Raine were going to appear on television, which he would invariably talk about when they next met. 'He always said he thought Raine had looked so beautiful and her hair was so lovely.'

The stroke was to affect Raine and Johnnie in very different ways, but it did not improve relations between Johnnie's children and their stepmother. Many felt that the fact that she had saved his life and her undoubted loyalty and devotion to him should have counted for more than her insensitivity towards them.

The stroke made Johnnie, in common with many who have been very close to death, adopt a more positive attitude to life. 'I now always look for the lighter side of life,' he said, 'find something that makes me laugh. There is quite a lot, you know.' It made him feel indebted to Raine for saving his life. Others also believe it clouded his judgment over the selling of family treasures.

It made Raine feel vulnerable about her future tenure at Althorp and even more protective towards Johnnie: a protection she was to maintain for the rest of his life.

13

The Wedding and Holidays by the Sea

If Johnnie's haemorrhage was the nadir of his life, the marriage of his third daughter Diana to the Prince of Wales was its highest peak. The royal marriage made Johnnie a household figure and the public took him to their hearts. Even the media loved him for keeping them constantly supplied with reminiscences about his daughter and making no attempt to hide his true feelings.

The touch-paper to the romance between Diana and the Prince of Wales was lit by Diana's sister Jane, although they had previously met when Sarah invited the Prince of Wales to a shooting party at Althorp in November 1977. Happily married to Robert Fellowes on the Queen's personal staff, Jane took advantage of one of the perks of his job and invited Diana to a royal shoot at Sandringham. The following year, in July 1979, Diana went to Balmoral to help Jane with her new baby and, once more, caught the eye of the Royal Family. In July 1980 she went back again, this time as a guest of the Queen. It was during this visit that Charles, acutely aware of the pressures on him to produce an heir, seemed to see her with new eyes and realise that the young, rather gawky adolescent was developing into a swan. Their romance began to blossom.

Nineteen-year-old Diana fell head over heels in love with Charles. He seemed to fulfil all her romantic ideals – a wise and worldly prince with a protective and gentle manner. He sent her innumerable bouquets of flowers and spend hours talking to her on the telephone. Romantic gestures apart, however, it was clear from the start that the Prince did not intend to change his life style to take account of his young love. Diana could hardly bear to be apart from him, but he insisted on going off on his planned skiing holiday to Klosters in Switzerland early in 1981. When he returned on 3 February, he then spent a couple of nights on HMS *Invincible*, the Royal Navy's latest aircraft carrier, before arriving at Windsor where he had arranged to meet Diana. She was thrilled to see him again and delighted with the romantic candlelit dinner he had organised. After the meal he formally proposed. Diana accepted without hesitation. After telephoning the Queen, Charles rang Diana's father. 'Can I marry your daughter?' he asked Earl Spencer. 'I have asked her and very surprisingly she said yes.' Johnnie replied 'Well done' and told him he was delighted for the two of them.

When recounting the telephone call, Johnnie joked mischievously that he had wondered 'what he would have said if I'd said "No". He spoke more seriously to Diana. 'When she told me she wanted to marry Prince Charles, I told her she must marry the man she loves.' Diana replied, "That is what I am doing." ' Her father assured the world: 'She loves him all right. There is no doubt about it.'

In spite of these noble words, several people close to Johnnie were only too aware of ripples beneath the surface of the royal romance. It was an open secret that Johnnie had set his hopes on Diana marrying Prince Andrew, the Queen's second son. When the ultimate prize of Prince Charles came within her reach, he was thrilled with the even greater prestige that such a match would bring to the Spencer family. The romantic plot was hatched, however, when the Queen Mother confided in her friend Ruth, Lady Fermoy, that the family was worried that Charles was over thirty and still unmarried and it was getting difficult to find a suitable bride for him. Lady Fermoy, perhaps with her daughter Frances's impulsive behaviour in running off with a commoner in mind, seized the chance of restoring the family's good name. She confided the Queen Mother's fears to Jane and the pair of them agreed that Diana, without a romantic blemish in her past, was in with more than a starting chance. They decided to place her within Charles's reach. Diana, too young to realise how she was being manipulated, became a willing sacrificial lamb both for the self-aggrandisement of the Spencer family and to provide an heir for Charles. 'It was all set up,' said a close relative. 'The poor girl didn't stand a chance.'

As a naïve nineteen-year-old, Diana received very little counselling in preparation for what she was letting herself in for. Nor was any consideration given to the fact that a girl deprived of her mother at an early age would have powerful emotional needs. Their failed relationship has become a cautionary tale to parents who aim for wealth and status above all else for their children.

The official engagement was announced on 24 February 1981. The following day huge crowds gathered outside Buckingham Palace, while Diana and Charles posed for photographs inside. The thronging reporters were surprised and delighted to find Earl Spencer wearing a red carnation in the buttonhole of his navy-blue suit, quite happily on the wrong side of the palace railings. With him was Raine and her twelve year-old son

Henry. 'We've come to photograph the photographers and get our own back,' he said. 'I have taken pictures of every event in Diana's life and I'm certainly going to snap this one.' He added later: 'I took them outside Buckingham Palace just as if it were a school's sports day.'

Crowds of well-wishers rushed up to congratulate him. 'I'm so excited about all this, I could burst,' he beamed to everyone's delight. He described Diana as 'a marvellous girl' and Charles as 'a very lucky boy', adding, 'When I told Charles the same thing he replied "I know."' His joy was only matched by Raine's megawatt beam. She made sure she stood out from the crowd by wearing a white mink coat and said they had known of the engagement for a week and that it had been a very hard secret to keep. 'We've been bursting to tell people,' she said. 'I just feel on top of the world.'

The event could not have happened to a more ambitious stepmother. A close relation said, 'I am sure she saw the engagement as an entrée to Buckingham Palace and the social scene she loves.' Despite the fact that Raine's relationship with Diana was cool at the best of times she declared that her and Johnnie's role in recent months, when Lady Diana's every movement had been the object of intense press speculation, was to be available if they were needed. 'We tried to provide a refuge from all the personal problems. She had to think over a very momentous decision.' Publicly she expressed her confidence that her stepdaughter could cope with the demands that would be made on her. 'She's got a marvellous, even temperament. She's not at all the sort of person to get highly strung or depressed. Everybody loves her,' she said. Privately, however, she showed considerable foresight, confiding in a close friend that she wondered how long it would take before Charles got bored with Diana and what would happen then. 'She didn't think it would take long,' according to the friend.

Johnnie's reservations about the match took a while to surface.

At the time of the engagement, he simply said how impressed he was with the mature way in which his daughter was handling the situation, a view which the Queen shared. 'Up to now she's been under tremendous pressure. But she will have a little protection from now on. It is a relief now and I am thankful for Diana ... She has come through it with flying colours.' He added, 'She never breaks down because Diana does not break down at all. She has great courage and resilience.' He had no doubt that she could cope with her new responsibility and would become a 'fairy-tale princess'.

After using up several more rolls of film, and dispensing beams and handshakes all round, Johnnie, Raine and Henry were whisked away in their bronze Rolls-Royce. Father and stepmother returned to Buckingham Palace later that evening for a private ninety-minute celebration with the happy couple which neither the Queen nor Prince Philip attended.

The following day, still flushed with happiness, Johnnie went to see his son Charles, then sixteen, playing the part of an Arab prince in Molière's *Le Bourgeois Gentilhomme* at Eton. During the play Charles had to ask for the hand of his love in marriage. The scripted reply was: 'She won't have you, she's set on marrying a title.' Not surprisingly, it brought the house down.

Johnnie's mood fluctuated in the months before his daughter's wedding. At times he tried to play down the consequences for himself and his family of Diana's prestigious marriage. 'Honestly, what do I get out of it? You'll say the glory, but is glory the word? My family go back to the Saxons, so that sort of thing's not a bit new to me. I'm happy for my girl because she's got the man she adores. For myself, in my heart, I wish she weren't marrying the Prince of Wales. I shall see so much less of her. She won't have the time to come here. Sometimes I feel very worried, as if I'll never see her again. Later, yes, but not for the first few years when I'll be watching her like everyone else on telly. There are times I wish she was marrying an ordinary chap so I could have her and my son-in-law living here with me in the park.'

On other occasions he seemed to revel in Diana's exalted position and his own small but significant part as her father. 'I always believed that whatever happened to her she would be all right. She was always a strong and sensible girl ... Prince Charles is very lucky to have found a girl of the right calibre ... There were very few girls who could have handled the job better than she has. There have been times when I think it might have been a little hard on her, but I know she has the qualities to handle it ... She comes from a good family and has certain qualities that come with the background, she has a natural dignity, she knows how to behave, how to treat people. She can see different points of view. The qualities are just there. It's heredity.'

In the aftermath of the wedding announcement much was made of the fact that the Spencers and the Queen were both descendants of Henry VII and James I and, depending upon which common ancestor the geneology was based, Charles and Diana were either sixteenth cousins once removed, eleventh cousins once removed or seventh cousins once removed via William Cavendish, the 3rd Duke of Devonshire. It was pointed out that they were also related through Charles II and his brother James II; Charles II had several illegitimate children and James II had one illegitimate daughter.

There was naturally a great clamouring for Johnnie to provide photographs of Diana as a young girl. He initially took a protective and moral stand, declaring that the Palace had his five green leather albums with Diana's name engraved in gold that contained most of his collection.

Those which he has kept back were for his eyes only. 'People have been battering down the doors dangling huge sums of cash,' he admitted. 'I never even thought of taking money for them, how could I? Some of these snaps no one is ever going to see. They're mine.' It was not a view he sustained for long. Soon after the marriage Johnnie was accused of trying to sell to newspapers for dowry-sized sums a snapshot of Lady Diana, aged six, in a bikini.

Ten years later, when the Spencers' finances were fully stretched, Johnnie sold several intimate photographs of Diana as a child – some have suggested for as much as £1 million – which appeared in Andrew Morton's biography *Diana: Her True Story*, published in 1992 soon after his death. This was a sober indication of how far his own judgment had declined in his latter years and greed had taken over.

The wedding of Prince Charles, 33, and Lady Diana Spencer, 20, which took place on Wednesday 29 July, 1981, in St Paul's Cathedral, was watched on television by an estimated 700 million people all over the world. The event turned Johnnie into a national hero, and secured for himself a permanent place in the nation's heart, as, weak and unsteady on his feet, he courageously climbed the steps of St Paul's before leading Lady Diana down the aisle of the cathedral. Much discussion had gone on as to whether Johnnie could manage such a long slow walk unaided, particularly on such a nerve-racking occasion and under the glare of the world's spotlight, but he was determined not to let either himself or Diana down.

The build-up of pressure as the wedding day approached made both Raine and Johnnie short-tempered. Just before the great day, local professional photographer Paul Martin turned up at Althorp hoping to take a photograph of the Earl and Countess. 'Lady Spencer informed me that cameras were banned. She was very aggressive, told me I was on private property and that she was going to call the police. I had to leave all my equipment with piles of other cameras and when I went back for it later, I found Lord Spencer had taken the film out.'

The wedding day, an occasion of unbridled romance, colour and celebration, started early. As Johnnie left his flat in Grosvenor Square to make his way to Clarence House to escort Diana to the cathedral in the royal Glass Coach, built when his grandfather, the sixth Earl, was Lord Chamberlain, he read out a touching statement: 'The Spencers have through the centuries fought for their King and country. Today Diana is vowing to help her country for the rest of her life. She will be following in the tradition of her ancestors and she will have at her side the man she loves.'

He arrived at Clarence House in good time for their 10.35 a.m. departure. Diana was dressed in an over-fussy crinoline dress of ivory silk taffeta with a 25-foot-train that creased during the short journey to St Paul's. On her head she wore the Spencer family diamond tiara held in place by a tulle veil. As the coach made its way first into Stable Yard Road and then out into the Mall, Johnnie was overwhelmed by the cheers of the crowd, many of whom had spent the night in the street to secure their positions. In the midst of his happiness at this outpouring of love for his daughter he remembered a promise to Timothy Clifford, now director of the National Galleries of Scotland. 'I told him I would be standing on a veranda overlooking the Mall and asked him to remember to wave,' says Clifford. 'To my astonishment he did. When he went by in his coach he waved like mad at me.'

On reaching St Paul's, the door of the coach was opened by a footman clad in the scarlet-and-gold state livery. Johnnie descended first, helped by his chauffeur, John Harmon, dressed in morning coat. Diana came next and waited while two of her five bridesmaids – Lady Sarah Armstrong-Jones, seventeen-year-old daughter of Princess Margaret and Lord Snowdon, and thirteen-year-old India Hicks, granddaughter of Lord Mountbatten – arranged her long train. She was carrying a bouquet of stephanotis, white orchids, lilies-of-the-valley, a sprig of myrtle from a bush planted from a spray in Queen Victoria's wedding bouquet, and gold roses in memory of Lord Mountbatten. When all was ready, father and daughter began to slowly climb to the cathedral door. Johnnie faltered briefly on one of the steps and commentators and spectators the world over held their breath. But he quickly recovered.

It took them three and a half minutes to walk down the 625-foot aisle of the great cathedral to the triumphant strains of Jeremiah Clarke's 'Trumpet Voluntary'. Leaning heavily on Diana's arm, Johnnie walked slowly and deliberately, making no attempt to hide his intense concentration. The world watched and waited, but his step did not waver. It was one of the ceremony's most moving moments.

A close relative says: 'No one can really know the sheer effort it took him on that wedding day. All the family willed him up those steps. He was so determined not to be taken up in a wheelchair even if he snuffed it at the end of the day.'

Raine had been desperately nervous on Johnnie's behalf. She had wanted to sit as close to him as possible, to give him moral, if not physical, support. She was not placed with the principal members of the family, however, but further back in the main seating area of St Paul's. It was Frances Shand Kydd, as Diana's mother, who was accorded all the red-carpet treatment. She was placed near the high altar with her other children and afterwards travelled from St Paul's to Buckingham Palace with the Duke of Edinburgh, while Johnnie returned with the Queen. Johnnie was as unforgiving as ever of Frances, and found her proximity difficult to bear. Raine's mother was not among the 2,500 wedding guests. Dame Barbara had turned down her invitation to the wedding, she said, in order to let 'young' people attend.

Johnnie later said of the occasion: 'If I was nervous, Raine was shaking worse than I was, especially since she couldn't be anywhere near me when I might have tripped on all those cathedral steps.' Reliving the moment in an interview with *Woman's Own* in 1988 he gave Diana full credit for his triumph:

I knew Diana would get me through, she's such a very strong character. She was so determined that she wanted me to do it, she was quite insistent. Most fathers support their daughters on their wedding day – certainly I did when my other two girls got married – but it was Diana who supported me. I knew that she believed that I could do it. She believed in me and that gave me the strength to get through it all. She's a quite remarkable girl in that way. It's funny because everyone remembers me taking her up the aisle, when it really wasn't that way at all, it was the other way round ... It was a long walk and a slow walk and I found the slow walk more difficult to do than a long walk. My daughter was very good to me.

After both the state and royal registers were signed, the bride and groom finally emerged from the West Door at 12.10 p.m. as a peal of twelve bells from the north-west tower of St Paul's was answered by church bells in the City. Johnnie, with other members of the Royal Family, stood for a while on the cathedral steps while photographs were taken. The Queen, well aware that he was tiring, then allowed him to precede her into the carriage before the procession returned to Buckingham Palace through the joyful crowds.

At the Palace over a hundred guests sat down to a three-course wedding feast of brill in lobster sauce, suprême de volaille Princess de Galles and strawberries and cream. The royal couple later cut the giant five-foot-tall, five-tiered, 255-lb official wedding cake with Charles's ceremonial sword.

In his wedding address, the Archbishop of Canterbury, Dr Robert Runcie, began with the words 'Here is the stuff of which fairy tales are made ...' This fairy tale, however, was one that turned sour very quickly. Diana lost a vast amount of weight in the run-up to her marriage, partly through coping with the strain of constant publicity, partly because she wanted to look glamorous and attractive to Charles. This was the beginning of bulimia nervosa, the addictive eating disorder, characterised by eating binges followed by induced vomiting that some medical experts believe has roots in family trauma, from which she was to suffer for several years.

Once married, she soon realised that it would take more than a svelte figure to sustain Charles's interest in her; equally, that married life was nothing like the Barbara Cartland novels she had enjoyed reading at school. There was a gulf between her and Charles, not just in age, but also in interests and friends. Nor did he seem able or willing to give her the emotional support she craved. It did not help matters when, like her mother before her, Diana became pregnant almost immediately. She suffered badly from morning sickness and felt wretched most of the time. This heightened her feelings of vulnerability and loneliness as she tried to adjust to the golden cage of royal life. At twenty she had to cope not only with her every word and move being watched by the media worldwide, but also with the unfamiliar restrictions on her freedom and the tight web of royal protocol that now surrounded her. There was one weekend during those first few difficult months of pregnancy when she felt that she just could not cope with the pressure she was under. She did not know where to turn, and finally decided to escape to Althorp for a couple of days in the hope of finding some peace.

She arrived ashen-faced, as thin as a rake and looking and feeling terrible. She spent most of her time sitting alone in what had been the day nursery which had already been redecorated by Raine in blue and white. Ironically, two white helium balloons from her wedding still floated from the ceiling. She had to be persuaded to come down for meals and when she did, she talked only to her father. She never once addressed Raine. 'It was terribly embarrassing,' says a friend who was also there. Diana stayed out of sight of the hordes of extra visitors who, in the aftermath of the wedding, poured into Althorp.

Johnnie thoroughly enjoyed his new celebrity status, as indeed did Raine, and they made every effort to be seen and dispense smiles to the visitors. 'After the wedding people do know the name more and my face,' he admitted, although he felt Althorp's own magic encouraged guests to come back. 'People come to Althorp once perhaps because I'm Diana's dad, but it doesn't explain why we get so many people coming back again and again.'

The additional publicity also encouraged cranks. Despite regular security checks by the Special Branch (in the event of visits by Diana, her husband and sons) an intruder, 21-year-old John Cashmore, who was said to have an obsession with Raine, was twice found in the private apartments at Althorp.

Raine's mental cash register worked overtime at the unexpected bonus of Althorp's increased popularity which inspired her to think up many imaginative money-making schemes such as musical evenings and corporate entertaining. This led to much talk of the Spencers' taking advantage of Diana's fame and position, which Raine hotly denied.

Raine and her mother had already conceived the idea of inviting parties of Americans over to England for what was billed as the 'Barbara Cartland Romantic Tour of England'. The cost of the trip was $1399 – air fare not included – and part of the tour was lunch with Earl and Countess Spencer at Althorp, followed by tea with Dame Barbara at her home in Camfield Place in Hatfield, Hertfordshire. The timing of the event so soon after Diana's engagement brought maximum criticism. Raine expressed concern that these attacks would put extra strain on Johnnie. 'All this cashing-in talk has upset him so much and it's lies, monstrous lies ... All this business of Mummy and I charging Americans millions to tour Charles and Diana's honeymoon route is so ridiculous. The trips were arranged two years before Charles even thought about marrying Diana.'

She was also criticised for selling cheap lookalike Diana engagement rings in the gift shop. This she again denied. 'Imagine selling plastic Charles and Di pendants on our jewellery counter – eeeuck,' she retorted. 'I was worried enough that one of the rings we've had for eighteen months looked a bit like The Ring. Thank God we'd run out of sapphires and only had emerald ones left.' Some years later, after the engagement of Sarah Ferguson to Prince Andrew, a remarkably similar ring to the one worn by Sarah also appeared in the gift shop, price £9.

Despite his earlier insistence on not cashing in on the royal connection, Johnnie was accused of asking a king's ransom for Diana's first school report and charging photographers huge sums to take a single picture at Althorp. He, too, denied the charge. 'I think it's terrible – I'd never make a penny out of my daughter's wedding. I've tried to behave like a gentleman and keep quiet, I'm not angry or bitter because I'm even-tempered, just like Diana, and not a bitter person. But I'm disappointed at the people who've tried to knock us and put my family down.'

The controversy even prompted Diana's mother to speak out. 'I'd never think of making a penny out of my daughter's wedding,' said Mrs Shand Kydd. 'I think it's terrible. I feel very strongly that it's not a time for any members of our family to consider making money out of the wedding. I have been asked to sell pictures of Lady Diana. But the answer is a very firm "No." Large sums have been mentioned, but the whole thing is totally alien to me.'

Six months after the wedding, on 15 January 1982, a pregnant Princess drove to Althorp with the Prince of Wales for a party given by Earl Spencer for two hundred tenants, farmers estate workers and their wives, most of whom had not been able to attend the wedding.

On 22 June 1982, after eleven months of marriage, Diana gave birth to her first child, a son, Prince William Arthur Philip Louis who became next in line to the throne after his father, the Prince of Wales.

The mellowing process that had begun in Johnnie with the birth of his own children and grew when he married Raine now continued with his grandchildren. They gave him an outlet for the part of himself that had always remained a child and he was able to build a loving and demonstrative relationship with them that he had never had with his own father. It was the role that seemed to suit his temperament best and he quickly became the country's favourite grandfather.

Prince Charles had rung the Earl shortly after William's birth and Johnnie described the new father as 'absolutely over the moon'. Johnnie also spoke to the Queen who was, he said, 'delighted'. He then amused waiting reporters by telling them he was going to celebrate by having a beer. He seemed a godsend compared to the uptight Royal Family who never showed their feelings in public. He and Raine got up at dawn to drive from Althorp to their flat in Grosvenor Square, to be on call to visit the Lindo Wing of St Mary's Hospital, Paddington, where the baby was born. After Johnnie had visited the baby prince, unsurprisingly, he pronounced him 'the most beautiful baby I've ever seen.' Once again he could not hide his pride in his daughter and his delight in his new grandson. 'Diana is absolutely marvellous,' he said. 'The baby is very lucky to have a mother like her. As long as the birth went all right I did not mind what the baby was ... even twins or triplets.'

Johnnie was a doting grandfather and as the little prince grew he developed a very close relationship with him. 'I do love him very much,' he said. 'He's such an open, affectionate child. The fact that he sees so much of his mother and father and they refuse to be separated from him, unless it is really necessary, is quite different from what even Prince Charles experienced.'

Johnnie talked about William at every opportunity, to anyone who would listen, and publicly supported his daughter's determination not to leave nine-month-old William behind when she and Charles went on an official tour to Australia. 'I knew that William would go to Australia and think it was quite right that he did. His mother and father would have been miserable without him.'

He was equally thrilled when William's brother Prince Harry was born two years later, on 15 September 1984. As soon as Johnnie heard the news, he ordered the Union Jack to be lowered from the roof of Althorp House and the Spencer personal standard in red, yellow and black run up in its place. Then he and Raine stepped excitedly, arm in arm, out through the front door of Althorp, to announce proudly that Diana had given birth to another boy. By that time almost all the visitors to the stately home had left the grounds, but reporters and television cameramen were waiting at the main entrance. Even before he reached the end of the long gravel drive, Earl Spencer was saying excitedly, 'We have had a boy ... Diana has had her second boy. She is very well and so is the baby.' Then, with Raine still clutching his arm, he said emotionally: 'I'm so pleased, particularly for Prince William. He will be thrilled. It will be lovely for him to have a companion, a playmate, and someone to fight with. It's lovely to have two boys. I hope one day he will play cricket for Gloucestershire. I hope he will one day become another Tom Graveney.'

He had heard the 'wonderful news', he revealed, direct from Prince Charles who had said that Diana was very well. 'He is a lucky little boy because he has such wonderful parents. He will have a very good start in life.' Then, with a sigh, he added, 'It's such a relief everything went off well, without complication.' The Spencers' mood towards the photographers mellowed on hearing the good news. 'After Harry was born,' remembers Paul Martin, 'they posed in front of the house and then invited all the photographers into their private drawing room for a glass of sherry.' This occasion apart, Martin never quite knew how the Spencers would react to him. 'Lady Spencer sometimes made you welcome and was sometimes very difficult.'

Johnnie and Raine visited Prince Harry when he was four days old, in Kensington Palace. They stayed just over an hour and emerged smiling broadly to declare: 'He's a lovely baby.' When little Harry was two months old, his parents brought him to Althorp for the weekend. As was their custom when they went to Althorp, Diana and Charles occupied the Prince of Wales Room. The babies helped create a short truce in the bad feeling between Diana and Raine, but this was only temporary.

With Johnnie's other daughters also producing offspring, the grand-children were coming thick and fast. In 1980 Lady Jane Fellowes gave birth to her first daughter, Laura, who was followed by a son, Alexander, born in March 1983 and a daughter, Eleanor, in 1985.

In July 1983, Lady Sarah McCorquodale gave birth to a daughter, Emily Jane. 'She's a darling little girl – very sweet with reddish hair,' pronounced Johnnie. 'It's another proud day for me.' It was a great relief for Sarah as there is always the danger that those who have suffered anorexia nervosa may not be able to conceive. Emily was followed by a son, George, in November 1984 and a daughter, Celia, in 1989.

Johnnie's grandchildren completed the mellowing process and he now viewed life without any bitterness. 'I would like twenty before I die,' he readily admitted. He lived to celebrate the arrival of another grandchild in December 1990, when Charles and his wife Victoria had their first daughter, Kitty. The news that Victoria was expecting twins was broken to him in the Humana Hospital Wellington, shortly before he died in April 1992.

One weekend in the summer of 1982, when Raine and Johnnie were staying at their flat in Brighton, Johnnie mentioned that he would like a 'proper' seaside home. Raine was delighted. She liked nothing better than a new project and particularly one that appealed to Johnnie. Why didn't they drive along the coast in the Rolls that very day and look around, she suggested. They eventually arrived at Bognor Regis where they stopped at the exclusive Aldwick Bay estate, a development to the west of the town that had been partly built before the Second World War as second homes for wealthy Londoners. It had not, however, become the Sussex Riviera that the developers had hoped, but there were some grand properties around, mainly owned by the *nouveaux riches*.

Raine and Johnnie went into a nearby estate agent's and explained that they were looking for a property. The estate agent suggested that she might have just the right house and offered to take them along to see it. They drove the short distance to Trade Winds, a large detached house right on the edge of a curving bay, on sale for about £125,000. The five-bedroomed, three-bathroomed house had been built in the early sixties by a retired glove manufacturer who had a passion for Spain. The house was built in a Spanish style, and has its own private beach, dotted with small bushes of kale, in the middle of a nature conservation area.

Raine and particularly Johnnie liked it immediately. A survey revealed problems with the roof and there was a great deal of negotiating over price before contracts were finally signed. The locals were delighted that Raine and Johnnie were acquiring a house in the area. The resort had tried in vain to attract royalty ever since George V came there to recuperate after an illness and, on his death-bed, uttered the immortal words, 'Bugger Bognor.'

Many believed a new chapter in Bognor's uneventful history might open with the appearance of the father and stepmother of the new Princess of Wales. The purchase of Trade Winds and subsequently Hacienda next door, and a third house, Water's Edge, on the adjacent estate began as a whim of Johnnie's, who had never had much idea about money, and developed into a grandiose and extravagant project. The purchase coincided with the first publicly-voiced complaints by the Spencers of the costliness of running Althorp, which would culminate in the controversial sale of art treasures.

As with the future restoration of Althorp, the redecoration of the houses at Bognor quickly got out of hand. Finding money to buy the properties was in itself a problem and in order to help do so Raine sold their Brighton flat. She contacted various friends, luckily found a buyer in businessman Peter Avia and the deal was completed without any publicity.

Once Trade Winds was bought, Raine enthusiastically embarked on extensive alterations. She employed an architect and asked her friend David Laws, of the interior design company Colefax & Fowler, to help redesign the property. All the rooms were fairly small, which wasn't to her liking. She wanted a large bedroom, dressing room and bathroom for herself, a bedroom and bathroom for Johnnie, a visitors' bedroom and bathroom and service quarters. It was only when work was in progress and the house was gutted, that she decided it would not be big enough for her needs.

This was why – for £65,000 – the Spencers bought Hacienda, the house next door, as an annex to Trade Winds and massive alterations began in earnest. The roof was replaced, doors taken out, new bathrooms and partitions put in and a sunroom built. 'Once she started, she couldn't stop,' says someone closely involved. About half-way through the alterations even Raine took fright at the amount of money that was being spent. She and David Laws fell out over escalating costs and she asked a local property dealer, Graham Burrows, to take over the redecorations.

Coincidentally Burrows's father had built Trade Winds and he himself had at one time lived in Hacienda. 'She obviously loved doing the houses up, but His Lordship was much more enthusiastic about living here than she was,' Burrows says. 'He made it clear, at the time, that he was looking forward to Charles and Diana bringing his newly-born grandson Prince William to the house for annual summer holidays.'

Raine made most of the decorative decisions. 'Sometimes,' says Burrows, 'she would ask Johnnie if he had an opinion of his own but he would reply "whatever you like, dear", promptly go off to another part of the house and leave her to it. He did keep telling me, "All I want is a bit of peace." '

Johnnie saw Trade Winds as a retreat and a bolthole from the visiting hordes at Althorp and a happy holiday home for his grandchildren. However, just as he failed to consult his children over the restoration of the family home and the sale of its treasures, nor did he check whether his daughters would actually want to spend their summers on the south coast. In fact they rarely came to Bognor. Some reports at the time maintained that Johnnie wanted to leave one of the houses to each of his daughters; others that they were to be a retirement home for Raine.

Anyone who knows Raine well realises that it would not suit the kind of person she is to be tucked away out of the limelight in Bognor; and that she is essentially a town person who has no wish to feel the seawind on her face.

Johnnie, however, loved looking out across the deep bay to the sea and watching the surfers and water-skiers pass by his window. And most of all he loved the garden. He called in a local landscape gardener, lavished money on getting it the way he wanted and filled it with beautiful statuary brought down from Althorp. He enthusiastically helped lay out a vegetable garden and was thrilled when he was able to take some of the produce back to Althorp for the cook.

179

The decor of Trade Winds was elaborate. The dining room had pink regency-stripe wallpaper. Raine and Johnnie had adjoining bedrooms with a door between the two. Raine's, with a double bed, was decorated in peach with pale green silk wallpaper, and the bathroom in matching colours. Johnnie's, with a single bed, was bright red and green. Those rooms that were not wallpapered were drag-painted, stippled and rolled, which in the early eighties was quite unusual. The house's swimming pool was restored and Johnnie insisted on putting a sandpit in the garden for the grandchildren. Raine ordered some purpose-built furniture, and filled the rest of the house with antiques from Althorp. Burrows noticed: 'Some of the furniture was heavily restored, they had some beautiful pieces that had been tarted up to the hilt.' The house was also filled with antique glass and paintings. The outside which had previously been painted white was changed to terracotta. 'In fact,' says Burrows, 'the only thing she left untouched was the Bullfighter weathervane on top of Trade Winds.'

Burrows found Raine 'a woman of fantastic energy who got a bit heated on occasions'. He also found she could be tactless. 'She knew my father had built Hacienda and when we went round it I showed her my old bedroom. She told me how dreadful she thought it was and how she was going to pull it apart. Fortunately I'm not very sensitive, but she didn't even consider that I might be.'

The bill for the alterations and his fees came to about £200,000 which Raine paid 'after a couple of reminders'. It was not, however, quite the end of their relationship. To Burrows's surprise Raine kept telephoning him. 'She'd call to tell me that two light bulbs had gone and would I come down and change them. I went a couple of times, but in the end I told her I was not a maintenance man and refused. She wasn't very happy about that, but I didn't have any rows with her.'

When the builders left, a local resident, Tricia Hopkins, was employed to give the houses a thorough clean. She then began to look after both houses while they were unoccupied and in July 1986 was asked to act as housekeeper for a month. She moved into the service flat in Trade Winds and remained as housekeeper until the following April. During that period Raine and Johnnie would come down for a few days every five to six weeks. Tricia would receive a telephone call from Althorp to say they had left and a member of staff would always call again to check that they had arrived safely. Raine liked the staff to line up inside Trade Winds when she and Johnnie arrived and to line up outside the door and wave when they left.

The one time Johnnie came on his own, he declined any ceremony. 'The occasion was just before a visit to Althorp by Charles and Diana and the tension over the preparations was so intense that Johnnie felt he had to get away,' Tricia remembers. 'He telephoned and told me, "I have to escape. Can you cope with me on my own?"' She was delighted to oblige. 'He wasn't full of airs and graces like her,' she says. 'On his first morning he asked me to cook him a big breakfast. I made bacon, eggs, the lot, but found out afterwards he shouldn't have had any of it as he was on a strict diet. He was like a naughty boy.'

Sometimes the Spencers would bring staff with them from Althorp who stayed both at Hacienda and Water's Edge, a third house on the estate bought for about £50,000 and again considerably altered to meet Raine's requirements. Bognor was the place where the Spencers came to unwind and Raine often stayed in bed until 1.00 p.m. Staff whose work schedule started at 8.00 a.m. had to remove their shoes and, Tricia remembers, 'creep along the gravel path so that you didn't make any noise. Nobody dare turn on a tap until they knew she was up and I wasn't allowed to flush my loo before lunchtime.' Raine rarely slept that late however, more often than not she would be lying in bed making phone calls. Tricia found Raine 'extremely difficult and rude. She regularly sacked people, although to be fair, you could say that some of her behaviour was because she is such a perfectionist. The staff stayed because you couldn't help falling in love with His Lordship. He was a wonderful gentleman, well bred all the way through.'

All cleaning had to be done very discreetly. Raine didn't like the cleaning staff to make their presence obvious. 'She was a great one for going round with her finger,' says Tricia, 'and a very tidy person who liked everything in its place. The only thing I really disliked was her potty, which she kept in the cupboard by the side of her bed. She didn't want to go to the ensuite bathroom at night, although his Lordship didn't mind going to his.'

If a member of staff wanted to speak to Raine about anything, she didn't like them to approach her without advance notice. 'You had to send a little card on a tray requesting permission to speak to her.'

Raine rarely left the house. 'She didn't like going out into the garden and never went on to the beach,' says Tricia. The clothes she brought with her reflected her life style. According to Tricia: 'Some weekends she would bring twelve nightdresses and negligées in silk and antique lace and just a couple of outfits, usually from Hardy Amies, in case she went out.' Just as Raine liked to change her clothes several times a day at Althorp, so she would change her negligées. 'She would have her lunch negligée, her tea negligée, her evening negligée and so on,' says Tricia. As at Althorp, everything Raine wore had to be ironed immediately it was taken off, and she liked all her negligées to be washed by hand.

In contrast Johnnie would 'slop around in any old clothes and didn't bother to change for dinner'. He could also be absent-minded. On one occasion when he was going to nearby Chichester for a book-signing he turned up in the kitchen in the morning with his trousers over his pyjamas. Tricia politely suggested that he had better go and change.

Raine liked the house kept very warm, which was not good for the furniture. 'Beautiful antique furniture would be stuck in front of the radiator which damaged them so much that Partridge's, the company restoring Althorp, would come down and taken them away to be restored,' Tricia remembers. 'Even the oil paintings would start to flake. I was told to put blocks of Oasis (used for flower arrangements) in the drawers to keep the atmosphere moist, but Raine wouldn't allow it.'

Although Raine and Johnnie were at Trade Winds to get away from it all, meals were still formal occasions, even when there were just the two of them. The table would have to be laid in a specific manner with fine china and solid silver cutlery. At tea-time scones and sandwiches had to be cut up to bite-size pieces. Tricia remembers, 'There was a terrific amount of wasted food.' Despite the fact that they liked to do different things, there was never any question about their feelings for each other. 'There was a big marble bench in the front garden,' says Tricia, 'and in the evening, when there was nobody to look at them, they would sit there, Raine in her evening negligée, holding hands. It was obvious he absolutely adored her.'

After a few years it became clear that Johnnie's plans for idyllic family seaside holidays with himself and Raine occupying one house the little princes occupying the other for a few weeks every summer were never going to be realised. Diana and the Prince of Wales came down only once and, even if they had wanted to come more often, the house was so open that they were advised that staying there would be too much of a security risk. Jane and Sarah hardly ever came. Taking account of the depth of bad feeling between his daughters and Raine, Johnnie should not have been surprised at this. He felt sadly disillusioned, however. Water's Edge was sold first. Then, in 1989, Hacienda was let out on a semi-permanent basis at a rent of £2000 a week in high season. Even Trade Winds, which the Spencers kept for their own use, was rarely occupied.

14

To Sell or not to Sell

The most controversial aspect of Raine and Johnnie's life together has been the sale of the Spencer family chattels and what they did with the proceeds. The selling started as a way of paying estate duty on Jack Spencer's death in 1975, but continued well after this seemed to have been paid off. While Johnnie was still in hospital recovering from his own life-threatening haemorrhage in 1978, the lifeblood of Althorp itself began draining away: until his death fourteen years later, paintings, silver, furniture and other treasures flowed out of the house at an alarming rate. Raine and Johnnie's actions had a devastating effect on both Althorp and the Spencer family, provoking fierce criticism, causing outrage among art historians and conservationists and giving a whole new meaning to the family motto: 'God defend the right.'

Robin Simon, editor of the influential art magazine *Apollo*, has called what occurred at Althorp 'the worst scandal that has happened to a country house in the last century. No one has ever put their hands on a collection and dealt with it so ruthlessly.' Timothy Clifford, director of the National Galleries of Scotland, agrees. 'It is one of the great tragedies of the eighties.' Richard Herner, managing director of the art dealers Colnaghi from 1976 to 1986, who bought many paintings from the Spencer collection, believes that 'things were being sold unwisely and in secretive circumstances without outside advice, which was unusual in a collection of that distinction and historical importance.'

Althorp House is one of the stateliest stately homes of England. It is a Grade 1 listed building whose 600-acre park is included in the register of parks and gardens of special interest. The original E-shaped Elizabethan house with moat was built in 1508 by John Spencer. Since then it has been owned by sixteen generations of Spencers. Robert, 2nd Earl of Sunderland, employed an Italian architect to redesign the house and was responsible for the famous staircase built between 1653 and 1662. His wife, Lady Anne Digby, kept Althorp in immaculate condition. The diarist John Evelyn wrote: '[She is] a lady who without any show of solicitude keeps everything in such admirable order, both within and without, from the garret to the cellar, that I don't believe there is any in this nation or anything ever that exceed her in such exact order.' In 1669 the Grand Duke Cosmo described Althorp as 'the best-planned and best-arranged country seat in the kingdom'.

After Robert died in 1702, Althorp was not used by the family, except very occasionally as a hunting lodge, for about eighty years. Robert's grandson Charles, an enthusiastic hunter, had the entrance hall decorated by John Wootten, the father of British sporting artists; in 1733.

Overall, however, Althorp was so badly neglected during the eighteenth century that in 1772 part of the roof collapsed and George John, the 2nd Earl Spencer (1758–1834), wrote that the house was very nearly blown down in a high wind. He decided to take matters in hand. He chose as his architect Henry Holland, responsible for the Royal Pavilion in Brighton. Holland's transformations, starting on a modest scale, gradually extended until the entrance hall with its magnificent seventeenth-century oak staircase was almost the only room left untouched. He applied the white facings to the building, filled in the dry moat and added a servants' wing.

At the time Althorp had northern-facing staterooms on the first floor, but Holland made reception rooms on the ground floor facing west. The cost of the alterations, which took three years from 1787–1790, amounted to £20,257.

John, the fifth Earl (1835–1910), made several structural and decorative changes, including hanging cherry-coloured silk in the drawing rooms and covering a gilt Louis XVI settee in cream silk brocade which was originally the skirt of a dress worn by his wife Charlotte at a fancy-dress ball at Buckingham Palace in 1848.

It was Johnnie's father who almost totally rebuilt Althorp in the late 1950s and early 1960s, with particular emphasis on displaying works of art from Spencer House, the family's London home. An article in the *Antique Collector* of August 1949 declared 'Few of the great mansions of England can show a family collection of paintings and furniture as superb in quality and as scrupulously cared for as Althorp.'

Jack Spencer's work was generally acknowledged as being one of the major post-war restorations of a country house. In order to help with the task, he received six repair grants from the then Ministry of Public Building and Works under the Historic Buildings Act which was passed to help safeguard the nation's architectural masterpieces.

In 1957 he was allocated £5,000, in 1959 £15,000, and in 1960 £7,500 for removing dry rot and repairing the roofs. He not only reroofed the house, but also replaced rotten beams that supported floors eaten away by deathwatch beetle. He reinstated the seventeenth-century staterooms on the first floor – which had been divided into bedrooms in the late eighteenth century. He redecorated the interior using historic fabrics and installed two chimneypieces which had been taken out of Spencer House during the Second World War.

Jack Spencer looked after Althorp meticulously in the traditional eighteenth-century manner. When rooms were not in use the blinds were pulled down, the furniture covered and even the damask on the drawing-room walls protected by dust covers. He was so fussy about the care of his treasures that he often cleaned the famous Marlborough silver himself. To save money on re-upholstery, he learned how to do needlepoint and became one of the country's top experts. After a day's work he would sit in his dark green sitting room in the west wing doing petit point in eighteenth-century patterns. When any maintenance work was carried out, he could see at a glance if it was up to standard. One of Jack's handymen remembers: 'He didn't need a spirit level to see if something was straight. He could see it with his eye.' He also restored several outbuildings, including the Palladian gardener's cottage and the stable block which he planned to use as a museum for the family papers and architectural drawings that were then kept at Althorp. (The papers were subsequently sold by Raine and Johnnie and the stable block used for the gift and wine shops.) He replanted the park with oak trees, and catalogued the archives (with free assistance from the Historical Manuscripts Commission) and the pictures.

Land agent Richard Stanley, who took over running the Spencer estates at Althorp, Wormleighton and North Creake a year after Jack's death, comments: 'Although Jack Spencer was said to have been imperious, he was an excellent steward of both the estate and the contents of the house. Compared with most houses of its size, Althorp was in extremely good order.' Trustee Viscount Coke, whose father was a friend and neighbour of Jack's, confirms that this was the case, particularly by the standards prevailing in the early seventies. 'In those days very few estates were business-orientated or commercially-minded,' he says. 'That came later with the enormous rise in inflation from the mid-seventies onwards which made us much more on the ball.' He also declares: 'Jack Spencer was a man of very great taste and would never interfere with his possessions in the house or indeed the house itself unless it was really necessary, simply because he understood the background of the house and its history. He knew every picture intimately, when it was bought and how it should be treated and looked after.'

Johnnie inherited Althorp to do with as he wished. Those acting as trustees for the land that went to his son Charles had no jurisdiction over the house, its contents or the park.

It is, of course, a valid argument that people have the right to sell their own possessions, and for most people who inherit a few heirlooms from a fond relative that right would seem to be absolute. For Lord Spencer, however, a vital link in the Spencer family chain, the absolute right to sell cannot be quite so clear-cut.

Before considering what was sold, whether it was necessary to sell so much, how objects were sold, whether Raine and Johnnie got the best price, how the proceeds were spent and whether any other options would have been open to them, it is worth looking a little more closely at the background of the Spencer family and Raine's own attitude to possessions.

Raine and Johnnie were by no means the first Spencers to sell part of their collections. On 14, 15, and 16 June 1785, George, the second Earl Spencer, put up for auction at Christie's a vast range of what the catalogue described as 'rich and elegant' household furniture and 'valuable effects' from the Spencer villa at Wimbledon Park, Surrey. He had a thorough clear-out, disposing of a vast array of goods that included a billiard table, thirteen solid mahogany doors, pea-green silk damask, crimson and yellow mixed damask, printed cotton, pier glasses, an elegant marble chimneypiece, mahogany sideboards and bookcases, rich inlaid commodes, Axminster and Wilton carpets, fenders, Venetian window blinds, nine black leather chairs, a dumb waiter, a mahogany polished table 12 ft 6 in. × 6 ft 6 in., five harpsichords, a bass violin, a guitar and 'a large assortment of exceedingly good feather beds'.

There is no record of any paintings being included in that sale, but shortly afterwards several valuable Old Master drawings were sold. The Earl also sold, at Christie's, a sideboard table designed by the architect John Vardy which was bought at auction nearly two hundred years later by the Victoria and Albert Museum and eventually found its way back to Spencer House when it was leased by Lord Rothschild in 1987. By way of compensation George Spencer added considerably to the Althorp library. He searched for rare books all over Europe and collected early printed editions of the Greek and Roman classics. By the time he died in 1834 he had collected what was regarded as the finest private library in the world, consisting of about 40,000 books including 58 Caxtons, 800 Aldines, and a coloured block-print of St Christopher dated 1423, an early example of European printing. The collection was sold in 1892 by John, the fifth Earl, known as the 'Red Earl', for £250,000 to Mrs John Ryland wife of the philanthropist. It is now part of Manchester University library.

In 1915 the sixth Earl sold his *Portrait of a Boy* by Rembrandt for £35,000 and, four years later, in 1919 his famous collection of etchings.

Even Johnnie's father sold valuable and irreplaceable works of art. In January 1925 six English masterpieces were sold to a wealthy New Yorker for more than £300,000: two full-length portraits of Georgiana, Duchess of Devonshire, by Reynolds and Gainsborough, a portrait of Lavinia,

Lady Spencer, by Reynolds, a portrait of Frances, Marchioness Camden, by Reynolds, a portrait of a man by Frans Hals, and *Daedalus and Icarus* by Van Dyck. Jack Spencer spoke publicly of his regret at having to sell these paintings to meet heavy death-duty demands (the fifth Earl had died in August 1910 and the sixth Earl in September 1922). 'The fact of the deaths of the two previous earls occurring within a comparatively short period has compelled the sacrifice,' he said, adding: 'I do not touch a penny of whatever I receive for the pictures.'

In 1937 he sold Holbein's famous portrait of Henry VIII, one of Britain's most important heritage items, to the industrialist and art collector Baron von Thyssen. In 1962 he offered a large oil sketch by Rubens, *David Sacrificing Before the Ark*, valued at £100,000, to the National Galleries of Scotland in Edinburgh for £70,000 in the hope that it could stay in this country. It was said at the time to be 'the finest Rubens painting ever likely to come on the market from a British private collection', but due to a bureaucratic rule which stipulated that the Government could not make a grant to the same gallery two years in succession, it was finally purchased by a private American collector.

It was Jack Spencer's death in 1975 that opened the floodgates through which an untold number of Althorp treasures escaped. Johnnie maintained he was left with death duties of over £2 million. It was a reason for selling, but not the only one. Other reasons given by Raine and Johnnie were that Althorp was in poor repair and badly in need of restoration. Whilst many conservationists deny that the house was in poor repair, they accept that the costs of running a stately home are crippling, although some feel that the Spencers relied on this too heavily. One expert says, 'There are some ennobled families who are in a terrible financial state, where it's a question of selling things to save the house. People didn't get the impression that that was the case at Althorp.'

Experts, relations and friends have proffered several less worthy reasons for the sale of the Althorp treasures, on the one hand Johnnie's lack of interest in his inheritance and obligations to his wife and, on the other, Raine's insensitivity and lack of knowledge. Many feel that she had become accustomed to, and wished to maintain, a lavish life style.

Raine's urge to sell might, however, even have been part instinctive. Well before she married Johnnie, Raine enjoyed the cathartic experience of a good clear out. She has never been a hoarder and there are several recorded precedents of her ridding herself of unwanted possessions. But what was doubtless good for Raine's soul as well as her bank balance in her youth, caused devastation when she became the chatelaine of Althorp.

In 1958 when Raine was still Mrs Gerald Legge, she gave a newspaper interview in which she talked about selling more than a hundred pieces of Staffordshire china, and a gold and silver powder case which her mother had given to her as a present ten years previously. 'I hate hoarding things that I have no real use for,' she said. 'I asked Mummy about selling [the powder case] and she told me she didn't mind. I have another one which I use so I saw no point in hanging on to it.' In one of her later clearing outs, she got rid of her mother's wedding dress without checking. Her mother was apparently none too pleased.

In 1960 Raine took advantage of David Hicks's redecoration of her smart marital home in Chester Street 'to get rid of lots of bits and pieces I have collected over the years. I am a very tidy person and can't bear cupboards to be full of things we no longer use.' Larger items of furniture went to Sotheby's but, rather than send smaller bits and pieces to a jumble sale or donate them to charity, she set aside a downstairs room and busily sold ornaments from prices that ranged from 10s (50p) to £10. It was to be useful practice for her assiduous selling when she later opened the gift shop at Althorp.

In June 1961 she sold some pictures at Sotheby's. 'We were left a lot of family pictures by my husband's uncle, the late Lord Dartmouth,' she explained, 'and now the house is just about full from top to bottom. I am selling a dozen, including some Venetian scenes I am very fond of. I hate to see them go but naturally the family ones must have precedence. Selling non-family paintings first was a rule she and Johnnie followed at Althorp. While this sentimental approach may be perfectly sound when dealing with the possessions of a wealthy but ordinary family, it is far too simplistic when dealing with a five-hundred-year-old inheritance.

Much later, in 1988, Raine temporarily turned her attention to her own extensive wardrobe and put up for auction at Sotheby's twelve of her dresses, some more than fifteen years old. Her action caused raised eyebrows and murmurs of disapproval among her upper-class friends. The dresses included six evening gowns by Pierre Balmain, three by Norman Hartnell and gowns by Christian Dior and Hardy Amies, most of which were studded with beads and sequins. She claimed it was to make way for some new outfits. It could also have been a gesture of solidarity with Johnnie and a way of raising some pocket money.

'All the dresses have a history,' she said. 'I wore the appliquéd silk gown by Balmain to the Queen of Denmark's wedding in 1967. It's terribly sad to part with them, but I do sometimes like to buy new things so I must make some space.' She was an enthusiastic saleswoman. 'You don't see such beautiful beadwork any more and the dresses are in immaculate condition. I'm a Virgo, passionately neat and tidy.' All but two of the dresses were sold, at prices ranging from £132 to £600, raising a total of £3,388.

Once Raine and Johnnie decided to raise funds there were several other practical options open to them.

They could have chosen to sell one or two significant and highly valuable items. Although these would have been a loss to the family heritage, they would have brought in sufficient income to maintain Althorp for several years. Richard Vander, director of the silversmith company C. J. Vander, explains: 'The more enlightened owners of great country houses try to realise as much as is necessary to keep their house in good order in an enlightened and sophisticated way. By selling one good thing you can do the place up and keep going for twenty years.' Instead Raine and Johnnie sold piecemeal. They broke up sets of furniture, which slashed their value as individual pieces and reduced the amount they would have been worth intact. It was not good business sense and ran counter to the traditional principal of conservation.

Althorp could have been set up as a private charitable trust, like, for example, Chatsworth in Derbyshire and Burghley House in Lincolnshire, whereby the family pays rent to live in the house but the property is owned by trustees. If they had done this the Spencers might have lost full ownership of Althorp, but would have kept many of the priceless treasures that have now been dispersed around the world. There would also have been tax advantages in that, broadly speaking, a charity is exempt from income tax, capital gains tax and inheritance tax.

They could have held a large house sale, which would have created considerable publicity and no doubt raised plenty of cash. There have been several precedents for this, including Castle Howard, the Yorkshire seat of the Howard family and the setting for the television adaptation of *Brideshead Revisited*. Or they could have sold selected items through major auction houses where the Spencer provenance would have generated worldwide publicity and been a major asset to the sale. These last two options would, however, have made it impossible to keep prices confidential and it would seem that the Spencers chose to sacrifice price for privacy.

Many feel that the trigger for selling the bulk of treasures was Johnnie's illness. For four long, lonely and traumatic months Raine had kept vigil at her husband's bedside as he struggled to emerge from the shadows of death. She had nearly lost him so many times and although she was thankful for what had been the narrowest of escapes, the prognosis for their future together looked bleak. Even if she had been on the best of terms with Charles Althorp, which she was not, the law of primogeniture meant that, on Johnnie's death, Charles would take over not only the title but the family home of Althorp with all its treasures. (When Johnnie died in 1992 Raine left Althorp within twenty-four hours.) The implications for her own financial future were considerable.

An eminent art historian believes: 'Raine got a terrible shock when Johnnie was so ill. If he hadn't had a stroke it might have altered the course of Spencer history and what happened to the treasures.' Art dealer Richard Herner was aware of a heightened atmosphere of tension when he went to Althorp soon after Johnnie's recovery. 'There was an element of panic at the beginning,' he says.

Raine always defended Johnnie's right to sell. 'It's absolutely unrealistic to think people don't sell things in their lifetime and it's ridiculous when people get dismayed by it,' she said, and that selling the treasures was following Johnnie's wishes. Nevertheless, few have any doubt that, despite Johnnie's repeated assertion that 'I'm the boss in our marriage', Raine exerted a strong influence over him. Viscount Coke says, 'She was much stronger a woman than he was ever a man. Johnnie was one for the quiet life. If she said that they must do this or that he would have said, "Yes darling, I'm sure you're right." ' Alan Jefferson, a colleague of Raine's at the British Tourist Authority where she has worked part-time since the early eighties, would disagree with that. 'Raine got the blame for selling things but it was Johnnie's property and he decided what needed to be sold.' He admits, however, that 'Raine has done the negotiation and you might argue that the negotiation was done badly, but the initiative to sell was very much his.'

The fact remains, however, that the first reports of sales of treasures appeared in the press while Johnnie was desperately ill. It is therefore difficult to judge to what extent his stroke affected his judgment and decision making at Althorp, because, although the haemorrhage itself had not damaged the intellectual part of his brain, many felt he was never quite the same afterwards, mentally as well as physically. He certainly knew that he owed his life to Raine, was justifiably grateful and anxious to repay her devotion. An image grew that Johnnie had become a doddering old earl, a view endorsed by Richard Herner. 'When I first went to Althorp soon after Johnnie's stroke to buy paintings, he only seemed to have moments of lucidity. I don't think he understood what was happening. I believe he thought he was acting in the best interests of the estate and that his wife was acting in his best interests. He seemed to rely on her for day-to-day decisions, negotiations and judgment.'

A common link running through most of the sales was the Spencers' insistence on secrecy. Although not in itself sinister, many believe that the secrecy with which deals were negotiated itself caused the low prices for paintings, silver, furniture and other treasures, which alarmed experts and the family almost as much as the sheer numbers of heirlooms sold. Paintings in particular were sold through dealers who then offered them privately to clients. 'Dealers will ring up a list of collectors who they know will buy a particular artist and a deal can be done out of the public eye,' explains Robin Simon. 'The dealers themselves can't be expected to act as moral guardians.'

The dealers loved the cloak-and-dagger transactions. 'Dealers make their living selling works of art and the more they can buy privately, the better,' explains Brian Allen, Director of Studies at the Paul Mellon Centre for Studies in British Art. He remembers that in 1982 the Centre was offered Sir Joshua Reynolds's portrait of the Swiss artist Angelica Kauffmann which, he says, 'was being very discreetly and quietly touted around'. (It was eventually bought by an American collector for £100,000.) 'I'm sure that if it had been sold at auction they would have got a higher price.'

The element of secrecy certainly increased the hostility Johnnie's children felt towards Raine. Charles Spencer told *Hello!* magazine after his father's death: 'I think that, in the past, too much was sold in the wrong way because, really, if you're going to sell something that is part of a great collection, I think you are duty bound to get the best price for it so you don't have to sell something else. But the sales that were done from here were done in such a way that many dealers in Bond Street in London profited enormously at the expense of my family. It was all done on the quiet and I hope those dealers are ashamed of what they've done to a family collection like this. My father was not an expert in the artistic field and they took advantage of his lack of knowledge and my stepmother's over eagerness to sell.'

Richard Herner, one dealer who is prepared to speak out, admits that all his transactions on behalf of Colnaghi had to be handled very quietly. 'Raine didn't want anybody asking any questions. The whole thing was shrouded in secrecy and they sold badly because of the secrecy.' He admits 'some paintings were ridiculously cheap'. He insists, however, that the dealer is not to blame. 'No dealer is responsible to the person from whom they are buying. Your trade as a dealer is the same as an estate agent – to get some sort of action between buyer and seller, and your loyalties are to your clients. The cheaper you can buy, the better you can sell. I wasn't a friend, I was a neutral agent trying to buy what was on offer from a famous collection in the best possible circumstances. It would have been stupid of me to give more than was asked.'

Herner denies, however, making vast profits on all his purchases. 'Not every picture I bought was a successful commercial transaction. Some paintings had great historical and cultural importance, neither of which is necessarily reflected in the market.'

Nor did the secrecy last long. The art world has sensitive ears and details of even the most confidential of sales were all round Bond Street in a morning. 'We were all whispering together and trying to get in on the act,' admits Herner. In any event the sale of a major work of art destined to go abroad is bound to be discovered as soon as an export licence is applied for: a licence is required to export a work of art that has been in the country for more than fifty years and is above a certain fixed value (in the early eighties this was £8,000). Licences are obtained through the Government's Heritage Secretary (formerly the Minister of the Arts) and can be withheld if the object in question is considered to be of national value.

The procedure followed is that either the owner, or the buyer of the picture or his agent appears before the Reviewing Committee to present his case for exporting the work. The committee has to decide whether it is of outstanding quality and interest to the nation and therefore worth saving, in line with the Waverley criteria which were drawn up in 1952 to safeguard valuable treasures from being lost to the country. The committee's judgment is based on the advice of more than forty experts in different areas. For example, Old Master paintings would be assessed by an expert at the National Gallery, portraits by the National Portrait Gallery, silver and porcelain by the V & A. The intention is to give British institutions the chance to make a comparable offer for the work of art and thus enable it to remain in Britain.

In practice, however, the application procedure is often no more than a holding operation. Prices for works of art have soared, British museums and art galleries have little cash available and the committee can only withhold the licence for a specified period. *Apollo* editor Robin Simon says: 'It's a great system, but it doesn't work. Huge amounts have gone which no one knows about.' Richard Herner agrees. 'There are ways round the committee. The seller can manufacture a buyer, export it at one price and have it resold at a higher price.' Now that Britain is subject to EC regulations, the procedure is changing. In France, for example, there are much stricter laws. The French Government has the power of veto at auction and attempts are currently being made to standardise regulations throughout the Community.

There were also moral considerations that perhaps should have exercised greater restraint on the Spencers' behaviour. Aristocrats lucky enough to inherit family treasures usually wish to maintain as much as possible of their inheritance in order to pass it on to the next generation. They are imbued with the notion that they are merely custodians of something older and greater than themselves. Addressing the Society for the Protection of Ancient Buildings in 1889, designer William Morris voiced the feelings of many when he said: 'These old buildings do not belong to us only; they have belonged to our forefathers and they will belong to our descendants unless we play them false. They are not in any sense our property to do as we like with. We are only trustees for those that come after us.'

Johnnie, inheriting a house and collection that, when his father died, was described as 'one of the country's jewels', could have been expected to feel a stronger sense of responsibility than most, particularly once Diana became Princess of Wales, making Althorp the ancestral home of the wife of the heir to the throne of England and the heritage of Prince William. Events proved that Johnnie was in this respect a weak link in the Spencer chain. 'Charles Althorp was brought up to believe that the most important thing is preservation and the continuation of Althorp,' says Viscount Coke. 'In practical terms Johnnie did remarkably little towards it. It is a tragedy for Charles that his father never thought of his son's inheritance or of the condition of Althorp as a grand house.'

An art expert who knew Johnnie most of his life feels that his childhood was largely to blame for his later attitude towards his inheritance. 'He had been crushed by a peppery, tiresome father who was deeply involved in his possessions. Johnnie's knee-jerk reaction was to do the opposite. Nor did he have a natural love of works of art. He was much more interested in country pursuits.' Apart from his lecture at Eton on the treasures of Althorp he showed very little interest in the collection. 'Johnnie let the art treasures go because they didn't mean anything to him,' said Michael Kitson, former Director of Studies at the Paul Mellon Centre for Studies in British Art. 'It seemed alas as if Johnnie, by all accounts a nice bloke, inherited none of his father's sensibilities and care for what he had inherited from his ancestors ... The general impression in the art world was that the Spencers went about the desecration of the Althorp collection in the most insensitive way imaginable.'

Brian Allen adds: 'No regard was shown for what had been a venerable tradition in the Spencer family of maintaining a collection. Family portraits have suffered least, but there was an Old Master collection of real quality and some of the most important pictures, which were not necessarily the most valuable, have gone. That is what upset the art establishment.'

Another moral obligation when selling a major work of art is to offer it to national institutions before attempting to sell it privately. This also has advantages for the seller. As a heritage expert explains: 'This can be done by a private treaty sale which not only has tax advantages but enables objects to be sold to the state but remain in the house they have been associated with. Sliding things off into the market without telling anybody isn't playing the game. The nation must have the opportunity of buying them. It's a moral thing. That being said, you are entitled to do what you like with private property.' The Spencers took advantage of this option when selling a couple of Van Dycks in 1976 as a way of dealing with death duties, but thereafter seem to have largely ignored it – to their own cost.

For example, in 1983 they sold *The Coronation of the Virgin* by the sixteenth-century German artist Johann Rottenhammer. Deeply influenced by Tintoretto, Rottenhammer did not work on large canvases and frescoes like his mentor, but created finely-wrought paintings on copper. This painting was bought by the art dealers Colnaghi for what Herner describes as a 'ludicrously small' sum. Colnaghi applied for an export licence to send the painting on a sale-or-return basis to the Karlsruhe Museum in West Germany but, because it was considered of special national importance, this was withheld for three months to allow a British gallery time to make an offer. The painting was finally bought by the National Gallery for an estimated £60,000. If the Spencers had sold it directly to the gallery or to another British public collection they would have gained substantial tax concessions which do not apply, once a painting is in the hands of a dealer.

Anna Somers Cocks, editor of *The Art Newspaper*, has clear views on the subject. 'It's considered to be unsporting not to consult or play ball with the authorities and always leads to people being frightfully unpopular. Overall there is an entente cordiale between great English private collections and the State who respect each other's rights and come to an agreement over works of art. They simply weren't interested. If, however, the law tried to appropriate people's stuff I would fight it tooth and nail, but I think there is a quid pro quo for the enjoyment of having these things. England has been brilliant at inculcating and encouraging the natural desire that people have to pass something on. There's really no equivalent to the English country house abroad whereby the house, its contents and parkscape are all capable of going on generation after generation.'

The Spencer children viewed the dispersal of their family treasures as a tragedy and the manner of its disposal, piecemeal and in secret, as nothing less than a catastrophe. They were angry that they were not consulted over the sales and held Raine responsible. Johnnie's aunt, Lady Margaret Douglas-Home, tried to talk to him about what was happening to the treasures. 'Sometimes I would say to Johnnie "Awful things in the paper again. What do you make of it?" But he would never even answer me. He was so loyal to her.'

Another close relative comments. 'The children should have been consulted and agreed to the reorganisation of the family home. It would have been much better to have had their co-operation.' Even Johnnie's son and heir was kept in the dark. 'It's very sad that Charles was never consulted,' says Viscount Coke. Raine and Johnnie's lack of sensitivity in this respect made family feelings all the more bitter. It is pure speculation, however, to assume that if Raine had considered the feelings of her stepchildren they would have liked her any the more.

Her position, as with all second wives and stepmothers, was extremely delicate. It might have improved family relations if she had trod gingerly, but to do so would have been out of character. Raine is made of robust stuff, a natural enthusiast who, when she takes on a task, does so with all cylinders firing. She is not known for her sensitivity.

Several aristocrats feel that the problem was compounded by the fact that Raine married into a tradition she did not understand. Although she adopted all the outward manifestations of being a countess and overwhelmed many with her regal manner, 'she was a countess one hundred percent instead of pretending like many do nowadays to be merely a farmer's wife' says a neighbour in Northamptonshire. She did not, however, convince the true blue. 'Raine wasn't brought up in the same sort of feudal landed society that the Spencers came from,' says one. 'The Spencers were courtiers in the old-fashioned sense of the word – people who had been connected with the Sovereign from time immemorial. Their tradition, with one or two exceptions, has been one of deep love and interest in the arts. Her life, however, has largely been a matter of getting ahead. She didn't have the background and never knew or understood that side of the role of the Lady of the house.' Another says: 'Raine is an arriviste. Her behaviour towards the collection exhibited the classic insecurity of the new rich McCorquodales and the smart Cart-lands, neither of which was landed.'

Nor was it felt that Raine understood the importance of the collection in heritage terms. David Laws believes 'Raine was educated about fur-niture, but not about art. She has an infallible memory, but one didn't know how much she remembered and how much she understood.'

The general timing of the selling added fuel to the fire. Johnnie inherited Althorp in the pre-Thatcherite 1970s, at a time when there was great concern about the number of country houses that were being broken up. In 1974, as part of European Architectural Heritage Year, which Raine was chairman of, the V & A held a major exhibition called 'The Destruc-tion of the English Country House' which dramatically drew people's attention to what was happening to many fine homes. The way Raine and Johnnie were selling off the family collection was generally perceived to run counter to the conservationist mood of the country.

Equally, their commercial approach to Althorp seemed inconsistent with Raine's earlier battles for conservation. One curator comments: 'Because she was involved in historic buildings, people thought she would have been responsible and that she of all people would do the right thing. It came as a particular shock that she didn't.' Sir Roy Strong remembers: 'Things just turned up. You found half the dealers of London had paint-ings from Althorp. This shook the Establishment rather badly because it was not the way someone who had spent her life working for preservation was expected to behave. Everyone would understand the problems of

Althorp, but they expected the pictures to be offered to the nation first. It was an odd anomaly.'

Another former colleague says: 'She had a public image of caring about the heritage on the one hand while on the other being involved in selling off the family heirlooms.' If Raine was aware of the discrepancy between her personal behaviour and her earlier public stands, she adopted the classic Cartland reaction of ignoring it.

As regards Johnnie, there seems no doubt that he treasured his wife far more than his inheritance.

15

Bargains at the Sales

It has been impossible to trace everything that has been sold by Raine and Johnnie. Although the disposal of major works of art has been well documented, not all of the less valuable paintings have been recorded. 'The [paintings] that have been publicly listed are probably the tip of the iceberg,' agrees art historian John Harris. 'No doubt in the cellars and the attic at Althorp, as in most stately homes, was a mass of material that is not on an heirloom list or on inventories and a lot of that has probably been syphoned out of the place.

'It's quite clear that there has been a mass of undocumented things that have been leaked out of Althorp and will only come to light when and if they are exported. There is no prohibition on selling things in this country. I think there are probably many minor things that they may have gained quite an amount of money for, but are not of a quality that would require an export licence.' It has also not been possible to establish the prices for all the Althorp treasures that were sold in secret. Many dealers keep quiet for fear of losing clients and many curators of museums and art galleries are prohibited from discussing private deals.

It is known, however, that several seventeenth-century religious pictures which were clearly not to Raine or Johnnie's taste were sold during the eighties, despite the fact that they had been in the family collection for three hundred years. 'They often pictured ecstasies and martyrdom which a conventional Mayfair lady like Raine would consider awful,' comments one art historian. Several miniatures have also disappeared. 'Miniatures are not terribly important, but look so nice accumulated in a house,' says editor Anna Somers Cocks.

Richard Herner admits to buying several paintings from the basement of Althorp. 'I think I bought about twenty that were brought up from the cellars dirty and unlooked-after. It's a mistake to sell these cheaply because they could be in the cellars merely because in historical terms they were not fashionable at a certain time.' One example is his purchase, in 1983 for about £30,000, of the painting *Agrippina with the Ashes of Germanicus*

by the Scottish artist Gavin Hamilton, a vast work commissioned by the
1st Earl Spencer in 1765. Hamilton had settled in Rome in the 1850s and
was one of the pioneers of neoclassicism. 'The painting was hanging in a
dark passageway and I nearly didn't see it,' Herner remembers. 'Raine
had no idea of its historical importance.' Several American museums
expressed interest in buying it but Herner successfully offered it first to
the Tate Gallery. Other basement purchases included a sixteenth-century
drawing after Raphael, a small copper engraving by Francesco Albani,
and a painting by Carlo Dolci.

Althorp contained works of art from the English, Italian, Dutch, French
and Spanish Schools, several of which are included in the National
Gallery's secret list of works of art of such outstanding importance that
they should never be allowed to leave Britain. It also had a remarkable
collection of Old Masters: 'one of the greatest collections of Old Masters
that was almost intact,' said Brian Allen.

Robert, second Earl of Sunderland (1641–1702), was the first major
collector of paintings in the family. All the portraits bought by Sunderland
had distinctly carved baroque frames, which it is thought he ordered
in Spain, hence the origin of the term 'Sunderland frames'. He also
commissioned Sir Peter Lely to paint the beauties of Charles II's court
and a portrait of his wife, Lady Anne Digby. Lady Anne added to the
collection several paintings she inherited from her brother, the Earl of
Bristol; these included Van Dyck's great double portrait of the second
Earl of Bristol and the first Duke of Bedford, Lady Anne's father and
uncle respectively.

Another important collector in the family was the Hon. John Spencer
(1708–46), who purchased several valuable works of art and inherited
more from the estates of his grandmother, Sarah, Duchess of Marlborough. These included Sir Godfrey Kneller's portraits of the Duke and
Duchess of Marlborough and Francesco Albani's *Holy Family*.

His son, the first Earl Spencer (1734–83) greatly enriched the collection
of portraits through his friendship with Thomas Gainsborough and Sir
Joshua Reynolds, who painted various members of his family, including
his favourite daughter Georgiana, later Duchess of Devonshire. The first
Earl also commissioned several sporting pictures by George Stubbs and
bought a number of paintings for Spencer House.

Just before Johnnie's father died, the Walpole Society published a
comprehensive list of more than seven hundred major pictures at Althorp,
compiled by Dr Kenneth Garlic. When the next probate valuation is
completed in the mid 1990s, it is expected that the total will be between
two and three hundred fewer than the number recorded twenty years ago.

While Johnnie repeatedly used the same excuses to justify the sales, the
fact is that many of these preceded expensive acquisitions which had

nothing to do with Althorp, including the purchase of a Rolls-Royce, three houses in Bognor and a large town house in Mayfair. 'Cheques for the purchase of paintings had to be written to coincide with other purchases, particularly with completions of property,' Richard Herner admits. He, too noticed a change in their attitude over the years. 'At the beginning they were very careful about what could be sold, but several paintings which they refused to sell on my first visit, including *The Five Apostles* by Van Dyck, were then sold on later visits.'

Art dealers are naturally entitled to make whatever profits they can. But there was often a huge discrepancy between what the Spencers received and what the dealers earned when they resold the Althorp masterpieces (sometimes they obtained several times as much as they had paid). Having Raine and Johnnie as clients must have been a dealer's dream come true. Yet, with a seemingly unending supply of works of art for sale, the Spencers were in a strong bargaining position and should have been able to dictate terms to dealers who would surely have agreed with them, enticed by the prospect of many hefty future commissions.

It is equally difficult to understand why, once Raine and Johnnie knew of the enormous profits being made from the resale of Althorp paintings, they returned again and again to the same dealers. The Spencers claimed that they were only selling the paintings because they desperately needed money for the refurbishment of Althorp. Selling their treasures at low prices would therefore seem self-defeating. The fact that Raine, who is generally acknowledged to have handled the transactions herself, accepted the situation would imply either that she was taken in by dealers, prepared to pay a heavy price for secrecy, or, as one friend believed, 'an awful negotiator because she doesn't understand other people.'

Certainly the first two propositions seem inconsistent with what one knows about Raine. She is canny, has a razor-sharp mind and a fine awareness of money which has been force-fed into her from childhood.

One member of the Reviewing Committee, who has to remain anonymous as its workings come under the Official Secrets Act, was so unhappy about the difference in price paid to the Spencers for several paintings and the price these paintings were eventually sold at abroad, that he tried to take the matter further. 'I urged the then Department of Trade and Industry to hold an inquiry because it happened with such alarming regularity. They were flabbergasted by this suggestion because Raine was then too close to the Crown.'

A spokesman for the DTI commented: 'The Department has no record of any investigation or any call for investigation into prices agreed in what would have been private contracts between vendor and purchaser(s) ... None of the officials, formerly with the DTI ... and now dealing with export controls for this department were involved in these responsibilities at the time of the [Spencer] sales and therefore they have no personal recollection to draw upon.'

Alarm bells rang in the art world in 1979 after Raine and Johnnie sold the paintings *Liberality and Modesty* by Guido Reni and *Apollo Crowning the Musician Marcantonio Pasqualini* by Andrea Sacchi to the London dealers Wildenstein. Wildenstein applied for a licence to export the paintings to Switzerland, giving their values as £15,000 for the Reni and £25,000 for the Sacchi, which proved to be a gross underestimate by any standards. The two paintings had been acquired as a pair by the first Earl Spencer in 1758 for the Great Room at Spencer House. Both had frames designed by Athenian Stuart to match the window architraves and door frames of the house. *The Times* reported that the Arts Minister, Norman St John-Stevas, 'has revealed none of the normal details ... neither the name of the dealer who applied for the licence, the foreign purchaser or indeed the price which any British gallery will need to raise to save them for the nation.' The report went on: 'Vendors are entitled to insist on secrecy, but surely this makes a mockery of any private attempts to raise money for important paintings.' It suggested that 'the secrecy increased speculation in the art world that the Spencers still have a financial interest in the sale of the two paintings, believed to be worth £100,000 each'.

The following day it was announced that galleries in this country needed to raise £250,000 by the end of July in order to safeguard the pictures. This proved an impossibility and both paintings are now in the United States.

'Their great big frames with wonderful neoclassical mouldings dominated the Great Room in Spencer House,' says Anna Somers Cocks. 'It was a case of a work of art that was right in that context and nowhere else. At the time no one thought that Spencer House would ever be restored, otherwise I'm sure they wouldn't have been allowed out of the country. Their sale abroad means that it is almost impossible totally to restore the Great Room'.

In 1982, a year after the Royal wedding an unprecedented number of paintings were sold, which led to much criticism of the Spencers in the press. Raine felt she had been sorely misjudged and misrepresented. 'If you believed everything you read in the newspapers you would think I married [Johnnie] for his money and that we were selling off all the family treasures to keep me in my old age,' she was quoted as saying in the *Daily Mail*. 'I sound like a monster. But I can't be that much of a monster, can I? Would such an idiot or a monster be asked by the Government three times to prepare reports for them? People don't realise I've been in public life for twenty-six years ... we do everything we can to keep [Althorp] going and all we get back is a pittance – 6,000 visitors a year at £1 a head.

Of course, we had a bit of luck with Diana ... but all the extra visitors have cracked the Library ceiling.'

In December that year *The Times* claimed in a front page story that Johnnie had sold treasures worth £2 million and that he was putting his family legacy under the auctioneer's hammer so that Althorp could be refurbished. 'We are doing up the house from top to bottom, so of course we have had to sell a few things,' Johnnie replied defiantly.

He also claimed that the sales were essential to help pay the running costs of Althorp and a £60,000 bill when he was being nursed back to health after his brain haemorrhage. The bill for convalescence was a one-off, and not used again as a reason for selling works of art. Maintenance costs were used repeatedly. In 1982 Johnnie stated that Althorp cost between £50,000 and £70,000 a year to run and highlighted the well-known dilemma of all landed nobility: the cracked ceiling versus the masterpiece. Few would disagree that in the last resort the ceiling is more important than the painting. The controversy over Raine and Johnnie's approach was, however, that they were inclined to use it as a first resort.

Johnnie explained through his solicitors that he was 'distressed and sad' about his need to sell, adding, 'I'm afraid you must blame the country's tax laws, not me. We still have some magnificent paintings, many of which have been restored. We have almost paid off those dreadful death duties and I am fairly sure we won't have to sell any more of our art collection. Running this place, which I love dearly, is eating into my private funds, but from the sales that have gone through, by opening to the public and having Americans and Germans to dinner and holding musical evenings we are keeping our heads above water.'

In September 1982 Raine and Johnnie were keeping their heads above a very different level of water with the extravagant purchase of the three seaside homes in Bognor Regis. The following year they splashed out again, this time buying a new Rolls-Royce Silver Spur for about £64,000. They also sold their small flat in Grosvenor Square and bought a 95-year lease on a larger first-floor three-bedroomed flat in the same block for approximately £300,000. Ironically the new flat had been the home for thirty years of Mrs Elsie Tritton, a hugely wealthy American who, because of a feud with Raine, was not on speaking terms with her, despite Raine apparently trying her best to heal the rift. The old lady died aged ninety-six leaving £4 million and would no doubt have been furious if she had known that Raine had secured her beloved flat just six hours after it went on the market.

Both purchases brought an avalanche of criticism. A duchess says: 'It was completely unnecessary for her to have lived in the same block as Gerald. We were also all very shocked when they bought the Rolls-Royce, especially when they were selling family heirlooms. No one needs to spend money on an expensive Rolls.'

There was another major exodus of paintings from Althorp in 1985. The sale of these, however, was handled with less secrecy than those of previous years. 'Once it was all out they blatantly sold the paintings at auction,' says an art historian. This time controversy raged over the sale of *The Duchess of Marlborough's Dogs*, painted by John Wootton in 1763; the duchess had written to her daughters, 'I am very fond of my ... dogs, they have all of them gratitude, wit and good sense: things very rare to be found in this country.' Although the work was not a masterpiece, it was a key painting in the Spencer family history. It was sold at Sotheby's for £143,000.

In September 1991 the Princess of Wales was said to have spotted a favourite childhood painting on sale at an antiques fair. Also for sale was a seventeenth-century painting by the Dutch artist Wouvermans for which the Spencers had received £120,000. It was being offered for three times that amount.

When Johnnie was asked about 'gaps on the wall' where once had hung great paintings handed down through generations, he shook his head slowly and said: 'Some of the things I've sold have been very dear to me. Selling them was not an easy decision. Very unpleasant. Horrid.' He denied that they were sold cheaply. 'We always get the best prices, but all the money has gone into the refurbishment of the house.' Second only to the collection of paintings was the remarkable Spencer collection of silver of which Johnnie was very proud. Betty Andrews, who was housekeeper in the seventies, remembers: 'A lot of the silver was laid out every day in exactly the same place even for His Lordship's breakfast. If the butler was out, I set the table. When there was a big dinner in the staterooms we looked at photographs so that we knew just where everything went and we always laid the table for the public.'

On 18 June 1978, three months before Johnnie's stroke, an estimated £50,000-worth of family silver was stolen in a robbery that remains a mystery to this day. 'The silver was left out just for one night ready for the next day, when it shouldn't have been,' Betty remembers. 'It was strange. It was always put away, except for that one Saturday night. There was no sign of any break-in. I don't know how they stole it and somehow managed to get across the park undetected. I've always wondered if someone hid in the room after the visitors went round. There was a nightwatchman who saw all the silver in place when he first went round, but the next time it wasn't there. In those days there wasn't any proper security apart from the nightwatchman. The whole thing was hushed up and we never heard anymore about it.'

The most significant part of the silver collection was the unique

Marlborough Plate given by Sarah, Duchess of Marlborough, to her favourite grandson, the Hon. John Spencer. The Spencers also inherited works by great eighteenth- and nineteenth- century silversmiths such as de Lamerie, Thomas Gilpin, William Pitts and Digby Scott. There was an unrivalled collection of silver candlesticks too. In 1963, silver expert Arthur Grimwade, who did the probate valuation on the death of Johnnie's father in 1975, wrote about the Spencer collection in the arts magazine, *The Connoisseur*. 'There is at Althorp one of the most extensive and representative ranges of candlesticks and candelabra, if individually not unique, that one may expect to find surviving in one house. Stretching as it does from the late years of Charles II down to the nineteenth century, it constitutes and epitomises in one collection the many forms of styles through which the candlestick passed in England over nearly two hundred years.' The earliest candlesticks dated from 1683 and were made by Pierre Harache, the forerunner of the immigrant Huguenots who strongly influenced the craft of goldsmithing in England. The collection also included the work of eighteenth-century craftsmen such as Lewis Mettayer and Thomas Farren, who made much of the Marlborough Plate, and William Pitts.

Grimwade described the Spencer collection as 'one of the greatest surviving groups of English ancestral silver', and the Marlborough Plate in particular as 'the most remarkable group of silver known to have been in one man's property ... The ceremonial plate of the great Duke of Marlborough is unique.' Much of this silver was issued by the Government to the Duke of Marlborough in 1701 as a status symbol when he was appointed Ambassador to the Netherlands, and almost all of it is engraved with his coat of arms, which increases its market value.

Although rumours began circulating that this magnificent Marlborough Plate, valued at about £1 million in 1978, was on the market and likely to go abroad while Johnnie was in hospital, the main furore over the future of the collection came to a head in 1982 when Johnnie offered for sale a pair of seventeenth-century gold wine coolers. Gold objects of the late seventeenth century are extremely rare and the wine coolers are thought to have been made by a Huguenot goldsmith driven into exile by Louis XIV. Tradition has it that the 22-carat gold coolers, which weighed 25 lb, were given to the Duke of Marlborough by Queen Anne after his victory at Blenheim. The sale of the coolers was negotiated by S. J. Phillips, the leading antique dealers in silver for most of this century, who have worldwide connections. Acting for Lord Spencer, Phillips sold them for about £1 million to the British Museum.

The sale prompted Grimwade to take the unusual step of writing a letter to *The Times* to express his 'deep concern' over the future of the Marlborough collection. He felt it was part of the national heritage that must not be dispersed, and that if the famous Marlborough Plate were sold piecemeal, it would make it almost impossible to secure it for the nation. '... If [Lord Spencer] was prepared to sell the wine coolers,' Grimwade wrote, 'he might sell items from the main collection.'

Johnnie's reply was that the coolers had been in a bank vault for the last hundred years and 'there was no income from them and no one could see them.'

'Quite a number of us were getting worried about the sales at the time,' remembers Grimwade. 'It was of course perfectly legitimate for him to sell what he liked, but the Marlborough Plate was exempted from death tax and works of art exempted from tax cannot be sold without settling up the taxes.'

Heather Wilson, head of Capital Taxes at the Museum and Galleries Commission, explains: 'If the owner of an exempted item sells that item, he should let the capital tax office know. If not, there are other ways we find out.'

Thorough investigations, however, only began after Johnnie's death. 'If any items have been sold on which tax is owed, the new Earl or the widow would have to pay, depending on the ownership of the item sold,' she says. 'If Earl Spencer owned something in his own right which he sold in his lifetime without paying tax, the executors on his estate would pay it.'

One of Johnnie's executors, Viscount Coke, is involved in this unhappy exercise, which involves paintings and other valuables as well as silver, and is likely to take several years. 'We have to discover what items if any have been sold that have not been notified to the tax office and then agree with the tax office what must be paid. It means that, in addition to the duty that must be paid on Johnnie's death, capital taxes may have to be paid that should have been paid during his lifetime. Johnnie never consulted Charles or his professional advisers. Things were just sold.'

Charles was kept so totally in the dark that he had to resort to asking for a copy of an article that appeared in *Harper's & Queen* in 1987, listing some of the Althorp sales. He also instructed agents to monitor auction houses and let him know when items from Althorp came up for sale.

In 1981 Johnnie tried to reassure those anxious about the valuable Spencer silver collection. He said: 'to sell the silver or part of it would be like selling my soul.' In practice, valuable chunks of his 'soul' were spirited out of Althorp. Much was bought in 1982 by the renowned American dealer, Arthur Gilbert via S. J. Phillips but only came to light when a catalogue of his collection, the Gilbert Collection of Gold and Silver, was published by the Los Angeles County Museum of Art in 1988. The lavish catalogue was compiled by Timothy Schroder, who worked at Christie's, then went to the Los Angeles museum and is now working at Partridge Fine Arts, the company responsible for the restoration of Althorp.

An unusual feature of the catalogue is that fewer Spencer heirlooms are noted in the index than appear in the catalogue itself: a curious act of carelessness. One particular omission from the index is a pair of valuable silver sauceboats considered to be so important that the description and photographs of them take up four pages in the catalogue itself. These two sauceboats with their ladles were made in 1813–14 by William Pitts and were described as 'an example of the return to taste of the rococo style during the Regency period'. They are elaborately engraved with birds, rabbits, fish and scrolls and the handle is in the form of an eagle standing on a tree-trunk and holding a lamb in his beak. The selling agent and date of purchase have been omitted.

In addition to purchases by Gilbert it is known that in 1983 twelve candlesticks engraved with the Duke of Marlborough crest were sold, and that the previous year two candlesticks by Farren were given as a present to the V & A by S. J. Phillips to mark the retirement of Claude Blair, keeper of the museum's Metalwork Department. Blair remembers: 'At the time there were lots of stories of things disappearing from the house, they were terribly secretive and no one knows how much Marlborough silver has gone. Although I naturally wish to see things conserved, I have a certain sympathy about selling. My personal feeling is that it's no use the Government telling stately-home owners that they should keep their possessions unless they make substantial provision to help them.'

Richard Vander, director of the silversmith company C. L. Vander, believes that 'at the end of the day what happened to the silver is probably a tragedy. Nor did the Spencers get decent prices.'

The selling of heirlooms was not confined to paintings and silver. The Spencer heritage was also stripped of furniture, archives, porcelain and property.

The furniture at Althorp is a combination of what has been accumulated by generations of Spencers for a grand country home, and what originally belonged to Spencer House and was removed to Althorp by Jack Spencer during the Second World War. The former was by and large unostentatious but of superb quality, the latter more glitzy and showy; the one not altogether at ease with the other. John Hardy, formerly of the furniture Department of the V & A, comments, 'The gold furniture that was originally at Spencer House was chosen because they wanted it to glitter and look wonderful in candlelight ... Such town furniture looks garish in the country.'

Hardy, together with his colleague Peter Thornton, who acquired several items of furniture in the sixties and seventies for the V & A in the hope that one day they could go back to a restored Spencer House, wrote a definitive article, 'The Spencer Furniture', in *Apollo* magazine in 1968 with the help of Johnnie's father. The furniture at Althorp is described as

'One of the most important collections of furniture in the country ... A collection which reflects each successive phase of English taste from the period of the Restoration up to Regency. Moreover, several of the pieces are in themselves cornerstones of the history of English furniture.' The collection contains important pieces designed for Spencer House by John Vardy and James Stuart – the latter's work being among the earliest neoclassical furniture in existence. Of the furniture that used to be in Spencer House, Hardy and Thornton wrote: 'It is difficult to appreciate its full grandeur now that it has been removed from its original setting. It must be remembered that each piece was intended to furnish a particular room and that its form and decor were influenced by the size and architectural detailing of the room concerned.'

Raine and Johnnie showed the same lack of strategy over the sale of furniture as they displayed with the sale of paintings and silver. Before Johnnie was taken ill he and Raine sold some items from Spencer House to the Victoria & Albert Museum, which have since been returned there on permanent loan. But once the desecration of Althorp was well under way in the 1980s, the Spencers chose not to sell to the V & A, or, more surprisingly, to Lord Rothschild who acquired a 124-year lease of Spencer House in 1987. It was estimated that Jacob Rothschild's investment company, J. Rothschild Holdings, invested more than £16 million in this last-remaining eighteenth-century London house where the building and contents had remained in the same family.

If Raine and Johnnie had sold the Spencer House furniture to Jacob Rothschild they would have raised much-needed funds and the furniture would have retained the family connection. According to one of the experts who worked on the restoration, 'Lord Rothschild was very willing to buy things.' Instead he spent considerable sums on creating reproductions of items kept at Althorp. Raine and Johnnie did however see this as a further source of revenue and charged hefty facility fees when Rothschild's restoration team came to look at originals. Items charged for included the Athenian Stuart saloon tables and mirrors originally made for the Great Room, several pictures frames and two chimneypieces which Johnnie's father removed from Spencer House in the 1940s and then had installed at Althorp.

Had the Spencers, when they wanted to sell furniture, approached the national heritage bodies, and particularly the V & A who were very keen on the Spencer House restoration, they would have received a fair price, tax concessions, the furniture would not have been scattered and the nation would have benefited. Instead they broke up valuable sets of furniture by selling items piecemeal and the V & A was reduced to keeping an eye on the dealers to see when pieces of furniture that originated from Spencer House came up for sale.

Peter Thornton was disappointed with Raine and Johnnie's attitude. 'It's a pity to have to make a lot of reproduction things for Spencer House, if the originals actually exist.' He is not, however, as critical of their behaviour as some. 'I'm a strong believer that private people can do what they like with their belongings, as long as they don't actually destroy them. There's always another opportunity with the next generation. There's no question of it being the last chance.'

The most controversial sale of furniture occurred in 1985 when the Spencers gave six armchairs from the Great Room at Spencer House, designed by Athenian Stuart, to John Partridge, chairman of Partridge Fine Arts, in payment for restoration work at Althorp. It was the cause of much consternation among experts. 'The sale broke up sets of chairs designed by architects as part of the architecture,' says Anna Somers Cocks.

Many other less valuable pieces of furniture were thought to have been sold secretly, some of which have turned up in unexpected places. During a trip to Scotland, Johnnie's daughter Jane and her husband Robert Fellowes found two chests of drawers in an antique shop that Jane recognised as coming from Althorp. Other items have been auctioned at Sotheby's. At one sale, antique dealer Christopher Hudson bought a nineteenth-century library desk and a square mahogany library table that came from Althorp. Although he knew the Spencers were anxious to sell furniture, he made no attempt to contact them directly with a view to acquiring more. 'I hardly buy anything privately because it is so difficult to give a fair price. I would rather people got everything valued properly to protect themselves.'

Archives, manuscripts and drawings were also sold. In 1984 an expert made an assessment of the family archives in the Muniment Room at Althorp and also of the old estate papers kept in a first-floor room in the stable block. Richard Stanley, then Althorp's land agent, recollects: 'The Spencer archives were said to be one of the finest still in private hands. It consisted of a very good collection of estate papers and also an enormous amount of personal correspondence going back over the centuries.' The family archives were sold to the British Library for about £1 million. Occupying 300 ft of shelving, they contain many important papers belonging to the fifth Earl, who served in Gladstone's Cabinet twice and was Lord Lieutenant of Ireland. Stanley's view is that 'the sale was opportunistic and unnecessary'. Fortunately some of the estate papers were retained.

Althorp also had a fine collection of china and porcelain. This began with the Hon. John Spencer's purchase of Meissen and Dresden china in the 1740s and was largely built up by Frederick, 4th Earl Spencer (1798–1857), who was an enthusiastic collector of ceramics. It includes Sèvres,

Chelsea, Capodimonte, Delftware, Chinese and Japanese porcelain, some of which had belonged to Sarah, Duchess of Marlborough.

It has been particularly difficult to trace these small treasures, although some ended up unexpectedly at the V & A. Sir Roy Strong, who was director at the time, remembers: 'We bought bits of porcelain that the people in the Ceramics Department recognised came from Althorp. It was quite clear that they had been sold off.'

Land and property were another potential source of income. Although initially the Spencers maintained a policy of not selling land, only surplus or vacant properties, over the years their attitude changed as their need for money increased.

They began in a small way by disposing of what was regarded as an Althorp anomaly, a Victorian primary school, St Ethelwold School in Shotton, North Wales, which they put up for sale for about £50,000 in 1982. The site had been given to the Church of England authorities by Johnnie's father and when the school closed, its ownership reverted to the Althorp estate. It was bought by a property developer.

As the eighties progressed, about one hundred and fifty further property deals were negotiated, either involving vacant buildings or small pieces of land released from restrictive covenants. Even this did not raise sufficient funds and in 1988 the Spencers sold 160 acres of land adjoining Althorp Park which was bought by the developers Costain Homes Ltd for the construction of a golf course. The purchase price was £1 million plus a further £2 million payable over the following five years.

It was, however, the sale of cottages on the family estate in 1991 that really outraged Johnnie's children and finally brought the rumbling family feud to a head amid a blaze of publicity. Some months after Richard Stanley's consultancy was terminated in late 1990, forty properties around Althorp – at Little Brington, Great Brington, Harlestone and Little Brampton – most of which were leased by tenants, were offered for sale at knockdown prices of between £35,000 and £60,000.

Letters were sent out to about thirty tenants offering them the chance to buy their homes. Most, however, wanted to continue renting their cottages and were devastated at the amount of money they would have to raise to become property owners. Rose Ayling, who lives in one of the cottages at Church Brampton that Johnnie wanted to sell, was shocked when 'right out of the blue' a letter came offering her an opportunity to buy her cottage. Part of the letter read: 'We understand that your short-holding tenancy has expired and Lord Spencer would like to offer you the opportunity to purchase the freehold for the cottage.' What was more worrying to Rose was that the letter said that if she was not prepared to buy, the Aylings would have to vacate the cottage when the lease expired.

It caused her great anxiety. 'I'd been here six years and had always been told that the cottage wouldn't be sold. I found out that my cottage was selling for £55,000 which was well out of my range.' Fellow tenant Mike Dodds helped to organise a petition. 'Many of us cannot afford to buy so we may face eviction,' he said at the time. 'The local authority cannot rehouse us until we are homeless.'

Enquiries were being handled by Miss Pauline Shaw, not an estate agent, but one of Raine's personal staff. She negotiated the sale of several cottages to local second-hand car dealer Dave Harvey. A senior member of staff said that at the time the Spencers needed funds for the purchase and re-decoration of the £1.6 million house in Farm Street, Mayfair, to which Raine moved within twenty-four hours of Johnnie's death. Part of the cost was also financed by the sale of the Spencers' flat in Grosvenor Square for £750,000.

When Viscount Coke heard what was afoot he personally wrote to Johnnie trying to prevent the cottages from leaving the family ownership by offering him a tempting proposition.

> I pointed out that as he claimed he was short of money, one way of increasing the price the cottages would fetch was to have competitive bids. I asked if he would give us, the trustees of his son's settlement, the chance to bid for the cottages. Unfortunately he wouldn't hear of it. I then wrote a further sharp letter and said it was a very great shame that he wouldn't allow the trustees to bid, which if we were successful would mean the cottages would stay within the Althorp estate. Johnnie didn't reply, but told his solicitor that he was very upset with my attitude. It was totally illogical, of course.

Johnnie justified his actions with the well-known excuses of his right to sell what was his, escalating maintenance costs and even his father's death duties which had already been settled. 'They are my houses – why shouldn't I sell them?' he said. 'If your grandfather leaves you a gold watch, you are perfectly entitled to sell it. My father left me this estate and I decided to sell some things to help pay our way. If I didn't we couldn't live [at Althorp]. We would all have to move out. It's a terrific problem that every stately home-owner faces these days. It's easy to criticise but we faced a very hard choice, to sell off some of our properties or to move out. And all this time I thought the family understood. My father left a big debt. We want to go on living here. One way to do it is to sell the cottages. Quite a lot of the tenants are very glad of the opportunity to buy. I believe people should live in their own houses, not rent. It's a property-owning democracy.'

Neighbours in Northamptonshire were shocked by this new development, which was directly contrary to the duty landowners usually felt towards their tenants. One comments: 'In the rural areas there is an old-fashioned attitude of noblesse oblige. That people look after their tenants, don't sell off their estate and don't charge very much for their property. There was the feeling that the estate was being decimated, which was so different to Johnnie's father, who was the old-fashioned squire, protective and caring towards his tenants and keeping up the estate.'

Johnnie claimed that he had only sold twenty cottages 'at the most', and denied the latest accusations against him. 'Our pensioners and widows stay in their houses till they die ... I should think I've got another two hundred cottages. Someone is trying to make out that I am a heartless landlord, on top of everything else. Everything I do is for my home, Althorp.' He called the reaction a 'storm in a teacup. You will always get someone who will try to cause trouble.' He even brazenly denied that the cottages had been sold cheaply. 'We always get the best prices.' Some believed that he was now quite ill and his grasp on reality weakened.

Examples of the poor prices realised include a Victorian almshouse in Upper Harlestone which Johnnie sold for £35,000 but which was back on the market six months later, after some modernisation, at £98,000. A cottage in Church Brampton, sold for £35,000, which was soon up for sale at £89,500; and one in Great Brington, also sold for £35,000, which was later offered for £78,950. One villager said: 'The sale of the cottages has cost the family a fortune. I think the Earl was a mug to sell them so cheaply and a lot of people round here think the same.'

It was the final straw for Johnnie's children, who now had proof from the trustees that the best prices for Spencer property were not being realised.

Before too many of the properties were sold, however, Johnnie died, the rest were immediately withdrawn from the market, and Charles Spencer has since been buying several cottages back.

16

Restoration Tragedy

'Surely we can keep a balance between old and new? It is one of the strengths of the British character that we continually search for compromise. Not revolution but gradual change. Not total destruction but a marriage between ancient and modern in our laws and in our Constitution.' So wrote Raine in the early seventies when she was chairman of the GLC Historic Buildings Board in her successful book *Are Historic Buildings Really Necessary?*

What a difference a few years make. Many feel that, at Althorp, the relationship between old and new was anything but balanced and that Raine's time there was marked by revolution rather than gradual change. Whereas most generations behave like custodians, Raine and Johnnie did exactly what they liked with the stately home. Whereas most generations repair, they revamped. She and Johnnie spent about £2 million doing up Althorp, raising much of the money through the sale of Spencer heirlooms.

Under the auspices of the Bond Street dealers Partridge Fine Arts, a hundred craftsmen worked for eight years imposing Raine's taste on the 121-roomed house. During her first three years at Althorp Raine's new broom whirled through the house until eventually everything down to the last doorhandle was cleaned, restored, rehung and repaired. Plasterwork was renewed, embroidery remounted, chairs re-upholstered, furniture and porcelain restored, marble treated with acid, carpets and curtains cleaned or replaced, double glazing installed, a seventeenth-century oak floor covered with wall-to-wall beige carpeting especially woven in Bradford, fire surrounds rebrassed, white columns painted to look like green marble, all remaining pictures cleaned and, in the words of one London craftsman, 'everything that didn't move, covered in gilt'.

It is estimated that some two thousand pieces of furniture were restored and regilded, five hundred paintings cleaned, and every chandelier brought down for repair and cleaning. It was a mammoth task and the result caused as much controversy as the sales.

Taste is, of course, subjective, but it is difficult not to compare the restoration at Althorp with Lord Rothschild's lavish but subtle restoration of Spencer House in London. By comparison Althorp looks decidedly tasteless. Unlike Raine and Johnnie, Jacob Rothschild gathered round him England's leading conservation experts including Dan Cruickshank, Gervase Jackson-Stops, John Martin Robinson, Peter Thornton and Joe Friedman. (Johnnie's children attended the opening party on 19 November 1990. Raine and Johnnie were conspicuously absent.)

A few saw Raine's work as a triumph. More, however, regarded it as a tragedy. Although Althorp looked immaculate and the new and cleaned carpets vied with the gilt to dazzle the eye, the general consensus was that it looked 'manicured', was 'over the top', 'rather vulgar' and best viewed through dark glasses. Viscount Coke feels 'Althorp looks too grand now. It's a country house not a London drawing room.' Timothy Clifford, director of the National Galleries of Scotland, voiced the feelings of many experts. 'Althorp and its restoration in many respects shows sadly how the Spencers were misguided in their choice of professional advisers. It no longer has that very special charm which is associated with a country house which has been built up from the layering of different generations of taste. By regilding the frames and furniture and chucking out old furnishings, you no longer feel that a house is the accretion of generations.'

Some criticism has been more vitriolic. Raine has been accused of doing 'more damage than the deathwatch beetle' and of having turned Althorp, 'one of the country's jewels', into what has been variously described as a 'summer pudding', 'a bordello', an 'Arab gin palace in Kensington', 'a Parisian brothel', 'a tart's boudoir', or 'a Monaco palace'. One art historian described the Great Hall with its crimson wallpaper as looking like a 'seventies Indian restaurant'.

Johnnie was no longer seen as the sunny, slightly vague charmer the nation fell in love with during the Royal Wedding, but a weak man who was allowing his family inheritance to be eroded.

There are a few, however, who feel Raine's restoration and redecoration not only look good, but will save several future generations of Spencers from having to do any further renovation. David Laws, then working for interior designers Colefax & Fowler, the company responsible for much of the restoration, is one of these: 'In a hundred years' time people will think how marvellous Althorp is. Raine brought the house alive and had a way of creating a marvellous atmosphere. She flowed into that house and made it live again as a proper grand country house with candelight, champagne and music. Everyone who came enjoyed themselves, even those who were a bit ashamed of knowing her.'

Raine has taken much of the criticism as a personal attack. 'People are jealous of success and [Althorp] is a success story,' she said. 'There's also personal jealousy of me because I am so lucky to have such a wonderful husband.'

Architectural historians, however, have stressed that jealousy and a 'wonderful husband' have nothing to do with it. One has said, 'The object is not to attack her, and not all that has been done is absolutely hideous, but the truth is in fifteen years she and Johnnie wrecked the house, undid three-hundred years of quality and certainly undid the work of the seventh Earl Spencer ... the work done at Althorp is absolutely appalling in historical and architectural terms.'

Raine's taste was not the only aspect of the restoration that caused controversy. Although Althorp was Johnnie's own property to do with as he liked, many experts doubted whether such drastic restoration was necessary and rejected the Spencers' allegations that they had to sell so many family heirlooms in order to raise funds to prevent Althorp falling down. As they had done over the sales, several architectural historians questioned whether Raine understood the inheritance she married into.

Ironically, in her book *Do You Care About Historic Buildings?*, Raine stressed the importance of passing on an inheritance to the next generation. 'Our children and grandchildren can respond as we have to the challenge of beauty created hundreds of years ago.' Sadly the restoration at Althorp has ensured that Spencer descendants will never see the beauty of the stately home as it once was. While Raine claimed that she was only acting on Johnnie's instructions, many felt the driving force came from her and that, like many men, Johnnie was happy to leave the decorating of his home to his wife. Lady Elizabeth Anson, the Queen's cousin, who knows the family well comments: 'I don't think he would have noticed if the rooms had been decorated in an over-lavish way. Lots of men don't. In the same way that they don't notice if their wives are terribly overdressed. I do know Johnnie absolutely adored Raine and depended on her totally.'

Raine saw her task very clearly. She told journalist Lynda Lee-Potter: 'When I married John he asked me to do everything to save the house. The walls were peeling, the pictures were damp, everything was painted in what used to be called Ministry of Works cream. It was going to cost £2 million we hadn't got.'

Johnnie went further. He called Althorp an 'uncomfortable ruin', and claimed that 'It had to be [restored] for the benefit of future generations, for my children and grandchildren.' His assertions are hotly disputed: 'Saying Althorp needed vast restoration is nonsense,' says Robin Simon. To this even David Laws agrees. 'There was nothing more wrong with Althorp than is normal in a house like that. There were a few rotten window frames and it needed rewiring and some new plumbing, not much more.' It might have benefited from a judicious lick of paint in some areas, however. Although Jack Spencer left Althorp in excellent order, he was not interested in the finer points of decor and after he had lived there alone for three years following his wife's death, some areas had become rather shabby. According to David Laws there were even lampshades from British Home Stores in the Library.

A family friend believes that although Raine was enthusiastic over the restoration and redecoration, nothing was done without Johnnie's consent. 'The children saw her as the architect of all the expenditure and to a very large extent she was, but it isn't fair for her to be blamed for all of it, because if Johnnie said "I don't want to do it" she wouldn't. She was, however, extremely capable of persuading him to go along with her ideas, but he wouldn't always. She was quite clever and knew when to back off, bide her time and try later.'

Johnnie himself was as ready as ever publicly to endorse Raine's work. 'It's all due to my wife. I am very proud of her. It was her brain, her energy, her knowledge, but most of all her eye for colour. That's the biggest change – colour.'

He also stressed his own involvement. 'People imply that I have very little to do with the running of Althorp and that my wife rules over everything. In fact everything we have chosen for the house has been done together.' He claimed they worked as a team 'right down to crouching on the floor for hours with bits of curtain' and that he had always wanted to restore the great house. 'Ever since I was a boy I have wanted to do up this house, but my father never had sufficient funds to do it. Now with the increased numbers of visitors coming here, it has given us an opportunity to refurbish. My wife has been a great help and a great source of energy for the work to be done.'

He even praised her plans for warming the place up. 'Who wants to live in a freezing old museum? ... We even have log fires which turn out to be gas. Such a clever idea of Raine's. She started out with five and then bought fifteen and stuck them in the bedrooms. I think she was mortified when one of our friends admitted she was so cold she slept the night in her mink coat.' Raine's efforts to make Althorp warm and comfortable included installing controversial double glazing. 'She refused to sit and freeze,' says Sir Roy Strong who believes Raine 'has made Althorp marvellous in many ways'.

Jack Spencer chose to live in a very small part of Althorp, using the rest only for important family parties. When Raine arrived on the scene she wanted to be able to enjoy the entire house. Nor was it her idea of fun to live in a museum. In an interview with Jean Rook of the *Daily Express* about the changes she had made at Althorp she said, 'All I've tried to do is make the place warm and cheerful so that every room feels like a home you'd want to linger in, instead of like one of those stiff stately places in which you daren't sit on a chair.'

Her attitude had architectural historians holding their heads in despair. 'Nobody is saying she should have slept on a seventeenth-century straw mattress,' said one. 'If she wanted onyx bathrooms and Dralon sofas it's perfectly all right. But not in the Long Room, which is of great historical interest. Althorp before Raine was like many great country houses, deliciously run down. She decided however that she was going to glitz it like a Monaco palace which is a sad tragedy as well as being stupid.'

Art historians hated the fact that paintings which weren't sold were put under spotlights described by one as 'the kind used to pick out Athena posters in Habitat interiors'; that a wonderful antique wooden floor was hidden by a fitted carpet; that strip lighting was put in some corridors and that antique chairs were covered in velvet Dralon.

Raine was also ridiculed for putting up a painting of herself which she commissioned at a price of £7,500 from the artist Carlos Sancha. 'She wanted it to be very glamorous,' Sancha explains. 'She wanted to look romantic and had her hair backcombed by her maid for every sitting.' The picture showed Raine in a pink halter-neck dress and received almost universal derision. It was described as 'so hideous it looks straight off the cover of a Terry's All Gold chocolate box'.

Raine placed the portrait of herself among the Spencer ancestors. 'She would have got Johnnie's agreement to do that,' insists David Laws. The only painting of Johnnie at Althorp was done by the artist Rodrigo Moynihan to mark his twenty-first birthday and presented to him by the agricultural tenantry. Although there were plans for Sancha to do a joint portrait of Johnnie and Raine this did not materialise.

One eminent art historian blames Raine's narrow upbringing for the way Althorp was redecorated and believes she is a victim of her generation. 'She is inbetween things. She was not a docile Victorian wife staying at home looking after the dogs, she did not have an academic education and she is not a modern woman. She had a suburban view of the high life. Certainly the way the house has been decorated is a scandal. It might be appropriate to a flat in Fulham, but not to an important country house with a complex building history. The pity was that it was left in such good condition by the seventh Earl. Of course some things were a little worn but so what?'

It was Raine's timing as well as her taste that aroused such ire amongst the experts. The trend prevailing in the late seventies and eighties was to discover what a stately home originally looked like and take it back to what the architect intended. Raine's flamboyant decor ran contrary to this. 'The way she was redecorating Althorp was absolutely in the teeth of what everybody was saying people should do to their country house,' says Anna Somers Cocks. 'Authentic decor was the cry from the scholarship front. If Raine had done her redecoration in the 1930s, no one would have lifted an eyebrow, but having professed to be so keen on conservation when she was on the GLC, the fact that she didn't really involve the scholars or experts but put herself in the hands of the trade, upset the scholarship world a lot.'

It has always been important to Raine that her surroundings are very clean and many felt her dislike of anything dirty affected her judgment at Althorp. When David Laws was walking around the house with her discussing the redecoration he came across 'marvellous and delicate' antique quilted silk curtains. 'They weren't in wonderful condition,' he remembers, 'but in a country house you could have kept them.' According to Laws, Raine's reaction was 'Darling, it is old, it is dirty' and the curtains were got rid of. This was an attitude she maintained with many old chattels unless they were extremely important and valuable. 'What was left had to be made very, very clean,' Laws says. 'That is why everything was regilded.' Sir Roy Strong noticed it, too, when he was taken on a tour of Althorp soon after Johnnie and Raine moved in. 'I remember my wife commenting on the beauty of some old Victorian patchwork. It was obvious that Raine had never looked at it properly and certainly didn't like it.' One expert believes her insistence on cleanliness is a symptom of her insecurity. 'It is a sign of fragility that everything has to look clean and new. You need to feel secure and be confident enough to show people that you can afford something to look tatty, faded and torn. That's part of the love of living in a great house.'

He also feels that although well-intentioned, Raine's ideas for improving Althorp were misplaced. 'She's bright – everything she's done to the house are the decisions of someone very dynamic and energetic, but they are untrained ideas. She doesn't know about the things in the way Jack Spencer did. You cannot replace an eighteenth-century chair with something that looks as if it came from an Knightsbridge store ... Her redecoration has been completely unhistorical. She has spoilt the house, wrecked the collection and not built up a good business.'

A museum curator goes further. 'I think the restoration has inflicted worse damage than the selling of treasures. At least if something is sold, it is being recycled and you can hope the museum or collector will leave it as it is. Whereas when it's restored badly it's ruined and nothing can be done about it.' Others take the view that Althorp will always be greater than the people living in it. 'Althorp is still a sensational house with sensational things in it,' says John Hardy, formerly of the V & A.

A dilemma for anyone inheriting a stately home nowadays is whether they want to live in a home or a museum. They have to decide whether inherited antiques should be left as they are, so that they can be passed intact to the next generation, or whether they should be restored. Those who favour restoration are faced with further problems. Do they put today's taste before authenticity, or so-called authenticity before taste? Do they conserve works of art only to prevent deterioration? Or do they go further and try to return them back to their original state?

Viscount Coke is quite sure on the matter. 'If something has completely gone you have to do something about it, but if it is not completely gone, look after it, conserve it, but don't over-restore it. I'm afraid in the eighties an awful lot of money was spent on the house, which has been done up from top to bottom. You really don't need to do all the rooms. So what if the silk on the wall is faded? Unless the wall-hangings are coming right off the walls, they should be left alone.'

John Hardy thinks the present-day situation is more complicated. 'If the house is open to the public you cannot keep the light and dirt out as you could in the past. There's also the problem of who do you go to for advice, which interior decorator do you choose, and once you start do you put the wallpaper back to its nineteenth-century blue or its eighteenth-century red?'

The catalyst of the restoration that was to spread throughout Althorp House was cracks in the Library ceiling, which the Spencers maintained were caused by extra visitors after Diana married the Prince of Wales. Raine called in an expert to examine the beams. She told *Architectural Digest*, 'He went upstairs, put on a boiler suit, took the floorboards up for a good look then told me the ceiling could fall down any minute.' A senior member of staff, however, describes it as 'a perfectly normal repair project. The problems were partly caused by low-flying aircraft.' He remembers a more major repair in 1990, when steel girders were used to reinforce the Library ceiling at a cost of about £40,000. 'The Library is situated under the Picture Gallery which had a floor of questionable strength. Raine wanted to have large numbers of people in the gallery at money-earning functions, as part of her commercialisation of the house. She wanted it reinforced so that there was no risk of injury to people or damage to the Library ceiling.'

Dealing with the cracks in the Library ceiling created such an upheaval that Raine and Johnnie decided they might as well do a little redecorating at the same time. After they had done one room, the others looked so shabby by comparison that it led on to redecorating them all.

Complaints have been made about the lack of action on the part of local authority with regard to the double glazing and some of the redecoration, neither of which should have been carried out without consent in a Grade 1 listed building. Daventry District Council, which did not have a conservation officer until 1987, states that no application for permission to make alterations to Althorp was ever received. The Council states that the first it heard about any alterations was when a journalist contacted them in November 1991. It was only then that conservation officer Ian Smith, with Neil Burton of English Heritage, went along to inspect the changes. Despite the fact that it is a criminal offence incurring heavy fines or even a prison sentence, to remove original wall-coverings, put in double glazing and generally alter the character of a Grade I listed building without listed building consent, they decided to take no action. Ian Smith claims that as the alterations had all been done about twelve years previously, 'it would be a bit churlish to do something about it so long afterwards'. Although the Department of the Environment state there is no time limit for bringing prosecutions, the Council's own guideline is that because of the time factor involved, their case would have been difficult to prove in court. Smith does admit, however, that 'if we had found out at the time we would have done something'.

Neil Burton, conservation officer for English Heritage, takes a more lenient view. 'One or two things were done to Althorp without listed building consent which should have been sought before they happened. When it was found out that they had been done, the feeling was that they were not unduly damaging and were for the most part reversible.'

Embarking on the work without obtaining permission was an extraordinary act of forgetfulness. William Bell, who was a member of the committee and worked under Raine on the GLC's Covent Garden Development Committee and Architectural Heritage Year was well aware of her legal knowledge. 'She knew the law regarding historic buildings and was very well acquainted with all the legislation concerned. She wasn't just an amateur, she would know which section of each act to quote. She found out from English Heritage what the regulations of Government historic buildings are and knew the consequence of those acts which are applicable.'

Ashley Barker, who was senior adviser to the Historic Buildings Board, agrees. 'I shouldn't think she was ignorant of any of these things. She had directed a fairly sharp intelligence to the law at the time.' Art historian Robin Simon says, 'If you had a house in London you would have had English Heritage come down on you like a ton of bricks. They should have been involved but weren't.' To make matters worse he describes the double glazing as 'ghastly hideous plastic sort of stuff which doesn't match the glazing bars'.

Non-academics take a less purist view of Raine's out-with-the-old-and-in-with-the-new approach. Alan Jefferson believes 'There's a feeling among conservationists that carpets and curtains have to be threadbare and nothing must be disturbed. Or that if a room has plain wooden boards that is the way it should be left for ever. There are very few historic houses that are totally lived in. Most people live in an apartment within the house. Althorp, however, was made comfortable for today and was not draughty. The windows were exactly the same, but there was an inner pane of glass on the thick sill to provide double glazing. So what if the gilding is shiny? So what if the walls were red before and are now blue silk? There's nothing to stop you changing the colour scheme.'

As experts have pointed out, redesigning a stately home is very different from redesigning a house. It requires considerable skill, a sense of history and a lot of money. The choice of the right adviser is essential. Many have criticised the choice of Bond Street dealers Partridge Fine Arts, and feel that Raine should have approached the redecoration with more caution.

Caution, however, is not a characteristic for which Raine is noted and even Johnnie admitted that the restoration project had got out of hand. 'Well, to tell you the truth we didn't intend to do so much,' he said. 'But after we'd tried out one room to see how it would look the rest looked so tatty we thought we'd better go the whole hog.' He loved it. 'I'm thrilled with it because when I was a small boy the house always looked so shabby. I'm only a link in a chain – there have been lots of past earls and I hope lots to come, so my job was to make life easier for Charles and my future daughter-in-law, when he finds her, by handing it on in a better state than I got it.' As usual, he gave his wife his full support. 'People have said nasty things about the restoration but many of them have not been to see it. It is the best restored house in England and my wife and I believe it has been done beautifully.'

Asked whether he endorsed what was going on, Johnnie said, 'I was ill a few years ago but my mind is perfectly sound. In fact, I can devote more time to the house and less to official engagements because I have been ill and at home.' David Laws, however, believes that once the redecoration was under way 'Johnnie began to pull the shutters down over his eyes over what was going on. If he didn't like it, he knew he couldn't stand up to her.' In reply to the criticism John Partridge says 'the proportion of praise for our restoration is undoubtedly far greater [than the criticism]. If I were given the opportunity of doing this project again I do not think there is anything I would change.'

During her marriage to Gerald Legge, Raine became used to ready money. She found the lack of cash at Althorp a difficult restriction and resented being criticised for the amount she was spending. David Laws admits that he had to adopt an on/off approach to the work, according to how much money was available. Money became increasingly scarce until Raine and Johnnie received a massive loan, estimated at about £2 million, from National Westminster Bank in Northampton. (If they had not been given the loan, no doubt even more Spencer treasures would have been sold.)

Raine and Johnnie preferred to raise money themselves rather than follow the practice of many stately-home owners and ask the National

Trust for financial help. 'We didn't apply for a grant from the National Trust because there are always strings attached,' explained Johnnie in an interview in *Woman's Own* in 1985. 'They send in their brigadier – and there's nothing I dread more than a National Trust brigadier.'

As time went on, however, even Raine admitted 'I became nervous about the costs.' In an interview with *Daily Mail* journalist Brian Vine in 1991, she said, 'I've even lent some of my own personal money to John when the interest rate looks too high on the loans. So some of me is in the house. Not many people know that.'

Raine justified their stand in an earlier newspaper interview. 'It's ironic that if we went whining to the Government for grants or tried to hand the house over to the National Trust, we'd be heroes and heroines. Certain people complain that my husband took an agonising decision to sell some treasures to make a go on the house. It's perfectly ridiculous.'

In time they learned not to worry about criticism. 'The more people criticise this house, the more people will come and see it,' said Raine. 'It's such an irony. They read the criticism and then come to see the "gaudy summer pudding" we've got here.'

One of the more expensive and wasteful projects was to convert the Muniment Room, which had housed the family archives, into a grandiose self-contained flat. Raine's idea was to provide a luxurious apartment inside the house that people attending conferences at Althorp could rent. Staff do not recall it ever being used for the purpose.

She also stripped the chapel, which precipitated the sale of many of the religious paintings, and used it as a lumber room. As well as the extensive redecorations in the public part of the house, Raine drastically altered the family's private wing, where she and Johnnie loved to escape. Here, Raine rejigged a whole series of rooms. She turned what was the night nursery into a boudoir with a sofa and two armchairs. She created a storeroom for her clothes and a bathroom for herself, leading off her very large bedroom, with turquoise walls and pink curtains. Her bedroom housed a huge king-sized canopied bed adorned with 14-foot-high draperies and lots of gilt furniture. Next door was Johnnie's rather masculine bedroom and dressing room decorated in pale fawn and stone. Raine brightened up the rather gloomy private drawing room where houseguests used to meet by painting it yellow and blue. This was the room where she kept her collection of silver-gilt boxes and Miró paintings and where Johnnie kept his collection of seascapes by the Norfolk artist Edward Seago whom he knew personally and liked. These paintings were Johnnie's only addition to the artistic heritage of his stately home.

Much of Raine's restoration was criticised because it has severely reduced the value of the remaining heirlooms. An expert comments:

She regilded things that should not have been gilded. She rebuilt bits of furniture that were already in good condition. In the Picture Gallery there is a whole series of eighteenth-century lacquer cabinets with brass hinges. They were rebuilt and all the metalwork was gilded including the hinges which were never gilded originally. They've been so messed around that they are no longer of museum quality which they were before. All the picture frames were gilded. A large set of mid-eighteenth century chairs have been rebuilt and covered in orange velvet and gilded, which has substantially reduced their value. They were originally designed by Athenian Stuart especially for Spencer House and were white and gold with green damask upholstery and in good condition as they were restored earlier this century with their authentic colours.

Experts were furious that the various relevant authorities seemed to be turning a blind eye to what was going on at Althorp. They singled out English Heritage who, they felt, could have done more to stop the restoration, in particular the Athenian Stuart furniture originally from the Great Room at Spencer House, which Raine considered dowdy and asked Partridges to restore. Because the furniture was of national importance and had been exempted from death duties in 1922, an application was made to English Heritage for a grant towards the 'restoration' costs. The Historic Buildings Committee of English Heritage asked the Department of Furniture and Woodwork at the V & A for its opinion. The reply was that the chairs did not need much restoration and certainly not much gilding as they had never been fully gilded.

The department went further, saying that the total restoration of the chairs would destroy their original quality. A grant was therefore refused on the grounds that the proposed work was neither necessary nor desirable. The work went ahead regardless. The set was also broken up. John Partridge was given six chairs for his work at Althorp, two of which he sold in an unrestored state to the V & A for £20,000.

A cupboard made by Athenian Stuart for Spencer House was also drastically altered. Over the years various architectural historians tried to examine this example of Stuart's fine craftsmanship but Raine always refused permission. One of her reasons might have been because it was converted to hold coats and kept in the family's private wing.

Expert restoration is extremely expensive. A pair of globes in the Picture Gallery, for example, cost £10,000 to restore. Chairs and picture frames cost about £2,000 each to regild. And it was the regilding costs which many felt had run wild in terms both of taste and expense. One expert said disparagingly, 'They squirted £2 million over the walls'.

Raine, however, had a predisposition for gilt which, like her interest in selling, has its roots in the early sixties. When still Lady Lewisham she found a family crest – a coronet out of which rise five ostrich feathers – in a Kensington antique shop. In what was described at the time as 'reckless disregard for the finer points of heraldry', she had the whole crest gilded before positioning it on the front door of her house in Hill Street, Mayfair. When questioned about her possible lack of taste she replied: 'The crest came off an old carriage door. It was in Sheffield plate and looked very nice, but I thought it would be even nicer gilded.' Several items of furniture were also brightly gilded.

Gilding is a difficult art; there is a big difference between commercial and historical gilding, and regilding or repainting antique furniture can cut its value by half, or even more. One expert believes: 'The way the gilt has been applied at Althorp has no subtlety and no depth. It is all wrong – opaque and garish – an abomination. And if you have enough money to throw around regilding things that don't need regilding, how can you then say you are preserving the house?'

Regilded picture frames also lose their value. Paul Mitchell, a renowned expert in antique picture frames, comments: 'From a purist point of view someone who sells antique picture frames would always prefer to have a frame with its original gilding. You cannot, for example, say it is a Louis XVI frame in its entirety if someone has regilded it in the twentieth century. It is not the same object and therefore does not have the same value.'

Furniture expert Peter Thornton, however, does not believe that the gilding at Althorp is that much of a disaster. 'I'm not so condemning as some people. Gilding is meant to look like solid gold. The idea that it must be cracked, battered and muted is just another way of looking at it. The gold was bright when it was new. The question is: Are you honouring your own taste or the person who bought the article originally? It is not clear-cut and once you start, some things will look brilliant, which in turn will make everything else around it look tatty.'

But even Johnnie recognised that the gilding at Althorp might have been overdone. 'The gilding may be a bit bright now, but in a hundred years' time it will tone down,' he said. That was certainly the view of John Partridge who was quoted in 1991 as saying, 'The brightness has already softened. I can see a difference every time I visit Althorp. What people must remember is that the furniture looks the way it did when it was first made. It wasn't meant to be seen by electric light, only candlelight and natural daylight. That makes a difference.'

Dame Barbara Cartland also supported her daughter's love of gilt. 'All Raine did was put back the rooms as they were originally. She made it look beautiful, absolutely right for the period. It was only the Victorians who made all their gold look antique.'

Johnnie also tried to justify the restoration on the grounds that it had provided work for skilled craftsmen. 'We kept a lot of craftsmen in business during a period of a recession and I'm very pleased about that too. We had people gilding, restoring leather, making tassels and braids. Many of those craftsmen could have gone under at that time.'

Raine's love of gilding is only matched by her strong views on colour. Like her mother, she likes colours bold. 'It is the most important thing to me,' she told *Architectural Digest*. 'I think being brought up during the war made me feel starved for it. People today don't realise how lucky they are to be able to buy paint in every colour. It totally influences the way people think. The important thing about colour at Althorp was to take clues from the paintings and carpets that were already in each room.

'In the Saloon for instance all the portraits give the hint that the walls should be terracotta – the heel of a shoe, a rose, a ribbon. The South Drawing Room had been a green that made people look seriously unwell. There the salmon pink comes from the Savonnerie carpet. In the Library the walls are a parchment colour because many of the books are that particular colour. I couldn't live with pretty, pretty colours.'

Even Johnnie was a little taken aback by some of Raine's colour schemes and John Partridge confessed to *Architecural Digest* that the strong blue Raine chose for the State Dining Room caused them both some anxiety. 'Lord Spencer and I were very worried about that blue,' he said. 'It seemed much too strong. But you know, she was plumb right. She had picked up the blue that was in two paintings by Salvator Rosa and it looks wonderful.'

Raine worked out a theme for each room and then decorated it to fit in with her ieas. 'The Library is a room for daytime, for wearing corduroy trousers,' she said. 'Not just stately-home things, but comfortable chairs and good reading lights, a good lamp next to the card table, a place to put down a cup of coffee.' She chose pink for the South Drawing Room so that people would say 'I'd love to give a party in that room.' 'The pink [is] for evening, a good colour for making women wearing silk dresses stand up straighter. The room is lit with candles at night, kept dim.'

David Laws remembers that Raine would do her research and then tell him what she would like. 'Sometimes I would turn it down,' he remembers. 'Once she even wanted silver on the walls.' He always felt happier if Raine didn't throw herself into the redecorating one hundred per cent. 'Then I could influence things.' He is particularly proud of the Library, Dining Room ('it was proper for the dinners she gave') and the Wootten Hall ('it looks good and is correct').

One of the ways Raine tried to make 'every room feel like a home' at Althorp was to order vast dried flower arrangements from Kenneth Turner. He first met Raine in the sixties when she asked him to do some flower arrangements for her Mayfair home. 'Countess Spencer adores flowers and for Althorp I had to create special decorations to enhance, but not take over, about ten rooms. Every room had a different character and the shape and colour were always discussed in detail first. Soon after she married Lord Spencer I went to Althorp and she gave me colour swatches and fabrics of the curtains and carpets. She had also bought the containers. She wanted the dried flowers to look very realistic and liked country flowers – delphiniums, peonies, larkspur, old-fashioned roses, love-in-the-mist, zinnias and dahlias. These were changed every two to three years.'

Turner also provided a 'huge hedge of flowers' for the house in Farm Street where Raine now lives. He is a great fan of hers. 'She is a poppet and a highly intelligent lady. She is an absolute perfectionist, has remarkable taste and a great eye for architecture. I love her to bits because she is the most enthusiastic person. I think most men get on well with her. But she doesn't suffer fools gladly.'

To maintain an atmosphere of cosiness even when Althorp was being used for functions, Raine would choose a room just a little smaller than was needed for the number of people expected. 'I don't mean it should be so crowded that you're likely to get champagne spilled on your dress, but certainly it shouldn't be like those cartoons of a stately home with two people at opposite ends of a huge table.' She and Johnnie used the State Dining Room if there were at least twenty-six guests, but felt it worked best with thirty to forty people. For musical evenings she liked to use the Great Room which had good acoustics. For dancing they used the Saloon.

Raine regularly acknowledged Johnnie's support in the refurbishment of Althorp. 'I couldn't have done it if I had a husband who was the kind who kept saying "You mustn't change that, Aunt Martha bought that in Hong Kong" or "Uncle Harry this that or the other." But he was wonderful. He just said "Let's do it." ' Alan Jefferson from the British Tourist Authority believes the comfort of the house should have impressed Johnnie's children. 'I think the children should have seen that although heirlooms have been sold, they have been left with a house that is very comfortable and the whole thing can be lived in and will be good for a long time to come.'

The children, however, did not see it that way. Diana in particular was outraged by her stepmother's 'gaudy' taste and on the increasingly rare occasions when she or her sisters visited Althorp to see their father, they refused to enter the private apartments if Raine was there. They preferred to stay in one of the houses on the estate where Johnnie could visit them. Charles was said to check that Raine was away before visiting his father and, if she returned unexpectedly, would not sit down at the same dinner table as her. Even Johnnie's aunt, Lady Douglas-Home, who had always loved Althorp had misgivings about the redecoration. 'It was meticulously done, but I don't know if I liked it,' she says.

At first Johnnie described the rumours of family arguments over the restoration as 'mischief-making tittle-tattle – sheer dry rot. It's absolute nonsense dredged up by people to stir up trouble and put my family down.' But he finally acknowledged that there was a problem in a rather undignified outburst to Brian Vine of the *Daily Mail*, on a flight to Nice in 1991, which people saw as a sign that he was not a well man.

17

Althorp Aid

If Raine's selling of the family valuables caused a sharp, disapproving intake of breath amongst fellow peers, her other money-making ventures left them quite breathless. She embarked on a wide range of commercial schemes, from charging for autographed postcards to marketing the family wedding dresses. Althorp was run like Aristocracy Plc as Raine set out to adapt what she had learned about improving product turnover and business tourism, during her time at the GLC and BTA, to her own mini-world at Althorp. Although some of her ideas were original they were often insensitive and inappropriate for a great country house. What fellow aristocrats and others wondered was why someone who had so longed for a title, was now selling cheap jewellery in the gift shop and, even worse, taking money herself at the till?

Even Raine has claimed that it was not always enjoyable. 'Some of it has been hell,' she said. 'It wasn't my idea of heaven to set up two shops and a tearoom and run functions, but my husband and I have done our best and if, at the end of the day, a few eggs have been broken, toes trodden on and a few people don't like it, then too bad.' To make her point, Raine would often insist that the air-conditioned Rolls-Royce picked her up from the front door of Althorp and drove her the 150 yards to the shop. Her overt friendliness to customers was deliberate, however, and she never lost her regal manner.

She even involved Johnnie in the operation, dressing him in an apron and handing him a broom to sweep the cobbles outside the newly-converted shops. It was a quaint his-and-hers situation. While she served in the gift shop, some said dispensing charm as if donating charity to the poor, Johnnie was to be found in the shop next door selling wine. Johnnie loved playing shopkeepers. It passed the time while the butler, cook and maids kept Althorp in order, and it made a wonderful photo-opportunity for tourists. To get the wine shop going, Johnnie raided the Althorp cellars and initially there were terrific bargains to be had. He sold vintage bottles at job-lot prices including fine brandy worth £50 for a mere £20. 'Several of us were regular customers when the wine shop first opened,' said a friend, 'we couldn't believe the prices.' Later these bargains were replaced by 'not very good wine' with the Spencer label.

Johnnie enjoyed both serving and chatting to his customers. He would hear many stories that amused him and sometimes, when the wine shop closed, would come into the house and say, 'I've had a good day today: three hysterectomies, a divorce and a bankruptcy!'

The neighbours, however, were not amused by Raine's middle-class marketing at Althorp. A local aristocrat said, 'They were not much liked in the area, not so much Earl Spencer, but Raine who, in trying to turn things around, brought a commercial streak into the estate. In the Northamptonshire area there are a lot of old landed families who have managed to turn their estates into a commercial enterprise.' She admits, though, that the disapproval was also 'partly resentment that she was so successful'.

Another described Raine as 'nouveau pushy especially as there were an awful lot of people in the area who have fallen on hard times whose estates were not paying but who have not gone to those lengths'. In answer to the criticism Raine fell back on the all-too-familiar excuses: 'The thing that makes me angry is how are we expected to settle death duties, pay for the upkeep and the restoration without doing things like selling wine and postcards?'

Raine adopted the principle of making every penny count, but a far less astute businesswoman could have told her that, as a way of funding the maintenance of a vast stately home, many of her schemes were as effective as feeding canapés to a giant. It would have made greater economic sense, and been far less trouble, if she had simply followed the practice of most stately-home owners and closed Althorp for the winter, thereby cutting down on heating costs and staff. Instead the house was kept open almost every day of the year, even though, there were hardly any visitors in the winter.

The Historic Houses Association estimated that in the late eighties it cost roughly £1 per square foot to keep a house like Althorp going per day – most of it spent on maintenance, particularly since English Heritage have cut back on grants to private house owners. Another stately-home owner believes, however, that 'although a house like Althorp needs a lot of backup, one never felt, unlike a lot of other big houses in the area, that there was a great lack of money there'.

Based on her experience in the tourist industry, Raine decided to develop Althorp as a much-sought-after location for functions both corporate and personal. She saw its potential as a glamorous place to hold lunches, dinners, wedding receptions, bar mitzvahs, musical evenings and for the launching of new commercial products. Even before the restoration was completed, there were so many bookings that the kitchen was breaking down under the strain. 'When there were fifty or so to dinner the kitchen couldn't cope,' David Laws remembers. 'Neither could the plumbing. In the evening houseguests had to be careful when they had a hot bath. It was hopeless when everyone came back after a day's shooting as they all wanted a hot bath right away.'

One of Raine's more successful ventures was the launch of musical evenings at Althorp. She started with a series of six musical soirées, beginning on 19 November 1982, which were described in the publicity brochure as 'a rare and delightful way of enjoying an evening', the ticket price of £30 to cover dinner and the concert. The first of three was well attended.

Local worthies, businessmen and retired teachers were among the one hundred guests who turned up in their evening best. The Spencers' relationship to the recently-wed and, at the time, phenomenally popular Princess of Wales, gave sales an obvious boost. 'I am not saying we wouldn't have come if they weren't the parents of the Princess of Wales, but it does make a difference,' said one guest. They were served terrine of game, roast beef and chocolate mousse, accompanied by Althorp wine. According to reports, guests were charmed by their hosts, who held hands from time to time throughout the evening.

After dinner, the guests went upstairs to the velvet-hung Great Room to listen to the London Operetta Ensemble perform selections from Gilbert and Sullivan. During the interval Althorp champagne, not included in the all-in price, was for sale and after the second half of the concert, guests were served hot soup before they left. Raine was reported to greet people with a smile 'which matched the porcelain beauty of her most delicate complexion'. Initially both she and Johnnie went out of their way to give their customers the social kudos of participating in a grand occasion. Johnnie was particularly amused to see them arrive dressed up to the nines. 'Johnnie loved to see people who were not to the manor born coming to Althorp dressed in their minks,' said a friend.

Raine could also be spontaneously generous. At a later dinner one of the guests, Sandra Hill from Preston, had hot gravy and horseradish spilt down the back of her cocktail dress when a waitress caught a tray on the back of her chair. She was being escorted upstairs when, by chance, Raine herself appeared. When she saw what had happened she immediately replaced Sandra's £60 dress with one of her own – a black velvet Dior gown originally worth at least £1000 which fitted Sandra perfectly. Raine even helped her into the dress, zipped her up and fastened the cuffs on the sleeves. She told Sandra to wear it home and post it back later, together with the bill for cleaning her own dress. In fact Sandra changed back into her own stained dress at the end of the evening.

In 1983 nine 'special evenings' with candlelit dinners and music recitals were offered for the all-inclusive, non refundable price of £430. One of these was a dinner for a hundred and seventy guests who, after eating, sat at the foot of the great Althorp staircase to listen to a performance of Cimarosa's *The Secret Marriage* by six English National Opera singers under the direction of Robert Carson of Glyndebourne. There were also twice-yearly champagne parties when one hundred and ten paying guests dined and danced for £55 a head.

Over the next few years there were several variations on the dinner theme including ceaseless corporate entertaining: groups of businessmen were ferried into Althorp by helicopter for meals, and shooting days were sold to Norwegians and Swedes. Stacks of tables and chairs were kept ready in the Wootton Hall which, said a friend, made Althorp look 'like a chain hotel'. One autumn, when a group of Japanese businessmen came for lunch, the centrepiece of each table was a gold tinsel mini-Christmas tree, which played a Christmas carol. Raine proudly showed these off to a friend, saying 'Aren't they the sweetest things you've ever seen?' The friend refrained from commenting.

Raine and Johnnie, Britain's highly commercial nobles, would entertain anyone if the price was right. In December 1982 eleven shoppers in the cut-price German supermarket chain Allkauf (the German equivalent of Kwiksave) picked up a leaflet at the checkout and, as part of a promotion competition, won tickets for a dinner party with Lord and Lady Spencer at Althorp. The lucky eleven were flown to London and transported to Althorp where non-German-speaking Johnnie could only smile his friendliest smile, while Raine did her best with her much better German to make them welcome. For their hospitality on this occasion the Spencers received a fee estimated in the region of £1,500.

When Raine was asked, at a later date, why she and Johnnie undertook such enterprises she replied, 'If you believe in Britain at all, it has got to show foreigners that things aren't all tumbling down. People are so eager to believe the bad things – Ireland and so on – it is nice to show them the other side.'

Johnnie had more success with American guests, who, as lovers of British royalty, were thrilled at the idea of dining with the Spencers for £50 a head. Johnnie had them eating out of his hand with anecdotes about Princes William and Henry.

Toastmaster Ivor Spencer, who runs a school for butlers, organised a day at Althorp for his trainees. For their fifty pounds they had morning coffee and a tour of Althorp followed by lunch, although no promises were made that they would meet the Earl and Countess. It was, Ivor Spencer said, appropriate for his students to see how the wealthy lived.

The Spencers also entertained Aramis, the makers of aftershave, during the launch of a new range of male toiletries called JHL. For two nights the 140 guests, mostly perfume-sellers more usually found on the ground floor of department stores, stayed at the stately home. 'Althorp was chosen because of the setting and ambiance,' said a spokesman at the time. 'JHL is for the man who appreciates the finer things in life.' Sadly there were not enough of these to make the range a going concern and it was discontinued. Later, in 1989, Raine and Johnnie entertained two hundred car dealers for a new model launch.

After a while the novelty of making small-talk to strangers wore off, and Raine and Johnnie became rather bored with spending the whole evenings in the company of their paying guests. They changed their routine and would appear formally dressed to greet guests on their arrival before disappearing into the private wing during the meal to eat their own supper on trays, usually watching television in the study. They would then return after dinner, still immaculately turned out, often to draw the raffle. The usual first prize was a hamper of Althorp champagne. After dinner, guests were able to wander through the main rooms.

Raine found a continuous supply of people to attend these occasions by putting the names of all the visitors to the house who spent well in the gift shop on computer and then sending them invitations. Many found a personal invitation from the Spencers irresistible. Raine also used mail-outs for a variety of other Spencer offers, sometimes to the great amusement of the recipients. One such was Claude Blair, former Keeper of the Metalwork Department at the V & A, who was responsible for the valuation of the Marlborough wine coolers which Johnnie and Raine sold in the early eighties. 'After my contact with them,' he says, 'I got several letters addressed "Dear valued customer" asking me if I wanted to purchase some wine.'

Johnnie was proud of Raine's organisational skills. 'My wife is a very good organiser of lunch parties and corporate hospitality to raise money for the house,' he said. This wasn't true of all functions, however.

Sandra Moss, from Milton Keynes, arranged for her thirteen-year-old son's bar mitzvah celebration to take place at Althorp House on 5 April 1992. When the occasion was booked eighteen months in advance, no one could have foreseen that it would take place a week after Johnnie's death. In the event, what should have been a celebration nearly turned into a fiasco. 'The Spencers were really pleased to take the booking,' she remembers, 'as it was to be the first bar mitzvah they would be catering. I paid my deposit but I didn't realise what I had let myself in for. When you go to an establishment like that you think it will be well run, but the organisation was chaotic. An answerphone was always left on and I had to fight to make an appointment to meet anyone.' Over the booking period four chefs came and went and, before a menu was even sorted out, Mrs

Moss claims she was asked to pay the full cost of the event in advance. She put her foot down. 'I told them that without seeing a menu, I wasn't paying.' Ironically it was Charles Spencer who saved the day. Despite having sacked Raine's caterers the day after his father died, rather than cancel the booking, he offered Mrs Moss the caterers he had used for his father's funeral. And although his father's ashes were being interned that same Saturday, he appreciated the importance of the event for the Moss family. 'He did everything he could, although he could find no record of our deposit,' says Mrs Moss. 'The paperwork was apparently in chaos.'

One of Raine's favourite promotional exercises was serving in the gift shop, where she also took the admission money. Here she could be found, even on Sundays, extolling the virtues of the reproduction jewellery to any visitor who would listen. The contrast between the immaculate and expensively turned out Countess and the poor-quality objects she was selling left some bemused, and others reaching for their wallets under the impression that if it was good enough for a countess it was good enough for them. Lady Elizabeth Anson, the Queen's cousin, loved Raine's reproduction jewellery and bought so much on her visits to Althorp that Johnnie gave her a jewellery box from Fortnum & Mason to thank her for supporting the shop. 'He was such a kind and lovable person,' she says.

Raine also hit upon the scheme of selling the jewellery by mail order. In 1982 she sent out thousands of colour brochures offering the so-called 'Althorp Jewels' to likely customers. She was delighted when, in the first week, £2,000 worth of orders arrived at the stately home. 'It's the best idea we've ever had,' she enthused. 'Quite honestly no one can tell the difference.' The jewels, which the catalogue made clear were not real, included 'emerald' earrings and brooches at £6.60 and an 'amethyst and rhinestone' necklace for £230. There was even a replica of Princess Diana's sapphire-and-diamond engagement ring for £7.82. An expert in Hatton Garden, the centre of London's diamond trade, said, 'Don't waste my time. It's something you find in a Christmas cracker. It's worth 50p, if that.'

The gift shop wasn't the consistent money spinner Raine had hoped and in 1991 she admitted that it had lost money.

Visitors could also buy autographed bottles of wine and books, and signed postcards for £1. Requests to autograph brochures of the house, however, would be met by a dazzling smile and a polite refusal. A visitor said, 'I was told they would never sign them because they could make more money by selling autographed pictures in the shop.' In 1988 Raine said: 'We worked out we'd written 30,000 signatures last year. We do them all ourselves. We don't cheat, that would be awful.'

Because Raine spent so much time in the shop, she had a first-hand view of the sort of visitors Althorp attracted. In 1987, noticing a marked increase in the numbers of Japanese tourists, she decided to learn Japanese. She employed a private tutor for several hours each week and studied hard. She began by learning basic instructions, then a simple conversation. Within a matter of months she had become so proficient that she could deliver a speech in Japanese, her mother, Dame Barbara, boasted. 'At fifty-eight I think it is marvellous.' Raine thoroughly enjoyed seeing the look of surprise on the faces of her Japanese visitors when she greeted them in well-pronounced Japanese.

But on yet another occasion her enthusiasm got the better of her. She was lunching with David Levin, the owner of the Capital Hotel in Knightsbridge and, after the meal, got up to go to the Ladies' room. As she left the restaurant she saw four Japanese businessmen sitting at the other end of the room. Without a moment's hesitation she went up to them and started talking Japanese. She welcomed them to London, talked about the hotel and herself. After a while one of the gentlemen said, 'Excuse me, but we are from California and none of us understand Japanese, which I assume is what you were speaking.' According to David Levin, 'She was mortified. She was giving her best.'

Raine had a love-hate relationship with visitors. She was delighted if they spent money in the shop, but she could also be unfriendly and tactless. Walking through the doors one day from the private wing into the public part of the house, she saw the end of a tour party walking down the corridors. 'Ah, the dreaded public,' she called and retreated behind the private door. David Laws, who was with her at the time, said her acerbic tones were heard by several in the group who looked shocked and upset.

Visitors were not encouraged to take notes as they walked around the stately home, even if they were conservationists and art historians who made their identity known. One art historian, working on a research project, was firmly tapped on the shoulder by Raine and told to put his notebook away. When he tried to explain his case to her, he was asked to leave.

Raine antagonised many by not allowing wheelchairs into Althorp, although disabled visitors were welcome in the teashop and could buy souvenirs. The Althorp brochure claims that disabled people are refused entry for reasons of safety and access, although a toilet has been adapted for their use. Raine justified the policy by saying, 'We do not have any sort of ropes or barriers and a wheelchair might easily roll over the carpets which are extremely valuable and we don't want that. A wheelchair is obviously a fire risk because, in case of a fire, it might block up an exit and be dangerous to other people visiting the house.'

One of her fiercest critics was Lord Snowdon, a keen campaigner for the disabled. Speaking at the London launch of a Charity Awards Scheme for premises with the best facilities for the disabled, in November 1991, he said in a barely concealed attack on Althorp: 'A privately-run stately home delights in welcoming fee-paying members of the public, but it is stressed in the brochure that people in wheelchairs are not allowed, let alone not welcomed. Not because of narrow doorways and passages, not because of steps but because, I quote: "Wheelchairs would damage the highly-polished floors and the person pushing the wheelchair might slip and hurt themselves." I find this attitude horrendous and totally unacceptable.'

Wheelchair athlete David Holding, a spina bifida victim since birth, and disabled winner of the 1989 London Marathon, was given a polite refusal when he asked to look round the house in November 1991. He was outraged. 'As far as I am concerned,' he said, 'it is blatant discrimination against disabled people.' It was felt that Raine's stand was particularly untenable in view of her long association with the British Tourist Authority whose job it is to encourage tourists of all kinds. It was another example of her private actions being at odds with her public stand. The Spencers were reluctant to make exceptions even for a party of old ladies, in the late eighties, in the care of Johnnie's favourite charity, SGBI. Johnnie's friend Grace Randall was among a group invited to Althorp for tea. As she was in a wheelchair she did not join the tour of the house, but Johnnie behaved like the gentleman he was and kept her company. 'He was so kind he stayed with me all the time,' Miss Randall said. 'After the tour they gave us a wonderful tea which Johnnie and Raine served and when we left we were all given a bag containing several small items including a pen and key-ring as a memento of our visit.'

Raine failed to take advantage of one important opportunity to increase the number of tourists to Althorp. Although Prince Charles and Princess Diana were opening an exhibition called 'The Treasure Houses of Britain' in Washington in 1985, the Spencers refused to loan a single heirloom from Althorp's historic collection, a decision which Raine put down to Johnnie. 'My husband decided not to lend anything because so often when you do, something gets broken,' she said. 'It's not worth it. In any event we are open to the public all the year round, so we need all the items in the house.' The exhibition, which featured seven hundred items from more than two hundred country homes, was planned as a showcase to encourage tourism to Britain, which Raine herself worked hard to promote. Prince Charles uncharacteristically spoke out on Diana's behalf. 'My wife is rather sorry to find there isn't anything in the exhibition from her family home,' he said.

Raine was also reluctant to let specialists study the Spencer archives before they were sold in 1984. 'There is a tradition of stately homes opening their archives to scholars,' explains an architectural historian. 'The seventh Earl was always corresponding with historians and societies in the process of historical research. Sometimes when scholars plough through papers they come up with interesting facts for the family. I wrote several letters to Raine in the course of some research – all of which were ignored. Eventually I managed to ask her directly, but my request was refused. If you somehow managed to get through to Johnnie himself, he would always let you come in.'

In 1983 Raine decided that money could be made by selling some old clothes that were hanging unworn in wardrobes around the house. These included a man's blue velvet jacket with satin lapels made in 1961, the year Diana was born, which was put on sale for £50. An enormous overcoat with a moulting fur half-lining that Johnnie's father had worn for twenty-three years was also on sale for £50 and a few of Raine's old frocks including a pure silk dress for £15. There are no records of what was sold but it was a venture she repeated on a grander scale in 1988.

Having enjoyed the success of both her musical evenings and her gift shop, Raine decided to combine the two money-making operations. She invited guests to Althorp and sold bits and pieces to them at the same time. Aware of the value of packaging the product, and to make the occasion seem as far removed as possible from a jumble sale, she asked people to wear formal attire. For one such party in the spring of 1984, the Spencers sent out four hundred 'At Home' invitations decreeing that guests wear 'Dark suits, cocktail dresses long or short'. Many who received them assumed they were being invited to a discreet and private gathering at Althorp, put on their finery and presented themselves promptly at 6.30 p.m. as requested. 'I thought it was a smart party and was clad to the nines,' one guest said. What a disappointment it turned out to be. After being greeted with warm smiles and lingering handshakes by the Spencers themselves, the guests were more than a little surprised to be shown into a room filled with tables laden not with the expected canapés, but all manner of knick-knacks, mementoes and souvenirs on sale to raise funds for Althorp. Johnnie personally mixed a punch which apparently soothed some of the ruffled feathers of the guests. The exercise was repeated several times, particularly in the months before Christmas when Raine hoped 'wallets would be full.'

In November 1989 two hundred 'friends' were invited to an 'At Home' for a Christmas preview of the gifts on sale in the Althorp shop. This time, under the chandeliers and Old Master paintings, waitresses in white gloves passed round canapés on silver salvers as guests sipped their drinks. At 8.00 p.m. sharp, however, Raine invited them to walk the short distance from the house to the stableblock, where the shop is situated. She managed to arrive before them in the chauffeur-driven Rolls and was able to greet everyone as they arrived. There they found a mountain of sandwiches, halves of Scotch eggs and cheese straws. To wash these down, guests were asked to pay 50p per cup of coffee – a commercial touch that soured the evening for many. Some guests refused to buy coffee on principle. One commented, 'We felt insulted. How could she? I was furious for a week. Lady Spencer was making so much money from the sale of her goods, it could have paid for the coffee fifty times over. It had been a pleasant social occasion until this jarred the whole evening.'

Johnnie, however, was delighted with Raine's business approach to his family home. 'I want to keep this place going and the best way to do it is to manage it as a business.' . . . 'I am the modern entrepreneurial aristocrat and proud of it.' . . . 'It's all commerce but it's got to be in order to survive.'

Asked whether he felt this was vulgar he replied, 'No, no. It all helps us to live here. If the house were taken over by the National Trust it would cost the taxpayer much more to keep it going than we spend on it. Besides, imagine all those beautiful rooms full of civil servants.'

Other fund-raising events included a series of activity days with clay-pigeon shooting, archery, cricket and go-kart racing. Each June there was a mini 'game' fair and a one-day horse event. 'It is very popular,' said Johnnie. 'People come from all over the Midlands because the riders like the old turf we have here. It has not been ploughed for years and years.' He declared in *The Field*: 'My wife and I are much more active in the different sports here than my ancestors would ever have been . . . We had a party of Koreans here recently who had never seen a sheep before – or at least that's what they said – and they had a high old time chasing them around the park.' He said he felt they were 'at the sharp end of the boat, earning the money all the time to keep this place going . . . I do not know what my ancestors would have made of it, but my view is that you have got to look ahead. There is no point in looking back.'

Despite all Raine's imaginative ideas, Althorp did not attract the numbers of visitors that some people felt it should. The owner of one of Britain's most successful stately homes said, 'Althorp was only getting about 35,000 visitors. If it had been properly managed it should have 150,000–200,000. Raine's efforts were a failure. When you are in the stately-home business, the most important thing is to promote an atmosphere of welcoming people. Many people didn't feel welcome at Althorp.'

Raine also tried to raise money through personal appearances, although not always successfully. Asked to open the 1991 Northern Antiques Fair in Harrogate, she stated that her fee would be £1,000 and that the money would be used for Althorp. With typical northern bluntness, she was told to forget it.

A major fund-raising idea of Raine's that backfired badly exploited the

Japanese connection which she had partly developed through her work for the British Tourist Authority. Some of her ideas showed promise and initiative but, like many of Raine's schemes, were marred by a lack of judgment and a tendency to run out of control.

Raine and Johnnie had been invited to Tokyo in March 1986 on an expenses-paid ten-day trip to promote Althorp and talk about tourism. They planned to extend this to about five weeks, also visiting Singapore, Malaysia, Thailand and Nepal. Johnnie was in his element and took around seven hundred photographs in all. These they decided to publish in a book, which they would produce and promote themselves. Entitled *Japan and the East*, they printed 10,000 copies of the book at a cost of £60,000. It contained 248 colour photographs and was priced at £14.95 – although it was briefly offered at a pre-publication price of £9.99. It was also available by mail order and in a special limited edition of 250 'bound in coral leather, tooled in gold and with silk endpapers' priced at £295 each.

Despite Raine and Johnnie's enthusiastic promotion of *Japan and the East* around the country, few copies were sold and the book was an expensive flop.

It was after this that they pushed the boundaries of taste beyond acceptable limits by outrageously claiming a royal connection and trying to raise funds by selling the rights to the family name. Plans were made to 'lend' the Spencer name, family crest and family motto 'God Defend the Right' for a hefty fee to a Japanese golf club. It was to be developed in Kushiro on the northern Hokkaido Island and called the Royal Spencer Golf Club. The idea was that the first four hundred members would be charged a reduced membership fee of £26,000 which would also entitle them to play at two British golf courses, including the one at Althorp.

There were, however, two problems. In the first place, the Spencers were not royal; secondly the would-be developer, Matasaka Takahashi of the Information Offering System Corporation was a man of dubious business connections to say the least. Takahashi was thought to have spent £54 million to buy or develop five golf courses and the estimated cost of the so-called Royal Spencer Golf Club was £15 million. The club was due to open in 1993 and was to have been launched with a lavish reception in Tokyo on 30 September 1991 at one of Tokyo's top hotels. Johnnie was intending to appear at the reception as honorary chairman of the golf club, when he got wind of the fact that the money behind the club might have been less than legitimately raised. He pulled out at the last minute. Takahashi was arrested in November 1991 on suspicion of illegally obtaining £500 million in loans. It was rumoured that he was to receive a large fee for his appearance and the use of the family name, but Johnnie refused to confirm this and merely said he was doing it for good relations with

Japan. One of the Japanese involved with the deal said, 'It is very unlikely that the Earl would have allowed his name to be involved for nothing by a man he knew very little about.' The development has been indefinitely postponed.

In this case the project not only antagonised Johnnie's children but incurred the wrath of Buckingham Palace. Using the word 'Royal' appeared to be a blatant breach of the Queen's golden rule that no one should exploit the royal name for cash. A constitutional expert said at the time, 'Johnnie has no right to lend his name to a golf club which wants to call itself royal. And he ought to know it.' What was worse, an insider said: 'He's ruined a lifetime's friendship by his foolish behaviour ... The Queen had never allowed the royal label to be used in this kind of commercial way.'

At about this time the Spencers began to market replicas of the wedding dresses worn by Princess Diana and her sister-in-law Victoria Lockwood, to be sold in Japanese chain stores. The dresses, to be made in Japan, were to be called the Spencer Wedding Dresses and were expected to be snapped up by Tokyo brides because of the Japanese love-affair with the British Royal family. They also offered a deal whereby a replica of Diana's ivory wedding dress made by David and Elizabeth Emanuel could be hired out and on each occasion the Spencers would receive a royalty payment.

The Takasago-den superstore in Nagoya, Japan's fourth largest city, took up the deal and rented the lookalike gown for the staggering sum of £1,100 a day. 'Since the product was launched, business has been booming,' said the store's managing director, Shoji Makina. 'We have acquired the right to the Royal Spencer name to sell our wedding dress hire service. Many young Japanese ladies dream of being like Princess Di.'

A family friend said, 'He must have taken leave of his senses.' The fashion world was equally stunned. Polish-born Tomasz Starzewski who created Victoria's unusual gold-tinged dress was quoted as saying, 'I am surprised, to put it mildly. No one has consulted me. I am not sure whether I should be upset or take it as a compliment. I shall want to check out the position with my lawyer.' Nor had the Spencers obtained permission from Diana, Victoria, or the Palace. It was the final straw and the Queen was so furious that in the last year or so of his life she made it plain that Johnnie was no longer welcome at Buckingham Palace.

18

A Lavish Lifestyle

Raine and Johnnie enjoyed a lavish life style at Althorp, despite their claims of being hard up. Raine was a grand hostess and Johnnie loved being lord of the manor and believed he was running the estate along traditional lines. In an article in *The Field* in 1991 he wrote: 'The estate is still the hub of the local community as it was in the past. I am very conscious of that as well as the need to set the other farmers a good example. We still have our tenants' parties here and all my children come down for those, including Princess Diana ... Things may have changed a lot, but the traditional values are still there.'

Raine particularly loved throwing balls for important family occasions and was an expert at making guests feel welcome. 'She had a way of creating a marvellous atmosphere with candlelight all over the place,' says David Laws. A member of the family adds: 'She ran Althorp brilliantly and her parties were fantastic. The whole house would be open and she would think about the seating plan for every single table even if five hundred people were coming. Mind you, you had to turn and talk to each neighbour at every course during the dinner, otherwise she would tell you off. For smaller dinner parties of about thirty, the rooms would be lit with real candles and there would be real fires burning. They were lovely glamorous occasions.'

Her big parties often had an unusual formula. 'She would send out a very smart invitation to perhaps two hundred and fifty to come to Althorp,' remembers David Levin. 'You then discovered that you were going somewhere else entirely – to a hostess who lived near by – who was giving a dinner party for about thirty. After dinner, at about 10.00 p.m., you all got into cars and off you went to Althorp, where you found Raine looking resplendent. You were given a glass of champagne, you could dance, and then you had breakfast – about a 50p-size portion of scrambled egg, which you ate with a very heavy silver fork. Then you went home.' Raine would always give her 'hostesses' a lavish present for their trouble.

The grand ball to celebrate Earl Spencer's sixtieth birthday, held on 11

May 1984, was a particularly happy event for Raine as her second son Rupert, thirty-three, had announced his engagement to Victoria Ottley, thirty, the previous day. Rupert, who is unpretentious and gentle, gave up a promising career as a maritime lawyer and underwriter to become a novelist. He and Victoria were married in October 1984 – his single brother William was not best man – and gave Raine her first grandchild, Edward, in December 1986, with a granddaughter, Claudia, following three years later. All Raine's children from her first marriage benefited from the extravagant parties thrown at Althorp, as, more surprisingly, did their father Gerald with his second wife Gwen.

Johnnie, however, was careful that his own increasing family did not mix with Raine's children and great pains were taken, except at very large parties, to ensure that they came to Althorp at different times. According to a member of the family this was not too much of a problem as, outside these grand occasions, Raine didn't see much of her children apart from Henry, the youngest, whom Johnnie liked very much.

In November 1985 there was a large 'Welcome Home' party for Raine's rather difficult eldest son, Viscount Lewisham, a chartered accountant, then thirty-six, who returned after working in America for nine years. Two years previously he had been jilted by an American heiress, Pamela Franzheim, daughter of the one-time American Ambassador to New Zealand, on the eve of their marriage. She mentioned 'meanness' as one of the reasons for her change of mind.

On 12 May 1989 a massive ball was held in honour of Raine as an advance celebration of her sixtieth birthday in September. Up to five hundred guests were invited, many of whom were telephoned by Raine beforehand, telling them not to divulge details to the press. Her love-affair with reporters was over. Raine was so determined that no photographs should be taken that every one of the lavish gold-embossed invitations contained a typed insert informing guests that cameras would not be welcome. Even the Princess of Wales – who felt she had to attend – and Prince Charles – who didn't accompany his wife – received the instruction, although this was sent in error. Staff at Althorp had automatically included the insert in the envelope to Kensington Palace.

Although only VIP guests dined at Althorp (the remainder were given dinner by various selected hostesses) the chefs apparently spent two days preparing for the ball, culminating in a forty-two-hour shift with just one four-hour break between two and six in the morning. And on the big night they had to stay on duty until 4.00 a.m., cooking breakfast for any remaining guests.

Raine, in her usual meticulous way, had thought of everything, including what presents she would like. Johnnie gave her a beautiful ruby necklace. Guests were asked not to give individual presents, but to make cash contributions to the silverware dealers, S. J. Phillips. Amounts varied from £10 to £750 and amply covered the cost of a pair of diamond drop ear-clips which were made up to Raine's own design.

Diana, Jane and Sarah arrived in the afternoon while the final preparations for the ball were under way. They chatted to each other for a while sitting on the steps at the bottom of the great staircase. It was not long before the conversation turned to Raine's excessive restoration work and the three of them decided to check out her latest changes. They trooped through the house, ending up with an inspection of the second-floor bedrooms. There, in a couple of rooms, they found piles of heavy brocade curtains that Raine had discarded. All three decided these were far too good to be thrown away, that they would come in useful in their own homes, and agreed to split them three ways. Jane went to get a van to take them away and Diana and Sarah, giggling together as they had when teenagers, waited until the van arrived and then hurled the heavy curtains out of the window. They then packed plastic bags full of linen and, so as not to be spotted by Raine, climbed out of the old nursery window and down a ladder with their bounty.

Raine, preoccupied with anxieties about the ball, had no idea what was going on in the bedrooms on the second floor. The electricity cut out at 6.30 p.m. and was only restored four hours later when many of the guests were arriving after their dinner parties. It did not, however, ruin the evening. Raine, her flawless complexion set off by a bright red Balmain gown, greeted them with her special-occasion megawatt smile. She admitted that she found this particular birthday a difficult hurdle to cope with. 'At sixty I feel very old. I said to Johnnie, "Do you want to change me for a young model?" ' Apparently Johnnie replied, 'No, No, No' which, added Raine, 'is all that matters.' She said that to help her stay young she took vitamins daily but not as many as her mother. 'If I did I'd rattle. What I do swear by is jojoba oil. I pour it on my face and hands.' Florist Kenneth Turner is one of many men who greatly admire Raine's looks. 'I think she's incredible for her age and has the most beautiful skin I have ever seen. It's like alabaster.'

Raine threw a large twenty-first birthday party for her youngest son, Henry, in 1990, then studying to be a barrister and the apple of his mother's eye. There was another party in April 1991 to celebrate her daughter Charlotte's marriage to Duca Don Alexander Paterno Castello di Carcaci the previous December. Charlotte, who had been brought up almost entirely by nannies, had never been particularly close to her mother, but once she gave up her acting career and married a man with a title the mother-daughter relationship moved on to a smoother footing.

Dame Barbara was seldom present at her daughter's parties. David Levin, who attended a couple of Althorp parties a year for fourteen years, never saw her there. He believes that Raine sometimes finds her mother 'an embarrassment'. 'Other times she talks about her as if she is a faith-healer. They don't spend a lot of time together because I don't think her mother asks her.' Raine's relationship with her mother is complex: although they make a great show of getting on in public, in private there have often been spells when they have not been on speaking terms. A close relation says: 'Barbara's great problem is that you are wonderful providing you fit into the chapter she is writing about you at the time, but it's trouble when you don't. She's never really understood that the people she writes about in her books will do what she wants them to do, and the people in real life won't. However, Raine has managed to remove herself far enough from her mother's control. They both have very strong personalities, a mutual respect for each other and their periods of not speaking don't usually last long. Barbara wanted Raine to telephone her every day like her brothers Ian and Glen do, wherever they are in the world. Raine refused and told her mother she would call her when it suits her. They would, however regularly meet for lunch at Claridges, but she rarely went to Barbara's home in Camfield Place.'

Just occasionally Dame Barbara's blanket support of her daughter would slip. 'You know very well children never consult their parents,' she said. 'Anything I say is always wrong anyway. She's very independent – every child likes to think they're independent. It's when you get old that you realise that your mother was right.'

In public Raine maintained that her mother was a regular visitor to Althorp. 'Mummy adores coming here,' she said. 'John gets out the pink champagne and she loves it. She always says, "I can just see one of my heroines tripping down the library steps and falling into the hero's arms."'

For overnight guests at Althorp, Raine's hospitality knew no bounds. She always checked the guest rooms herself to make sure that each had a supply of chocolates, tissues and cotton wool, were full of flowers, that the towels were clean and a new bar of soap and an unused toilet roll were ready for use. On the desk in the bedroom guests would find notepaper, envelopes, stamps, postcards and a supply of new magazines. 'Raine thought of everything,' says interior designer Nicky Haslam. 'You've never seen a desk like it. There was even every possible size of envelope and a supply of air mail stamps of different values to various countries in the world.'

Although Raine's hospitality was second to none, she is not always an easy person to have as a friend. Her regal manner and sharp tongue, which gave rise to the nickname 'Acid Raine', made it difficult for people to feel relaxed in her company, particularly when inviting her to their own homes.

Sir Roy Strong believes: 'She's a tremendous shot in the arm when you see her, but it's very difficult when people live at the scale she lived to be friends. I remember someone asked her to dinner and his poor wife went out of her mind getting things ready. She felt she was having the Queen Mother round. It's hopeless in the twentieth century to be made to feel so completely inadequate.'

When Raine was invited out, she would often make her displeasure felt if the evening did not come up to her high standards. A wealthy Northamptonshire neighbour says, 'Having her to dinner was a nerve-racking experience. She would always come dressed up to the nines, glistening with jewellery. You had to get it right or she would smile graciously and tell you how nice it was to come to such a casual evening.' She could also be awkward. According to the wife of a well-known peer, 'Raine once went to stay with a family for the weekend and found the wardrobe in her room wasn't tall enough to hold the full-length ballgown she had brought along. She made such a fuss that in the end the host agreed to call in a carpenter to alter the cupboard.' Yet after every social occasion she has attended, Raine has always been meticulous about sending a handwritten thank-you note.

A colleague at the British Tourist Authority feels that, perhaps because of the hundreds of guests who came regularly to Althorp, Raine's relationship with people was largely superficial. 'She strikes me as having remarkably poor antennae about the way people receive her, which often goes with a dominant personality,' he says. 'She got very little feedback from other people. That promotes loneliness because you tend to get few relationships which are warm and enduring. People are also frightened of saying if they have been offended by her, which perhaps doesn't do her a service.' He considers that Raine herself is partly to blame. 'If she perceives that she can achieve her ends by keeping people in their place she will, but I don't think there is anything personal in it, it is a way of achieving the object in sight.'

She can be very tactless. A friend from Gloucester bought a country house and mentioned to Raine that she and her husband were thinking of employing Colefax & Fowler, the interior designers who redecorated Althorp, to handle their own redecoration. According to the friend, 'Raine said, "I wouldn't if I were you. They only work on large houses."' She also offended Lady Wardington, wife of Johnnie's childhood friend, when she wrote to Raine, whom she knew quite well, asking if she would contribute to a charity book called *Superhints* which even the Queen Mother had agreed to help. She did not receive a reply from Raine, but from her secretary, who wrote to say that Lady Spencer was inundated with such requests and unable to contribute. 'We had known each other so long, I think she could have had the courtesy to tell me herself,' Lady Wardington says.

David Levin prefers to see Raine *à deux*. 'I like to have lunch when there's just the two of us because she is so much easier to talk to. When there are more people about she tends to put on a performance, but to be fair, the performance is very nearly demanded of her. She has a lot of presence with her handbag, gloves and scarf, but it's a sort of overkill. She loves you to say she looks sensational and to admire her perfume.' Levin has never found her tactless. 'I have never spent any time with her and thought "how can you be so insensitive".' Johnnie would often ask Levin's wife Margaret, who is a similar size to the Princess of Wales, to go with him to Harrods and help him buy presents for Diana and his grandchildren. 'He used to smile at everyone in Harrods,' remembers Levin. 'He thought they all knew him, which they didn't. Sometimes he would strike up a conversation in the lift asking people if they were visitors to Britain. He did it one day and the woman replied, "No, I'm from Balham."'

Another friend believes that, despite Raine's close relationship with Johnnie, she was often lonely at Althorp. 'She realised Johnnie's limitations only too well in a perfectly nice way. He couldn't think of more than one thing at once, his concentration span was extremely short and if he wanted something done, he wanted it finished straightaway and wouldn't be happy until it was.'

In the years that followed his stroke, Johnnie's eyesight gradually deteriorated. He found it difficult to read, though he still managed to drive locally and to shoot. When there were no evening engagements at Althorp he liked to listen to Radio 2 and particularly enjoyed *Your Hundred Best Tunes* on Sunday evenings. By 1988 he found he had increasing trouble focusing and no longer watched television. Raine enjoyed listening to opera, reading and watching television. She 'adores' cops and robbers and used to relax watching *Dynasty*, the American soap opera ('marvellous escapism') despite its similarities with her own life style. 'I don't want television to educate me,' she said. At bed-time she says she reads her mother's romantic novels which 'lull' her to sleep.

Although Johnnie never forgot that he owed his life to Raine, and became increasingly dependent on her, he was an obstinate man given to occasional uncontrollable bursts of tempers. Initially Raine used to give in to these, coaxing him round to her point of view later, when the rage had passed.

Sir Roy Strong: 'She was marvellous with him and it was marvellous to see them together. They absolutely depended on each other. He was absolutely sweet – such a nice man. And obviously attracted to strong women. Both Frances Shand Kydd and Raine are very tough.' A close member of the family adds: 'Johnnie was a stubborn, opinionated individual and not easy to live with. Raine was brilliant with him.'

A colleague of Raine's agrees: 'They had a very warm, close, inter-dependent relationship and were aware of each other all the time in the way close people are.'

Nevertheless, it was in character for Johnnie to put on a macho front, particularly when interviewed by journalists. He was regularly quoted as saying how important it was for the man to be in charge: 'It's better for the man and for the woman.' He called most women 'bird-brained' and admitted that it was Raine's 'brain power' that had first attracted him. 'It's rare to find a woman with the very good mental agility which she's got. We've both been married before so we value the benefit of a good marriage. In our case marriage has been better second time around.'

He admitted to finding Raine a challenge and was even prepared to discuss their arguments. 'She's an amazing person, but you've got to control her,' he said. 'I don't touch her physically or even shake her. When I'm cross I'm very direct with her. I shout "Now bloody well listen to me for a minute" and she does. I sit her down and say, "You're a tremendous person, Raine, and a very special person, but you've got to judge it a bit and limit your output." Then she says "I'm sorry, I love you." She is very good.'

He didn't mind when Raine argued back. 'When I jump on her, she jumps back at me, but it doesn't worry me. She always comes round to my decision in the end.' Occasionally, he said, 'She grumbles that I am too soft and kind and nice with people. And that I'm too idle and I don't work hard enough. But I've very strong steel underneath.'

Interviewed five years after their marriage Johnnie said, 'We're still passionately in love ... At our age ... you either become very dependent on each other or you grow apart. We're very dependent. She'd do anything to help me and she's much better at dealing with problems and getting to the root of things than I am. In my little way I think I guide her and keep her calm and steady. The longer we go on together even just working side by side on the house, selling things in the shop – the closer we get. I hope Raine and I will go on together for a long, long time.' His allegiance to Raine was never in doubt. 'Loyalty to your nearest and dearest is the most important thing in life. And what counts most is supporting and being loyal to your wife, isn't it?'

The annual Althorp charity cricket game, based on the happy matches Johnnie played when he lived at Sandringham, was a major family event. It took place in the grounds and was followed by a barbecue which Johnnie liked to cook himself. 'He's a dab hand at it and his barbecues have become something of a ritual,' says Charles.

Family relationships, however, often cast a shadow on the event. One year Charles was so furious with his stepmother that he could not bear to be anywhere near her; in the middle of the festivities Charles whispered to his father than if he would not ask Raine to leave, then he would walk out himself.

The highlight of the Althorp social calendar for Johnnie was his Christmas party, which became legendary even in his lifetime. His childhood enthusiasm for the festival remained undiminished in adulthood, as housekeeper Betty Andrews recalls. 'He loved it first with his own four children, even more when Jane and Sarah used to come with their husbands, and particularly once he had grandchildren. Wrapping up his Christmas presents was a major operation. There were so many things which he would collect all year. We used to put them into sacks, one for each child, then put the sacks against different chairs in the library for the children to open on Christmas Day. Once he remarried he treated Her Ladyship's children just the same.'

Each year Johnnie's Christmas party would cater for a larger number of grandchildren as the size of his family increased, and the children of friends would also be invited. He would excitedly organise every detail of the party for weeks beforehand. Every time he went to London he would stop at Harrods to buy more gifts for his grandchildren and other small guests.

'My idea of heaven on earth is the children's party we have a week before Christmas,' he said. 'We have about thirty children, conjurors, clowns turning somersaults, a wonderful tea, and Father Christmas arriving in a donkey cart.'

The little princes William and Harry became regular attenders. One year they arrived in fancy dress. William came as George Michael, in sunglasses, with his hair slicked back and designer stubble painted on his chin. Harry came as a Ninja Turtle wearing a green suit, Ninja mask, and a shell strapped to his back.

When the children arrived all the staff lined up to meet them. Then came a clown on stilts, a pink elephant who made the children laugh by falling and rolling about and the magician, Smartie Artie, performing tricks. Instead of place cards, the children all had a cup-cake with their names on the icing and after tea – a wonderful display of jellies, sandwiches and superb wooden musical table decorations – they were given chocolate coins to buy small furry toys, sweets and little gifts from the wooden shops that had been set up. At one point in the party bells could suddenly be heard tinkling. The entertainers would shout 'Children, listen, listen' and then usher them to the window and there in the distance, seeming miles and miles away, would be a little light. All the children were encouraged to ask, 'What can the light be?' Gradually the tinkling got louder and louder and, as the light came closer, the children saw a little pony pulling a marvellous old coach with Santa Claus – one of the members of staff – sitting in it. The children always got very excited as it came clip-clopping up the winding driveway.

Meanwhile a ramp was put on the steps and, as the coach approached, the front doors would be thrown open and it would bring Father Christmas right into the main hall. Climbing out of the coach with his sack, he would say hello to all the children and give each one of them even more presents.

Often Johnnie would then lift William and Harry into the coach, climb up beside them and go for a ride round Althorp's enormous entrance hall. It was difficult to say who enjoyed it more – the children or Johnnie. In 1991, when the rift between Johnnie and his children was at its peak over the selling of cottages on the estate, there were press reports that William and Harry would not be going to their grandfather's party that year. They did, in fact, attend what turned out to be the last Christmas party before the Earl's death. The Princess of Wales, however, did not on this occasion accompany them. It was reported that she was detained in London on private charity business at Kensington Palace and taking the opportunity of the boys' absence to do some last-minute Christmas-present wrapping. Nor did her brother Charles appear, although Victoria brought their little daughter Kitty. It was said that Charles had not spoken to his stepmother since they had had a blazing row during the summer.

As the Cartland family traditionally celebrate Christmas together, Johnnie and Raine joined Dame Barbara at her home in Hertfordshire. A festive lunch was followed by another Cartland tradition of the youngest person present making a speech extempore. 'That's why all my children and grandchildren speak so well, of course,' explains Dame Barbara. Each year, too, Johnnie would make a point of standing up and saying how much he loved Raine and how much he owed to her. 'He would say. "Here's Raine. I love her so much," ' says Dame Barbara. A close relation says, 'Johnnie always enjoyed the occasion and would make hilarious asides in a loud stage whisper during the speeches.'

If the Christmas party was the highlight of Johnnie's year, the pinnacle of Raine's time as chatelaine of Althorp was reached in November 1982 when the Queen came to tea. Some months previously Raine and Johnnie had been fellow guests at a charity drinks party and Raine was thrilled when the Queen made a point of coming over to her to talk about the refurbishment at Althorp. Her joy knew no bounds when the Queen said that she would soon be making her first official visit to Northampton and that she wished to see the changes at Althorp. The tea date was fixed.

On the great day Raine and Johnnie were given a police escort to rush them back after the official luncheon as the Queen would be following hot on their heels. Raine could hardly contain her excitement. 'It was such an honour for her to be acknowledged,' says a friend. In anticipation of the Queen's visit Raine gave orders for the outside of Althorp to be repainted. It was a particularly wet November, and although exteriors of houses should never be painted when it rains, Raine insisted that the work went ahead. Men were to be seen up ladders with a sponge in one hand wiping away the rain and a paintbrush in the other. It was all unnecessary as, by the time the Queen arrived, it was already dark.'

Raine was determined that this vital social occasion should go well and there was a full dress rehearsal beforehand. Tea was to be traditional, with cucumber sandwiches and chocolate cake. The cook made a sample chocolate cake in advance but Raine had doubts about it and finally decided to have it made by someone in the village. On the day itself, the staff had never seen Raine so nervous. It was a typical grey November day and she went round the house closing the curtains and trying various lighting arrangements, with and without candles, until she felt the atmosphere was right. A tea-table was set up at the end of the Library. Raine decided that, despite her nerves, she wanted to pour out the Queen's tea herself.

Everything went according to plan. Raine and Johnnie arrived back at 3.45 p.m., thirty-five minutes before the Queen, who was due at 4.20 p.m. Johnnie changed into an old, shabby tweed suit and Viyella shirt because he said he wanted to be comfortable for the occasion. Although it was a private visit, the staff lined up to greet the Queen who had disposed of her official limousine and arrived punctually in a Range Rover accompanied by a detective and bodyguard.

As the car drove up, the butler put down the red carpet and Johnnie opened the door. The Queen greeted Johnnie and Raine, who curtsied, and smiled at all the waiting staff. Raine then escorted her upstairs to a bathroom where new soap and clean towels had been put out. The plan was that Raine would then wait in the Library and Johnnie would stand by the great staircase ready to escort the Queen down. In the event, Raine couldn't wait. 'I had to see my Johnnie, my husband, escorting the Queen of England down the staircase,' she later said. At tea Raine served the cucumber sandwiches, cut the chocolate cake and poured the tea herself. Everyone, it seemed, had a marvellous time and the visit that was scheduled to last forty-five minutes overran and lasted an hour and a half. There is, however, no record of the Queen's opinion of Raine and Johnnie's restoration.

The visit dashed rumours, rife even in those early days, that Raine was persona non grata with the Palace. Indeed the Queen, who had always been very fond of Johnnie, was said to prefer Raine to Frances, with whom she had never got on. Soon afterwards Raine was invited to lunch at the Palace where she was given the great compliment of being placed next but one to the Queen. She and Johnnie also attended several royal garden parties. The relationship, however, deteriorated over the next few years when one of their money-making schemes broke the Queen's golden rule of never allowing the royal tag to be used for commercial purposes.

Aside from the Christmas party, Johnnie was always delighted when Prince William came to Althorp. Like many grandparents, he looked for any of his own characteristics that William might have inherited. 'I like to think there's a lot of me in him,' he said when William was five years old. 'Whenever William's around there's always something happening. He's very high-spirited, tremendously energetic and always getting into trouble. But you can't get annoyed with him, however naughty he's been, because he's got such charm. For a five-year-old he's tremendously cunning, he knows how to get his own way. He's very bright and quick-witted and he's got a terrific sense of humour.' Johnnie had a treehouse built for William about six feet above the ground. There were steps up to the front door and inside a sink with running water and miniature utensils.

Johnnie admitted that the grandchildren 'fought like mad', although 'It's marvellous how well they get on, but if there's ever any trouble, then it's always William who's the ringleader. I love it when they're here because they fill the place with their noise and energy. The moment they arrive they are everywhere, up and down the stairs, in and out of all the rooms, climbing over everything.'

Raine, whom the boys called 'Aunt', is not the sort of person to enjoy entertaining children. She worried about them touching her antiques and sometimes retired to her boudoir with a 'headache'. Johnnie was more relaxed and let William and Harry race pedal-cars along the elegant passageways of Althorp. However, even he confessed that William 'frightened the life out of us' when he took a toboggan to the top of the grand staircase and 'whizzed all the way down' or when he climbed up the steps in the Library and hurled himself off the top.

There was one scare when William went missing for a couple of hours; the detective started panicking and actually went down to the lake to look for him. Eventually he was found hiding in the Library with Harry. Johnnie loved the prank. 'If I can't find either of them, I'll know where to look,' he said. He was delighted that they were 'very affectionate children'. He felt they had been well brought up, were well-mannered, polite, and charming, a state of affairs he gave his daughter full credit for. 'They behave very well when they are on duty and when they're off duty, they're normal little boys. There's no sibling rivalry between them,' he said. 'They're very lucky to have Diana as a mother. They lead fairly normal lives really, as Diana has lots of girlfriends of her own age, all of whom have children.'

Diana had a special place in Johnnie's heart. 'Diana has always been a wonderful daughter to me,' he said. 'She's always been very loving and she's brought up her little boys to love their grandfather – and for some reason they do.' He was equally proud of her work and it gave him enormous pleasure to be told that the two most popular people in the world were the pope and his daughter. Interviewed by the *Chronicle Herald*, the local newspaper in Halifax, Nova Scotia, on the eve of Princess of Wales's eighteen-day tour of Canada in 1983 he warned the world that Diana was a strong character. He was quoted as saying, 'Marriage has changed her. She is not shy any more and knows her own mind. She is very determined indeed and always gets her own way. I think Prince Charles is learning that now.' He did not, however, make quite such an accurate forecast over his royal grandson's allegiances: 'William will grow up very close to the Spencer family and be influenced by them as much as by the others ... I know the Royal Family can seem to swallow people up when others marry in and the other family always looks as if it has been pushed out. But that can never happen to us. We can cope with the pressures. We have been brought up with royalty and there is no question of us being pushed out.'

After admitting there were initial difficulties between his children and Raine, Johnnie tried to paint a glossy picture of family life. In October 1986 he told Jean Rook: 'These raked-up old stories about the Family Feud and all of us living here in the park without visiting one another are terribly upsetting. No step-relationships are easy. It was hard on my children and hard on Raine moving into a family as close as we are. You couldn't expect it to work wonders at the start. But things are so much easier now. We just have to keep our sense of humour – though it's hard at times.'

Raine equally continued to put a brave public face on her poor relationships with her stepchildren and particularly with Diana. In 1987 she insisted, 'It's totally untrue that we don't get on,' adding that Diana had invited her to Prince Harry's birthday party and when it was her birthday Diana took the time to send her 'wonderful' flowers and a 'loving' card, even though she was in Spain at the time. 'She wouldn't have done that if we didn't like each other.' In 1988 she declared, 'Diana and I don't hate each other. It's such a bitchy thing to say ... People see her as a heroine figure and then I'm cast as an awful woman that she hates.' In 1989 she went further. 'Everything passes. We get on well now, but we all lead busy lives – we don't live in each other's pockets.'

In fact Diana disliked her stepmother so strongly that she rarely visited Althorp, even to see her father whom she did care about.

Raine felt that her years working for the GLC had helped toughen her up and enabled her to cope with criticism. 'We don't go out of our way to read anything disagreeable,' she said. 'If people want to believe what they read in the papers, there is nothing we can do. If you took notice of these things, you might just as well lie down in your coffin. I don't get cross. I just laugh.'

Johnnie, however, confessed that this wasn't quite true. 'She pretends not to mind,' he said, 'but underneath she's very hurt.'

19

A Working Life

Raine's lack of interest in her career after she married Johnnie did not last long. And once Johnnie had recovered from his brain haemorrhage, she tried to pick up the threads of her life outside Althorp. 'The only thing that bugs me,' she said, 'is that now I'm only associated with this house and the Spencers. It's only part of my life. I have been eighteen years in local government.' She became restless and bored when she stayed at Althorp too long. David Laws remembers her saying: 'I cannot just sit in this great pile all the time, I have to get out.'

Johnnie, however, was not keen on her spending too much time away from him. 'He didn't want her to develop an independent life and perhaps repeat what happened with his first wife,' says Laws. 'But he didn't like to confront her.'

Raine looked around for a new challenge to exercise her talents and her friend Norman St John-Stevas came to her aid. In 1979, as Chancellor of the Duchy of Lancaster and later as Minister for the Arts, he suggested to Prime Minister Margaret Thatcher that Raine be appointed chairman of the newly established National Heritage Fund. With £15 million to disburse to preserve historic houses and estates, the appointment was, at the time, a coveted position in the art world. Opposition to her appointment was strong, however, not least because, as she and Johnnie were already selling Spencer heirlooms, it was felt that a conflict of interests could have arisen. Labour MP Andrew Faulds was one of those against the idea. 'Raine was the flavour of the month,' he remembers. 'But she seemed to me to be totally inappropriate for such an appointment. I didn't think she had the capability to run a major national institution which was then just being brought into being. Its whole success was likely to rest on whoever ran it. The fact that she was disposing of things at Althorp didn't help. She's a gutsy girl but I am not impressed by her intellectual and academic capabilities.'

In the end Raine's name did not even appear on the short list. In his book *The Two Cities*, published in 1984, St John-Stevas wrote of the incident: 'The opposition proved too strong. Unfortunately she arouses jealousy among smaller and less-talented fry. This is a sad reflection on the meaner side of human nature.' Instead he appointed Raine to the Advisory Council of the V & A, on which she served from 1980 to 1982 and where once again she managed to impress Sir Roy Strong, then the museum's director. 'Most of the trustees didn't read the minutes from the various heads of departments, but she always did because she said that told her the pulse of the way the place was run. I respect her for that.'

Raine relaunched herself into public life in 1981 when she switched on the Christmas lights of Northampton, swiftly followed by an appearance at the Royal Opera House on 4 December 1981 when she publicised a new guidebook to stately homes. 'This is my first speaking engagement since my husband's illness,' she confided. 'I'm really getting back into the swing from now on. My husband is better and now we're going to do our own thing.'

In 1982 she offered her services to the British Tourist Authority. (She had worked for the English Tourist Authority from 1970–75.) Although her work was highly regarded, colleagues found she often treated them as if they were members of her staff. She had always been regal and imperious but since acquiring a stately home and a stepdaughter who had become the Princess of Wales, many found her increasingly intimidating. A BTA colleague says, 'She has always been a demanding woman, setting high standards for herself and everyone around her. She's difficult and becomes imperious with people who give less than their best.' David Levin, another of Raine's BTA colleagues, remembers their first meeting. 'I was completely bowled over by her. I had never met anyone quite like her and at first I thought she was too much. Everybody has a strong view one way or another about Lady Spencer. She instils a positive view on both sides. Everything about her is extreme. At our first meeting at the BTA she took out paper tissues from her handbag as if she was a conjurer producing a rabbit out of a hat. She laid six on a chair, then sat on them, saying "People just don't know how to clean furniture."'

Once Levin got to know Raine better, he admits, 'I sort of fell in love with her. I think she's just marvellous. I'm an enormous fan. She's completely misunderstood, which is absolutely her own fault. She's enormously professional, marvellously attractive and extremely kind.' Although he has never seen the other side of her, he agrees, 'You would certainly get the message that you were not being well received. She is capable of being glacial and tight-lipped. She's very regal in the way she bears herself and when you confront her, either in a meeting or one to one, I'm sure she plays on it. She's very aware of the effect she's having on people'.

Raine had conflicting attitudes towards her male colleagues, sometimes demanding that they behaved like medieval knights, at other times that they obeyed her orders without question. 'She tends to rely on certain men, not just for bag-carrying, but for the support in her different BTA roles,' says an executive. 'She also uses her power and standing as a woman – she requires to be shown out, found a taxi and to be looked after in the old-fashioned sexist sense like a lady would have been treated a hundred years ago. On the other hand, she is perfectly capable of dropping that role and is a powerful and capable woman. She needs a lot of attention in the sense that anything that is done for her or with her needs scrupulous attention to detail and to be done in an impeccable style.' Like her mother, Raine is none too keen on female colleagues. David Quelch, managing director of the Burberry fashion store, states: 'She is a man's woman rather than a woman's woman. I do sense a slight talking down, slightly dismissive attitude to any females who are present. She certainly doesn't tolerate fools.'

Raine has held several positions within the BTA organisation since 1982, having been chairman of its former Hotels and Restaurants Committee, Development Committee, Accommodation Committee and Commendation Schemes Panel. While her skills as chairman are highly regarded, her regal manner resulted in some members of her committees becoming very obsequious towards her, while others resigned because, one commented, 'They couldn't take all the grovelling.'

Raine comes well prepared for meetings, arrives early and ensures that they always finish on time. Apart from the tissues which she puts on her chair, she also comes equipped with lorgnettes, white gloves, a gold Cartier travelling clock and a gold pen which was a present from Johnnie; all of which she lays out very precisely in front of her. When she chairs a committee, even when as many as forty people are present, she ensures that everyone makes a contribution. 'No one gets out of the door without having said something,' says Michael Medlicott, a BTA executive. 'Some members just come for their names to be on the headed notepaper, others want to do nothing but talk. Raine, however, is a great disciplinarian and manages the committee so that everybody puts in their tenpenn'orth. It is a very impressive performance.'

As always when she has a project she cares about, Raine is an undeniable asset to the British Tourist Authority. She was very generous in allowing the BTA to use Althorp, without charge, to entertain foreign visitors. She organised a dinner in the State Dining Room for the Japanese Minister of Tourism, the Assistant Minister, and a group of Japanese travel executives, and insisted on paying half the cost of the food. She donated a solid silver coffee pot from the Althorp collection to be used by the BTA for their Bed and Breakfast Awards Scheme and so enjoyed her role that when she and Johnnie went abroad for personal reasons, she would often fit in a press conference to promote British tourism.

During the eighties Raine and Johnnie travelled widely, often at his suggestion. 'Johnnie got very restless,' a friend says. They always travelled with at least one member of staff and Raine ensured that Johnnie was cosseted and that the pace was not too rushed. A trip that might take the average person ten days would often stretch to four weeks for the Spencers. 'Johnnie was such a keen photographer and loved new visual experiences, but they had to take it very slowly as he didn't have much stamina,' says a friend. He nearly always brought back presents from his trips for members of the Althorp staff. Raine too knows how to pace herself and when she cannot do any more 'she will tell you and disappear'.

Working for the BTA not only gave Raine a welcome escape from Althorp but also helped her to keep Johnnie stimulated. When she was chairman of the BTA's Spa Committee she agreed to write a book on the eleven spas of England and suggested to Johnnie that he took the photographs. For six months in 1982 the pair of them, Raine uncharacteristically dressed in walking shoes and mackintosh, toured Britain's spa towns getting copy and taking pictures. They had, said Raine 'great fun doing it all'. In Cheltenham Johnnie was invited to join a group of ladies bathing in a whirlpool. 'They shouted to me to jump in,' he chuckled afterwards. 'The bath was made for eight and there were only seven of them. I thought I would never get out again so I ran for it.'

The Spencers on Spas was published in December 1983, price £9.95, and distributed to twenty-two countries. Johnnie and Raine were not paid for this public-spirited exercise; royalties were donated to the spas, with Tunbridge Wells receiving the sum of £1,000 to help restore one of its spa buildings. Raine knew the value of publicity in selling copies and, despite her newly acquired royal connection, set about promoting the book with fervour.

The promotion lasted for months as Raine and Johnnie made their almost royal progress round the country in their Rolls-Royce. In Tunbridge Wells they received special mayoral dispensation to drive across a 'pedestrian only' precinct to be set down in front of the W. H. Smith for a signing session. One hundred and sixty-six copies went in two hours.

The travelling was so intense that Raine laughingly said at one stage, 'It's almost a case of if it's Tuesday, it must be Manchester.' Johnnie coped well. 'He's very fit now, really enjoying it,' she said. She put all her energy into the promotion. In a lull at a signing session at Hatchard's bookshop in Piccadilly, Raine was heard to trill loudly, 'It's a nice book. It makes a lovely Christmas present. It's only £9.95,' to encourage customers.

During one book-signing in Nottingham, however, Johnnie showed the crusty side of his nature. Jack Tye, his ex-batman from army days, came up to him while he was signing copies with ten pounds he had saved from his pension to buy the book. He asked Johnnie if he recognised him. 'No,' Johnnie said. 'Royal Scots Greys,' Jack prompted. Johnnie did not reply. The local newspapers were delighted with the picture potential, but Johnnie only reluctantly agreed to be photographed. 'Now for God's sake can we get on with what I'm here for,' he said as soon as the photo session was over.

The reviews of the book were mixed. *The Times* pronounced Lord Spencer's photographs 'quite exceptionally good whether of architecture or of people or of both'. And that Lady Spencer was 'artlessly artful. She combines history with personal reminiscence in the most engaging way.' *The Guardian*, however, described her writing as 'drivel', condemning her Cartland style and quoting as an example her description of Bath: 'Titania would have been bewitched as are so many visitors by the unexpected fantasy and surprises . . . of the place.'

Inspired by the moderate success of *The Spencers on Spas*, Raine and Johnnie toured Japan and Asia in the mid-eighties. Johnnie took innumerable photographs which they later published in the glossy book called *Japan and the East*. According to a member of staff, this did not sell well.

Raine works hard for the BTA. A colleague, Alan Jefferson, claims: 'She gives more time to her duties than any other BTA board member. Whenever she is asked to open something or speak she does it so beautifully that she is invariably wanted back.' Not all her work is glamorous, however. As the current chairman of BTA's Development Committee she is concerned with European community legislation, immigration, customs and licensing and, according to Jefferson, not only runs the committee like 'a military operation' but 'fights a tireless battle with immigration and customs people to shorten queues of incoming visitors. Equally, when she finds that customs officers are not as well looked after, in terms of rest rooms and sitting rooms when they are off duty, she will then fight their corner and try to get something done.'

She has also chaired the BTA's Awards Scheme committee and, whereas other chairmen have relied on the written reports of committee members, Raine insists on seeing and judging the short list of tourist attractions for herself; she even paid an incognito visit to Rock Circus, a zany visual presentation of the history of rock music, at Piccadilly Circus.

In 1990 she became chairman of the BTA's three-year 'Britain Welcomes Japan' campaign which aims to increase the number of Japanese visitors to this country. Fellow committee member David Quelch admits to being 'slightly in awe' of Raine when he first met her. 'Her reputation precedes her, not only because she is of high peerage, but I thought how am I going to satisfy her?' He believes, 'You couldn't ask for a better ambassador to sell Britain to the Japanese,' and admits he has learned a lot from her style. 'She could have had a great career in industry. She has a marvellous way of telling you off at meetings by complimenting others, which encourages you to do better. She made me want to aspire to the highest compliment she paid to someone else. I took a few notes for my own management meetings. I have even copied her way of having a watch in front of her to keep track of time, although mine isn't gold.'

Quelch believes Raine's presentation of herself is fundamental to her success. 'She portrayed her role of the countess in an elegant way. The Japanese think she is magnificent and everything they imagined a countess would be.'

Early on in the campaign a high-level Japanese ministerial delegation came to England and one of their stops was Althorp. Raine made a five-minute speech of welcome in Japanese without a note, which according to BTA executive Michael Medlicott 'left them thunderstruck'. 'The Japanese are very sensitive about the way the West behaves towards them and few people manage to do what Raine did, particularly people associated with the Royal Family. Such things probably achieved more for Anglo-Japanese relations than anything else you could think of.'

Occasionally her sense of humour misfires. 'She made a wonderful speech in Japanese to some businessmen,' remembers David Levin. 'She told them they were famous for their television sets, but that we British have royal television sets like Philips and Fergusson. The Japanese sat there absolutely po-faced, but I thought it was very funny.' According to Jefferson, the one thing the Japanese did not like about Raine was the fact that during their visit she was serving in the Althorp gift shop. 'They found it rather tacky because a countess shouldn't be in a shop. She also mistakenly tried to sell them her reproduction jewellery – segments of the Japanese market have a lot of money and are not interested in fakes.'

Jefferson and Quelch both remember occasions when Raine surprised them with her kindness. Once, when Jefferson was in hospital, she not only sent him bouquets of flowers and organised a card for colleagues to sign, but also sent Johnnie to Fortnum & Mason for Stilton cheese, smoked salmon and peaches that were delivered to his bedside. When Quelch was taken ill at Althorp during a lunch for the Japanese, Raine sent him home in a chauffeur-driven car. 'She's so kind and sensitive,' he says. 'I would never describe her as hard or thick-skinned. She can give the appearance of being tough, but I think that's good management.'

Despite the considerable demands Raine makes of her colleagues, at BTA 'She's worth every piece of heartache or problem she has created,' says one, although she can be very forthright in her criticism of staff, sometimes even putting their jobs on the line 'for quite small offences'. Also, although Raine writes her own speeches, she always requires a detailed briefing and full itinerary before any visit. 'Someone else would either be more used to finding out things for themselves or fighting on their feet,' a colleague explains. 'You certainly wouldn't need to prepare an itinerary to show what was happening at every second.'

Johnnie often accompanied Raine to BTA functions and was a great success, his gift for remembering people's names endearing him to many. He took his socialising seriously. A friend explained: 'He didn't just rely on his memory. He had a notebook where he made comments about individuals he had met, although he didn't always need to refer to them.'

'Johnnie was terrific on these occasions,' remembers Alan Jefferson. 'He came in a supportive role and never wanted the limelight.' Occasionally when Raine was ill he would even chair meetings on her behalf. In 1984 Raine had laryngitis and lost her voice on the day she was due to present some BTA awards. She was so determined not to let people down that she turned up with Johnnie who, much to the delight of everyone present, read out her speech before the awards were presented. Because his balance was still affected by his stroke, Raine stood with a supporting arm around him. Several colleagues commented on their close relationship. 'There was very strong mutual dependence between them,' says one. 'She was also always concerned about his physical well-being which was precarious. When he got tired he held her arm very firmly when they stood together. You could see the strain of holding him.'

Raine would often talk about Johnnie in loving terms to Alan Jefferson. 'They were very close,' he says. 'She would be relating some story and often break off to say "then Johnnie looked at me with those incredible blue eyes of his". You could see how much they cared for each other.' Johnnie for his part did not like Raine to be away from him even for one night. If she had to go to attend an evening function in the north of England he would invariably accompany her and whenever they were apart for more than a few hours she would always telephone him.

Raine, who could be irascible, rarely lost her temper with Johnnie. 'I have never seen her cross with him,' says David Levin, 'although I have seen her tease him. They got on marvellously.'

Jefferson had occasion to witness one of Johnnie's bursts of ill-humour. 'He was not such a sweetie, he had quite a temper,' he remembers. 'I've seen the odd flash. Raine often tried to get round him saying "Johnniekins, come on, please." But often he would say "no" and mean no. He often got very impatient at the end of the evening while Raine was going round kissing everyone on both cheeks and would loudly tell her to stop the kissing because he wanted to go home.'

Johnnie was also known to lose his temper with journalists. One day in April 1983 when he and Raine arrived for lunch at the Dorchester, he was outraged when an opportunist press photographer took a picture of them both. He demanded, unsuccessfully, that the film be removed and handed over and was furious when later that afternoon the same photographer took further snaps of the two of them shopping. He instinctively gave chase and passers-by were astonished to behold the father of the Princess of Wales doing a curious wobbly run, during which, at every few paces, he attempted to kick the photographer from behind. The photographer escaped injury by scuttling into the London crowd.

Even with her BTA activities, Raine was keen to return to political life. Offering her services to Conservative Party Headquarters in the run-up to the June 1987 election, she called herself 'Oddjob' and said, 'I am only a cog in the machine and am very happy to help. Everyone I know is working for the Party in some way or another and I would be embarrassed to be singled out from all the hundred of thousands of people helping.' According to friends, however, she hoped her efforts would lead to other work for the Conservatives and was very disappointed when they did not. She was also saddened that her son, Viscount Lewisham, who had earlier unsuccessfully fought two elections for the Conservatives, failed even to be selected to fight a seat in 1987, despite attending a Tory training course for prospective candidates.

Raine had been taught to develop a sense of her own importance on her mother's knee. This took a nasty knock when she was subjected to a body search at Heathrow Airport in October 1985 on her way to Paris for one of her regular shopping trips. 'Do you know who I am?' she stormed in front of dozens of Terminal Two passengers. Two senior security officers were called to explain that a certain percentage of passengers had to undergo random searches. She protested vigorously as she was escorted to a side cubicle and only finally agreed to be frisked by a female officer after it was explained that she would not otherwise be allowed on the flight. A Heathrow worker commented, 'She kept on arguing, totally under the impression that she should be exempt because of who she was. In fact she didn't have a leg to stand on. She did not get VIP status.'

Raine said afterwards that she felt 'disgusted and degraded'. 'How naïve of the airport's security officers to think I was a terrorist. Can you imagine anything more stupid? ... I can think of nothing worse than having a strange woman running her hands over your whole body. Unless you're gay you don't need that treatment ... I am convinced it was done through sheer spite to take me down a peg or two. I am not concerned for myself but for a possible adverse reaction from other tourists who might have to face the same ordeal. I made a fuss, not so much for myself, but on behalf of other women. Subjecting women to this kind of degrading physical abuse can only be bad for tourism.'

The episode threatened to create as much fuss as 'the storm in the dirty teacup' at Heathrow at the start of Raine's political career. She claimed she received 'massive support from the public plus a number of foul letters from people demanding to know who the hell I think I am'. She also received what she described as a 'pompous' letter from the British Airports Authority intimating that she had overreacted. Her reply to that is perhaps indicative of her approach to life in general. 'The truth is,' she said, 'that I don't care what people think of me, except those I respect. It has been suggested that I shall regret my outburst. Well, I never have regrets. If you're right about something what is there ever to regret?'

20

The Price of Loyalty

In the late eighties, Spencer family loyalties were stretched as never before, although in public Johnnie and Raine tried to present a united front. 'John and I have been married for twelve years and all his children are perfectly friendly towards me,' Raine always maintained. 'We see each other either at Althorp, in London or at their houses. We recently had lunch with Diana. She rings up all the time. Of course she asks for her father, but if I answer, we have a lovely chat. Anything else is complete fabrication.' Every once in a while, however, the thinnest crack would appear in this façade and she would admit that the rumours of family disharmony sometimes got her down. Fortunately, an antidote was always to hand. 'When I get depressed John says "You have a husband who loves you."'

Johnnie's feelings for Raine were touching and unwavering and he was always eager to tell anyone who asked how much she meant to him. 'Raine has made me very happy and given me a reason for living,' he said. 'The happiest time of my life has been with Raine. We're never apart, never spend a night away from each other.' He tried to be equally loyal to his wife under siege from his family, to his daughter, the Princess of Wales, whose marriage was the subject of increasing speculation, and to his son Charles who confessed publicly to an extramarital tryst with another woman in the first year of his marriage to former model Victoria Lockwood.

Johnnie tried to protect Raine from the humiliations and insults to which his children subjected her. By unspoken mutual agreement he and his daughters saw each other less and less often and he was particularly anxious to avoid any confrontation between Raine and Diana, the second most special person in his life. He knew Diana was reluctant to visit Althorp when her stepmother was there, so Johnnie devised a way of seeing her and his grandsons without offending Raine. He would first arrange to have tea with Diana at Kensington Palace and then organise a visit to the SGBI in Chislehurst – the one place he went on his own –

where he would pop in on elderly resident Grace Randall. He would, however, only tell Raine about the SGBI visit. In this way he could do a good turn by visiting Miss Randall and manage to see Diana and the grandchildren without offending his wife all in the one afternoon.

Like many who have been close to death, Johnnie viewed life with unfailing optimism and the family tensions only occasionally got him down. 'Remember I might be seeing nothing,' he said. 'I could be underground. The last ten years have been packed with pleasures, like getting up and pulling back the curtains on a sunny morning which I never thought I would see again.'

In the latter years of his life Johnnie tried to show that he was more active than people believed. In a newspaper interview in 1988, he said, 'Some people think I am just an old man sitting at home, but actually I am very active. We farm in quite a big way. We have five thousand acres and produce quite a lot of food ... We have mixed farming, a beef enterprise, herds of milk cattle and sheep.'

Although history might take a dim view of the eighth Earl's time at Althorp, in an article in *The Field* magazine written towards the end of his life Johnnie maintained that he, in contrast to his ancestors, was very interested in environmental matters. 'The one thing I am keen on is conservation. They were not in the old days. I have two keepers (there were five in the old days). They are loyal and dedicated young men, who help rear the young pheasants and generally protect the environment by controlling the vermin, in particular rats, grey squirrels and mink, which do so much damage among our wild duck. We have ninety different varieties of birds in the park and a heronry which is quite rare. The herons have fifty nests a year which we protect. They have been here for two hundred years, always in one particular corner of the estate, but when the railway came in the 1840s they upped sticks and moved to where they are now.'

Unlike Raine, he loved to walk round the park and stop for a chat with any visitors he came across. 'My ancestors were rather remote really. I enjoy meeting the many country people who come and visit the park. I walk two or three miles a day and swim too. Trouble is it makes me so hungry I eat more. Also my wife keeps me young. I am sixty-four but I only feel about fifty.'

Despite this assertion, some of Johnnie's friends noticed a considerable deterioration in his health in the few years before he died. 'He changed dramatically from the young boy I knew,' says schoolfriend Lord Wardington. 'Then he was all drive. In the last years of his life there wasn't any drive, although there was a certain obstinacy.'

It does seem, however, that although Johnnie became physically quite frail, he had more of a grasp on reality than he was given credit for. If he lacked the willpower to restrain Raine's decorative ideas, he did so from choice. He certainly remained acutely aware of the problems that beset his children. Running parallel to the troubles at Althorp was the cloud hanging over the marriage of Diana and the Prince of Wales. Johnnie was fiercely protective of his youngest daughter. In an interview with *Woman* magazine in 1988 he dismissed reports of her marital problems with a wave of the hand. 'They're trivial just like mosquitoes,' he said. 'Of course they're not true. Of course Charles and Diana have their rows, what couple doesn't, but they are nothing out of the ordinary. What makes it so different for them is that they're on show the whole time. They might have had a disagreement, then they have to step out in front of the cameras and pretend that everything is going well and that's not easy, as any couple would know.'

He claimed that Diana found rumours of a rift 'very hurtful' and regretted that her every movement and expression was watched by the world. 'There are times when I wish she could have a couple of years off just to bring up her two children and be at home with them and not worry about anything else apart from them and her husband,' he said. 'Instead it's a bit like a nonstop circus and I don't like that. I don't think the Royal Family should be turned into some sort of soap opera, which is what the media is making it. Luckily the public don't see her like that. I've stood in the crowd at one of her engagements and I've felt the warmth they have for her. It's not been spoilt by any of the smear campaigns. To them she's still the fairy-tale princess which she really is. She's the fairy-tale princess because she does a wonderful job, she's very genuine, she's very beautiful, and she's still very much in love with Charles.'

In private, however, Johnnie knew that the fairy tale was turning into a nightmare. He was aware that the marriage had failed long before the publication of Andrew Morton's controversial biography and the 'Dianagate' tapes of alleged telephone conversations between James Gilbey and the Princess. He confided his anxieties to a long-term male friend at a dinner party at Althorp a couple of years before he died. 'Johnnie was terribly unhappy and said the worst thing that had happened to Diana, and therefore to him, was her marrying into the Royal Family,' the friend says. 'He thought when Diana and Charles married it was going to be for the best, and certainly the best thing for the Spencer family. But he knew it wasn't working out. In fact he said the marriage was a disaster. He also acknowledged that his earlier confidence that Diana wouldn't be taken over by the Royal Family was wrong and how sorry he was that he hardly saw his grandchildren.'

Despite this, Johnnie continued to maintain his loyal family front even though Diana was making little effort to hide her own feelings in the increasingly public rift. 'I am sure she can rise above it,' he said. 'She was born with great courage and if you see her with two beautiful charming children you can see she's happy.'

He also became increasingly concerned about his son Charles. In 1984, when he was nineteen and a history undergraduate at Magdalen College, Oxford, Charles, with help from his trustees, bought a £200,000 house a short step away from Kensington Palace. He had previously used his mother's flat in Pimlico when he was in London. 'It's my first house and I am very happy with it,' he said. He was an active socialiser, well known at nightspots and nicknamed Champagne Charlie although he denied that he even liked the drink.

On 20 May 1985 Charles threw a no-expense-spared party to celebrate his twenty-first birthday. Not wanting the event to take place at Althorp and under Raine's control, he chose the then unrestored Spencer House as a venue instead. He spent about six weeks organising the party and paid a large part of the estimated cost of £100,000 himself. The evening began with dinner at the Mirabelle for his family, including his mother and stepmother who were thoughtfully seated well away from each other. They dined on galette of duck and orange sauce, consommé with celery, fillets of sole served in a cream sauce with lobster mousse and fresh fruit. After dinner the family went on to the all-night party at Spencer House where the three hundred guests included several of the younger members of the Royal Family, nightclub owner Peter Stringfellow, the disc jockey Kenny Everett, the late gender-bender pop singer Divine, and even Lord St John of Fawlsey, Raine's friend.

Workmen had spent all day on the preparations for the party, including putting up a 120-foot blue-and-white canopy along the balcony of the sixty-roomed mansion in case of rain and rigging floodlights on the lawn.

Jazzman Ronnie Scott and soul singer Janice Hoyte were booked to perform in a ballroom lavishly decked out with thousands of roses, carnations, daffodils and lilies. At three o'clock there was a show by dancing girls in Janet Reger bras, slips and suspenders and the party did not end until six in the morning. 'I thoroughly enjoyed every minute of it,' said Charles.

After university Charles became a contracted television reporter for the giant American NBC network, operating both from England and the United States. In spite of his wealth and walking into a plumb job straight from Oxford, several colleagues felt sorry for him. One comments: 'You couldn't help it. You could tell he had been affected by his parents' divorce and was emotionally insecure. He was in a very difficult position and had been thrust into the limelight because of his sister. Being a celebrity was the bane of his life. He was very protective of his father although it was a difficult relationship. He used to say that his father was all there but he couldn't express himself terribly well.' In contrast, Charles made little attempt to hide his feelings for his stepmother. 'He never showed any affection for her at all,' his colleague says.

In 1989 Charles met 24-year-old model Victoria Lockwood at a friend's party. They became virtually inseparable and six weeks later announced their engagement. 'When I met Victoria it was love at first sight,' Charles explains. 'I didn't think such things happened but they obviously do.' When a seventeen-year-old schoolgirl, Victoria was chosen as Girl of the Year by *The Tatler* after a series of semi-professional photo shoots. She had also, like Charles's sister Sarah, suffered from anorexia nervosa. More significant was the fact that she was not an aristocrat but came from a fairly ordinary upper-middle-class background.

Johnnie was astute enough to warn his son about rushing into a hasty marriage, urging him to make the engagement last a little longer. Charles, however, did not want to wait and the couple were married on Saturday 16 September, 1989, at the twelfth-century St Mary's Church at Great Brington, in the middle of a torrential downpour. Victoria looked a frail waif, painfully thin with long lank hair and constantly puffing on Marlboro cigarettes. Her unconventional wedding dress, designed by Tomasz Starzweski, was made of gold lace trimmed with fur which some said was reminiscent of curtain material.

The wedding and reception, which reportedly cost £200,000, turned into a nerve-racking affair. Charles's best man, fellow Old Etonian and Oxford graduate Darius Guppy, who was later jailed for fraud, failed to deliver his speech. He seemed well enough in church, but as the afternoon wore on, succumbed to a sudden indisposition and efforts to find him were fruitless.

After the wedding Charles sold his London house and he and Victoria moved into the Falconry on the Althorp estate. His close proximity to the big house increased family tensions over the sale of heirlooms. A friend says, 'It made things much more difficult because he could see the removal vans pulling up.' A year later, Charles persuaded his father to oust the Althorp land agent, Richard Stanley, who had managed the estate for fifteen years and the job was put in the hands of the property dealers, Savills. Although Stanley was never given a reason for his dismissal, the assumption is that Charles saw him as his stepmother's lieutenant.

Charles's marriage nearly broke up in its first year when he confessed to *Daily Mail* gossip columnist Nigel Dempster that he had had an affair with journalist and cartoonist Sally Ann Lasson, having learned that she was about to sell her story to the *News of the World*. Not surprisingly, both gave very different accounts of the relationship. Ms Lasson claimed that it was based on deep friendship, Charles said it was of little significance. His version was that in February 1990, a few months after their wedding, he and Victoria went through 'an extremely messy patch' when a separation 'seemed possible'. In despair he confided his marital problems to Sally Ann Lasson with whom he had had a 'one-night stand' in 1986, believing that, as she had had a failed marriage herself, 'she might be in a position to give advice'. On 28 March 1990, 'after a particularly unpleasant series of quarrels with my wife', Charles rang the sympathetic Ms Lasson and asked if she would come with him to Paris. 'I sincerely thought my marriage was over,' he said. She agreed and Charles admitted, 'We went to Paris and had our second one-night stand four years after the first.'

The experience 'so sickened' him that he did not stay on at the Hotel Balzac in Paris with Ms Lasson but returned to London, eager to patch up his marriage.

Johnnie was 'very saddened' when he heard about the affair and that his son's marriage was in trouble. He told Charles in no uncertain terms to pull himself together, make the marriage work and, ironically, that on no account could he embarrass the Princess of Wales by getting divorced. Despite the fact that by now Diana could hardly bear her own husband's presence, she stepped in and persuaded her brother and sister-in-law to join her for a holiday on the Caribbean island of Necker to help patch up their differences. There were reports that the Queen too was astounded that Charles, her godson, had publicised his problems in the newspapers.

Whether he followed his father's advice or his relationship with Victoria sorted itself out naturally, in February 1991, a month after the birth of his first daughter Kitty, Charles declared that he and his wife were 'deeply in love'. He admitted he had caused Victoria 'more grief than I would wish her to have in a lifetime with me. I accept full responsibility for the folly of my actions.' In public, Johnnie loyally supported his son and admitted his relief that the marriage seemed to have weathered the storm. 'They are very happily married and they have got a lovely little girl. If you get married you have got to take the rough with the smooth.' In private, however, he confessed to a friend that 'Charles has always been difficult' and that he found Victoria 'odd'. The friend says: 'There was always an enormous gulf in what both families expected from one another.'

Family relations were not calm for very long before the children's anger and bitterness dramatically erupted over the sale of cottages on the Althorp estate. Charles had a shouting match with his father and step-mother that several members of staff could not help overhearing. An employee says, 'Charles accused them of destroying five hundred years of family heritage. He said that in the past fifteen years more damage had been done at Althorp than in the last four centuries. He reminded his father that his role should be to look after the house during his lifetime.' A family friend said at the time: 'The sales have created tremendous distress. The children are desperately loyal to their father, but he is not in the best of health and disposing of assets which really he should hold on to.'

When the row was at its peak Raine and Johnnie took the wise decision to leave the country. They flew to Nice to join a luxury yacht for a Mediterranean cruise and in doing so fell neatly into the journalistic hands of Brian Vine of the *Daily Mail* who managed to board the same British Airways flight and secure a seat on the opposite aisle. He waited for the plane to reach an altitude of about ten thousand feet before broaching the delicate subject of family relationships and found an abscess ready for lancing. Raine defended Johnnie staunchly, saying he had been very generous to all his children. 'I know that for a fact,' she added. 'People never seem very grateful whatever you do.' While she could 'do without all this bad blood', she stressed that she personally was immune from the slings and arrows thrown by her stepchildren. 'No one can hurt me now. I've been through all sorts of hurt. John's stroke and nursing him, a career in politics at the old LCC and GLC – and a step-family.' She said she was well aware of her nicknames. 'Yes, I've heard myself called wicked stepmother and Acid Raine and Raine Drain ... but all these names go over my head. I'm only interested in my love for John and what he is trying to do for posterity. He loves Althorp and everything we have done with it.' She told Brian Vine that she felt sad for Johnnie who only wanted to 'spread a little happiness among his family'.

In answer to allegations, repeated over sixteen years, that she was selling off the Spencer heritage she trotted out her familiar line. 'I don't make those decisions to sell paintings or cottages. I get my orders from him,' pointing at her husband. 'He tells me what to do and I do it. This idea that I am some great influence is not right. These possessions are his to do what he likes with.'

Johnnie seemed to pour his heart out too. He claimed he had made ample provision for his children, including leaving Diana nearly £1 million, and he put the family dispute down to Diana's dislike of the new-look Althorp, admitting that she only visited at Easter and Christmas.

Although Johnnie's two younger children could just about cope with his tunnel vision regarding the changes at the family stately home, they were incensed by his subsequent personal remarks about them. Denying that he and his children were not on speaking terms, Johnnie said of Charles, 'He is married to a splendid girl in Victoria but I think he's a little immature. He'll get over it all, just you wait and see. I love my children, but they have gone a bit haywire. My son must know the problems involved [at Althorp]. We've spent millions here. You know children aren't grateful. They never even thank you for pocket money – apparently.' He then turned his attention to the Princess of Wales. 'Diana doesn't understand about money. She has no experience of money. She's too young.'

Not unnaturally Diana did not take kindly to being told she had no grasp of money and relations between her and her father and stepmother reached breaking point. Charles, equally displeased at being publicly denounced as 'immature', chose to speak out. 'I fully understand that stately homes are extremely expensive to maintain,' he said 'but there are other issues which go slightly deeper which I don't think my father has addressed.'

Friends saw Johnnie's outburst as evidence of his declining health. They knew that in his prime Johnnie would never have publicly made such wounding and insensitive remarks about any of his children, and particularly not about Diana.

Johnnie and Raine prolonged their holiday for two months until matters had calmed down. When, following letters written by each of the girls to their father appealing to him to think again about the Althorp sales, they received assurances that he would not dispose of any more furniture or paintings for the time being, the family decided to call a halt to their public squabbles. While remaining publicly defiant, Johnnie admitted that the selling 'could now probably stop'. It was a deeply upsetting episode for all concerned. A friend said, 'The children decided they had achieved their aim of highlighting what they saw as a very worrying situation. Everyone's sorry people have been hurt and Countess Spencer has come out of it looking like the wicked stepmother. But the fact this row surfaced shows the depth of feeling involved.'

The hammering by the press hardly seemed to dent Raine's cast-iron surface. She told Lynda Lee-Potter, 'I'm not at all concerned with that overworked word, my image' and viewed the criticism, as she often does, in narrow, personal terms. 'You see, friends are always friends and enemies are always your enemies. I've lived by that all my life. It's no use longing to be loved, that's very transient. What I think one minds is one hates being betrayed. You trust friends and obviously you trust the people who work for you ... Lies are always a nuisance, always corrosive, but they hurt the people who tell them most. We weren't angry, just sad, at the betrayal. You have to be strong. You're not allowed in life to have the lot. Things like this are just pinpricks. I don't turn to people for help. I'm not like that. I cope on my own.'

Always adept at putting her point of view, Raine could now blame the recession, which in 1991 was beginning to bite, for many of the financial problems at Althorp where, she admitted, the takings were down. 'Selling things you own, especially in this recession – it hits stately homes too, you know – is the right of everyone.' What she failed to mention was that, despite the recession, Johnnie had just bought a £1.6 million five-storey house in Farm Street that had been gutted and was being totally redecorated to Raine's high standards. She installed air-conditioning, organised a lift for Johnnie – as he found climbing stairs increasingly difficult – created a special room for him to relax in which led on to a sunny terrace and had a tiny extra kitchen built where they could make coffee for themselves. David Levin and his wife Margaret were one of the first visitors. 'Raine is a perfectionist and the house is immaculate, very, very cosy and in marvellously good taste,' Levin says. 'It's all very *Upstairs, Downstairs*. All the staff bedrooms are individually furnished, they have their own kitchen, airing cupboard and a special cupboard designed for the television.'

Johnnie was not destined to enjoy many hours sitting in the sun. Members of the Althorp staff noticed that he seemed under the weather and not his usual cheerful self for some days before he was taken into hospital at the end of March 1992. They were not surprised when he spent an increasing amount of each day resting on his bed, but they began to get truly anxious about him when he failed to appear to welcome paying guests. He had always been meticulous about greeting visitors, particularly if they were likely to spend money in his wine shop. He stayed in his room during a party for Japanese guests at the beginning of March, but struggled up for the group photograph before they left. A few days later, despite feeling no better, he went with Raine to London for a dinner party. The journey did him no good and on arrival he started to shake and looked so drawn that his doctor was called. Johnnie was told that he had a chest infection and must rest at Farm Street for at least a week.

He kept pleading to be allowed to return to Althorp and arrived back in the middle of frantic preparations for a Romantic Evening function. (Female guests were to receive a free Barbara Cartland novel and the men a bottle of wine.) Johnnie took no notice of the preparations, which was unusual, but retired to his room. The staff became really worried when Raine told them that as Johnnie was not well, she would in future take charge of the wines. 'We knew he must have been ill because not in a million years would he have let Her Ladyship near his beloved cellars if he could help it,' says one employee.

During that day his condition deteriorated and the family doctor was called. The GP decided that the Earl should go to hospital for tests and an ambulance took him back to London, to the Humana Hospital Wellington in St John's Wood. He was diagnosed as having pneumonia but in fact the doctors were more concerned about the weak state of his heart. It was closely monitored, and after a few days seemed to be under control. The pneumonia responded well to treatment, Johnnie's zest for life aiding his recovery.

Johnnie, who has never liked hospitals, claimed he was bored, missed his daily routine of feeding the birds, with leftover toast from breakfast and nagged to be allowed to go home. The doctors agreed to a provisional date but on 29 March, the day before he was due to return to Althorp, he had a heart attack and died.

Postscript

On his father's death, 27-year-old Charles became the ninth Earl Spencer and inherited a fortune worth approximately £89 million. He immediately closed Althorp to the public as a mark of respect for his father, but behind the bright blue wrought-iron gates frenzied activity was under way. His first task was to exorcise the presence of his stepmother. A meeting was called and staff were told that the dowager countess was no longer welcome in the house. A senior member of the household says: 'We were told that Her Ladyship could take only what belonged to her and not one thing more.' Charles fired several members of staff including the chef, the catering staff and Raine's personal assistant and hairdresser, Sue Ingram, who had been with the family for seventeen years. In addition Ingram was also told that she could not have her forthcoming wedding reception in the house as previously planned. Charles issued instructions to halt any further sales of estate cottages, removed Barbara Cartland's books and the signed postcards from the gift shop, and all photographs of Raine from the premises.

Diana was at Althorp with her brother when Sue Ingram arrived to collect some of Raine's possessions. Initially she was not allowed to touch anything but she refused to leave without some of Raine's clothes and eventually an agreement was reached that any further visits would be supervised. On returning the following day she was prevented from removing Raine's papers.

Two days after Johnnie's death, Raine herself turned up at Althorp with a Land-Rover to remove some of her things. She brought with her a pile of red stickers with which to identify larger possessions. These, plus her portrait by Sancha, would, she was told, be despatched to her Mayfair home. In its place on the great staircase Charles had already hung a portrait of the third Earl, painted in 1845.

Following that visit, Raine's maid, Pauline Shaw, who had negotiated the sale of cottages, came to collect the remainder of Raine's clothes, which she packed into four new, expensive, Louis Vuitton suitcases.

Diana and her brother demanded to see the contents of the suitcases before they would allow them to leave the house. When Diana noticed an 'S' embossed on the cases she said they belonged to her father and ordered Raine's clothes to be taken out and put into black bin-liners instead. A member of staff then saw Charles Spencer kick the bags down the stairs. 'He had kept his anger pent up for so long that he grabbed possession after possession and threw them down. I think it made him feel much better,' he says.

Although Diana made no attempt to hide her dislike and distrust of Raine, her husband took an entirely independent, even disloyal line. After Johnnie's death the Prince of Wales wrote Raine an eight-page handwritten letter of condolence, which so delighted her that she showed it to several friends. 'It couldn't have been more sympathetic, understanding and loving,' says one. Their warm relationship continued to blossom after the Prince and Diana separated with regular visits and long telephone calls.

Within a few days of his father's death Charles Spencer began the melancholy task, aided by the executors of his father's will, of matching an inventory of past treasures with what was now left in the great house. It was a daunting operation to try to establish what had been sold.

Charles opened Althorp again on 17 April 1992, three weeks after his father's death. Five hundred people queued to see the changes. The entrance fee had gone up 20 per cent from £2.95 to £3.50, but two more bedrooms were now open to the public. Many visitors quizzed the guides on the alterations Charles had already made and about his feeling towards his stepmother, but they remained tight-lipped. Within a year the family home was to provide Diana with a refuge after her marriage had officially broken down and she spent her first Christmas there with her brother and sisters and their families but without her own children.

On 19 May a memorial service of thanksgiving for the life and work of Earl Spencer was held at St Margaret's Church, Westminster. Charles organised the event and took pains to ensure that the two sides of the family were segregated. Johnnie's first wife Frances, with her children and grandchildren, entered the church from the east and sat to the left of the aisle. Raine and her family, this time including Dame Barbara – dressed unusually in black – entered from the west side and sat on the right. The Princess of Wales, on this occasion accompanied by her husband, sat with their children in the front pew with the new Earl and Countess Spencer. The Queen, Duke of Edinburgh, Queen Mother, Duke and Duchess of York, Prince Edward, Princess Royal and Princess Margaret were all represented. The hymns could not have been more English – 'I Vow to Thee My Country' and 'Thine Be The Glory'. Canon Donald Gray officiated, assisted by the Dean of Westminster, the Very Revd Michael

Mayne. Bandsman Craig Kidd of the Royal Scots Dragoon Guards played Gigue-Vivace from the Sonata in B flat for Trumpet and Organ by Jean Baptiste Loeillet.

Charles read the lesson which he had felt unable to do at his father's funeral and Mr Robin Leigh-Pemberton, Governor of the Bank of England, gave the address. He tactfully made light of the family feud. 'Both sides may have found fault with each other,' he said, 'but in what family does that not happen? I take this opportunity to say that there never was a split.' Canon Gray described the Earl as 'an open, courageous man who was a loyal husband, a loving father and a uniquely wonderful grandparent'.

After the service the two branches of the family met outside on the steps. Raine looked splendid in black and white, her hair winged perfectly along the lines of her wide-brimmed hat. For their last act of togetherness the Spencers had, in public at least, decided to paper over the chasm that divided them. Even Princess Diana, who wore the same black Chanel suit and wide-brimmed hat that she had worn at her father's funeral, walked directly up to Raine, put her arms round her and kissed her. Prince William and Prince Harry did likewise. Raine returned their affection while Mrs Shand Kydd manoeuvred herself away from a confrontation. Sisters Jane and Sarah were also in black, both wearing almost identical pearl chokers to their mother who was dressed in black and bright pink. Victoria, pregnant with twin girls, wore a black and peach jacket.

Once the Prince and Princess of Wales had left, two greeting lines formed outside the church. On one side, Raine kissed mourners or shook their hands with smiling cries of 'Darling' while on the other the new Earl, his wife and his mother formed a more subdued group. Raine stayed until the last of the four hundred guests had left. Asked how the service had gone, she said: 'He would have loved it.'

The extent of Raine's inheritance from Johnnie will never be exactly known. He showered her with jewels and gifts throughout their marriage and made ample financial provision for her including an estimated £4 million. Raine retains ownership of their two houses in Bognor, the luxury house in Mayfair and money from various trust funds. In addition, in Johnnie's last will, finalised in January 1992, she was given the choice of one of his cars; all the contents of their houses in Bognor, with the exception of an ivory inlaid travelling box, a writing table and three stools, which after her death must be returned to Althorp; all the contents of the house in Farm Street except for the Claude Vignon painting, *A Man with Bagpipes*; all Johnnie's cash and investments in his Coutts Bank account under the management of Global Asset Management and an annuity of £10,000. Johnnie left each of his daughters a memento to be chosen by his trustees and each of his grandchildren £1,000. He left his collection of Third Reich postcards to his grandson Alexander Fellowes, a selection of books from his private collection to his granddaughter Laura Fellowes, and the money in his Halifax Building Society to Laura's sister Eleanor.

Not long after the memorial service Raine publicly declared that she wanted privacy and a new life. She put out an emotional statement to the Press Association, saying: 'I do not wish to comment to any newspaper or journalist on Althorp or the Spencers as a family now or ever. I am a widow and I would be grateful if the press would leave me alone to rebuild my life.' She didn't stand a chance. The press, with whom she had built up such a volatile love–hate relationship over so many years, ignored her regal command and continued to monitor her movements, speculate about her in the gossip columns and boldly call her 'the merry widow'.

There was plenty to talk about as Raine is not the self-sufficient female she makes herself out to be. Like her mother she enjoys male company and within weeks of Johnnie's death was seen out and about, lunching at Claridge's and dining at the exclusive Harry's Bar. Lord St John of Fawsley comments: 'Johnnie said she would make a very bad widow. She needs another person with her. She is not totally independent.' It was even said that she had never looked better, which Michael Cole, public relations director at Harrods, attributes to the fact that she no longer had the burden of dealing with Johnnie's children. 'She would never have been less than polite,' he says, 'but she told me she was pleased she no longer had to maintain relations with the volatile Spencer children which she found very wearing.' She also felt at ease with herself. 'She said she had nothing to reproach herself for and knew she had made Johnnie so very happy.'

Several friends reported having received telephone calls from Raine telling them she would like to come for dinner or for the weekend. Some have accommodated her, others have found her too demanding. 'She takes over when she comes,' says one friend Raine contacted. 'Insists you provide her with a personal maid and on the last occasion she stayed with us, took so long to get ready that she came down at ten thirty for dinner that was schedule for eight. Nor did she seem to mind a bit that she kept all the other guests waiting.' Another friend, knowing how insistent Raine was on fresh orange juice for breakfast, rose early and drove to the village nearby to find the necessary oranges. 'I don't know how she manages to persuade everyone to run round her like she does,' she says.

Michael Cole sees nothing wrong with her behaviour. 'Just because she doesn't cry on cue doesn't mean that she is not a good person. She is. She could have done the widow's weed act, but she chose not to. She is totally professional. A remarkable woman.'

In May 1992, two months after Johnnie's death, Raine travelled to Rome to visit her daughter Charlotte and her son-in-law the Duca Don

Alexander Paterno Castello di Caraci. She did not, however, stay with them, but chose instead the five-star Hassler Hotel. She began to see a lot more of her family and was often escorted by her brother Ian whose marriage had broken up after twenty years. Raine was a guest of Greek billionaire John Latsis for a cruise on his yacht *Alexander*, stayed with friends in Paris, dined with Prince Rainier of Monaco, went out with retired hotelier Douglas Barrington, aged seventy-one, and only eight months after Johnnie's death was seen dancing cheek to cheek in the Manhattan nightclub Doubles with American cereals heir Francis Kellogg who was seventy-five. It wasn't long before rumours began to circulate that she wanted to marry again. However, a member of the family commented that she would never marry a plain 'mister'. 'She wouldn't want to lose her title, which she has never had in her own right. She was trained for that from the cradle.'

Raine, now two stones lighter, justified her social whirl: 'I am just terribly, terribly happy rebuilding my life,' she said. 'I live in the present and the future. I never want to forget the past because I adored my husband and we had such happy times together. But now I have to get on with my life.'

Get on with it she did. On Monday 10 May, 1993 a mere thirteen months after Johnnie's death, Raine announced that she was to re-marry. Her third husband was Jean-François de Chambrun, a French count with a chateau in Nice and a home in Paris. Like Raine's two previous husbands when she married them, he is heir to a fortune and has the requisite title although at fifty-seven, the count is seven years her junior. They met at a dinner party in Monte Carlo a mere thirty-three days previously and for the third time in her life the romantic Raine fell in love at first sight. She showed no coyness or reserve at the well organised photo-call. When her future husband was asked to give Raine, in kingfisher blue dress with a white organza corsage on her shoulder, a peck, he replied 'I do not do pecking' and passionately kissed her neck. Then, much to the gathered journalists' surprise and delight, the joyful pair then kissed fully on the lips with such force that Raine only just managed to keep her balance. Members of the aristocracy were less than impressed. 'I couldn't believe her behaviour,' said one. 'And how could she at her age put an engagement announcement in *The Times* and get an engagement ring, that is so similar to Diana's.'

Raine, however, relished the limelight, seemingly delighted that the press, despite her requests earlier in the year, hadn't deserted her after all. She proudly showed off her antique ring, a sapphire surrounded by eight diamonds, which came from S. J. Phillips and which she had already earmarked before she even met Jean-François as the ring she would like if she ever re-married. She also announced that the wedding would take place in July. A second photo-call with her mother followed at Dame Barbara's home in Camfield Place, where the amorous pair went for tea. Raine had by this time changed into a sleek navy dress with white trim and positively glowed even when Jean-François admitted they had already had their honeymoon. 'Well, at our advanced age,' she blushed, 'no-one would think we'd only just held hands.' She even revealed to journalist Valerie Grove that despite her earlier weight loss and losing a further half stone since she met him, Jean-François was keen to see 'another sliver off the derriere.' She mentioned that she had already taken her husband-to-be to lunch at Highgrove with her close friend Prince Charles and had telephoned her other admirers including Francis Kellog with her news. She expressed confidence that Jean-François and Johnnie would have liked each other tremendously and admitted that she had already started to re-organise the Count's chateau. Confidently gliding into a glowing sunset she offers this message to all. 'There is hope, even if you're an ancient like me. Never worry what age you are, look for adventure, grasp at life. What you give out, you get back, like a boomerang!'

Treasures Sold from the Althorp Collection

This list is by no means complete, but it is known that the following items were sold:

1976

PAINTINGS

Sold by agreement with the Inland Revenue in lieu of Capital Transfer Tax (death duties):
• *Albert de Ligne, Prince of Brabaçon and Arenberg* by Van Dyck, dated 1630. Private treaty sale to the Tate Gallery.
• *Viscountess Andover and Lady Elizabeth Thimbleby* by Van Dyck. Bought by Robert, 2nd Earl of Sunderland. Private treaty sale to the National Gallery.
• *Penelope Wriothesley, Wife of William, 2nd Lord Spencer* by Van Dyck. Transferred in lieu of Capital Transfer Tax to the Treasury in 1976. Now in York City Art Gallery.
• *Rachel de Ruvigny, Countess of Southampton* by Van Dyck. Transferred in lieu of Capital Transfer Tax to the Treasury in 1976. Now in the Fitzwilliam Museum, Cambridge.

FURNITURE

• An armchair from Lady Spencer's bedroom in Spencer House. Sold to the V & A.

1977

PAINTINGS

• Several portrait drawings by Gainsborough, commissioned by the 1st Earl Spencer. Sold to a private collector.
• *An Album of 102 Scenes from Contemporary Life* by Adriaen Pieters van

der Venne, acquired by the 1st Earl Spencer. Sold to the British Museum for £148,000.

FURNITURE

• A suite consisting of six armchairs, two settees and two sofas designed by Athenian Stuart for the Painted Room, Spencer House. The sides of the sofas are formed by winged lions with long necks carved in gilt. The chairs are supported by lions' legs. Sold to the V & A.

CHINA AND PORCELAIN

• A Frankenthal coffee pot with a painting by Osterpey of a naked girl asleep at the foot of a tree, dated 1762–70. Sold to the V & A for £4,950.
• In the late 1970s twenty pieces of porcelain were transferred to the Treasury for £71,530 in lieu of Capital Transfer Tax. They were distributed to eight different museums.

1979

FURNITURE

• Mahogany washstand, inlaid with padouk and boxwood, from Lady Spencer's bedroom in Spencer House, made by Athenian Stuart in about 1760. Sold to the V & A.

PAINTINGS

• The paintings *Liberality and Modesty* by Guido Reni and *Apollo Crowning the Musician Marcantonio Pasqualini* by Andrea Sacchi were sold to the London dealers Wildenstein. The Reni painting was bought by the collector Peter Jay Sharp, owner of the Carlyle Hotel in New York, who died in 1992. The painting by Sacchi, for which Wildenstein paid about £40,000, was acquired by the Metropolitan Museum of Art, New York, for an estimated £270,000.

1980

• Five Apostles: *St Bartholomew, St James the Greater, St Simon, St Matthew* and *St Mathias*, painted by Van Dyck in about 1620. These paintings were bought by Colnaghi as a 'joint venture' with an anonymous client who has retained two. *St Simon* was sold to the J. Paul Getty Museum in California and two to the Swiss art collector Peter Nathan.

1981

FURNITURE

• 17th-century black lacquer table with Japanese lacquer panels, mirror and a pair of matching candle-stands. Sold via Partridge Fine Arts to the V & A for about £150,000.

1982

PAINTINGS

• *St Jerome in Penitence*, an oil sketch painted in about 1620 for the painting in Dresden by Van Dyck. Sold to Colnaghi.
• *Icarus* by Van Dyck. Sold to Colnaghi.
• *Holy Family and Angels* by Francesco Albani, inherited from Sarah, Duchess of Marlborough. Sold to Colnaghi, who sold it to an Italian dealer.
• *The Marriage of St Catherine* by Carlo Dolci, acquired by the Hon. John Spencer in 1740. Sold to Colnaghi.
• *Scene on Ice* by Hendrick Avercamp, collected by the 2nd Earl of Sunderland. Sold to dealers Harari & Johns.
• A portrait of the Swiss artist Angelica Kauffman by Sir Joshua Reynolds. Sold to the dealers Artemis and bought by an American collector for £100,000.
• *Noah's Sacrifice* by Giovanni Benedetto Castiglione, now in the Los Angeles County Museum.
• *Two Cherubs in Clouds* by the 17th-century Italian master Il Guercino. Sold to Colnaghi.

FURNITURE

• A six-foot-long George II giltwood console table, designed by John Vardy for Spencer House, was nearly sold to an American but the export licence was blocked. It was subsequently bought by the National Heritage Memorial Fund for £38,000.

SILVER AND GOLD

• Pair of 17th-century gold wine coolers from the Marlborough collection. Sold by S. J. Phillips to the British Museum for about £1 million.
• Pair of valuable 19th-century sauceboats and ladles made by William Pitts. Bought by American dealer Arthur Gilbert. Date of purchase and selling agent unknown.
• A sideboard dish, 26 in. diam., made in 1677 by William Harrison, with

an engraving of Fitzgerald impaling Ranelagh. Sold by S. J. Phillips to Arthur Gilbert.

• A bowl and standing dish 'of the highest quality and grace' made by Paul de Lamerie, dated 1723, for the Hon. John Spencer who in 1734 married Lady Georgina Carteret. The pieces were traditionally known as Lady Carteret's porridge bowl and stand and had been used as a christening bowl by many generations of the Spencer family. Sold by S. J. Phillips to Arthur Gilbert.

• A small fish-kettle, dated 1801, made by John Edwards 'for special circumstances such as a picnic'. It is described as 'very rare' and was part of the official plate given to the Duke of Kent on his appointment as Governor of Gibraltar in 1802; the kettle is engraved with the royal arms of the badges of the Order of the Garter and the Order of St Patrick. Sold by S. J. Phillips to Arthur Gilbert.

• Two candlesticks designed by Thomas Farren, given to the V & A by S. J. Phillips, to commemorate the retirement of Claude Blair.

PROPERTY

• St Ethelwold School in Shotton, North Wales, sold to a property developer for about £50,000.

1983

PAINTINGS

• *Agrippina with the Ashes of Germanicus* by the Scottish artist Gavin Hamilton. Sold to Colnaghi, who sold it to the Tate Gallery. Now on loan to Spencer House.

• Three minor Italian Old Masters were auctioned by Christie's in New York, including *Christ Reproving his Disciples* by Niccolo Berrettoni, for $4,620.

• *The Coronation of the Virgin* by the 16th-century German artist Johann Rottenhammer. Sold to Colnaghi, who sold it to the National Gallery for about £60,000.

• *St Luke Painting the Virgin* by Il Guercino. Sold to Colnaghi. The 87 in. × 71 in. painting, then valued at £310,000, was executed specifically for the church of Réggio d'Emilia in 1662 and had been in the Althorp collection since 1750. Despite an embargo on the sale to a client in New York by the then Arts Minister, Paul Channon, no British institution could raise the money to buy the painting and it was eventually exported to Kansas City.

• *Witches at their Incantations* by Salvatore Rosa. Sold to Wildenstein who applied for a licence to export it to an anonymous purchaser in

Switzerland. The painting, dated 1646, was considered by Rosa to be the best of a series on witchcraft that he painted in Florence where there was a vogue for the occult in intellectual circles. It has been in Britain since at least 1761 when it was acquired by the 1st Earl Spencer. The sale was blocked for six months by the then Arts Minister, Lord Gowrie, and only hours before the time-limit expired the National Gallery made an offer of £350,000 for the masterpiece.

SILVER

• A cup and lid in silver-gilt, dated 1608. Bought by Arthur Gilbert from the dealer S. J. Shrubsole in New York.
• Twelve candlesticks engraved with the Duke of Marlborough crest.

1984

FURNITURE

• Two armchairs carved in giltwood, designed for Spencer House by J. Gordon in about 1760. Sold via Partridge Fine Arts to the V & A.

ARCHIVES, DRAWINGS AND MANUSCRIPTS

• The Spencer family archives were sold by private treaty to the British Library for about £1 million. The British Library was helped in the purchase by grants of £128,398 from the National Heritage Memorial Fund and £5,000 from Friends of the National Libraries.

1985

PAINTINGS

• *The Duchess of Marlborough's Dogs*, painted by John Wootton in 1763. Sold at Sotheby's for £143,000.
• *Madonna and Child with St John the Baptist* by Jacopo Bassano, initially recorded in the collection of the Hon. John Spencer, father of the 1st Earl Spencer, in 1765. Sold at Sotheby's for £35,000 to an anonymous American collector.
• *Christ and the Woman of Samaria* by Lo Scarsellino, which was in the collection of the Hon. John Spencer and inherited in 1746 by his son John. Sold at Sotheby's for £12,500.
• Portrait of Mary Musters, wife of Sir Richard Spencer of Offley, and her son John when a child (1677–78 to 1699) by John Riley. Sold at Sotheby's for £4,800.
• *The Rt Hon. Stephen Poyntz* by Jean Baptiste Van Loo bequeathed to

Georgiana, Countess Spencer, by Poyntz's widow. Sold at Sotheby's for £12,100.

• *Frances Worsely, Countess Grenville* by the Studio of Thomas Hudson. Sold at Sotheby's for £3800.

• *The Hon. John Spencer* by Stephen Slaughter. Sold at Sotheby's to Colnaghi for £4180.

• *The Reception in the Kitchen of the News of Master Bobby Shandy's Death* by Edward Bird, RA, bought by the 5th Earl Spencer in 1862. Sold at Sotheby's for £8200.

• Two other paintings, *The Drowned Leander Borne by Nereids* and *Hermits in a Cave*, both by David Teniers the Younger, were put up for auction at Sotheby's but did not reach their reserve price.

• A folio of 18th-century views of Rome sold to dealers Hazlitt, Gooden & Fox.

• Raine also put up for auction one of her own paintings, *St Christopher with the Infant Christ and St Peter* by the Italian Old Master known as Cima, which she acquired before she married Johnnie. Sold by Sotheby's for £230,000.

FURNITURE

• Six armchairs from the Great Room, Spencer House, designed by Athenian Stuart, were given to John Partridge, chairman of Partridge Fine Arts, in payment for restoration work at Althorp. Partridge sold two chairs to an American collector, two to the V & A for £20,000, and the remaining two, regilded and reupholstered, for £75,000.

A commode which belonged to Louis XV was put up for auction at Sotheby's but failed to reach its reserve of £200,000.

SILVER

• A double cup (two cups which join at the lip) made of silver and silver-gilt, dated 1600. Double cups first appeared in southern Germany during the fifteenth century and this one was presented to Robert, 1st Baron Spencer of Wormleighton, by Frederick, Duke of Württemberg, and is thought to be the only surviving piece of plate of the first Baron. Bought by Arthur Gilbert from S. J. Phillips.

ARCHIVES, MANUSCRIPTS AND DRAWINGS

• A collection of musical manuscripts which had been collected and inserted into an album in the late nineteenth century by Lady Revelstoke, bequeathed to her daughter, wife of the 6th Earl Spencer, was sold at Christie's for a total of £107,881. The collection included a lithography portrait of Charles-Auguste de Bériot, which sold for a mere £86, and a love-song by Mozart, written in his own hand, for £51,840. There was also a three-page letter from Beethoven to his publisher, arranging the opus numbers for a group of his most famous works, which was sold to a Berlin dealer for £28,000.

• Approximately 185 architectural drawings for Althorp by Henry Holland and others were sold to Artemis. An application for a licence to export them to the J. Paul Getty Museum in California, giving their value as £17,500, was refused and they were later purchased by the British Library for £26,000

• John Vardy's drawings for Spencer House were sold to Artemis. These are now in the J. Paul Getty Museum in California.

MISCELLANEOUS

• In the mid-1980s a gold snuffbox from the renowned Spencer collection of 18th-century gold boxes was bought by Arthur Gilbert from S. J. Phillips. Dated 1750, this rectangular gold and ivory snuffbox has a miniature of the 1st Earl Spencer by Jean-Etienne Liotard mounted inside the lid.

1986

ARCHIVES, MANUSCRIPTS AND DRAWINGS

• Northamptonshire estate papers which had been kept at Althorp were sold to Northampton Record Office.

CHINA AND PORCELAIN

• A mid-18th-century Capodimonte ewer and basin was up for sale to the J. Paul Getty Museum. A licence to export it was refused, however, and the ewer and basin were bought by the British Museum for £100,000.

PROPERTY

• During the 1980s about 150 property deals were negotiated, involving vacant properties or small pieces of land released from restrictive covenants.

1988

• 160 acres of land were sold to developers Costain Homes Ltd for £1 million plus £2 million payable over the following five years.

1990

PAINTINGS

• *Portrait of a Sculptor* by Nicolas de Largillière was sold to Colnaghi.

1991

PROPERTY

• Over forty cottages on the Spencer estate were put up for sale at prices ranging from £35,000 to £60,000. About twenty were sold before Johnnie's death.

Bibliography

Second to None, The Royal Scot Greys 1919–1945 by R. M. P. Carver. Published by the regiment.

The Royal Family and the Spencers, 200 Years of Friendship by Nerina Shute. Robert Hale.

Barbara Cartland, Crusader in Pink by Henry Cloud. Weidenfeld and Nicolson.

Barbara Cartland, by Gwen Robyns. Sidgwick & Jackson.

We Danced All Night, by Barbara Cartland. Arrow.

I Seek the Miraculous, by Barbara Cartland. Sphere.

The Ithmus Years 1919–1939, by Barbara Cartland. Hutchinson.

The Years of Opportunity 1939–1945, by Barbara Cartland. Hutchinson.

The Princess of Wales, by Barbara Maxwell. Queen Anne Press.

Princess, by Robert Lacey. Hutchinson.

Diana, Princess of Wales, by Penny Junor. Sidgwick & Jackson.

The Year of the Princess, by Gordon Honeycombe. Michael Joseph/Rainbird.

Diana In Private, The Princess Nobody Knows, by Lady Colin Campbell. Smith Gryphon.

Diana Her True Story, by Andrew Morton. Michael O'Mara.

The Definitive Diana, an A–Z Guide, by Sally Moore. Sidgwick & Jackson.

Diana: One Of The Family, by Paul James. Sidgwick & Jackson.

Princely Marriage, Charles & Diana The First Ten Years, by Anthony Holden. Bantam Press.

The Spencers on Spas, by Raine Spencer, with photographs by John Spencer. Weidenfeld and Nicolson.

Charles Darwin by John Bowlby. Hutchinson.

Acknowledgements

Writing this book coincided with the astonishing revelations about the marriage of the Prince and Princess of Wales and I suffered from a noticeable backlash each time a fresh wave of allegations broke. Even Dame Barbara Cartland, who is notoriously helpful to journalists, withdrew her initial co-operation, although this I later discovered was on the express instructions of her daughter. She told me that Raine had called a family conference and told the family not to speak to me. Dame Barbara, ever loyal to her daughter, then took the opportunity to scold me for even contemplating the project. 'Raine doesn't want this book done. Why do you want to upset her?' she asked. When I tried to justify myself suggesting an eminent author like herself might understand, she relented slightly by suggesting 'Why don't you do what I do when I write a biography and wait until she's dead?' Assuming Raine follows in her mother and grandmother's footsteps and survives into her nineties, I decided to forge ahead. Just as the book was going to press Raine announced her engagement to Count Jean-François de Chambrun and in an astonishing about-turn seemed to open her heart to the Press.

Despite her non co-operation there have been many who have been very helpful and I have had much valuable information from museum curators, conservationists, art historians, staff, family and friends of both Raine and Johnnie. Some, however, have wished to remain anonymous. Of those I can name, I would particularly like to thank Dr Brian Allen, Jenny Allsop, Betty Andrews, Lady Elizabeth Anson, Lord Archer, Ashley Barker, the Duchess of Beaufort, William Bell, Ruth Birchall, Claude Blair, Simon Blow, Lieut. Commander Henry Bruce, Graham Burrows, Sir Roger Cary, Sir Hugh Casson, Nigel Chamberlayne Macdonald, Patrick Cherrier, Alan Claridge, Timothy Clifford, Viscount Coke, Michael Cole, John Darling, Brigadier Davies-Scourfield, Jonathan Dawson, Lady Margaret Douglas-Home, Clive de Paula, the Earl of Dudley, Andrew Faulds, Lady Glenconner, the Duke of Grafton, Arthur Grimwade, the Hon Lady Goodhart, Rupert Hambro, John Hardy, John Harris, Nicholas Haslam, Richard Hayward, Richard Herner, David Hicks, Christopher Hodsall, Tricia Hopkins, Imperial War Museum, Brian Jackson, Alan Jefferson, Simon Jenkins, Stephen Jones, Professor Michael Kitson, David Laws, David Levin, Sir Julian Loyd, John Lowther, Lady Olga Maitland, Paul Martin, Michael Meddlicott, Michael Middleton, Paul Mitchell, Lord Montagu of Beaulieu, Major Morton, Sir William Morton, Sandra Moss, doctors at the National Hospital, Russell Nash, Sir Robin Nugent, Pat O'Rourke, John George Phillips, David Quelch, Grace Randall, Major Jim Randall, Anthony Rowe, Gary Shaeffer, Lord

285

Shelburne, Page Shepherd, Robin Simon, Anna Somers Cocks, Richard Stanley, Sir Roy Strong, Sir Peter Studd, Major Michael Trasenster, Peter Thornton, Peter Townend, Charles Trueman, Kenneth Turner, Richard Vander, the Victoria and Albert Museum, Anna Vinton, Brian Vine, Peter Watson, Lady Anne Wake-Walker who also gave me permission to use family photographs, Catherine Walwyn, Lord and Lady Wardington, Lord Walker and Heather Wilson.

I am very grateful to David Betts for letting me see his late father's diaries, to *Architectural Digest* for letting me quote from their magazine. Also of particular help was John Bowlby's book on Charles Darwin.

I would specially like to thank Susan Hope for her perseverance and patience in researching and checking facts; my husband Robert Low for his infinite tolerance and understanding and much needed good advice; my sons Jeremy, Daren and especially Daniel for their patience with a preoccupied mother who did not always fulfil her duties as she should. I am grateful to my agent Caroline Dawnay for her much needed encouragement, to Jane Birkett for her painstaking copy editing and most of all I am indebted to my publisher Ion Trewin for his involvement at every stage of the book; his wisdom and continual support have been invaluable.

Index

Wardington, Lady, 242
Wardington, Lord (Christopher
    Pease), 23, 23–4, 25, 39, 153
  quoted, on Johnnie etc., 23, 23–4,
    24, 25, 39, 43, 51, 97, 130, 135,
    153, 261
Waring, Derek, 128, 134
Water's Edge (house at Bognor),
    181, 182
Webb, Jessie, 8
West Heath, 47, 136
West Lewisham, 104–6, 115
Westminster, Dean of, 39
Westminster, Duke of, 128, 151

Westminster City Council, 99–100,
    104, 108, 112, 115
What is Our Heritage? 133
William, Prince, 6, 175–6, 245, 246,
    248, 249, 272
Willis, Lord, 116
Wilson, Dr, Bishop of Chelmsford,
    73
Wilson, Heather, 204
Windsor, Duke of (formerly Prince
    of Wales, then King Edward
    VIII), 16, 18–19
Wormleighton, 59, 185